Here Comes The Guide

Third Edition

Cover Photos

Over the years we've looked at a wide variety of wedding photographs, and Stephanie Tabachnikoff's are some of the most original and captivating we've seen.

Stephanie only photographs a small number of weddings every year, developing a very personal relationship with each client. "I like to get to know the couple, their family connections and their vision of the wedding," she says. "That knowledge enables me to see people the way they'd like to see themselves, and make them look the very best they can."

Stephanie's work reflects the unique character of each wedding. She uses black and white film as well as color to best convey the essence of a given moment. We like to call her pictures "professional candids"—they combine the artistry of a professional photo with the natural warmth and spontaneity of a snapshot. And she has such an uncanny ability to capture unexpected, whimsical and sentimental moments, we wonder how she manages to be in the right place so much of the time.

Whatever your expectations of wedding photography, Stephanie's photos will transcend them. Her pictures are beautiful. They are elegant. They are funny and tender. They are imbued with the spirit of the day, and when you look through an album of them, you can't help but celebrate a little bit yourself.

Stephanie is one of the foremost believers in the notion that a picture is worth a thousand words. We think her photos speak volumes.

S.F. Tabachnikoff ©1993
Shadows and Light Photography
Piedmont Avenue, Oakland CA
(510) 632-5886

Here Comes The Guide

Northern California

Over 300 Exceptional

WEDDING & RECEPTION
LOCATIONS

Lynn Broadwell
Jan Brenner

Hopscotch Press · Berkeley · California

Here Comes The Guide

This is the third edition of Here Comes The Guide ™

Library of Congress Cataloging-in-Publication Data

Broadwell, Lynn 1951—

Here Comes The Guide ©
Third Edition
Includes Index

Library of Congress Catalog Card Number Pending
ISBN 0-9625155-4-X

Inside Illustration: Michael Tse, Lynn Broadwell

Printed in the U.S.A.

For information, write or call:

HOPSCOTCH PRESS
1563 Solano Ave., Suite 135
Berkeley, CA 94707
510/525-3379

For Matthew.
You've been a really good boy.
Uncomplaining and patient throughout.
Although you're too young to understand exactly why
Mommie has to stay at the office at night and on weekends,
you already know how to be supportive.
Thanks.
I love you.

Contents

Regions and Cities

Acknowledgements

I'd like to thank Doug Broadwell
for his consistent support and
unwavering confidence in me.

I can only hope that
at some point, mine sweet,
I will be able to make your dream
come true.

A Personal Note

If you're like me, you love to have really good information at your fingertips—the kind that's intelligently compiled, easy to assimilate and most importantly, easy to use. *Here Comes The Guide* is designed with this in mind, so I know you'll find it to be an invaluable resource.

But no matter how hard I've tried to make the information in *Here Comes The Guide* completely accurate, it isn't. Some facilities give us incorrect data. Some go out of business. And when places change ownership or management, everything can be turned upside down overnight. If you add that to normal changes that occur over time, you'll understand why it's difficult to make a large body of data absolutely perfect.

So what can you do to insure you're getting correct information? The answer is simple:

ALL YOU HAVE TO DO IS CALL AND CONFIRM OUR DATA WITH THE FACILITY COORDINATOR OR MANAGER.

Read them the text from *Here Comes The Guide* that pertains to their location, and get them to *verify* that it's still current. If it isn't, jot down the new information directly into your book.

I can't stress enough how important is it to take this final step.

If you do your research using our guide, and confirm everything with each facility you contact, you can't go wrong.

Preface

Searching for a place to get married is not easy and usually not much fun. The amount of time consumed in calling up places, asking questions and compiling information can be mind-boggling. And who has that kind of time nowadays? Certainly not two people who work full time. *Here Comes The Guide* is intended to cut your search time by over ninety percent!

The first edition of *Here Comes The Guide* grew out of my own frustration in finding a wedding location. I tried to locate magazine articles about the best places. I called up wedding consultants and I networked a lot, asking all my friends and acquaintances where they got married.

What I was trying to do was examine all my options and there was no resource to help me. I was absolutely amazed that *nobody* had a comprehensive list with the kind of detailed information I needed!

What I discovered was a patchwork quilt of information. Each Chamber of Commerce was different. Some had wedding location lists all organized and ready to mail out; others had nothing and knew nothing. Wedding consultants had information, but it was usually limited and without all the details one needs to make a decision. Florists, cake bakers and caterers were usually too busy to take the time to describe over the phone all the places in their respective repertoires.

I became anxious. With a full time job and limited time to conduct an exhaustive search, I realized that I would never be able to thoroughly examine or *even find out* about interesting or unusual wedding sites! My frustrations were exacerbated by the fact that it was August and the wedding date in October was drawing closer with each passing day.

As luck would have it, my sister mentioned that her hairdresser had gotten married on a yacht in San Francisco Bay. Hallelujah! That's it, I cried! What a great idea! I had never even thought about a floating facility and had no idea you could do such a thing.

We got married behind Angel Island, by the captain, on a hot, sunny day. After the ceremony on the bow, the yacht tooted its horn, the crew let loose multi-colored balloons, and a "just married" sign was thrown over the stern. As we swept past Alcatraz, Sausalito, the Golden Gate and Bay Bridges, our guests relaxed in the sun, enjoying drinks and hors d'oeuvres. What a wonderful day! Even my parents' friends took time after the wedding to write, genuinely enthused about how much they loved their outing on the water.

Doug and I have been married over seven years now, but we wish we could do it all over again. It was the place that made all the difference.

Introduction

This is a unique guidebook.

The response to the first and second editions of this guidebook has been overwhelming. All 5,000 copies of the first edition were sold out in less than a year! The second edition has been also been successful.

Since 1990, I've received hundreds of 'thank you' calls and letters, not only from brides and grooms-to-be, but from others who have used *Here Comes The Guide* to find non-wedding locations! Clearly, there is a genuine need for a comprehensive guide that includes places for ceremonies, receptions and rehearsal dinners.

So here it is—the updated essential resource for anybody planning a wedding in Northern California, with extraordinary sites for everybody and every pocketbook. *Here Comes The Guide* offers practical tips and step-by-step guidance for reviewing, selecting and evaluating both event sites *and* services. This book will save you an enormous amount of time, and since detailed information about fees, deposits and in-house catering costs are included, you can comparison shop and save money, too.

This book is loaded with invaluable information that has been compiled with your needs in mind.

We've tried to anticipate the questions you'd ask and collect data that is important for decision-making. If you find that the most popular spots are already booked (especially June through October), you'll still have a long list of wonderful locations from which to choose. You'll discover delightful places that you might not have found on your own and wedding ideas that you might never have considered. This book is intended to open your eyes to a variety of new possibilities. We give you tips to help you quickly select and evaluate dozens of sites and their services, and no matter what kind of place you finally select, *Here Comes The Guide* is designed to make all your planning efforts *a lot* easier.

Our service directory is different—we've screened everyone for you!

If you worry about locating top-notch services, don't. *We've done the legwork for you.*

Finding a first-rate caterer, DJ, florist, cake maker or photographer can be difficult. How do you know they're really good at what they do? We developed a *screened* service directory at the back of this guide in order to bring you the best services we could find. Screened means that we did our homework so you don't have to. We required 10 to 30 trade references to qualify each of these service providers for our publication because we wanted to make sure that the people we recommend are not only technically competent, but professional, personable and serious about providing good service.

Unlike other publications that take ad dollars indiscriminately, we wouldn't allow a vendor to advertise with us until they'd received a great review from other professionals in the industry. When you ask 10 to 30 people in the event industry about the quality of someone's product or service, ultimately you figure out who's good and who's not. Given the enormous amount of work we did to qualify our advertisers, we feel very confident about giving a *personal endorsement* to each and every one of the companies that made it into our service directory. We think you'll save lots of time and aggravation if you call these folks first, before you search through the yellow pages or elsewhere. These service providers are not ordinary—they're the best in the business.

If you can't find the perfect spot in *Here Comes The Guide*, just call us.

I can't publish the names of all the sites I've discovered, so I keep computer files that include locations that missed our print deadlines as well as exclusive locations that want to be known strictly by word-of-mouth. I've personally inspected, screened and reviewed hundreds of places. As a consequence, I'm often sought after as a location scout, conducting searches for clients seeking particularly hard-to-find spots. Even with over 300 places in this book and over 900 in the computer, I'm still finding out about more sites because people like you call in with new leads. And I'm always impressed by the countless variations in ambiance, price and services available to those willing to explore a bit further. So if you can't find what you're looking for in this guide, call us. We'll explain how our location scouting service works and you can decide if you want more help.

Use our helpful matrix to speed up your search.

One of the greatest benefits of using *Here Comes The Guide* is the enormous amount of time you'll save. And, you can save even more time using the *find-it-fast* feature. Because of the sheer number of facilities included in this book, we've designed a helpful matrix, placed conveniently in front of the main body of *Here Comes The Guide*. It enables you to breeze through all of the entries by city, capacity and other important criteria, and pre-select those sites you wish to read about in more depth.

Here Comes The Guide covers Northern California.

Take advantage of the fact that Northern California is home to some of the most outstanding facilities in the United States. There are so many locations that offer exceptional environments, top-notch cuisine and professional event services, you're sure to find a special place that suits your needs. So grab this guide and explore! We've covered

Sacramento, Tahoe, the Gold Country, the North Coast and the Monterey Peninsula as well as the central Bay Area. When you discover the perfect spot for your wedding, you'll feel confident that you made the right choice because you did your homework using *Here Comes The Guide*.

It takes a lot of work to create a memorable wedding. Don't pick a place that's just so-so when you can select one that's a cut above. Whatever your tastes, whether you're a newcomer or native to Northern California, I hope you'll find this an entertaining, comprehensive and indispensable guide.

Coming next—honeymoons in paradise.

If you're going to take a honeymoon after the wedding, you'll be delighted with our next big project—a series of guidebooks focusing on *warm water locations* for honeymooners. We're off to explore and then tell you about honeymoon places in a way no one has done before. Instead of featuring the usual motels, hotels and packages, we're going to highlight interesting and unusual places to stay, including sites that can accommodate weddings and receptions, too. You can honeymoon at villas, bed and breakfasts, private homes, hidden cabins and splendid resorts. We'll avoid plastic fantastic hotels and stick to spots that offer interesting features, exceptional ambiance and service. And, of course, we'll give you plenty of information (including prices) so you can compare and contrast options. We'll find special rates for our readers and point out those locations where air and car packages apply. The first guidebook in the series will be *Here Comes The Guide, Hawaii* to be followed by *Here Comes the Guide, Florida; Mexico; Bahamas and Caribbean.*

If you would like to be put on our *Here Comes The Guide, Hawaii* mailing list, just call or fax us your name, address, phone number and projected wedding date so we can keep you informed about our progress. Since we find many unusual and special spots through our readers, we'd like to know if you have any special suggestions for the Hawaii publication. We look forward to hearing from you.

Private dining rooms are a hot commodity.

In addition to requests for wedding and reception spots, we're getting phone inquiries from all over the U.S. for private dining rooms. People want to know where they can go for rehearsal luncheons and dinners, bachelor parties, wedding showers and family get-togethers. It's not too hard to understand why. They just don't have extra time to plan a wedding *and* an additional party. Private dining rooms in restaurants are the perfect solution for smaller celebrations. Often, one call does it all. If the standard menu isn't exactly what you want, many restaurants will customize one for you. Staff, tables, chairs, linens and silver are included at no extra charge. Cakes, flowers and special wines can be arranged, too. There is hardly a faster, more efficient way of hosting an event than going through a restaurant that has a private dining room.

To help you, we've compiled a list of high-quality Northern California restaurants that love to host special events. Some are included in *Here Comes The Guide*, others are highlighted in our guidebook, *Perfect Places*, which identifies spots for parties, special events and business functions. We've also listed some others that are available for private functions, but are in neither book.

Restaurants in Here Comes The Guide

San Francisco	Page	Phone	East Bay, cont.	Page	Phone
Asta	47	415/495-2782	Piemonte Ovest, Oakland	231	510/601-0500
Atrium	48	415/788-4101	Scott's Gardens, Walnut Crk	251	510/934-0598
Blue Fox, The	51	415/981-1177	Scott's Seafood, Oakland	236	510/444-5969
Cafe Majestic	53	415/776-6400			
Carnelian Room	59	415/433-7500	*Wine Country*		
Cliff House	63	415/386-3330	Cafe Kinyon!, Yountville	317	707/944-2788
Lascaux	84	415/391-1555	Depot 1870, Sonoma	305	707/938-2980
MacArthur Park	85	415/398-5700	Mark West Lodge, Santa Rosa	303	707/546-2592
Miss Pearl's Jam House	89	415/775-5267			
Palio d'Asti	95	415/395-9800	*South Bay*		
Portico	98	415/861-2939	La Pastaia, San Jose	266	408/286-8686
Splendido	113	415/986-3222			
Square One	115	415/788-1110	*Sacramento Valley*		
			Casa de los Niños, Sacto.	366	916/452-2809
North Bay			Haman House, Roseville	359	916/791-2545
Deer Park Villa, Fairfax	131	415/456-8084	Shot of Class, Sacramento	381	916/447-5340
Guaymus, Tiburon	151	415/435-6300			
Lark Creek Inn, Larkspur	132	415/924-1602	*Carmel Valley*		
Ross Garden, Ross	137	415/457-2151	The Ridge Restaurant	331	408/659-0170
East Bay			*Tahoe*		
Cafe Fontebella, Oakland	219	510/452-2508	Cottonwood, Truckee	408	916/587-5711
Mudd's, San Ramon	245	510/837-9387	Sunnyside, Tahoe City	404	916/583-7200
Oliveto, Oakland	230	510/547-5356	Zina's, Truckee	411	916/587-1771

Additional Restaurants in Perfect Paces

San Francisco	Phone	East Bay	Phone
Cypress Club	415/296-8555	Bette's Diner, Berkeley	510/601-6939
Delancy Street	415/257-9800	Spiedini, Walnut Creek	510/939-2100
Elka	415/922-3200		
La Fiametta	415/474-5077	**South Bay**	
L'Olivier	415/981-7824	Campbell House, Campbell	408/374-5757
Modesto Lanzone	415/928-0400	Il Fornaio, San Jose	408/271-3366
Postrio	415/776-7825		
Stars	415/431-2716		
Stinking Rose	415/781-ROSE		
Vinoteca	415/983-6200		

Other Restaurants Available for Private Parties

San Francisco	Phone	East Bay	Phone
1001 Nob Hill	415/441-1001	Bridges, Danville	510/820-7669
Bistro Roti	415/495-6500		
Cafe Oritalia	415/346-1333		
Etrusca	415/777-0330		
Fleur de Lys	415/673-7779		
Hayes Street Bar & Grill	415/863-5545		
La Folie	415/776-5577		
La Pergola	415/563-4500		
Le Piano Zinc	415/431-5266		
Monsoon	415/441-3232		
Ristorante Donatello	415/441-7182		
Salud	415/864-8500		

How To Use This Guidebook

A Few Thoughts On Picking a Geographical Location

Your first *big* decision is to select a geographical location that will make sense for you, your family and the majority of your guests. Most people get married close to home, so there's little to consider. But if you pick a spot out of town, you need to think about the logistics of getting everyone to your wedding site.

If there are few financial or other constraints, then it really doesn't matter how far from home you go. If, however, you live in Napa and want to get married in Carmel, it's worth considering the total driving time to and from your destination, whether people are bringing children or whether an overnight stay will be required. When the distance is over two hours driving time, an overnight stay may be in order. A distant event location may limit you to a Saturday night event since guests may have to spend many hours traveling. And if you have guests arriving by plane, it's certainly helpful if there's an airport nearby. If you'll be serving alcohol, and you know your friends and family enjoy drinking, try to house them close to the wedding site. Check out the average temperatures where you plan to hold your event—it may be sunny in Marin in June but foggy and cold in Monterey.

There's no reason why you can't contemplate a wedding in Napa Valley or in the wilds of Big Sur. Just remember that the further out you go, the more time it will take—and you may end up having to delegate the details of party planning to someone else.

Selecting a Wedding Location

Identify What Kind of Wedding You Want and Establish Selection Criteria Early

Before you jump into the facility descriptions in *Here Comes The Guide*, take stock of all your needs and wants. Here are some basics:

Being Realistic: Your Budget

You'd think that it's an obvious consideration, but you'd be surprised how many brides and grooms are unrealistic about what they can afford. Weddings can be *very* expensive. Part of the problem is that most couples aren't very experienced with event budgeting and don't know how to estimate what locations, products and services will finally cost.

Part of being realistic means that couples must learn some simple arithmetic. For instance, the bride that has $5,000 dollars for 250 guests should know that $20 per guest is not much. And what is that $20 supposed to cover? Tax and gratuity together can range from 22–28% of the food and beverage cost (15% gratuity plus 8% tax equals 23%). That means budgeting $16.29/person plus 23% tax and gratuity will equal $20/person. But you've forgotten something expensive. Understand that any alcohol, let's say $6/person, would take the total available for food down to $10.30/person. For a seated meal, that's an unrealistic figure. Here's a graphic way to look at the costs for 250 guests:

Guests	_Food Cost_	_Alcohol Cost_	_Subtotal_	_Tax_	_Gratuity_	_Total_
250	$10.29/guest +	$6/guest =	$16.29/guest +	8% +	15% =	$5,006.78

Make sure you have a grand total in mind before you start budgeting. Of that total, how much will you spend for your location, food and beverage, band or DJ, flowers, cake, alcohol or other elements? When the grand total does not look like it will cover all the costs, it's time to make some hard decisions. If you have a very large guest list and a small pocketbook, you may need to scale down the event or simplify some of the amenities offered. Can you cover the price of a costly, seated dinner, or should you opt for hors d'oeuvres and a champagne reception only? Who is paying for the event? If parents are involved, make sure you keep them informed of anticipated costs. Whoever foots the bill, be advised that doing the homework here really counts. Pin down your costs early on in the planning stage and get all estimates in writing.

Style

Do you know what kind of wedding you want? Will it be a formal or informal affair, a traditional wedding or a creative, innovative party? Will it be held at night or during the day, indoors or outdoors? Will guests be dressed in black tie or in Western country garb? Know what you want _before_ you look for a location or the sheer number of options will be overwhelming. Remember, you can set the ambiance or tone of your wedding by selecting the right location.

Guest Count

How many people are anticipated? Many facilities want a guaranteed guest count 60 to 90 days in advance of your function—and they will want a deposit based on the figure you give them. It's important to know what the numbers are early on in order to plan your budget. Once you have a firm number in mind, use it to select the right ceremony or reception spot.

Seasonal Differences

The time of year and hours of the day may be major factors in wedding site selection, so be clear about the seasonal temperatures where your reception is planned. There's a good reason why most places are booked spring through fall. If you're arranging an outdoor winter party, make sure you have a backup plan that includes an inside space. If your budget can cover the costs, tents are another option to insure against inclement weather.

Special Requirements

Sometimes, places have strict rules and regulations. If most of your guests smoke, then pick a location that does not restrict smoking. If alcohol is going to be consumed, make sure it's allowed and find out if bar service needs to be licensed. If dancing or a big band are critical, then limit yourself to those locations that can accommodate it and the accompanying decibels. Do you have children, seniors or disabled guests on your list? If so, you need to plan for them, too. It's essential that you identify the special factors that are important for your wedding before you sign a contract.

Parking

Where to put your car is usually not a critical factor if you get married outside an urban area. However, if you're planning a wedding party in downtown Sacramento, San Francisco, Monterey or Carmel, make sure you understand what arrangements need to be made to facilitate parking.

Professional Help

If you are a busy person with limited time to plan and execute a party, pick a facility that offers complete coordination services, from catering and flowers to decorations and bar service. Or better yet, hire a professional event or wedding consultant. Either way, you'll make your life considerably easier by having someone else handle the details.

Food Quality

Food accounts for the greatest portion of the wedding budget. Consequently, menu selection is a big deal. Given the amount of money you will spend on this item alone, you should be concerned about the type, quantity and quality of meals. If in-house catering is provided, we suggest you pay critical attention to the facility's choices and services offered prior to paying a facility deposit. Try sampling different menu options in advance if you can. If you'd like to see how a facility handles setup and food presentation, arrange with the caterer to visit about a half an hour prior to someone else's wedding party.

Hidden Costs

This may come as a surprise, but not all services and event equipment are covered in the rental fee. Get it in writing! The cost of all extraneous elements can really add up. Watch out for those facilities that hide the true cost of renting their space by having a low rental fee. It's possible to get nickeled and dimed for all the extras: tables, chairs, linens, glassware, valet service and so forth. You can also end up paying for security and cleanup beyond what's normal. Save yourself a big headache by understanding exactly what's included in the rental fee and what's not before you sign any contract.

The important point we're trying to make here is that if you know what kind of wedding you want, and are clear about the essentials, your search will be made faster and easier. If you try to pick a location before you've made basic decisions, selection will be a struggle and it will take longer to find a spot that will make you happy.

Understanding the Information in Here Comes The Guide

Each location description in *Here Comes The Guide* follows the same format. To help you understand our thinking, what follows below is an explanation of the main headings in the same order as they appear.

Reserve In Advance

What we've indicated here is only a *suggested* time frame for making reservations in advance. Naturally, if a popular spot books 12 months in advance and you want to have a wedding there next week, your choice may prove unrealistic. If the *reserve in advance* information seems in conflict with your plans, don't despair! Find out if your particular date is available. Who knows? There are always cancellations and occasionally a popular date is not booked. If there's a location you really like, take a chance and call, even if it seems an unlikely possibility.

Description

Once you've selected a geographical area and you're clear about your needs, then thoroughly review all the sites listed in your area of preference. If you're pressed for time, you can read through the *find-it-fast* matrix first to preview facilities for location, capacity and other critical factors. Then, you can forge ahead to the main body of *Here Comes The Guide* and read the descriptions of *only* those sites that seem to be a good fit, based on your preliminary preview. If the facility still appeals to you after you've read the description, and it fulfills your location requirements, mark it with a ✔ and then move on to capacity.

Capacity

By now you should have a rough idea of how many people will be attending. If not, you may be in trouble, since many facilities want a deposit based on an estimated head-count. Look at the capacity figures for each event location. *Seated* or *sit-down* capacity refers to guests seated at tables. *Reception* or *standing* capacity refers to a function where the majority of guests are not seated, such as a champagne/hors d'oeuvres reception. Put a ✔ next to those facilities that fit your guest requirements. If you're planning well in advance and don't have your guest list whittled down yet, then you'll just have to estimate and refine the count as the date draws near. There is a world of difference in cost and planning effort between an intimate party of 60 and a large wedding with over 500 guests. Pin down your numbers as soon as you can.

Fees and Deposits

We've tried to give accurate costs as best we can. Where we haven't mentioned pricing, it may be because the facility's fee schedule was changing at time of publication or that the fee schedule was too complicated to fit into our set format. Some facilities want the flexibility to negotiate prices, and prefer not to state prices until they know exactly what kind of function you have in mind.

Look at the data regarding fees and deposits and remember that *these figures change regularly and usually in one direction—up*. It's a good idea to confirm the information we give in *Here Comes The Guide* with the facility you're calling, just to make sure it's still valid. If you're planning far in advance, anticipate increases by the time your function occurs. Once you are definite about your location, try to lock in your fees in a contract, protecting yourself from possible rate increases later. Make sure you ask about every service provided and are clear about all of the extras that can really add up. What can be extra? Facilities can charge you for tables, chairs, linens, plateware and silverware, glassware and fees for extended hours and other major items. Don't be surprised to see tax and gratuity (or service charges) in fixed amounts applied to the total bill if the facility provides restaurant or catering services. Although it may seem redundant to indicate that tax and service charges are *additional* in each entry, we find that most people forget (or just don't want to accept the painful reality) that 23%–28% will be applied to the food and beverage total.

Sometimes deposits are non-refundable. If the deposit is a large percentage of the total bill, make sure you know whether it's refundable or not. If it's refundable, then read the cancellation policy thoroughly. Also make sure you understand the policies which will ensure you get your cleaning and security deposit returned in full.

Food costs vary considerably. Carefully plan your menu with the caterer, event consultant or chef. Depending on the style of service and the type of food being served, your total food bill will vary dramatically, even if provided by the same caterer. Expect a multi-course seated meal with beverages to be the most expensive part of your wedding.

Alcohol is expensive, too. Look closely at the alcohol restrictions. Can you bring your own wine or champagne? Does the facility charge a corkage fee? Some facilities discourage you from bringing your own (BYO) by charging exorbitant fees for removing the cork (corkage) and pouring. Other places have limited permits which do not allow them to serve alcohol or restrict them from serving certain kinds; some will let you or the caterer serve alcohol, others will require someone with a license. Make sure you know what's allowed. Decide what your budget is for alcohol and determine what types you're willing to provide. And keep in mind that *the catering fees you are quoted rarely include the cost of alcohol*. A comment about trends in alcohol consumption is warranted. People are drinking less wine and hard alcohol than ever before and consumption of mineral water is on the rise. If you provide the alcohol, make sure you keep your purchase receipts so you can return any unopened bottles.

How much money can you afford to spend? Facility deposits are usually not large, but sometimes the rental fees plus food and beverage services can add up to $30,000 or more, depending on the location and number of guests. Be sure you have a sensible handle on your budget and read all the fine print before you sign any contract.

Availability

Some facilities are available 7am to 2am for wedding functions; others offer very limited "windows." If you'd like to save some money, consider a weekday or weeknight reception. Or, think about having your nuptials planned for the off season—the month of November, or January through March. Even the most sought-after places have openings midweek and during non-peak months, and at reduced costs. *Facilities want your business and are more likely to negotiate terms and prices if they have nothing else scheduled*. Again, read all the fine print carefully and ✔ those facilities that have time slots that meet your needs. If you inquire about the date you have in mind, and the reply is that it's already booked, it doesn't hurt to ask if someone actually *confirmed* that date by paying a deposit or signing a contract. If they haven't, you may be in luck.

Services/Amenities

Most facilities provide something in the way of services. We've attempted to give you a brief description of what each individual location has to offer. Because of space limitations, we have shortened words and developed a key to help you decipher our abbreviated notations. Please refer to the *Services/Amenities and Restrictions Key* for clarification and explanation. When you become familiar with our notation style, go back to *Services/Amenities* and put a ✔ where your requirements are met by the facility. You'll be able to quickly see what essentials on your list are covered and which ones are not.

Previewing a Facility

Once you've tallied up all your ✔ marks, you should have a handful of sites that merit a personal preview. If you plan to visit a lot of locations, here are some handy tips.

Appointments

Should you attempt to drive by first or schedule an appointment? If you reviewed the description and liked what you read, then we recommend you make an appointment to see each location. Sometimes the exterior of a great building looks worse than the beautiful and secluded garden it hides from the street. And sometimes, vice versa—a stunning facade will attract you and upon entry you discover an interior that doesn't appeal to your taste.

When you call for appointments, don't forget to ask for cross streets. Some places are hidden and take forever to find. Try to cluster your visits so that you can easily drive from one place to another without backtracking. Get a good, detailed street map of the area, and before you go to the sites, locate each one on the map in red or another contrasting color. Schedule at least 30 minutes per facility and arrange for ample driving time in between each stop. The key here is efficiency. Don't over-schedule yourself, however. It's best to view places when you're fresh. If you've reached your saturation point after five visits and you still have several more to go, those last places might get "bad reviews" simply because you're looking at them through bleary eyes and can't absorb any more information. While you want to accomplish as much as you can in as brief a time as possible, you will ultimately do yourself a disservice if your judgment is clouded by fatigue.

When you're previewing a facility, make sure to check out the restrooms, dance floor and kitchen facilities. Sometimes it's easy to get carried away by a great view or an extraordinary gold ceiling so that you forget a major item—like a place for the band.

Be Organized

Whether you're visiting a handful of facilities or canvassing an entire region, be organized. After you've decided on your wedding requirements, selected the facilities you want to see and arranged a workable visiting schedule, there are still things you can do to make this process easy on yourself.

Bring a camera. Take pictures of whatever you want to recall about a place—the front exterior, the garden, etc. A Polaroid is wonderful because it gives you instant "memories." Also, bring extra film. If you're using a 35mm camera, we recommend asa 200 print film which is fast enough to take interior shots. Make sure to write the name of the facility on the back of the photo. If you have a video camera, by all means, bring it along. You'd be surprised how easy it is to confuse various sites when you've got a dozen of them competing for space in your mind and you can't remember which garden or dining room corresponds to which place.

Bring a tape recorder. During or after each visit, record your immediate impressions. Your likes, dislikes and any other observations can be quickly recorded. You can write up your notes when you have more time. If you don't have a recorder, jot down your comments in *Here Comes The Guide* itself or in a notebook. Observe not only the physical surroundings, but pay close attention to how you are treated by the manager, the owner or the event coordinator. No matter how you do it, thorough note-taking is crucial if you want to be able to adequately evaluate everything you have seen and heard.

File everything. Many facilities will provide you with pamphlets, menus, rate charts and other materials. One good way to handle the deluge is to put each facility's paperwork in a 9" x 12" manila envelope with its name on it. A binder with plastic pocket inserts is also handy. The idea is to avoid having to sort through a pile of things later. You want to keep your notes, photos and handouts clearly identified and easily accessible.

Bring snacks. Driving from place to place can make you hungry and thirsty. If you take a little something to eat, you can munch en route and keep your energy level up.

Working with a Facility

Confirm All the Details

We can't over emphasize the importance of accurate information. *When you make the initial phone call, confirm that the information presented here is still valid.*

We have asked each site to give us current information, but we know from long experience that *facilities can change prices and policies overnight.* Show or read to the site's representative the information that refers to his/her facility, and have them inform you of any changes. If there have been significant increases in fees or new restrictions that you can't live with, cross it off your list and move on. If the facility is still a contender, request a tour.

Once you have determined that the physical elements of the place suit you, it's time to discuss details. Ask about services and amenities or fees that may not be listed in the book and make a note of them. Outline your plans to the representative and make sure that the facility can accommodate your particular needs. If you don't want to handle all the details yourself, find out what the facility is willing and able to do, and if there will be additional fees for their assistance. Facilities often provide planning services for little or no extra charge. If other in-house services are offered, such as flowers or wedding cakes, you need to inquire about the quality of each service provider and whether or not substitutions can be made. If outside vendors are called in to supply these services, you might want to ascertain whether the facility receives a commission. If you prefer to use your own vendors, will the facility charge you an extra fee?

The Importance of Rapport

Another factor to consider is your rapport with the person(s) you are working with. Are you comfortable? Do they listen well and respond to your questions directly? Do they inspire trust and confidence? Are they warm and enthusiastic or cold, businesslike and aloof? If you have doubts, you need to resolve them before embarking on a working relationship with these folks—no matter how wonderful the facility itself is. Discuss your feelings with them, and if you're still not completely satisfied, get references and call them. If at the end of this process you still have lingering concerns, you may want to eliminate the facility from your list even though it seems perfect in every other way.

Working with a Caterer

Get References and Look for Professionalism

If you're selecting your own caterer, don't just pick one at random out of the yellow pages. Get references from friends and acquaintances or, better yet, call the caterers listed in the *Here Comes The Guide* service directory. We've thoroughly screened these companies and can unequivocally assure you that they are in the top 5% of the industry in terms of quality and service. We keep all of their references on file, just in case you'd like to get more details about them. Feel free to call and ask questions.

Every caterer is different. Some offer only preset menus while others will help you create your own. Prices and menus vary enormously, so know what you want and what you are willing to spend. After you've talked to several caterers and have decided which ones you want to seriously consider, get references for each one and call them. Ask not only about the quality of the food, but about the ease of working with a given caterer. You'll want to know if the caterer is professional—fully prepared and equipped, punctual and organized. You may also want to know if the caterer is licensed and whether he/she has a kitchen approved by the Department of Health. Ask the caterer where the food is being prepared. Does he/she carry workmen's compensation and liability insurance? Although this level of inquiry may seem unnecessary or complicated, these questions are intended to increase your critical thinking about your catering choices.

Facility Requirements

Often the facility you have chosen will have specific requirements regarding caterers. Whether they have to be licensed and bonded, out by 11pm or fastidiously clean—make sure that before you hire a caterer, he or she is compatible with your site. In fact, even if the facility does not require it, it's a good idea to have your caterer visit the place in advance to become familiar with any special circumstances or problems that might come up. You'll notice throughout *Here Comes The Guide* the words "provided" or "preferred" after the word *Catering*. Sites that have an exclusive caterer or only permit you to select from a preferred list do so because each wants to eliminate most of the risks involved in having a caterer on the premises who is not accustomed to working in that environment. Exclusive or preferred caterers have achieved this exalted status because they provide consistently good services. If your facility has confidence in them, generally you can, too. Whether you are working with one of your facility's choices or your own, make sure that your contract includes everything you have agreed on before you sign it.

Working with an Event Planner or Consultant

Consultants Handle Details

Opting to hire a professional may be a wise choice. If you can afford it, engaging someone to "manage" your event can be a godsend. A good consultant will ask all the right questions, determine exactly what you want, and put together your entire affair. Although your role will largely be to select from the options presented and write checks, you should not give up being a decision-maker. It's your wedding—no one else should decide what's right for you.

A consultant is also valuable if you have difficulty coping with the often overwhelming number of details and decisions involved. He or she can provide whatever guidance, support and decision-making you need. Wedding consultants and event planners can be hired on a meeting-by-meeting basis, too. If you don't need much more than some advice and structure, this arrangement can be extremely beneficial.

So if the planning process is just too much for you to handle, and you don't mind the expense, definitely consider hiring a professional. Most of the principles used in selecting a caterer apply to hiring an event coordinator. Try to get suggestions from friends or facilities, follow up on references the consultants give you, compare and contrast service fees and make sure you and the consultant are compatible. The range of professionalism and experience varies greatly, so it really is to your advantage to investigate consultants' track records. Again, once you have found someone who can accommodate you, get everything in writing so that there won't be any misunderstandings down the road.

Insurance Considerations

You may want to get extra insurance coverage for your event. Since this is now a major consideration for many facilities (and service providers), you may not have an option. More and more facilities are requiring either proof of insurance or a certificate guaranteeing additional coverage.

Deep Pockets

These days, if someone gets injured at a party or something is damaged at or near the event site, it's likely that somebody will be sued. Unfortunately, that's the way it is. Event sites and service providers are very aware of their potential liability and all have coverage of one kind or another.

In the past, usually the facility was sued. Nowadays, everybody gets sued, and that may mean you. Whoever has the most insurance is said to have the "deepest pockets" and will be pursued to pay the bulk of the claim. To protect themselves, facilities have begun to require additional insurance from service providers *and* their clients. The goal is to spread the risk among all parties involved. Don't panic. Although *event insurance,* per se, is impossible to obtain, extra insurance for a specified period of time is easy to get and relatively inexpensive.

Obtaining Extra Insurance

Facilities often require between $500,000 and $1,000,000 worth of extra coverage. If you are a home owner, just ask your insurance agent to tack on a rider to your home owner's policy to cover the event date and time period. The company will issue you a certificate of insurance specifically for your function in the amount selected. To finalize your rental agreement, you will have to present this certificate to the facility owner or representative as proof of insurance.

If you're not a home owner, many facilities are able to offer additional insurance through their own policies. You will pay an extra charge, but it's usually nominal.

It Can't Happen To Me

Don't be lulled into the notion that it can't happen to you. Naturally, there is more likelihood of risk with a late night New Year's Eve party or a high school prom night than at a wedding. But we could tell you stories of upscale parties where something did happen and a lawsuit resulted. Many event sites have plenty of coverage and are willing to assume the "deep pocket" risk. Others don't and won't. Take into account the type of event and the factors that may affect liability. Even if extra insurance is not required, you may want to consider additional coverage anyway, especially if alcohol is being served. You are the best judge of your guests' temperaments. If you plan on having a wild wedding, a little additional insurance could be a good thing.

Do Your Part: Recycle

You wonder why we're including a brief item about recycling in a book like *Here Comes The Guide*? Because most of the time, special events generate recyclable materials and excess food. Many caterers often have leftover food that the bride and groom don't want to take home. Nowadays, you and the caterer can feel good about doing your part by donating the excess. You also can recycle plastic bottles, glass, metal and paper. An added benefit is that food donations are tax deductible for either you or the caterer. And, if you recycle, the cost for extra garbage containers (bins) can be eliminated or reduced.

Food donations are distributed to teenage drop-in centers, youth shelters, alcoholic treatment centers, AIDS hospices, senior centers and refugee centers throughout the region. You should also know that a 1989 state law protects the donor from liability.

Your packaged food can be picked up the day of the event or brought back to the caterer's kitchen to be picked up later on. Place food in clean plastic bags, plastic containers or boxes. Perishables should be refrigerated. Other recyclable materials must be separated. Food must also be edible. For example, if dressing has been poured over a salad, most likely it won't be worth eating the next day.

How do you make a donation? Call your local recycling center to arrange a pickup. You can look through your phone book to find a local Food Bank or you can call the following organizations to make advance arrangements.

San Francisco:	Food Runners	415/929-1866
	Food Bank	415/957-1076
	The Episcopal Sanctuary	415/863-3893
Berkeley:	Daily Bread Project	510/540-1250
Oakland:	Oakland Pot Luck	510/272-0414
San Mateo & Santa Clara Counties:		
	Second Harvest	408/266-8866
Marin County:	Food Bank	415/883-1302
Sacramento:	Food Bank	916/452-3663
	Loaves & Fishes	916/446-0874

Services/Amenities & Restrictions Key

SERVICES/AMENITIES

Restaurant Services

yes: the facility has a restaurant available on site for catering your wedding or that is accessible to your guests

Catering

provided: the facility provides catering • *provided, no BYO:* the facility arranges catering; you cannot arrange your own • *preferred list:* you must select your caterer from the facility's approved list • *provided or BYO; provided, BYO ok:* the facility will arrange catering or you can select an outside caterer of your own • *BYO, must be licensed:* arrange for your own licensed caterer • *provided, if BYO buy-out required:* a fee will be charged to "buy-out" the facility's preferred caterer if you wish to make your own arrangements

Kitchen Facilities

ample or fully equipped: major appliances and space, large and well-equipped • *moderate:* medium-sized and utilitarian • *minimal:* small with limited equipment, may not have all basic appliances • *setup only:* room for setup, but not enough space or utilities to prepare food • *n/a:* not applicable when facility provides catering

Tables & Chairs

some provided or *provided:* facility provides some or all of the tables and chairs • *BYO:* make arrangements to bring your own

Linens, Silver, etc.

same as above

Restrooms

wca: wheelchair accessible • *no wca:* not wheelchair accessible

Dance Floor

yes: an area for dancing (hardwood floor, cement terrace, patio) is available • *CBA, extra charge:* you can arrange for a dance floor to be brought in for a fee

Bride's Dressing Area

yes: there is an area for changing • *no:* there's no area for changing • *limited:* smaller space not fully equipped as changing room • *CBA:* can be arranged

Parking

descriptions are self explanatory; *CBA:* can be arranged

Overnight Accommodations
if overnight accommodations are available on site, the number of guestrooms is listed; • *CBA:* the facility will arrange accommodations for you

Telephone
restricted: calls made on the house phone must be local, collect or charged to a credit card • *guest phones:* private phones in guestrooms • *house phone:* central phone used by all guests

Outdoor Night Lighting
yes: indicates that there is adequate light to conduct your event outdoors after dark • *access only* or *limited:* lighting is sufficient for access only

Outdoor Cooking Facilities
BBQ: the facility has a barbecue on the premises • *BBQ, CBA:* a barbecue can be arranged through the facility • *BYO BBQ:* make arrangements for your own barbecue

Cleanup
provided: facility takes care of cleanup • *caterer:* your caterer is responsible • *caterer, renter:* both you and your caterer are responsible for cleanup

Other, Special
description of any service or amenity not included in above list

RESTRICTIONS

Alcohol
provided, no BYO: the facility provides alcoholic beverages (for a fee) and does not permit you to bring your own • *BYO:* you can arrange for your own alcohol • *corkage, $/bottle:* if you bring your own alcohol, the facility charges a fee per bottle to remove the cork and pour • *WCB only (or any combination of these three letters):* only wine, champagne and/or beer are permitted

Smoking
allowed: smoking is permitted throughout the facility • *outside only:* smoking is not permitted inside the facility • *not allowed:* smoking is not permitted anywhere on the premises • *designated area:* specific areas for smoking have been designated

Music
Almost every facility allows acoustical music unless stated otherwise. Essentially, restrictions refer to amplified music • *amplified ok:* amplified music is acceptable without restriction • *outside only:* no amplified music allowed inside • *inside only:* no amplified

music permitted outside • *within limits or restrictions:* amplified music allowed but there are limits on volume, hours of play, number of instruments, etc.

Wheelchair Access

Accessibility is based on whether a facility is wheelchair accessible or not • *yes:* the facility is accessible • *limited:* the facility is accessible but with difficulty • *no:* the facility is not accessible

Insurance

Many facilities require that you purchase and show proof of some insurance coverage. The type and amount of insurance varies with the facility, and some facilities offer insurance for minimal charge. *required, certificate required or proof of insurance required:* additional insurance is required • *not required:* no additional insurance is required

Other

decorations restricted: the facility limits the use of tape, nails, tacks, confetti or other decorations

Find-It-Fast

We know your time is valuable.

If you've got to find a place to get married *fast* and you don't have enough time to leisurely read through all the location descriptions, use this convenient chart. It lists each facility by *region* and *city* in alphabetical order and highlights essential information for each one. This makes it easy to quickly identify the wedding locations that are most appropriate for you.

Once you've identified a handful of places that seem to meet your needs, read each *Here Comes The Guide* entry for more complete information.

Target your area of geographical preference first.

Pick the cities that are best for you, your family and guests, keeping in mind the location selection advice in the "How To Use This Guidebook" section.

Identify the facilities that fit your needs.

Read through the columns, from left to right noting which features are essential to your wedding. If a site seems to offer what you need, put a light check mark next to it or better yet, *xerox the pages and use color highlighters.* In this edition, we've added another handy feature; the *Here Comes The Guide* page number that helps you find the lengthier description fast. Now you can easily look up the ones you've checked. If you still need more information, call the facility.

Remember, the find-it-fast section is not perfect.

The purpose of this matrix is to reduce your searching time. However, because the information presented is abbreviated, it won't be perfect. A bullet • in the *Amplified Music Restricted* column, for example, may mean that amplified music is not allowed, or it may only mean that you can't have it outside. To find out how the restriction will affect your party, *you have to read the full description.* The following is a brief explanation of the matrix headings.

Matrix Headings

Maximum Capacity

Most of the numbers shown are for standing receptions. However, some might be for a combination of seated and standing events. If the capacity looks *about* right, it's important that you read the corresponding *Here Comes The Guide* entry to confirm. The numbers marked with asterisks * indicate that the figure may be very inexact. For instance, we may have been given the maximum capacity for *only* the largest room in a multi-room facility. Consequently, the maximum capacity if all the rooms are combined is unknown. A facility with a large total capacity may also be able to comfortably accommodate a small event in one of its rooms. If a location seems perfect but the numbers are not quite right, we suggest you read the entry and then call to make sure.

Indoor and Outdoor Facilities

These columns are self explanatory.

In-house Catering and BYO Catering

In-house means that the facility can cater your event or arrange to have it catered. BYO indicates that you can make arrangements for your own caterer.

Alcohol Provided or Alcohol BYO

If you see a • in the *Alcohol Provided* column and a • in the *Alcohol BYO*, that means the facility can provide alcohol *and* they will also let you bring your own. Note that many facilities charge a corkage fee if you BYO. If there's a • in the *Alcohol Provided* column, but not in the *Alcohol BYO* column, you cannot bring your own alcohol. If there isn't a • in either column it means that alcohol is not allowed.

Restaurant On Site and Guestrooms Available

These columns are self explanatory.

Event Coordination

Many facilities provide wedding planning and coordination, everything from catering to flowers and custom party favors. This service may be free or there may be an additional charge. Be sure to ask.

Wheelchair Access Restricted

Indicates access problems ranging from a single step into a building to total inaccessibility. It doesn't mean you *can't* get into a site—it just denotes that there may be some degree of difficulty.

Smoking Restricted

Means no smoking or smoking in designated areas only.

Insurance Required

Proof of insurance or a certificate of insurance may be required.

Amplified Music Restricted

Means amplified music is not allowed or is permitted with inside/outside constraints and/or volume limits.

FIND-IT-FAST MATRIX

FACILITY	PAGE	MAX. SEATED CAPACITY	MAX. STANDING CAPACITY	Indoor Facilities	Outdoor Facilities	In-house Catering	BYO Catering	Alcohol Provided	Alcohol BYO	Restaurant On Site	Guestrooms Available	Event Coordination	Handicap Restricted	Smoking Restricted	Insurance Required	Amplified Music Restricted
SAN FRANCISCO																
Alamo Square Inn	44	125	200	•	•	•		•	•		•	•	•	•	•	•
Aquatic Park Bayview Room	45	150	190	•		•		•						•		
Archbishop's Mansion	46	50	100	•		•		•	•		•	•	•	•		•
Asta Restaurant	47	110	200	•		•		•	•							
Atrium	48	175	300	•	•	•		•	•	•		•				
Balclutha	49	125	300	•	•		•							•	•	
Blue and Gold Fleet	50	200	300	•	•	•		•				•	•			
Blue Fox, The	51	80	150	•		•		•	•	•		•	•	•		•
Cable Car Barn and Museum	52	400	800	•			•	•							•	
Cafe Majestic	53	120	n/a	•		•		•	•			•	•			•
Caffe Esprit	54	125	300	•	•	•		•				•				
California Academy of Sciences	55	550	3000	•		•	•	•				•				
California Culinary Academy	57	200	500*	•		•		•	•	•		•				•
California Spirit, The	58	80	149	•	•	•		•				•		•		
Carnelian Room	59	300	500	•		•		•	•	•		•				
Casa de la Vista	60	180	300	•	•	•		•	•			•				
Casa San Gregorio	61	50	80	•	•	•	•	•	•		•	•	•		•	•
City Club, The	62	200	700	•		•		•		•		•				
Cliff House, The	63	135	160	•	•	•		•				•	•			
Conservatory of Flowers, The	64	70	200	•			•							•	•	
Contract Design Center	65	250	500	•			•	•				•			•	
Delancey Street	467	300	500	•	•	•	•	•	•	•		•		•		•
Eureka, The	66	250	600	•	•		•	•					•	•	•	
Ferryboat Santa Rosa	67	500	500	•	•	•	•	•	•			•	•	•		
Flood Mansion, The	68	300	450	•	•		•	•					•	•		
Forest Hill Club House	69	100	200	•	•		•	•				•				•
Fort Mason Conference Center	70	230	350	•			•	•				•		•		
Galleria Design Center	71	1200	2500	•		•	•	•				•			•	
GiftCenter Pavilion	72	300	450	•		•	•	•				•			•	
Ginsberg Collection, The	73	100	350	•			•	•				•		•	•	
Golden Gate Park Gardens	74	200	200		•		•	•								•
Golden Sunset	75	40	100	•	•	•		•	•		•	•	•	•		
Green Room, The	76	300	500	•			•	•				•	•	•	•	•
Greens	77	150	250	•		•		•		•		•				
Haas-Lilienthal House	78	80	200	•			•	•				•	•			•
Hamlin Mansion	79	200	350	•		•		•				•	•			•
Herbst & Festival Pavilions	80	3500	5000	•			•	•				•			•	
Hornblower Dining Yachts	81	800*	1000*	•	•	•		•	•		call	•	call			

FACILITY	PAGE	MAX. SEATED CAPACITY	MAX. STANDING CAPACITY	Indoor Facilities	Outdoor Facilities	In-house Catering	BYO Catering	Alcohol Provided	Alcohol BYO	Restaurant On Site	Guestrooms Available	Event Coordination	Handicap Restricted	Smoking Restricted	Insurance Required	Amplified Music Restricted
Julius' Castle	83	100	n/a	•		•		•		•		•				•
Lascaux	84	140	n/a	•		•		•	•	•		•		•		•
MacArthur Park	85	280	500		•		•		•	•	•	•		•		
Mansions Hotel, The	86	90	150	•	•	•		•	•	•	•	•				
Marines' Memorial	87	250	250	•		•		•	•	•		•		•		
Mark Monroe Productions	88	200	600	•		•		•				•		•	•	
Miss Pearl's Jam House	89	400	800	•	•	•		•	•	•	•	•				
Miyako Hotel, The	90	500	600	•		•		•	•	•	•	•				
Nimitz Conference Center	91	389	500*	•	•	•		•				•				
Old Federal Reserve Bank Bldg.	92	400	800	•		•	•	•	•	•		•		•		
Pacific Spirit, The	93	35	90	•	•	•		•	•		•	•	•	•		
Palace of Fine Arts, The	94	300	500		•		•		•			•			•	•
Palio d'Asti	95	250	300	•		•		•	•	•		•		•		•
Pan Pacific Hotel	96	360	500	•	•	•		•	•	•	•	•				
Park Hyatt San Francisco	97	150	300	•	•	•		•	•	•	•	•				
Portico	98	100	150	•		•		•		•	•	•	•			•
Queen Anne, The	99	85	150	•	•	•		•	•		•	•				
Rincon Center Atrium	47	200	500	•		•		•	•	•		•				
Rock & Bowl	100	n/a	300	•			•	•								
Rococo Showplace	101	140	350	•			•		•			•		•	•	•
Rotunda, The	102	200	350	•		•		•	•	•		•				
Sailing Ship Dolf Rempp	103	400	800	•	•	•	•	•		•		•				
San Francisco Maritime Museum	104	120	400	•			•		•			•		•	•	
San Francisco Mart	105	500	800	•			•	•	•	•		•			•	
San Francisco Spirit, The	106	300	700	•	•	•		•	•			•		•		
Sharon Arts Center	107	80	100	•	•		•		•			•		•	•	•
Sheraton Palace Hotel	109	600	1000	•		•		•	•	•	•	•				
Sherman House, The	110	60	100	•	•	•		•		•	•	•		•		•
Showplace Design Center	111	250	500	•		•	•	•				•	•		•	
Spectrum Gallery	112	400	650	•			•	•	•			•			•	
Splendido	113	200	200	•	•	•		•	•	•		•		•		•
Square One	115	45	n/a	•		•		•	•	•		•				•
SS Jeremiah O'Brien	116	210	300	•	•		•		•				•	•	•	
Stanford Court, The	117	550	800*	•		•		•		•	•	•		•	•	•
St. Francis Hotel, The	118	1000	1500*	•		•		•	•	•	•	•				
St. Paulus Church	119	250	450	•		•	•	•					•	•		
Swedenborgian Church	120	115	150	•	•		•		•				•	•		•
Trocadero, The	121	125	150*	•	•		•		•			•				
Wattis Room, The	123	100	200	•		•	•	•	•			•				
1409 Sutter	468	150	275	•		•		•	•			•		•	•	

FACILITY	PAGE	MAX. SEATED CAPACITY	MAX. STANDING CAPACITY	Indoor Facilities	Outdoor Facilities	In-house Catering	BYO Catering	Alcohol Provided	Alcohol BYO	Restaurant On Site	Guestrooms Available	Event Coordination	Handicap Restricted	Smoking Restricted	Insurance Required	Amplified Music Restricted
HALF MOON BAY																
Douglas Beach House	124	95	150	•		•		•				•				
Mill Rose Inn	125	125	125	•	•	•		•			•	•	•	•		
Montara																
Montara Gardens	126	150	150	•	•	•		•						•	•	•
Point Montara Lighthouse	127	60	60	•	•	•		•			•			•	•	
San Gregorio																
Rancho San Gregorio	128	125	125	•	•	•		•			•	•	•	•		
NORTH BAY																
Belvedere																
China Cabin	130	48	65	•	•	•		•						•	•	•
Fairfax																
Deer Park Villa	131	300	500	•	•	•		•	•	•		•				•
Larkspur																
Lark Creek Inn, The	132	200	250*	•	•	•		•	•	•		•	•			•
Mill Valley																
Mill Valley Outdoor Art Club, The	133	120	200	•	•		•	•								•
Mountain Home Inn	135	80	110	•	•	•		•	•	•	•	•				
Ross																
Caroline Livermore Room	136	130	500	•	•		•	•							•	•
Ross Garden Restaurant	137	75	150	•	•	•		•	•	•		•				•
San Rafael																
Dominican College	138	340	500	•	•		•	•							•	•
Falkirk Mansion	139	60	125	•	•		•	•						•	•	•
Forty Twenty Civic Center Drive	140	300	500	•	•		•	•						•	•	
Foster Hall	141	250	500	•	•	•		•	•			•		•		•
Marin Beach and Tennis Club	142	75	175	•	•	•		•	•			•	•		•	
San Rafael Improvement Club	143	125	160	•	•		•	•						•	•	
Sausalito																
Alta Mira, The	144	150	200*	•	•	•		•	•	•	•	•			•	•
Casa Madrona Hotel	145	100	140*	•	•	•		•	•	•	•	•	•	•		
Sausalito Woman's Club	147	175	200*	•	•		•	•						•	•	•

FACILITY	PAGE	MAX. SEATED CAPACITY	MAX. STANDING CAPACITY	Indoor Facilities	Outdoor Facilities	In-house Catering	BYO Catering	Alcohol Provided	Alcohol BYO	Restaurant On Site	Guestrooms Available	Event Coordination	Handicap Restricted	Smoking Restricted	Insurance Required	Amplified Music Restricted
Stinson Beach																
Stinson Beach Creekside Center	148	200	400	•	•		•		•			•		•	•	
Tiburon																
Corinthian Yacht Club	149	250	400	•	•	•		•	•	•		•	•	•		•
Guaymas	151	100	150	•	•	•		•	•	•		•	•			•
Lyford House, The	152	125	125	•	•		•	•						•		•
Old St. Hilary's	153	125	n/a	•									•	•	•	•
# NORTH COAST																
Bodega Bay																
Bay Hill Mansion	154	50	50	•	•	•	•	•			•	•	•	•		•
Cazadero																
Timberhill Ranch	155	40	40*	•	•	•		•	•	•	•		•	•		•
Fort Bragg																
Mendocino Coast Botanical Gardens	156	30	30		•		•		•	•				•		•
Shoreline Properties	157	call	50*	•	•		•		•		•			•	•	•
Jenner																
Murphy's Jenner Inn	158	call	90*	•		•	•	•	•	•	•	•	•	•		•
Little River																
Inn at School House Creek	159	70	100*	•	•	•	•	•		•	•		•	•		•
Rachel's Inn	160	30	125	•	•	•		•	•	•	•	•	•			•
Mendocino																
Ames Lodge	161	30	30	•	•		•		•		•		•	•		•
Mendocino Hotel	162	110	150	•	•	•		•		•	•	•		•		•
Monte Rio																
Huckleberry Springs	163	65	65	•	•	•	•	•			•		•	•	•	
# PENINSULA																
Atherton																
Holbrook Palmer Park	164	250	250	•	•	•	•		•			•	•	•	•	•
Belmont																
Ralston Hall	165	200	250	•	•		•		•				•	•	•	

FACILITY	PAGE	MAX. SEATED CAPACITY	MAX. STANDING CAPACITY	Indoor Facilities	Outdoor Facilities	In-house Catering	BYO Catering	Alcohol Provided	Alcohol BYO	Restaurant On Site	Guestrooms Available	Event Coordination	Handicap Restricted	Smoking Restricted	Insurance Required	Amplified Music Restricted
Burlingame																
Kohl Mansion	166	250	450	•	•		•		•					•	•	•
Hillsborough																
Crocker Mansion, The	168	100	300	•	•		•		•				•	•	•	•
Menlo Park																
Allied Arts Guild Restaurant	169	155	200	•	•	•				•		•	•	•		•
Latham Hopkins Gatehouse	170	45	100	•	•		•		•			•	•	•		•
Stanford Park Hotel	171	250	250	•	•	•		•	•	•	•	•		•		•
Mountain View																
Rengstorff House	172	24	85	•	•		•		•				•	•		•
Palo Alto																
Gamble Garden Center, The	174	75	75	•	•		•		•				•	•	•	•
Garden Court Hotel	175	250	300	•	•	•		•	•	•	•	•		•		
MacArthur Park	176	222	120	•	•	•		•	•	•		•		•		
Stanford Barn	178	290	350	•	•	•	•	•	•			•		•		
Portola Valley																
Fogarty Winery & Vineyards	180	200	225*	•	•		•	•				•	•	•	•	•
Ladera Oaks	179	350	350	•			•		•							•
Redwood City																
Hotel Sofitel	182	200	400	•	•	•		•	•	•	•	•		•		
Pacific Athletic Club	183	600	1000	•	•	•		•	•	•		•		•		
Woodside																
Green Gables	185	call	1200		•	•		•				•			•	
Pulgas Water Temple	186	150	n/a		•									•		•
EAST BAY																
Benicia																
Camel Barn Museum	188	154	330	•			•		•				•			
Captain Walsh House	189	175	175	•	•		•	•	•		•	•		•	•	•
Fischer-Hanlon House	190	50	100	•	•		•		•				•	•		•
Berkeley																
Bancroft Club, The	191	250	350	•		•		•	•	•	•	•		•	•	•
Berkeley City Club	192	300	325*	•	•	•		•		•	•	•		•	•	
Berkeley Conference Center	193	220	350*	•		•		•	•	•		•		•		

FACILITY	Page	Max. Seated Capacity	Max. Standing Capacity	Indoor Facilities	Outdoor Facilities	In-house Catering	BYO Catering	Alcohol Provided	Alcohol BYO	Restaurant On Site	Guestrooms Available	Event Coordination	Handicap Restricted	Smoking Restricted	Insurance Required	Amplified Music Restricted
Berkeley Rose Garden	195	n/a	150*		•								•			•
Brazilian Room	196	150	225	•	•	•	•		•				•	•		•
Hillside Club	197	150	200	•			•		•				•	•		
Concord																
Centre Concord	198	400	400	•			•		•				•	•		
Crockett																
Crockett Community Center	199	350	400	•	•		•		•			•				
Danville																
Behring & UC Museums	201	500	600*	•	•		•		•				•	•		•
El Rio	202	150	300	•	•	•	•	•	•		•	•	•	•	•	•
Victorian & Executive Estate, The	203	200	500*	•	•	•	•	•	•		•	•	•	•	•	•
Fremont																
Ardenwood Historic Preserve	204	call	500		•	•		•				•				•
Palmdale Estate, The	205	150	1000	•	•		•	•				•		•		•
Shinn Gardens	207	200	200		•		•	•						•	•	•
Vallejo Adobe Historical Park	208	49	100	•	•		•	•					•	•	•	•
Lafayette																
Lafayette Park Hotel	209	280	500	•	•	•		•		•	•	•		•		•
Livermore																
Concannon	210	500	750	•	•		•	•				•		•		
Ravenswood	212	150	150	•	•		•		•					•	•	•
Tri Valley Aahmes Activity Center	213	540	1000	•			•		•			•		•	•	
Wente Bros. Estate Winery	214	250	500	•	•	•		•				•				
Wente Bros. Sparkling Wine Cellars	215	700	200	•	•	•		•		•		•				
Montclair																
Montclair Woman's Club	216	188	360	•	•		•		•				•	•		
Moraga																
Hacienda de las Flores	217	128	200*	•	•		•		•					•	•	•
Oakland																
Athenian Nile Club	218	250	350	•			•	•	•			•	•			
Cafe Fontebella	219	275	1000	•	•	•		•	•	•		•		•		
California Ballroom	221	350	600	•			•		•			•		•		
Camron-Stanford House	222	call	250	•	•		•		•				•	•	•	•
Claremont Resort, The	223	350	400*	•	•	•		•		•	•	•				

FACILITY	PAGE	MAX. SEATED CAPACITY	MAX. STANDING CAPACITY	Indoor Facilities	Outdoor Facilities	In-house Catering	BYO Catering	Alcohol Provided	Alcohol BYO	Restaurant On Site	Guestrooms Available	Event Coordination	Handicap Restricted	Smoking Restricted	Insurance Required	Amplified Music Restricted
Commodore Dining Cruises	224	350	450	•	•	•	•	•	•		•	•	•	•		
Dunsmuir House	225	3000	3000	•	•		•	•	•			•		•	•	
Lake Merritt Hotel, The	227	225	275	•		•		•	•	•	•	•	•	•		•
Mills College Chapel	228	175	n/a	•									•			•
Morcom Rose Garden	228	n/a	200		•								•			•
Oakland Hills Tennis Club	229	110	200	•	•	•	•		•			•		•	•	•
Oliveto	230	26	n/a	•		•		•	•					•		
Piemonte Ovest	231	110	200	•	•	•		•	•	•			•	•		•
Preservation Park	232	185	400	•	•	•		•				•		•	•	
Sailboat House	234	155	225	•			•		•				•	•		
Scottish Rite Center	235	1500	1300*	•		•	•	•						•	•	
Scott's Seafood Restaurant	236	250	450	•	•	•		•		•		•				
Sequoia Lodge	237	100	150	•	•		•	•						•		

Piedmont
| | | | | | | | | | | | | | | | | |
| Piedmont Community Center | 238 | 200 | 300* | • | • | | • | • | | | | | | • | • | |

Pleasanton
Century House	239	125	125	•	•		•	•						•	•	•
Pleasanton Hotel, The	240	300	400	•	•	•		•	•	•		•				

Point Richmond
East Brother Light Station	241	250	250	•	•	•	•	•	•		•	•	•	•		
Linsley Hall	242	60	110	•	•		•		•				•	•		•

San Leandro
| | | | | | | | | | | | | | | | | |
| Best House | 243 | 150 | 150 | • | • | | • | | • | | • | | • | • | | |

San Pablo
| | | | | | | | | | | | | | | | | |
| Rockefeller Lodge | 244 | 250 | 500 | • | • | • | | • | • | | | • | | | | • |

San Ramon
Mudd's Restaurant	245	150	70	•	•	•		•	•	•		•		•		•
San Ramon Community Center	246	250	450	•	•		•		•			•		•	•	•
San Ramon Senior Center	248	115	250	•	•		•		•			•		•	•	•

Sunol
| | | | | | | | | | | | | | | | | |
| Elliston Vineyards | 249 | 240 | 300 | • | • | • | | • | • | | | • | | • | | • |

Vallejo
| | | | | | | | | | | | | | | | | |
| Foley Cultural Center | 250 | 500 | 600 | • | • | | • | | • | | | | | • | | |

FACILITY	PAGE	MAX. SEATED CAPACITY	MAX. STANDING CAPACITY	Indoor Facilities	Outdoor Facilities	In-house Catering	BYO Catering	Alcohol Provided	Alcohol BYO	Restaurant On Site	Guestrooms Available	Event Coordination	Handicap Restricted	Smoking Restricted	Insurance Required	Amplified Music Restricted
Walnut Creek																
Scott's Gardens	251	200	300	•	•		•		•			•		•		
Shadelands Ranch	252	50	250	•	•		•		•					•	•	•
SOUTH BAY																
Campbell																
Martha's Restaurant and Cafe	254	180	180	•		•		•	•	•		•				
Gilroy																
Hecker Pass	255	300	400		•	•		•				•				
Los Gatos																
Byington Winery	256	150	250	•	•		•	•				•	•	•	•	•
Mirassou Champagne Cellars	257	120	200	•	•		•	•				•		•	•	
Opera House	258	500	750	•			•	•				•				
Village House & Garden Restaurant	260	130	200	•	•	•		•	•	•			•	•		
Morgan Hill																
Oak Valley Vineyards	261	200	200		•		•		•			•	•		•	
San Jose																
Briar Rose, The	262	150	150	•	•	•	•	•	•		•	•	•	•	•	•
Fairmont Hotel, San Jose	263	1000	1000	•		•		•		•	•	•		•		
Hotel De Anza	264	150	170	•	•	•		•		•	•	•		•		
Hotel Sainte Claire	265	280	450	•	•	•		•		•	•	•				
La Pastaia	266	175	175	•		•		•		•	•	•		•		
O'Connor Mansion	268	100	200	•	•		•		•			•	•	•		•
San Jose Athletic Club	269	300	400	•		•		•				•				
San Jose Historical Museum	270	1000	1000*	•	•		•		•			•		•	•	•
San Jose Municipal Rose Garden	271	200	200		•		•									•
Santa Clara																
Adobe Lodge Faculty Club	272	100	300	•	•	•		•	•			•		•	•	•
Decathlon Club	273	400	600*	•	•	•		•		•		•		•		
Madison Street Inn	274	75	75	•	•	•	•		•		•	•	•	•	•	
Saratoga																
Chateau La Cresta	275	1500	1500	•	•	•		•		•		•	•	•	•	•
Saratoga Foothill Club	277	126	185	•	•		•		•			•	•	•	•	•
Villa Montalvo	278	175	200	•	•		•		•				•	•	•	•

FACILITY	PAGE	MAX. SEATED CAPACITY	MAX. STANDING CAPACITY	Indoor Facilities	Outdoor Facilities	In-house Catering	BYO Catering	Alcohol Provided	Alcohol BYO	Restaurant On Site	Guestrooms Available	Event Coordination	Handicap Restricted	Smoking Restricted	Insurance Required	Amplified Music Restricted
WINE COUNTRY																
Alexander Valley																
Chateau Souverain	280	150	250	•	•	•		•		•				•	•	•
Calistoga																
Mount View Hotel	281	100	125	•	•	•		•	•	•	•	•		•		•
Geyserville																
Trentadue Winery	282	300	300		•		•	•				•			•	
Guerneville																
Surrey Inn, The	284	500	1500	•	•	•	•		•			•	•	•	•	•
Healdsburg																
Madrona Manor	285	135	135	•	•	•		•		•	•	•		•		•
Villa Chanticleer	286	600	600	•	•		•		•						•	
Kenwood																
Kenwood Inn	287	125	125	•	•	•	•	•			•	•	•	•		
Landmark Vineyards	288	500	700	•	•		•	•				•		•		•
Napa																
Blue Violet Mansion	289	49	100	•	•		•	•	•		•	•		•	•	•
Chimney Rock Winery	291	250	250	•	•		•	•	•			•		•		
Churchill Manor	292	150	150	•	•	•			•		•	•	•	•		•
Inn at Napa Valley	293	250	250	•		•		•	•	•	•					
MacDonald Farm	294	150	150		•		•		•			•	•	•	•	•
Napa River Boat	295	90	100	•	•	•		•	•			•		•		•
Versant Vineyards	296	250	250		•		•		•					•	•	
Petaluma																
Fairbanks Mansion	297	100	250	•	•		•	•	•		•	•	•	•	•	
Garden Valley Ranch	298	250	250		•		•		•							
Rutherford																
Auberge du Soleil	299	110	180*	•	•	•		•		•	•	•				•
Rancho Caymus Inn	300	115	150	•	•	•		•	•	•	•	•				
Santa Rosa																
Chateau DeBaun Winery	301	800	800	•	•		•	•					•			
Mark West Lodge	303	200	500	•	•	•		•	•	•		•	•			•

FACILITY	PAGE	MAX. SEATED CAPACITY	MAX. STANDING CAPACITY	Indoor Facilities	Outdoor Facilities	In-house Catering	BYO Catering	Alcohol Provided	Alcohol BYO	Restaurant On Site	Guestrooms Available	Event Coordination	Handicap Restricted	Smoking Restricted	Insurance Required	Amplified Music Restricted
Sonoma																
Buena Vista Winery	304	200	400	•	•			•	•			•	•	•		
Depot 1870 Restaurant	305	140	140	•		•		•	•	•						
Gloria Ferrer Champagne Caves	306	90	150	•			•	•	•			•		•		•
Las Castañas	307	300	500*	•	•	•	•	•	•	•		•	•	•	•	•
Mission San Francisco	308	n/a	100	•									•	•	•	•
Sonoma Mission Inn and Spa	309	150	275	•		•		•	•	•	•	•		•		•
Vallejo Home	310	100	100		•									•		•
Viansa Winery	311	112	275	•	•	•		•				•		•		•
St. Helena																
Charles Krug Winery	312	1500	1500	•	•		•	•	•			•		•		•
Meadowood Resort	313	250	300*	•	•	•		•	•	•	•	•				•
Merryvale Vineyards	314	160	160	•	•	•	•	•				•		•		
V. Sattui Winery	315	250	350	•		•		•	•			•		•	•	
White Sulphur Springs	316	250	300	•	•	•	•	•	•		•		•	•	•	
Yountville																
Cafe Kinyon!	317	400	400	•	•	•		•	•	•						
LAKES BASIN																
Clearlake																
Windflower Island	319	60	60	•	•	•		•	•		•	•	•		•	
SANTA CRUZ AREA																
Aptos																
Veranda, The	320	80	175	•	•	•		•				•	•	•		
Ben Lomond																
Highlands House & Park	321	200	200	•	•		•		•					•		•
Santa Cruz																
Babbling Brook Inn	322	40	60		•		•	•	•		•		•	•		•
Chaminade	323	180	225	•	•	•		•		•	•	•				•
Cocoanut Grove	324	400	600*	•		•		•	•	•		•		•	•	
Hollins House	325	45	250	•	•	•		•	•	•		•				
Terrace Hill House and Gardens	326	200	200		•	•		•				•	•	•		

Facility	Page	Max. Seated Capacity	Max. Standing Capacity	Indoor Facilities	Outdoor Facilities	In-house Catering	BYO Catering	Alcohol Provided	Alcohol BYO	Restaurant On Site	Guestrooms Available	Event Coordination	Handicap Restricted	Smoking Restricted	Insurance Required	Amplified Music Restricted
MONTEREY PENINSULA																
Carmel																
Highlands Inn	328	100	180*	•	•	•		•		•	•	•	•			•
La Playa Hotel	329	100	150*	•	•	•		•	•	•	•	•				
Mission Ranch	330	180	300*	•	•	•		•		•	•	•		•		•
Carmel Valley																
Ridge Restaurant, The	331	60	300*	•	•	•		•	•	•	•	•				
Monterey																
Monterey Bay Aquarium	333	250	2000	•		•		•	•		•		•		•	•
Old Whaling Station	334	150	150	•	•		•		•					•	•		•
Pacific Grove																
Martine Inn	335	125	125*	•	•	•		•				•		•		•
Pebble Beach																
Beach & Tennis Club	336	250	250*	•	•	•		•	•	•		•				
Inn at Spanish Bay, The	337	300	300*	•	•	•		•		•		•				
Lodge at Pebble Beach, The	339	250	330*	•	•	•		•	•	•	•	•				
GOLD COUNTRY																
Amador City																
Imperial Hotel	340	60	75	•	•	•		•		•	•					•
Auburn																
Auburn Valley Country Club	341	150	400	•	•	•		•	•	•						
Power's Mansion Inn	342	75	75	•	•	•		•	•		•		•	•		•
Columbia																
Angelo's Hall	343	150	200	•		•	•	•					•	•		
Avery Ranch	344	250	250	•	•	•	•	•	•		•		•	•	•	
City Hotel	345	60	100	•		•		•	•	•	•	•	•	•		•
Foresthill																
Monte Verde Inn	346	250	250	•	•	•		•				•	•	•		
Jackson																
Windrose Inn	347	100	100	•	•	•	•		•			•	•		•	•	•

FACILITY	PAGE	MAX. SEATED CAPACITY	MAX. STANDING CAPACITY	Indoor Facilities	Outdoor Facilities	In-house Catering	BYO Catering	Alcohol Provided	Alcohol BYO	Restaurant On Site	Guestrooms Available	Event Coordination	Handicap Restricted	Smoking Restricted	Insurance Required	Amplified Music Restricted
Jamestown																
Historic National Hotel	348	60	100	•	•	•		•	•	•	•	•	•	•		
Jamestown Hotel	349	84	140	•	•	•		•	•	•	•	•		•		
Railtown 1897	350	325	450	•	•	•		•				•		•		•

YOSEMITE AREA

Groveland

Iron Door Saloon, The	352	75	150	•		•		•		•		•		•		

Oakhurst

Estate by the Elderberries	353	125	150	•	•	•		•		•	•	•	•			

Yosemite

Yosemite Facilities	354	168	300*	•	•	•		•		•	•	•		•		•

SACRAMENTO VALLEY

Rancho Murieta

Rancho Murieta Country Club	356	200	350	•	•	•		•	•	•		•	•	•		•

Rocklin

Finnish Temperance Hall	357	144	309	•			•		•							•
Sunset Whitney Country Club	358	300	300	•	•	•		•		•					•	

Roseville

Haman House Restaurant	359	200	300	•	•	•		•	•	•		•	•	•	•	
Maidu Community Center	361	280	450	•	•		•		•					•	•	
Roseville Opera House	362	250	320	•			•		•			•	•	•	•	

Sacramento

Amber House	363	65	65	•			•		•		•	•	•	•		•
California State Railroad Museum	364	400	600	•			•		•					•	•	
Capitol Plaza Halls	365	300	500	•		•	•	•	•			•		•	•	
Casa de los Niños	366	93	150	•	•	•		•	•	•		•		•		
Driver Mansion Inn	367	100	100	•	•	•		•			•	•	•			•
Fairytale Town	368	500	3500		•		•		•					•	•	•
Governor's Mansion	369	150	200	•	•		•				•	•	•			•
Hyatt Regency Sacramento	370	1075	1650*	•	•	•		•		•	•	•				•
Matthew McKinley, The	382	150	150	•	•	•		•	•			•	•	•		•
McKinley Park Rose Garden	371	200	200		•											

FACILITY	PAGE	MAX. SEATED CAPACITY	MAX. STANDING CAPACITY	Indoor Facilities	Outdoor Facilities	In-house Catering	BYO Catering	Alcohol Provided	Alcohol BYO	Restaurant On Site	Guestrooms Available	Event Coordination	Handicap Restricted	Smoking Restricted	Insurance Required	Amplified Music Restricted
Penthouse, The	372	240	300	•		•		•	•	•		•		•		
Radisson Hotel, Sacramento	373	1000	1800	•	•	•		•	•	•	•	•				
Rancho Arroyo	374	2400	6000*	•	•	•		•	•	•		•		•	•	
Riverboat Delta King	375	150	150*	•	•	•		•		•						•
Sacramento Ass'n of Realtors' Bldg	376	325	325	•			•	•				•		•	•	
Sacramento Grand Ballroom	377	500	700	•		•	•	•				•		•	•	
Sacramento History Center	379	call	700	•			•	•						•	•	
Sacrmento Horsemen's Ass'n	380	200	200	•	•		•	•						•	•	
Shot of Class, A	381	250	400	•		•			•	•		•				
Spirit of Sacramento	382	350	350	•	•	•		•	•			•		•		•
Sterling Hotel	383	110	200	•		•		•	•	•	•			•		•
Towe Ford Museum	384	300	500	•			•	•						•	•	
Traveler Centre, The	385	300	300	•			•	•							•	
William Land Park Amphitheater	386	150	n/a		•		•						•			•

Yuba City

Harkey House	387	60	125	•	•		•	•				•	•	•		
Moore Mansion	388	60	60	•			•	•				•	•	•	•	•

THE DELTA

Ryde

Grand Island Inn	390	250	700	•	•	•		•	•	•	•	•				

Walnut Grove

Grand Island Mansion	391	200	1000	•	•	•		•	•			•	•	•		

SAN JOAQUIN VALLEY

Lodi

Japanese Pavilion & Gardens	393	175	175	•	•	•	•	•						•		
Wine & Roses Country Inn	394	400	400	•	•	•		•	•	•	•	•		•	•	

Stockton

Boat House	395	32	50	•	•	•	•	•						•		

LAKE TAHOE REGION

Facility	Page	Max. Seated Capacity	Max. Standing Capacity	Indoor Facilities	Outdoor Facilities	In-house Catering	BYO Catering	Alcohol Provided	Alcohol BYO	Restaurant On Site	Guestrooms Available	Event Coordination	Handicap Restricted	Smoking Restricted	Insurance Required	Amplified Music Restricted
Big Bend																
Rainbow Lodge	396	120	150	•	•	•		•	•	•	•	•	•			
Carnelian Bay																
Gar Woods Grill and Pier	397	200	300	•	•	•		•		•						•
Norden																
Sugar Bowl Resort	398	400	400	•	•		•	•			•	•	•	•		
South Lake Tahoe																
Tallac Vista	399	75	75	•	•		•	•						•		•
Valhalla	400	125	125	•	•		•	•					•	•		•
Squaw Valley																
Resort at Squaw Creek	401	500	700*	•	•	•		•		•	•	•				
Tahoe City																
River Ranch, The	403	200	200	•	•	•		•	•	•	•	•		•		
Sunnyside Restaurant & Lodge	404	100	100*	•	•	•		•	•	•	•	•	•			
William B. Layton Park	405	300	300*		•		•	•							•	•
Tahoe Vista																
La Playa	406	100	175	•	•	•		•	•	•						
Tahoma																
Ehrman Mansion	407	150	150		•		•	•						•	•	•
Truckee																
Cottonwood	408	230	230	•	•	•		•	•	•				•		
Northstar	409	200	300*	•	•	•		•	•		•	•				
Zinas!	411	75	90	•		•		•	•	•		•		•		•

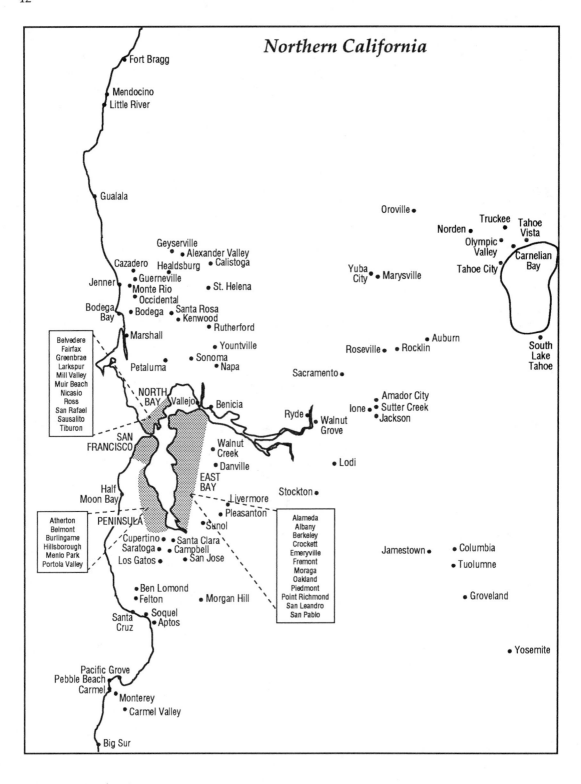

Northern California

Fort Bragg

Mendocino
Little River

Gualala

Oroville

Norden
Truckee
Tahoe Vista

Olympic Valley

Carnelian Bay

Yuba City
Marysville

Tahoe City

Geyserville
Alexander Valley
Calistoga

Cazadero
Healdsburg

Jenner
Guerneville
Monte Rio
Occidental

St. Helena

Bodega Bay
Bodega
Santa Rosa
Kenwood

Marshall

Rutherford

Auburn

Roseville
Rocklin

South Lake Tahoe

Belvedere
Fairfax
Greenbrae
Larkspur
Mill Valley
Muir Beach
Nicasio
Ross
San Rafael
Sausalito
Tiburon

Yountville

Petaluma

Sonoma
Napa

Sacramento

NORTH BAY
Vallejo
Benicia

Ryde

Amador City
Ione
Sutter Creek
Jackson

Walnut Grove

SAN FRANCISCO

Walnut Creek
Danville

Lodi

Half Moon Bay

EAST BAY

Livermore

Stockton

Pleasanton

PENINSULA

Atherton
Belmont
Burlingame
Hillsborough
Menlo Park
Portola Valley

Sunol

Cupertino
Santa Clara
Saratoga
Campbell
Los Gatos
San Jose

Alameda
Albany
Berkeley
Crockett
Emeryville
Fremont
Moraga
Oakland
Piedmont
Point Richmond
San Leandro
San Pablo

Jamestown
Columbia

Tuolumne

Ben Lomond
Felton
Morgan Hill

Groveland

Soquel
Aptos

Santa Cruz

Yosemite

Pacific Grove
Pebble Beach
Carmel
Monterey

Carmel Valley

Big Sur

Here Comes The Guide
Locations

San Francisco

ALAMO SQUARE INN

719 Scott Street at Fulton
San Francisco, CA 94117
(415) 922-2055 Wayne Corn
Reserve: 1–6 months in advance

Located along the perimeter of the much photographed Alamo Square, made famous by the row of restored, colorful Victorians, the Alamo Square Inn is a special place for wedding events. Built in 1895, the mansion combines both Queen Anne and Neoclassical Revival styles with rich woodwork and oak floors, high ceilings, chandeliers and a stately staircase illuminated by a stained glass skylight. The Inn is actually a bed and breakfast complex of 2 houses adjoined in back by a garden and solarium/atrium. All of the downstairs rooms in both houses are available for ceremonies or receptions. Of special note are the triple bay windows in the drawing room (a great backdrop for ceremonies) and the formal parlor which has a vista overlooking Alamo Square.

CAPACITY: The Inn can accommodate 200 people for a stand-up reception or 125 for a sit-down affair.

FEES & DEPOSITS: For special events, $1,000 is required to secure your event date; $500 of this is a refundable security deposit. For events, the facility costs $250/hour with a 3-hour minimum rental required. Event staff run $15/hour/person (5 hour min.). Catering is provided. Mid-afternoon buffets start at $25/person and sit-down functions start at $35/person. Tax and a 15% gratuity are additional. The remaining balance, based on an estimated head count, is due in full at the beginning of the event week.

AVAILABILITY: Anytime. Events must end by 10:30pm with guests out by 11pm.

SERVICES/AMENITIES:

Restaurant Services: no
Catering: provided, no BYO
Kitchen Facilities: n/a
Tables & Chairs: provided
Linens, Silver, etc.: provided
Restrooms: no wca
Dance Floor: yes
Bride's Dressing Area: CBA

Parking: off street lot, valet CBA
Overnight Accommodations: 15 guestrooms
Telephone: guest phone
Outdoor Night Lighting: yes
Outdoor Cooking Facilities: no
Cleanup: provided
Other: audio-visual equipment

RESTRICTIONS:

Alcohol: provided, corkage $3/bottle, no red wine at standing functions
Smoking: smoking porch only

Music: amplified within reason
Wheelchair Access: no
Insurance: events binder required

AQUATIC PARK
BAYVIEW ROOM

890 Beach Street at Aquatic Park
San Francisco, CA 94109
(415) 775-1866
Reserve: 2–6 months in advance

Imagine your reception a stone's throw from the water's edge! Make your vision a reality by renting the Bayview Room which occupies the east end of the Maritime Museum building, across from Ghirardelli Square. The entire structure was cleverly designed to resemble a cruise ship, even down to the nautical looking decks (loggias) with railings. Constructed in the round, the Bayview Room has a high ceiling, inlaid terrazzo floor and large glass windows on almost all sides providing sensational views overlooking the Aquatic Park pier, Alcatraz, Sausalito and historic ships berthed nearby. An additional benefit is the adjacent open-air loggia (balcony) which resembles a long, narrow deck except that it has a tile floor. Bay breezes will enliven any celebration and the loggia's nautical paraphernalia will capture your guests' attention. They'll be able to touch parts from old ships, look at the dry-docked nineteen-foot sloop *The Mermaid*, Benny Buffano sculptures and unblemished examples of 1930s Art Deco tile murals along the wall facing the Bay. You can extend your party by bringing tables onto the loggia—or just have the bar set up here so everyone can enjoy the views.

CAPACITY: The Bayview Room seats 150 guests; 190 for a standing reception. Use of the loggia increases the number of guests. For larger parties, the Maritime Museum may also be rented in conjunction with the Bayview Room.

FEES & DEPOSITS: A refundable $200 cleaning and security deposit is required when reservations are confirmed. The rental fee is $700 for the Bayview Room plus $10/hour for an Event Staff person. Rental fee for the loggia is an additional $100. All rental fees are due 2 weeks prior to the event.

CANCELLATION POLICY: With 60 days' notice, the deposit is refunded.

AVAILABILITY: Year-round. Weekdays after 5pm. Saturdays 9am-12:30am, Sundays 4pm-12:30am.

SERVICES/AMENITIES:

Restaurant Services: no
Catering: BYO
Kitchen Facilities: setup only
Tables & Chairs: provided
Linens, Silver, etc.: BYO
Restrooms: wca
Dance Floor: yes

Parking: on street, adjacent public lot
Overnight Accommodations: no
Telephone: pay phone
Outdoor Night Lighting: yes
Outdoor Cooking Facilities: no
Cleanup: caterer or provided, extra fee
Bride's Dressing Area: CBA

RESTRICTIONS:

Alcohol: BYO
Wheelchair Access: yes
Smoking: outside only

Music: amplified within reason
Insurance: may be required

ARCHBISHOP'S MANSION

1000 Fulton Street at Steiner
San Francisco, CA 94117
(415) 563-7872 Kathleen Austin
Reserve: 2 months in advance

Built in 1904 as the residence for the archbishop of San Francisco, this elegant historic landmark with hand-painted ceilings, fine woodwork and distinguished period furnishings, has been restored to its original splendor. The first floor dining room, main hallway and parlor are available for ceremonies and receptions. The great hall stairway landing is a terrific spot to take your vows, allowing the bride to make a grand entry. Facing Alamo Park, the Mansion is a regal bed and breakfast inn.

CAPACITY: For a standing reception, 100 people, or for a sit-down meal, approximately 50.

FEES & DEPOSITS: A non-refundable deposit of 50% of the estimated fee is needed in order to secure your event date. A $375 refundable security deposit is also required. This facility is rented at $150-200/hour, measured from the arrival of the caterers to their departure. A 4-hour minimum rental is required. The balance and security deposit are due 1 week prior to the event.

AVAILABILITY: Sun–Thurs, all day up to 11pm; Fri & Sat up to 5pm only.

SERVICES/AMENITIES:

Restaurant Services: no
Catering: CBA or BYO, must be licensed
Kitchen Facilities: ample
Tables & Chairs: some provided
Linens, Silver, etc.: caterer
Restrooms: no wca
Dance Floor: no dancing
Bride's Dressing Area: yes

Parking: on street, valet CBA
Overnight Accommodations: 15 guestrooms
Telephone: house phone
Outdoor Night Lighting: access only
Outdoor Cooking Facilities: no
Cleanup: caterer
Other: baby grand piano

RESTRICTIONS:

Alcohol: provided, corkage fee if BYO
Smoking: outside only
Music: no amplified

Wheelchair Access: no
Insurance: not required
Other: decorations restricted

ASTA & THE RINCON CENTER ATRIUM

One Rincon Center
101 Spear Street
San Francisco, CA 94105
(415) 495-2782
Reserve: 3-6 months in advance

If you like the sultriness of the Thin Man movies, you're gonna like Asta. Taking its name from the feisty terrier who often upstaged detectives Nick and Nora Charles (William Powell and Myrna Loy), this sleek and sophisticated restaurant pays homage to the supper clubs of the thirties and forties. In fact, old movies (with the sound off) run continuously on small screens over the bar. Like most of the decor, they're in classy black and white. Everything here is custom designed—the period furniture, metal and glass light fixtures, and unusual 3-D wall sculptures. The main dining room curves around the lower level of the restaurant, while the bar occupies the upper level. The area in front of the bar can be used as a dance floor, and there is a place for a small band. One of the greatest things about Asta is that it's located right next to the Rincon Center Atrium, a phenomenal setting for a large wedding reception. This circular space glows under a skylight roof, soaring 80 feet or more overhead. In the center of the skylight, a fountain of water descends like soft rain, filling a shallow pool below—a unique backdrop for a wedding ceremony. Palms and other plants add to the sensation of actually being outdoors. Terraced seating follows around the perimeter of the Atrium, and the spacious main floor has plenty of room for additional dining and dancing. With its indoor waterfall and year-round view of the sky, the Atrium is definitely a unique spot.

CAPACITY: Asta Restaurant can hold 110 seated or 200 standing guests. The Atrium can seat 200 or 500 standing guests.

FEES & DEPOSITS: A deposit in the amount of 25% of the estimated total is required four weeks prior to the event. 50% of the estimated total is due on the day of the event, and the remaining charges are due within two days of the event's conclusion. There is a 10% facility fee for all parties of less than 18 guests in Asta's private room, and for events held in the Rincon Center Atrium or the entire Asta Restaurant where the number of guests is less than 120 people. Per person food service rates are: $15-25 for luncheons, and $30-40 for dinners. Tax and an 18% service charge are additional.

CANCELLATION POLICY: The deposit is refunded only if the date can be rebooked with a party of equal or greater value.

AVAILABILITY: Asta is available Monday night, all day Sunday and Saturday during the day. Other times can be arranged. The Atrium is available Monday-Friday after 4:30pm, and all day Saturday and Sunday year-round.

SERVICES/AMENITIES:
Restaurant Services: yes
Catering: provided, no BYO
Kitchen Facilities: n/a

Parking: Rincon Center Garage, valet CBA
Overnight Accommodations: no
Telephone: pay phone

Tables & Chairs: most provided
Linens, Silver, etc.: provided
Restrooms: wca
Dance Floor: yes

RESTRICTIONS:
Alcohol: provided, corkage $9/bottle
Smoking: allowed
Music: amplified ok

Outdoor Night Lighting: access only
Outdoor Cooking Facilities: no
Cleanup: provided
Bride's Dressing Area: yes

Wheelchair Access: yes
Insurance: not required

ATRIUM

101 California Street
San Francisco, CA 94111
(415) 788-4101
Reserve: 3–6 months in advance

Located in the award-winning 101 California building, Atrium is one of the most elegant restaurants we've seen. As you enter the foyer, an oriental runner leads you past a marble-topped bar into the main dining room. The soothing atmosphere created by gray carpet, deep mauve upholstered chairs and light peach walls is punctuated dramatically by the exotic colors of azaleas, orchids and palms. Polished marble dividers define the dining areas in this split-level room, creating separate, homey spaces. One mirrored wall reflects the light and greenery of the atrium on the opposite side. The glass-enclosed atrium is ideal for rehearsal dinners, cocktails and hors d'oeuvres or after-dinner dancing. Hanging pots of kangaroo ivy provide a lush canopy, and bud vases with festive seasonal flowers complete the greenhouse effect. The adjacent plaza, lined with hundreds of planters overflowing with impatiens, is a lovely spot for a champagne reception or a ceremony. Tiered granite steps in the middle of the plaza are perfect for group wedding photos. And during the Christmas season, a 50-foot redwood Christmas tree with 35,000 lights, surrounded by a sea of red poinsettias creates a dazzling display. For very intimate prenuptial dinners, or a private getaway for the wedding party, the executive dining room offers a warm, secluded retreat. Behind plantation shutter doors, an oriental carpet, cherrywood buffet, antique mirror and striking contemporary pastel artpiece produce a rich, tasteful decor. With its special touches, imaginative cuisine, and convenient downtown location, Atrium can satisfy even the most demanding clientele.

CAPACITY:

	Seated	Standing		Seated	Standing
Main Dining Room	40–130	100–300	Executive Dining Room	14	—
Atrium	34	80	Entire Restaurant	175	300

FEES & DEPOSITS: A $500–1,000 non-refundable deposit (depending upon the number of guests) is required at the time of booking and is applied to the total bill. Payment schedules are individually arranged with the final bill due at the conclusion of the event. Buffets, lunches and dinners range from

$15–40/person. Beverage, tax and gratuity are additional. There is no minimum number of guests, and the final guest count is due 48 hours before the event.

AVAILABILITY: Year-round, daily, 7am–2am.

SERVICES/AMENITIES:

Restaurant Services: yes

Catering: provided

Kitchen Facilities: n/a

Tables & Chairs: provided

Linens, Silver, etc.: provided

Restrooms: wca

Dance Floor: yes (in greenhouse)

Bride's Dressing Area: yes

Parking: validated in large lot for $75 for entire party weeknights, $175 on weekends

Cleanup: provided

Overnight Accommodations: no

Telephone: pay phone

Outdoor Night Lighting: yes

Outdoor Cooking Facilities: no

RESTRICTIONS:

Alcohol: provided, $10/bottle corkage

Smoking: allowed

Music: amplified ok

Wheelchair Access: yes

Insurance: not required

BALCLUTHA

San Francisco Maritime National Historic Park
Hyde Street Pier
San Francisco, CA 94109
(415) 929-0202 Daria Booth
Reserve: 1–2 months in advance

The Balclutha, a 3-masted, square-rigged sailing ship, made her maiden voyage from Wales to San Francisco in 1887. After her long and varied career, the ship was purchased and restored by the San Francisco Maritime Museum in 1954, as a memorial to the by-gone days of sailing. This impressive and historic floating landmark is available as a public exhibit *and* for private functions. Wedding ceremonies often take place on the top (poop) deck or in the 'tween deck, which is covered. This is a very unusual wedding site.

CAPACITY: For a standing reception, 200-300 guests; for a seated function, 125 guests.

FEES & DEPOSITS: A $1,500 refundable security deposit is required and is usually returned within 2 weeks after the event. The rental fee is $900 minimum. The total fee will depend on the length of your event and the number of guests. Work out the details with the National Maritime Museum Association. Fees include a National Park Ranger on duty during events.

CANCELLATION POLICY: Deposits are refundable 21 days prior to your event.

AVAILABILITY: Nov-May, 5pm-midnight; June-Oct, 6pm-midnight.

SERVICES/AMENITIES:

Restaurant Services: no
Catering: BYO
Kitchen Facilities: no
Tables & Chairs: BYO
Linens, Silver, etc.: BYO
Restrooms: none, restrooms on pier
Dance Floor: deck

Parking: on street, garage nearby
Overnight Accommodations: no
Telephone: pay phone nearby
Outdoor Night Lighting: deck lighting
Outdoor Cooking Facilities: no
Cleanup: caterer
Bride's Dressing Area: yes

RESTRICTIONS:

Alcohol: BYO
Smoking: only allowed on pier
Music: amplified until 11pm

Wheelchair Access: limited
Insurance: not required

BLUE AND GOLD FLEET

Pier 39
San Francisco, CA 94133
(415) 705-5555
Reserve: 2–3 months in advance

Ready to accommodate big and small parties alike, the Blue and Gold Fleet proudly offers three vessels available for private charter. The Golden Bear, Old Blue and Oski make it possible to have a scenic and entertaining event while cruising San Francisco Bay. Note that there are alternate docking sites available for your party for a minimal extra charge. The B&G staff are extremely helpful with DJ selection, live entertainment, flowers and decoration, plus theme party planning.

CAPACITY: These boats usually carry over 100 people. Each vessel can accommodate 200 for a buffet dinner dance or 300 for standing receptions.

FEES & DEPOSITS: A $500 deposit is required 10 working days after arranging a tentative date. The fees vary depending on season and day of the week:

	Friday	Saturday	Sunday	Mon–Thurs
April–October	$2,700	$3,000	$2,500	$2,300
November–March	2,400	2,700	2,300	2,100

The above rental fees are for a 4-hour minimum cruise. Fees are increased for major holidays. Catering is provided. Blue and Gold catering costs range from $7/person to over $20/person, depending on menu arrangements. Sales tax and a 15% service charge are additional.

CANCELLATION POLICY: Your deposit is returned if a cancellation is made 60 days prior to the event.

AVAILABILITY: June–Sept 5, no charters are available before 6pm. Sept 5–May 30, one boat is available during the day, with a 4-hour minimum rental required. Evenings are generally available for private functions.

SERVICES/AMENITIES:

Restaurant Services: no
Catering: provided, no BYO
Kitchen Facilities: no
Tables & Chairs: provided
Linens, Silver, etc.: provided
Restrooms: no wca
Dance Floor: yes

Parking: Pier 39 garage
Overnight Accommodations: no
Telephone: emergency only
Outdoor Night Lighting: yes
Outdoor Cooking Facilities: BBQ
Cleanup: provided
Bride's Dressing Area: no

RESTRICTIONS:

Alcohol: provided, corkage $3/bottle
Smoking: allowed
Music: amplified ok

Wheelchair Access: on main deck only
Insurance: not required

THE BLUE FOX

659 Merchant St.
San Francisco, CA 94111
(415) 981-1177
Reserve: 2 weeks–12 months in advance

A long-time San Francisco institution, The Blue Fox is a restaurant with a history. Located on the first block of San Francisco, it began as a popular bohemian cafe and became a well-known speakeasy during prohibition. In 1933, an Italian from Viareggio opened the original Blue Fox, naming it after the restaurant he'd left behind in Italy. Today, it's still a family business. Nationally recognized for its elegant Italian and Continental cuisine, the restaurant also offers several dining areas that are perfect for rehearsal dinners or receptions. The Palatina and Alfieri rooms are classic, with crystal chandeliers, ambered mirrors and softly draped wall panels. The decor is soothing, in peach, mauve and cream tones. In complete contrast, the private dining rooms downstairs are two of the most unique spaces we've seen. Both serve as wine cellars, and guests are surrounded by thousands of wine bottles. The Large Wine Cellar has brick and stone walls and a dark wood-beamed ceiling. Guests dine by lantern light, kept low to protect the wine. As you survey the elaborately carved, high-backed chairs with their scarlet upholstery, and the deep red carpet, you feel like you're in the depths of a castle. The Original Wine Cellar is smaller, but similar in style. It's a bit more whimsical, however, with chianti bottles, salamis, grapes–and even a fox–suspended from the ceiling. Whether you want an ambiance that's formal and sophisticated, or one that's unconventional and fun, The Blue Fox delivers the best of both worlds.

CAPACITY:	Room	Seated	Standing	Room	Seated	Standing
	Palatina Room	80	—	Original Wine Cellar	30	—
	Alfieri Room	65	100	Large Wine Cellar	80	150

FEES & DEPOSITS: A non-refundable deposit is required when reservations are confirmed. The deposit is $250 for groups under 25, $500 for 25–50 guests and a minimum of $1,000 for over 50. There is a room charge of $100 for groups of 12 or less in the Wine Cellars. A guaranteed guest count is required 48 hours prior to the event. The balance is due 15 days after receipt of invoice. Luncheons start at $30/person, dinners at $50. Tax and a 20% gratuity are additional.

CANCELLATION POLICY: The deposit is not refundable.

AVAILABILITY: Monday–Saturday, flexible hours. Special events may be arranged on Sundays.

SERVICES/AMENITIES:

Restaurant Services: yes
Catering: provided, no BYO
Kitchen Facilities: n/a
Tables & Chairs: provided
Linens, Silver, etc.: provided
Restrooms: no wca
Dance Floor: CBA

Parking: valet ($5/car), inexpensive garages
Overnight Accommodations: CBA
Telephone: pay phone
Outdoor Night Lighting: access only
Outdoor Cooking Facilities: no
Cleanup: provided
Bride's Dressing Area: CBA

RESTRICTIONS:

Alcohol: provided, corkage $15/bottle
Smoking: designated areas
Music: amplified ok w/approval

Wheelchair Access: main floor only
Insurance: not required

CABLE CAR BARN AND MUSEUM

1201 Mason St. at Washington
San Francisco, CA 94108
(415) 923-6202　Jim Tomes
Reserve: 3–24 months in advance

Looking for something a bit different? The Barn and Museum are two really unusual sites to hold a reception. For a very dramatic entry, you and your group can even arrive riding a cable car! The cavernous Barn is a working "corporation yard" for the cable cars. The Museum houses historical displays and has an interesting view down into the drive wheels that run the cable car system. During special events, cable cars are lined up in the Barn to section off actual working areas from the party spaces. Note that neighborhood parking is impossible; guests may arrive by cable car or other forms of public transit. A Muni-approved parking plan must be in place before they'll allow the rental to occur.

CAPACITY: Barn and Museum, combined, can hold 800 for a standing reception and 400 seated guests.

FEES & DEPOSITS: $1,000 plus a $500 refundable cleaning deposit are required to secure a date. The deposit is payable 2 weeks after booking. The refundable portion is usually returned with a week after the event. The rental fee is $1,850 for Barn and Museum combined. Any remaining unpaid balance plus use permit and insurance paperwork are due 2 weeks prior to the event.

CANCELLATION POLICY: During the holiday season or peak use periods, you must cancel at least 2 months in advance to receive a full refund.

AVAILABILITY: Year-round, everyday. The Barn 5pm–10:30pm; the Museum, during the summer 6pm–11pm, during the winter 5pm–11pm. Guests must be out by 11pm. No events are scheduled on major holidays.

SERVICES/AMENITIES:

Restaurant Services: no
Catering: BYO
Kitchen Facilities: no
Tables & Chairs: BYO
Linens, Silver, etc.: BYO
Restrooms: wca
Dance Floor: no
Bride's Dressing Area: no

Parking: no
Overnight Accommodations: no
Telephone: office phone
Outdoor Night Lighting: access only
Outdoor Cooking Facilities: no
Cleanup: caterer
Other: cable car arrivals CBA

RESTRICTIONS:

Alcohol: BYO
Smoking: allowed
Music: amplified to 10pm

Wheelchair Access: yes
Insurance: event liability required
Other: permit required

CAFE MAJESTIC

1500 Sutter Street at Gough
San Francisco, CA 94109
(415) 776-6400
Reserve: 6 weeks in advance

Cafe Majestic, built in 1902 and authentically restored, is an appetizing restaurant in both cuisine and decor. We were surprised to learn that many of the menu selections are derived from old San Francisco cookbooks. The owner, Tom Marshall, has a penchant for 'vintage' recipes, and is enthusiastic about offering a dining environment reminiscent of the City's genteel past. For receptions or prenuptial dinners, this is a splendid spot. The refreshing bright and airy interior has peach walls, a high ceiling and tall windows along the street side of the room. The warm wall color contrasts nicely with light teal wainscotting, shutters and trim. Small Kentia palms provide the perfect green accent next to the crisp white table settings. In addition to a charming ambiance and superb food, overnight accommodations are available in the adjacent Hotel Majestic.

CAPACITY: The Main Dining Room can hold 20–120 seated guests, the Board Room, 10–20 for smaller groups.

FEES & DEPOSITS: To rent a portion of the restaurant, a refundable deposit of $300 is required when the date is confirmed. To rent the entire restaurant (75 guests minimum to waive rental fee), a non-refundable $500 deposit is required. With food, there's usually no rental fee. Meal service per person rates: luncheon entrees $10–14, dinner entrees $15–23, first courses $4–8, hors d'oeuvres start at $6. The balance is due the day of the event. Tax and service charges are additional.

CANCELLATION POLICY: With 2 months' notice, your deposit will be refunded.

AVAILABILITY: Year-round, everyday from 7am–midnight. Closed Memorial Day, July 4th, Labor Day, December 26th and January 2nd. You can reserve the entire restaurant and bar on Saturday or Sunday afternoon, from noon to 5pm.

SERVICES/AMENITIES:

Restaurant Services: yes
Catering: provided, no BYO
Kitchen Facilities: n/a
Tables & Chairs: provided
Linens, Silver, etc.: provided
Restrooms: wca
Dance Floor: yes
Bride's Dressing Area: no

Parking: valet
Overnight Accommodations: 60 guestrooms
Telephone: pay phone
Outdoor Night Lighting: access only
Outdoor Cooking Facilities: no
Cleanup: provided
Other: nightly pianist, grand piano, flowers provided

RESTRICTIONS:

Alcohol: provided, corkage $12/bottle
Smoking: in bar only
Music: amplified restricted

Wheelchair Access: yes
Insurance: not required

CAFFE ESPRIT

235 16th St.
San Francisco, CA 94107
(415) 777-5558
Reserve: 3 weeks–12 months in advance

Caffe Esprit is far more than just a delightful place for lunch, cappucino or a snack. It's a great space for a wedding reception. The front of the café is actually two enormous glass roll-up doors which connect the attractively landscaped patio with the open two-level interior, flooding it with light. The high-tech style of burnished metal fixtures is softened by the serpentine bar and tables finished in natural ash. A curved staircase can showcase the bride's entrance, or provide an unconventional stage for toasts and photo opportunities. An oversized wire basket of lemons and large jars of pickled olives and peppers add spots of color behind the bar. Caffe Esprit's spacious patio with large round tables, umbrellas and curved benches is ideal for day or evening functions. When the weather obliges, the roll-up doors can be raised, allowing both partygoers and breezes to mingle. The semi-private area upstairs overlooks the café's main floor below, and has a bank of windows with a view of the bay, occasional sailboats and sea lions, and the East Bay hills. An artful combination of functionality and elegance, Caffe Esprit can host a casual or formal reception with equal ease.

CAPACITY: Indoors, the café can seat up to 125 guests, 300 standing. The Patio can seat up to 64 guests.

FEES & DEPOSITS: A $250 deposit is due at the time of booking to reserve your date. Half the total is payable 2 weeks before the function, and the balance is due on the evening of the event. Per person food costs are $10–25 for lunch and $18–75 for dinner. Tax and a 15% service charge are extra.

CANCELLATION POLICY: With more than 1 week's notice, the deposit is refundable.

AVAILABILITY: Monday–Saturday, 5pm–2am; all day Sunday. Closed Thanksgiving, Christmas and New Year's Day.

SERVICES/AMENITIES:

Restaurant Services: yes
Catering: provided, no BYO
Kitchen Facilities: n/a
Tables & Chairs: provided
Linens, Silver, etc.: provided, fee for extras
Restrooms: wca
Dance Floor: yes

Parking: large lot (no fees)
Overnight Accommodations: no
Telephone: pay phone
Outdoor Night Lighting: yes
Outdoor Cooking Facilities: no
Cleanup: provided

RESTRICTIONS:

Alcohol: provided, corkage $9/bottle
Smoking: allowed
Insurance: not required

Wheelchair Access: yes
Music: amplified ok
Other: no mylar balloons or tape

CALIFORNIA ACADEMY OF SCIENCES

Golden Gate Park
San Francisco, CA 94118
(415) 750-7221   Deidre Kernan
Reserve: 3 months in advance

Although first and foremost a public museum, the California Academy of Sciences offers an incredibly wide range of sensational spaces for private parties. Located in Golden Gate Park, the museum is one of the largest natural history museums in the world and the oldest in the Western U.S. Use the dynamic and dramatically lit exhibits as backdrops for your wedding photos and reserve well in advance for parties scheduled between September and Christmas.

African Hall: Authentic sights and sounds of a busy savannah watering hole, featuring majestic dioramas filled with exotic birds and animals.

Earth and Space Hall: Features celestial bodies, a neon solar system and earthquake simulation. Note that laser shows at night have public access.

Hall of Human Cultures: Otherwise known as Wattis Hall, this large room holds dioramas depicting man's adaptation to his natural environment.

Temporary Exhibit Space: Special exhibits, like the most recent Caribbean Festival Arts show, are changed often. Call to find out what's current.

Life Through Time: Dinosaur fossils and moving models demonstrate the evidence for evolution. Available for cocktail receptions only.

Wild California: Wild California is remarkable for its lifelike exhibits. The battling sea lions and coastal dioramas are terrific.

Aquarium: Sensational exhibits of reptiles and amphibians, exotic fish, penguins, dolphins and seals. The fish roundabout is a spiral ascending ramp with tanks along the outer wall. The top platform, a circular space surrounded by blue-green lit tanks, with large fish swimming in one direction, is one of the most extraordinary party spaces we've seen. Also, check out the swamp with crocodiles—it's a favorite spot for unique celebrations.

Museum Store: Can be opened on request. Guests must be notified in advance so they can remember to bring funds and credit cards for purchases.

CAPACITY, FEES & DEPOSITS: A non-refundable deposit of 30% of the estimated fee is due within 21 days of contract receipt. The remaining 70% and a $500 refundable security deposit are due three weeks prior to the event. For holiday rentals (December 1–24) the remaining fees are due 90 days prior to the event. The security deposit is returned after your function, pending assessment of the facility's condition. If cleanup assistance is necessary, $150/hour will be billed.

	Fees	Standing Capacity	Seated Capacity	Standing & Seated
African Hall	$3,500	400	300	150
Hohfeld I & II	1,500	capacity varies	—	—
Lovell White	1,500	capacity varies	—	—
Space Hall	1,500	150	100	60
Wattis Hall	3,500	400	150	100
Aquarium, Swamp, Roundabout Combo	3,500	400	200	—
Roundabout Only	1,500	125	60	60
Wild Calif.	3,500	300	150	150
Life Thru Time/Oceans	3,500	capacity varies	—	—
Auditorium	1,000	—	400	—
Planetarium	1,200	—	300	—
Entire Academy	8,000–12,000	to 3,000		

Combinations of different halls can be arranged for any sized gathering. The above fees include an Academy representative and security guards.

AVAILABILITY: The Academy is available September 1st–July 3 from 6pm–12:30am; July 4–September 1 from 8pm–12:30am; and the first Wednesday of every month from 10pm–12:30am. With prior notice, you can extend your party for an extra $150/hour.

SERVICES/AMENITIES:

Restaurant Services: no
Catering: provided, or BYO from approved list
Kitchen Facilities: no
Tables & Chairs: BYO
Linens, Silver, etc.: BYO
Restrooms: wca
Dance Floor: CBA

Parking: museum lot
Overnight Accommodations: no
Telephone: pay phones
Outdoor Night Lighting: access only
Outdoor Cooking Facilities: no
Cleanup: caterer and museum janitorial
Bride's Dressing Area: no

RESTRICTIONS:

Alcohol: BYO, license required
Smoking: not allowed
Music: amplified ok except for aquarium

Wheelchair Access: yes
Insurance: indemnification clause required
Other: decorations need approval, catering restrictions

CALIFORNIA CULINARY ACADEMY

625 Polk Street
San Francisco, CA 94102
(415) 771-3500
Reserve: 1–12 months in advance

Located in the lovely and architecturally significant California Hall, a 1912 historic landmark, the California Culinary Academy makes available a number of interesting and varied spaces for wedding receptions. The main dining room, Careme, is like a formal theater. It's ornate, large and formal with an awesome ceiling extending up three floors. When dining here, you can observe hundreds of young, aspiring chefs cooking for you. Circling above the main floor is a balcony called Cyril's, a dining area with fabulous views of the lower dining room and ceiling. The main bar is lovely, warm and intimate with dark wood, mirrors and an old bar. The Private Dining Room is small and intimate without ornamentation. The Academy Grill is a more informal space. Wine-tasting, cooking demonstrations and a Grand Buffet are offered in addition to sensational chocolate and Viennese desserts. Note that the food service here is really exceptional; the Academy is one of the world's foremost culinary schools.

CAPACITY, FEES & DEPOSITS: To secure your date, a refundable $1,000 deposit is required when you book reservations. You need a minimum of 100 people to open the Culinary Academy on a weekend, for which there is an additional $750 charge. The Academy office will determine when 50% of the estimated fee total is due prior to the event. Also note that for private parties, a combination of rooms with special rates can be arranged. Food service is provided. Hors d'oeuvres start at $5.50/person, luncheons at $18.50/person and dinners at $25.95/person. Sales tax and 18% service charge will be applied to the final bill.

	Standing Capacity	Seated Capacity	Fees
Main Dining Room	500	280	$1,000
Main Bar	150	60	350
Private Dining Room	60	30	150
Cyril's	150–175	80	500
Academy Grill	200	200	500

CANCELLATION POLICY: Your deposit will be refunded up to 30 days prior to your event.

AVAILABILITY: Weekends, all day. There's no minimum rental block, but there's a 5-hour maximum. On weekdays, since the Academy operates a school, guests must arrive between 11:30am–1:30pm for lunch and 6pm–8:30pm for dinner.

SERVICES/AMENITIES:

Restaurant Services: yes

Catering: provided, no BYO

Kitchen Facilities: n/a

Tables & Chairs: provided

Linens, Silver, etc.: provided

Restrooms: wca

Dance Floor: $350 setup charge

Bride's Dressing Area: CBA

Parking: garage nearby

Overnight Accommodations: no

Telephone: pay phone

Outdoor Night Lighting: access only

Outdoor Cooking Facilities: no

Cleanup: provided

Other: ice sculpture and wedding cakes

RESTRICTIONS:

Alcohol: provided, corkage $7.50/bottle

Smoking: allowed

Music: amplified after 7:30pm

Wheelchair Access: yes

Insurance: not required

THE CALIFORNIA SPIRIT
Pacific Marine Yacht Charters

Berthed at Pier 39, East Basin
San Francisco, CA 94133
(415) 788-9100
Reserve: 1–9 months in advance

The 100-foot custom designed California Spirit is one of four luxury yachts in Pacific Marine's elegant fleet. This yacht features a grand salon with dance area, a plush observation salon with leather couches and an upper salon in rich woods complemented by soft colors. A spacious outdoor deck sets the stage for a truly memorable ceremony. First-class service and award-winning cuisine ensure that you and your guests will have an experience you won't soon forget.

CAPACITY: The California Spirit can accommodate up to 149 guests for cocktails and hors d'oeuvres. Formal seating is available for 80.

FEES & DEPOSITS: A $2,000 deposit is required to reserve your date; half the food and beverage cost is due 30 days prior to your event.

	Weekdays (before 6pm)	*Weekdays (after 6pm)*	*Weekends/Holidays*
Yacht rental rates	$625/hr	$750/hr	$900/hr

A 3-hour minimum rental is required, 4 hours on Saturday evenings and holidays. A guaranteed guest count is required 7 days prior to departure and the remaining balance is due 5 days prior to your event.

Special packages, starting at $24/guest, include wedding ceremony performed by the captain, gourmet menu, champagne toast, customized wedding cake and a wedding coordinator's time. Yacht rental, beverage service, tax and gratuity are additional.

CANCELLATION POLICY: With 60 days' notice, 85% of the deposit will be refunded; with less notice, the deposit will be forfeited.

AVAILABILITY: Anytime, no limits.

SERVICES/AMENITIES:

Restaurant Services: no
Catering: provided, no BYO
Kitchen Facilities: on board
Tables & Chairs: provided
Linens, Silver, etc.: provided
Restrooms: wca
Dance Floor: yes
Bride's Dressing Area: yes

Parking: Pier 39 garage, validations available
Overnight Accommodations: no
Telephone: cellular phone & radio
Outdoor Night Lighting: yes
Outdoor Cooking Facilities: no
Cleanup: provided
Other: complimentary wedding coordination

RESTRICTIONS:

Alcohol: provided, corkage $7/bottle
Smoking: outside only
Music: amplified ok

Wheelchair Access: yes, CBA
Insurance: not required
Other: no rice

CARNELIAN ROOM

555 California Street, 52nd Floor
San Francisco, CA 94104
(415) 433-7500   Private Dining Dept.
Reserve: 2 weeks–6 months in advance

The Carnelian Room is truly a "room with a view." Occupying an enviable location on the top floor of the Bank of America building, it overlooks the Bay, both bridges, the Embarcadero and the East Bay hills. Inside, the atmosphere is reminiscent of an English manor, warm and elegant with rich walnut paneling and masterworks of 18th and 19th century art and cabinetry. Complementing the view from the main dining room is an equally imposing backdrop: the West's finest wine cellar, some 40,000 bottles in all.

Imaginative menus are available featuring American cuisine—or consult with the catering director and create your own. Experienced staff are also on hand to coordinate any details of your special event.

CAPACITY: The Main Dining Room and 11 private suites, each with a glittering vista of the Bay Area, can be scaled for groups as small as 2 or as large as 500 guests.

FEES & DEPOSITS: A refundable deposit of $150 is required when reservations are confirmed. Small suites rent for $50/event and the large suites, $150/event. Pre-selected menus are developed in advance of any event. Dinners start at $34/person and substantial hors d'oeuvres start at $16/person. 80% of the estimated event total is payable 10 days prior to the function. The balance is due the day of the event. Tax and a 15% service charge will be applied to the final bill.

CANCELLATION POLICY: With 14 days' notice, the deposit will be refunded.

AVAILABILITY: Year-round, Monday–Friday from 3pm, Saturday and Sunday all day. Closed most major holidays.

SERVICES/AMENITIES:

Restaurant Services: yes
Catering: provided, no BYO
Kitchen Facilities: n/a
Tables & Chairs: provided
Linens, Silver, etc.: provided
Restrooms: wca
Dance Floor: CBA

Parking: garage, $7 after 5pm or on weekends
Overnight Accommodations: no
Telephone: pay phones
Outdoor Night Lighting: access only
Outdoor Cooking Facilities: no
Cleanup: provided
Other: full event coordination

RESTRICTIONS:

Alcohol: provided, corkage $10/bottle
Smoking: allowed
Music: amplified ok

Wheelchair Access: yes
Insurance: not required

CASA DE LA VISTA

410 Palm Ave., Building 271
Treasure Island
San Francisco, CA 94130
(415) 395-5151
Reserve: 1–18 months in advance

If Treasure Island actually possesses any treasures, Casa de la Vista could very well be one of them. This is a good choice for a reception if you can find a sponsor (Military person on active duty, retired or reservist). Situated on the edge of the island, it has unobstructed views of the entire San Francisco skyline, both bridges, Alcatraz, and Marin. The facility itself is quite pleasant. It's light and airy with a long wall of floor-to-ceiling glass that overlooks the Bay. Painted in a soft mauve overall, the vaulted ceiling is accented by light blue beams and pink pillars provide colorful support. A modern fireplace with brass chimney and a convenient bar are located near one end, leaving the majority of the room open for flexible arrangements. In back, olive trees shade a large brick patio which can also be set up for your event. Casa de la Vista is a terrific spot because it's very private *and* has knockout views. Additionally, there's the benefit of having a central location, great for guests coming from either San Francisco or the East Bay.

CAPACITY: This facility can hold 300 for a reception or 180 guests for a seated affair.

FEES & DEPOSITS: A non-refundable deposit is required at the time of booking (25% of the estimated total cost of the event). The balance and a final guest count are due one week prior to the event. There is a $200 setup fee which may be waived with meal service. After 11pm, overtime hours are available for an additional charge. Per person rates: dinners/buffets $10–30, hors d'oeuvres trays $35–200. Any menu can be customized, no tax is required and the service charge is 15%.

AVAILABILITY: Year-round, everyday from 11am–4pm and 6pm–11pm.

SERVICES/AMENITIES:

Restaurant Services: no
Catering: provided
Kitchen Facilities: n/a
Tables & Chairs: provided
Linens, Silver, etc.: provided
Restrooms: wca
Dance Floor: yes
Bride's Dressing Area: CBA

Parking: large lot
Overnight Accommodations: no
Telephone: pay phone
Outdoor Night Lighting: yes
Outdoor Cooking Facilities: CBA
Cleanup: provided
Other: event coordination, piano

RESTRICTIONS:

Alcohol: provided, corkage $6.50/bottle
Smoking: allowed
Music: amplified ok

Wheelchair Access: yes
Insurance: not required

CASA SAN GREGORIO

398 Pennsylvania Avenue
San Francisco, CA 94107
(415) 641-1902
Reserve: 3–6 months in advance

Located in the sunny Potrero Hill District, this bed and breakfast inn offers a unique location for intimate ceremonies and receptions. The inn's modern design features an indoor pool, a well-appointed second level dining area plus a remarkable rooftop deck which offers incredible, 360-degree views of The City and surrounding Bay Area. The enclosed patio area is ideal for small celebrations and outdoor buffets. The adjoining Cottage is perfect for out-of-town family or friends who plan to spend the night.

CAPACITY: The Inn can hold 50–80 for a standing reception or 30–50 guests for a seated affair.

FEES & DEPOSITS: $1,000 is required to secure your date, $500 of which is a refundable security deposit. Rental fees are $175/hour with a 3-hour minimum rental required. Event staff run $15/hour per person (5-hour minimum).

CANCELLATION POLICY: With less than 2 weeks' notice, $300 of the deposit will be forfeited.

AVAILABILITY: Year-round, everyday. The event must end by midnight, with guests out by 11:30pm.

SERVICES/AMENITIES:

Restaurant Services: no

Catering: provided or BYO

Kitchen Facilities: ample

Tables & Chairs: provided

Linens, Silver, etc.: CBA or BYO

Restrooms: no wca

Dance Floor: no

Parking: on street

Overnight Accommodations: 3 suites

Telephone: guest phone

Outdoor Night Lighting: yes

Outdoor Cooking Facilities: BBQ

Cleanup: provided

Bride's Dressing Area: yes

RESTRICTIONS:

Alcohol: provided, corkage $3/bottle, no red wine at standing functions

Smoking: allowed

Music: amplified within reason

Wheelchair Access: no

Insurance: required

THE CITY CLUB

155 Sansome Street
San Francisco, CA 94104
(415) 362-2480
Reserve: 1–12 months in advance

Just walking into the lobby of the Stock Exchange Tower, situated in the heart of the financial district, gives you an inkling of what's to follow. The entry has highly polished black and green marble floors and black and white marble walls, gold ceiling and finely detailed metal elevators that whisk you up to the 10th floor. Here you enter the former watering hole for the Pacific Stock Exchange which has been painstakingly restored to its original beauty. The Club is located on the 10th and 11th floors and features one of the most striking and exquisite Art Deco interiors we've seen. The Club's 10th floor entry is through bronze-framed elevator doors decorated in silver, bronze and brass appliqué. A remarkable interior staircase complete with an original 30-foot high Diego Rivera fresco leads to the 11th floor. Furnishings are original Art Deco pieces and appointments are generously clad in black marble, silver and brass. The ceiling is stunning, covered with burnished gold leaf squares. The white baby grand piano is indicative of this facility's elegance and attention to detail. This is a truly exceptional place to hold a wedding reception.

CAPACITY: For weddings, the entire club (10th and 11th floors) may be reserved. The total capacity is 700 for a standing reception or 200 for a seated function.

FEES & DEPOSITS: A deposit is required, the amount dependent on several variables, so make sure you get specific information over the phone. For Saturday parties, the minimum rental fee is $1,250 for a 4-hour block. For Sunday, the rental fee is $500/4-hour block. Should you desire more time, additional fees may apply. On week nights, Monday through Friday, the fee for the Main Dining Room is $300 and for both floors, $500.

CANCELLATION POLICY: The deposit refund will vary depending on when you notify the Club of cancellation.

AVAILABILITY: The Club's dining rooms are available everyday after 4pm. On Saturdays and Sundays, they are available earlier. Call for more specific information.

SERVICES/AMENITIES:

Restaurant Services: yes

Catering: provided, no BYO

Kitchen Facilities: n/a

Tables & Chairs: provided

Overnight Accommodations: no

Telephone: pay phone

Outdoor Night Lighting: access only

Bride's Dressing Area: yes

Linens, Silver, etc.: provided

Restrooms: wca

Dance Floor: yes

Parking: CBA

Outdoor Cooking Facilities: no

Cleanup: provided

Other: white baby grand piano

RESTRICTIONS:

Alcohol: provided

Smoking: allowed

Music: amplified ok

Wheelchair Access: yes

Insurance: not required

THE CLIFF HOUSE

1090 Point Lobos
San Francisco, CA 94121
(415) 386-3330 Betty or David
Reserve: 3–6 months in advance

From here you can smell the salt air, feel the ocean breezes and watch the sea lions cavort on the rocks below. This historic spot has actually been the home of several Cliff Houses. The first, a modest 1863 structure, the second a grand and elaborate Victorian resort built in 1896, and the current restaurant, built in 1909, which is now part of the Golden Gate National Recreation Area. The upstairs restaurants are favorite destinations for both tourists and locals to eat (and have a few martinis) while experiencing a California sunset. Downstairs, however, is the Terrace Room, a private, contemporary dining room which can be reserved for prenuptial dinners or receptions. Painted in cool grays, with window treatments in burgundies, pinks and grays, the Terrace Room has some terrific benefits. Let's start with the views—three sides of this space have multiple windows which overlook the Pacific. It also has a small, outdoor terrace for al fresco dining. Next, it's large enough to handle a crowd. And there's more. This room is separated from the rest of the Cliff House's public spaces, so it's completely private and quiet. If you've been searching for a special spot next to the ocean, the Terrace Room is worth a look.

CAPACITY: The Terrace Room can hold 135 seated guests; 160 standing guests.

FEES & DEPOSITS: To reserve, a $250 non-refundable deposit (which is applied towards the final bill) is required when reservations are confirmed. Half the estimated event total is due 4 weeks prior to the event, the balance payable at the end of the function. A guest count confirmation is due 48 hours in advance. Food service is provided. Per person costs are approximately $30, minimum, for buffets, $24-31 for seated dinners. Tax and 15% service charge are additional.

AVAILABILITY: Year-round, daily.

SERVICES/AMENITIES:

Restaurant Services: yes

Catering: provided, no BYO

Kitchen Facilities: n/a

Tables & Chairs: provided

Linens, Silver, etc.: provided

Restrooms: wca

Dance Floor: CBA, extra charge

Parking: on street, 2 free lots, valet CBA

Overnight Accommodations: no

Telephone: pay phones

Outdoor Night Lighting: yes

Outdoor Cooking Facilities: no

Cleanup: provided

Bride's Dressing Area: CBA

RESTRICTIONS:

Alcohol: full service available

Smoking: allowed

Music: amplified ok

Wheelchair Access: limited

Insurance: not required

Other: no rice or birdseed

THE CONSERVATORY OF FLOWERS

Golden Gate Park
San Francisco, CA 94117
(415) 641-7978
Reserve: 6–9 months in advance

This large, graceful, ornate and mostly glass structure is the oldest existing building in Golden Gate Park and probably the best example of Victorian Greenhouse Architecture in the United States. Built in 1879, it's a California historic landmark, visited by thousands of people a year. (Be careful that you don't confuse this structure with the Hall of Flowers building.) The entire Conservatory is available for wedding events. The West Wing is particularly well-suited for ceremonies, featuring an interior patio with trellis and displays of seven seasonal flower types. The East Wing features two ponds, waterfalls, rare aquatic plants and flowers. Palms and orchids abound in exotic profusion. The Conservatory is such a sensational and historically unique facility, your guests will never forget your event!

CAPACITY: The Conservatory accommodates 200 standing guests or 70 seated.

FEES & DEPOSITS: A non-refundable $300 deposit is due when the contract is signed. The rental fee is $250/hour for a minimum 3-hour rental, Monday–Thursday; 5-hour minimum Friday–Sunday. A refundable $500 damage deposit is also required. These fees are payable 30 days prior to your party and include the services of 2 security guards and 1 staff person. A special charge applies for any rental between 4pm–6pm.

AVAILABILITY: Year-round, from 4pm–midnight. May be closed on major holidays; call for more information.

SERVICES/AMENITIES:

Restaurant Services: no

Catering: BYO, licensed

Kitchen Facilities: minimal

Tables & Chairs: BYO

Linens, Silver, etc.: BYO

Restrooms: wca

Dance Floor: CBA

Parking: large lot

Overnight Accommodations: no

Telephone: office phone

Outdoor Night Lighting: access only

Outdoor Cooking Facilities: BYO BBQ

Cleanup: caterer

Bride's Dressing Area: no

RESTRICTIONS:

Alcohol: BYO

Music: amplified ok

Wheelchair Access: yes

Smoking: outside only

Insurance: liability required

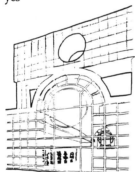

CONTRACT DESIGN CENTER

600 Townsend Street
San Francisco, CA 94103
(415) 864-1500
Reserve: 3–6 months in advance

The Contract Design Center Atrium has a crisp, cool, clean style. White terrazzo flooring leads to a wall of uniquely constructed glass and a white vaulted ceiling gives the center height and interest. And behind the atrium, visible through the glass wall, is a very versatile courtyard. Tented or left open to the sun, the spacious white aggregate patio lends itself to a variety of outdoor events, including ceremonies and receptions.

CAPACITY, FEES & DEPOSITS:

Area	Seated	Reception	Rental Fees
Atrium	225	500	$3,000*
The Courtyard	250	500	—
Atrium & Courtyard	—	—	$3,500*
Conference Center	—	—	$500

*The basic rental fee may vary depending on the specific details of your event.

A non-refundable deposit of 50% of the rental fee is required when the contract is submitted. The balance is due 30 days prior to the event. Fees include a house technician.

CANCELLATION POLICY: The fees and deposits can be applied toward another event within a 90-day period.

AVAILABILITY: Year-round, Monday–Friday after 3pm, Saturday and Sunday from 8am. The Conference Center, daily from 8am.

SERVICES/AMENITIES:

Restaurant Services: no

Catering: preferred list or BYO w/approval

Kitchen Facilities: minimal

Tables & Chairs: provided

Linens, Silver, etc.: BYO

Restrooms: wca

Dance Floor: terrazzo floor

Bride's Dressing Area: CBA

Parking: street, garage

Overnight Accommodations: no

Telephone: pay phones

Outdoor Night Lighting: yes

Outdoor Cooking Facilities: yes

Cleanup: provided

Other: event coordination, technician provided

RESTRICTIONS:

Alcohol: provided, no BYO

Smoking: allowed

Music: amplified ok

Wheelchair Access: yes

Insurance: certificate required

THE EUREKA

San Francisco Maritime National Historic Park
Hyde Street Pier
San Francisco, CA 94109
(415) 929-0202 Daria Booth
Reserve: 1 month in advance

The 277-foot side-wheel paddle steamboat, the Eureka, was once the world's largest passenger ferry. It is now permanently docked at the end of the Hyde Street Pier along with other historic vessels of note. Built in 1890 as a railroad ferry and later converted for passenger service, the Eureka is one of the few remaining relics of San Francisco's grand era of ferry transport. Unbelievably, she was still in service as recently as 1957. Now the old girl is a museum of sorts, available as a public exhibit and as a very unique space for wedding functions. (Due to repairs, the Eureka will not be available until Fall, 1993.)

CAPACITY: The Eureka can accommodate up to 600 guests.

FEES & DEPOSITS: A $1500 refundable security deposit is required and is usually returned 2 weeks after your function. The rental fee is $900 minimum. The total fee will depend on the length of your event and the number of guests. Work out the details with the National Maritime Museum Association. Fees include a National Park Ranger on duty during events.

AVAILABILITY: Available November–May from 5pm to midnight and June–October from 6pm–midnight.

CANCELLATION POLICY: Deposits are refundable 21 days prior to your event.

SERVICES/AMENITIES:

Restaurant Services: no

Catering: BYO

Kitchen Facilities: no

Tables & Chairs: some provided

Linens, Silver, etc.: BYO

Restrooms: wca limited

Bride's Dressing Area: CBA

Parking: on street, adjacent garage

Overnight Accommodations: no

Telephone: pay phone

Outdoor Night Lighting: yes

Outdoor Cooking Facilities: no

Cleanup: caterer or renter

Dance Floor: wood deck

RESTRICTIONS:

Alcohol: BYO

Smoking: only on the pier

Music: amplified until 11pm

Wheelchair Access: limited, lower deck only

Insurance: required

Other: decorations restricted

FERRYBOAT SANTA ROSA

Permanently moored at Pier 3
The Embarcadero
San Francisco, CA 94111
(415) 394-8900
Reserve: 2 weeks–12 months in advance

Permanently moored at Pier 3, this historic 1927 ferryboat has been meticulously restored to her former grandeur and now commands a stately presence at the foot of San Francisco's financial district. 240 feet long, the Ferryboat Santa Rosa's main deck has 10-foot ceilings, two open air fantail decks and floor-to-ceiling windows that wrap around the entire facility. Wedding ceremonies are often held in front of the East Fantail Deck, where the view of the bay is spectacular. Try a champagne reception on the Sun Deck and take advantage of the sea air and a 360-degree panorama of downtown, Telegraph Hill, Treasure Island and the Bay Bridge. At night, your guests can enjoy dining and dancing beneath a glittering city skyline and the Bridge's necklace of lights. And the Santa Rosa's convenient dockside location allows everyone to come and go as they please, while enjoying the unique ambiance of the waterfront.

CAPACITY:

Area	Seated	Standing
Entire Ferryboat	500	500
East Deck	200	300
West Deck	300	500

FEES & DEPOSITS: A $2,000 deposit is required within 7 days after booking, and the balance is due 5 days before the event. On-board charges must be paid the evening of the function. Rental fees are as follows:

Day	Hours	Fee	Min. Rental
Mon-Fri	Before 5pm	$150-250/hr	3 hours
Sun-Thurs	After 5pm	$300-500/hr	3 hours
Weekends	5pm Fri-5pm Sun	$300-500/hr	4 hours Sat eve
			3 hours Sun

CANCELLATION POLICY: The deposit is fully refundable with 120 days notice, or if the date can be rebooked.

AVAILABILITY: Year-round, anytime.

SERVICES/AMENITIES:

Restaurant Services: no
Catering: select from list or BYO
Kitchen Facilities: setup only
Tables & Chairs: provided, extra charge
Linens, Silver, etc.: caterer
Restrooms: wca
Dance Floor: CBA, extra charge
Other: event coordination

Parking: on street
Overnight Accommodations: no
Telephone: boat phone
Outdoor Night Lighting: CBA for extra charge
Outdoor Cooking Facilities: allowed
Cleanup: provided
Bride's Dressing Area: private ladies' room

RESTRICTIONS:

Alcohol: provided, corkage $7/bottle
Smoking: designated areas only
Insurance: required with own caterer

Wheelchair Access: main deck only
Music: amplified ok

THE FLOOD MANSION

2222 Broadway
San Francisco, CA 94115
(415) 563-2900 Mrs. Hackman
Reserve: 3–12 months in advance

The Flood Mansion is a symphony of classical styles—Italian Renaissance, Rococo, Tudor and Georgian. This elegant marble building, constructed in 1915, has remained well preserved since Mrs. Flood donated her home to the Religious of the Sacred Heart in 1939. Although the building is now used as a private school, it is available for special events after school hours. Receptions are welcome, but wedding ceremonies need advance approval. The Mansion is impressive. Its Grand Hall is 140 feet long with marble floors and great views of the Bay. The Adam Room, near the entry, is quite lovely with high, ornate ceilings, specially designed wood tables and chairs plus a marble fireplace. The beautiful Reception Room, at the end of the Grand Hall, boasts magnificent coffered ceiling, painted murals in golds, blues and greens, and hardwood parquet floors. This room is architecturally complex and detailed. A pretty, enclosed courtyard off of the Grand Hall is available for outdoor gatherings, weather permitting. The Mansion is definitely the place for a stately and elegant wedding party.

CAPACITY: The entire main floor has a standing capacity of 450 people or a seated capacity of approximately 300. Individual seated capacities: the Grand Hall, 200; the Adam Room, 60; and the Reception Room, 80–100 people. In addition, there is a theater area downstairs.

FEES & DEPOSITS: 50% of the total rental fee is the deposit required to secure your event date. Also required is a $1,000 custodial and security fee, some of which may be reimbursable. The rental fee is $5,000 for the facility. The final balance is due 2 weeks prior to the event.

CANCELLATION POLICY: Should you cancel, the rental deposit is not refundable. The $1,000 custodial and security deposit is refundable.

AVAILABILITY: Fridays after 3pm, Saturday and Sunday all day. All events must end by midnight. No hourly minimum rental block is required.

SERVICES/AMENITIES:

Restaurant Services: no
Catering: select from list
Kitchen Facilities: ample
Tables & Chairs: BYO
Linens, Silver, etc.: BYO
Restrooms: wca
Dance Floor: yes
Bride's Dressing Area: CBA

Parking: valet parking required
Overnight Accommodations: no
Telephone: pay phone
Outdoor Night Lighting: access only
Outdoor Cooking Facilities: no
Cleanup: caterer
Other: 2 baby grand pianos

RESTRICTIONS:

Alcohol: BYO
Smoking: outside only
Music: amplified until 11:30pm

Wheelchair Access: yes
Insurance: extra liability required

FOREST HILL CLUB HOUSE

381 Magellan Ave.
San Francisco, CA 94116
(415) 664-0542 Will Connolly
Reserve: 4–6 months in advance

The Forest Hill Club House is an architectural gem designed by Bernard Maybeck, is tucked away in a very nice neighborhood of private residences. Completed in 1919, the building's exterior and interior are decorative yet rustic, representing the final phase of the turn-of-the-century American Arts and Crafts movement. The interior features a large, long room with hardwood floors and a sizeable fireplace. The furniture in several rooms may have been designed by Bernard Maybeck. The adjacent brick patio and garden, completed in 1966, is a great spot for outdoor ceremonies if the weather cooperates. For weekday functions, the Club House is available with little advance notice. This is a small but charming facility.

CAPACITY: The Club House can accommodate 200 standing guests or approximately 100 seated guests. The dance floor is large enough for 50 dancers.

FEES & DEPOSITS: 50% of the total rental fee is required when you reserve your date. A $350 refundable security/cleaning deposit is due 6 weeks prior to the event and is usually returned within 30 days after the event. On Friday, Saturday and Sunday, the fee is $1,100. Weekdays, it's $500. Overtime is permissible at $75/hour. The remaining 50% balance is due when the contract is signed, about 6 weeks before the event.

CANCELLATION POLICY: 50% of the rental fee is retained if the date can not be rebooked. If it can, the entire rental deposit will be refunded.

AVAILABILITY: Anytime, up to midnight. An 8-hour block is the required minimum.

SERVICES/AMENITIES:

Restaurant Services: no
Catering: BYO
Kitchen Facilities: moderate
Tables & Chairs: some provided
Linens, Silver, etc.: BYO
Restrooms: wca limited
Cleanup: caterer or renter

Dance Floor: yes
Parking: on street
Overnight Accommodations: no
Telephone: pay phone
Outdoor Night Lighting: yes
Outdoor Cooking Facilities: BYO BBQ
Bride's Dressing Area: CBA

RESTRICTIONS:

Alcohol: BYO
Smoking: allowed
Music: amplified inside only

Wheelchair Access: limited
Insurance: not required

FORT MASON CONFERENCE CENTER

Fort Mason Center
San Francisco, CA 94123
(415) 441-5706 Conference Center Director
Reserve: 6 months in advance

Located at the south end of Landmark Building A at Fort Mason, the Conference Center is well situated to provide an extraordinary environment for ceremonies or receptions. Three different-sized rooms, with track lighting, carpets, high ceilings and hanging banners offer varied party opportunities. The view of the Golden Gate Bridge is outstanding, as is the view of the nearby yacht harbor, especially when lit up at night. If you just want to get married here, note that Greens Restaurant, a first class place to hold your reception, is located close by.

CAPACITY: The Conference Center can accommodate 350 guests for a reception; 230 for seated functions.

FEES & DEPOSITS: A $300–350 security deposit is required, depending on the size and type of event, and is returned after the function. The deposit is payable when you book your date. Rental rates vary depending on the type of event, day and number of rooms rented. For the largest room, the rental fee is $685. For that room plus two additional adjacent rooms, the fee is $785. The rental fee is due 30 days prior to the event date.

CANCELLATION POLICY: Call for cancellation policy.

AVAILABILITY: Everyday from 8am. Guests and caterer must vacate the premises by midnight; 1am by request.

SERVICES/AMENITIES:

Restaurant Services: no

Catering: BYO

Kitchen Facilities: no

Tables & Chairs: provided

Linens, Silver, etc.: BYO

Restrooms: wca

Dance Floor: CBA

Parking: large lot

Overnight Accommodations: no

Telephone: pay phone

Outdoor Night Lighting: access only

Outdoor Cooking Facilities: CBA

Cleanup: caterer & Fort Mason

Bride's Dressing Area: CBA

RESTRICTIONS:

Alcohol: BYO

Smoking: outside only

Music: amplified ok

Wheelchair Access: yes

Insurance: not required

GALLERIA DESIGN CENTER

101 Henry Adams Street
San Francisco, CA 94103
(415) 864-1500
Reserve: 3–6 months in advance

The Galleria Design Center is renowned throughout the Bay Area as *the* place to celebrate. This spectacular four-story atrium soars 60 feet to a retractable skylight. Daylight floods the building, and at night you really can see the stars. Hundreds of glittering lights, giant palm trees and lush indoor gardens create a unique environment, and a large, theatrical stage is ready-made for superb parties. Tiered levels provide dining or standing reception space with excellent views of the stage. Vast and inviting, the Galleria is a distinctive wedding location.

CAPACITY, FEES & DEPOSITS: The Atrium seats 1,200 (4 floors), and accommodates 2,500 for a standing reception. The basic rental fee of $6,000/day may vary, depending on the specific details of your event. A non-refundable deposit of 50% of the rental fee is required when the contract is submitted. The balance is due 30 days prior to the event. Fees include a house technician.

CANCELLATION POLICY: If you cancel, the fees and deposits can only be applied toward another event within a 90-day period.

AVAILABILITY: Year-round, Monday–Friday after 3pm, Saturday and Sunday from 8am except for seasonal market periods when the Galleria has trade shows.

SERVICES/AMENITIES:

Restaurant Services: no

Catering: in-house caterer or BYO w/approval, extra fee

Kitchen Facilities: minimal

Tables & Chairs: some provided

Linens, Silver, etc.: BYO

Restrooms: wca

Dance Floor: terrazzo floor

Bride's Dressing Area: CBA

Parking: street, garage

Overnight Accommodations: no

Telephone: pay phones

Outdoor Night Lighting: access only

Outdoor Cooking Facilities: yes

Cleanup: provided

Other: event coordination, stage, equipment & technician provided

RESTRICTIONS:

Alcohol: provided, no BYO

Smoking: allowed

Music: amplified ok

Wheelchair Access: yes

Insurance: certificate required

GIFTCENTER PAVILION

888 Brannan Street
San Francisco, CA 94103
(415) 861-7733   Evelyn Marks
Reserve: 1–12 months in advance

The GiftCenter Pavilion is one of San Francisco's most appealing event spaces. Four stories high, its colors are a light dusky peach and teal, and it is capped by a skylight that covers the ceiling and opens to the stars. The center of the room makes a great area for dancing. Seating is often arranged above on the surrounding tiers, giving guests a great view of the activities below. The GiftCenter also has a large stage and a quarter of a million dollars in state-of-the-art sound and lighting equipment. We like this space! It's impressive and spacious, yet designed well enough to make a smaller party here feel comfortable. And what's also nice is that everything can be arranged for you—from flowers and cake to wedding decorations.

CAPACITY: The Pavilion can hold 150–450 for a standing reception or 300 seated guests.

FEES & DEPOSITS: A non-refundable deposit of 50% of the total rental package is due when the contract is submitted. The total balance is due 10 days prior to the event. Rental fees range from $3,500–6,000 depending on the day of the week, level(s) rented and guest count. The fee includes setup, janitorial services, 2 security guards, lighting/sound equipment. Extra fee for technical personnel.

AVAILABILITY: Year-round, everyday from 6am–2am, except during gift shows.

SERVICES/AMENITIES:

Restaurant Services: no

Parking: large lots, street

Catering: in-house caterer, BYO w/approval
Kitchen Facilities: fully equipped
Tables & Chairs: provided
Linens, Silver, etc.: provided or BYO
Restrooms: wca
Dance Floor: yes

RESTRICTIONS:
Alcohol: provided, corkage $5-7/bottle
Smoking: allowed
Music: amplified ok

Overnight Accommodations: no
Telephone: pay phone
Outdoor Night Lighting: access only
Outdoor Cooking Facilities: no
Cleanup: provided
Bride's Dressing Area: yes

Wheelchair Access: yes
Insurance: certificate required

THE GINSBERG COLLECTION

190 San Bruno Avenue
San Francisco, CA 94103
(415) 621-6060 Norman List
Reserve: 1–12 months in advance

And now for something completely different.... The Ginsberg Collection showroom is the handiwork of world-renowned designer, Ron Mann, who brings together an enticing mix of Mediterranean, North African and Southwest influences. The two primary event rooms look as though they might have been hewn from an upscale cave. Their uneven, textured adobe walls reveal dozens of niches—all filled with artifacts, antiques and decorative objects from around the world. And even though every nook, raised surface and corner overflows with exotic items, the showroom appears spacious thanks to 30-foot ceilings and a fluid floor plan. A built-in concrete, serpentine table is perfect for seated dinners or buffets, and multi-leveled platforms create unique spaces for ceremonies, dancing, or just plain mingling. The kitchen is another fascinating element—it blends in so thoroughly with the overall interior design that it's practically invisible. Want to have a private conversation? Two spiral staircases take you upstairs, where several slightly mysterious and angular rooms, offer a quiet retreat. There's always something to discover at the showroom, and if you happen to be smitten with an oversized urn or Thai rain drum, take it home with you—everything is for sale!

CAPACITY: The showroom can accommodate 100 for a seated meal and 350 for a standing buffet.

FEES & DEPOSITS: The facility rents for $3,000. A $500 deposit is required to reserve your date, and the balance is due 10 days prior to the event.

CANCELLATION POLICY: The deposit is not refundable.

AVAILABILITY: Weekdays, 3pm–12am; weekends anytime.

SERVICES/AMENITIES:
Restaurant Services: no

Parking: lot, on street

Catering: preferred list or BYO
 Kitchen Facilities: ample
Tables & Chairs: BYO, some gallery pieces avail.
Linens, Silver, etc.: BYO
Restrooms: wca
Dance Floor: yes
Other: wedding coordination

RESTRICTIONS:
Alcohol: BYO
Smoking: outside only
Insurance: required

Overnight Accommodations: no
Telephone: emergency phone
Outdoor Night Lighting: access only
Outdoor Cooking Facilities: no
Cleanup: caterer
Bride's Dressing Area: yes

Wheelchair Access: yes
Music: amplified ok

GOLDEN GATE PARK WEDDING GARDENS

Golden Gate Park
San Francisco, CA 94117
(415) 666-7035
Reserve: 1–12 months in advance

All through the peak months of the wedding season, May through August, up to 6 weddings a day are performed in Golden Gate Park. Three small gardens are particularly in demand for wedding celebrations.

The Shakespeare Garden: Founded in 1928, this garden, located west of the California Academy of Sciences, features many of the plants mentioned in Shakespeare's plays. It is a small, relatively enclosed space surrounded by hedges and shrubs.

Queen Wilhelmina Tulip Garden: In full bloom in early spring, this fabulous collection of tulips and circle of green lawn provides a backdrop to the Dutch Windmill, located in the northwest corner of the park. It is also a small, enclosed space surrounded by larger vegetation.

The Rose Garden: Although roses do bloom year-round, the most spectacular display of blooms and fragrance occurs during late spring/early summer. The rows of roses in full color make a great promenade for bride and groom and a wonderful background for wedding photos. The Rose Garden is available for ceremonies only.

CAPACITY: The standing capacity in the Shakespeare Garden is 200, in the Queen Wilhelmina Garden, 100 and in the Rose Garden, 100 guests.

FEES & DEPOSITS: 10% of the total anticipated fee is required as a deposit for the Tulip and Shakespeare Gardens. The Rose Garden deposit is $25. Deposits are payable within 5 days of making your reservation. The rental fee for the Tulip and Shakespeare Gardens is $225 for the first 2 hours and $35/hour thereafter. The Rose Garden fee is $125 for the first 2 hours and $25/hour thereafter.

CANCELLATION POLICY: If you cancel 30 days prior to the event, 90% of the deposit is refunded; if less than 5 working days prior to your event, no refund.

AVAILABILITY: The gardens are available from 9am to dusk everyday.

SERVICES/AMENITIES:

Restaurant Services: no

Catering: BYO

Kitchen Facilities: no

Tables & Chairs: BYO

Linens, Silver, etc.: BYO

Restrooms: location and wca varies

Dance Floor: no

Parking: on street

Overnight Accommodations: no

Telephone: pay phones in park

Outdoor Night Lighting: access only

Outdoor Cooking Facilities: no

Cleanup: caterer or renter

Bride's Dressing Area: no

RESTRICTIONS:

Alcohol: BYO

Smoking: allowed

Music: no amplified

Wheelchair Access: yes

Insurance: not required

Other: you must provide your own security

GOLDEN SUNSET
Pacific Marine Yacht Charters

Berthed at Pier 39, West Basin
San Francisco, CA 94133
(415) 788-9100
Reserve: 1–9 months in advance

The sleek, 75-foot Golden Sunset is one of four luxury yachts in Pacific Marine's elegant fleet. This yacht features three decks, an open air wing bridge with wet bar and an intimate private stateroom with a queen bed, VCR and marble bath with jacuzzi. A state-of-the-art sound system with compact disc and cassette capabilities is also available.

CAPACITY: The Golden Sunset can accommodate up to 100 guests, weather permitting, and can seat up to 40 guests.

FEES & DEPOSITS: A $1,500 deposit is required to reserve your date. Half the food and beverage cost is due 30 days prior to your event.

	Weekdays (before 6pm)	*Weekdays (after 6pm)*	*Weekends/Holidays*
Yacht rental rates	$500/hr	$550/hr	$625/hr
Groups of 20 guests or less	425/hr	475/hr	550/hr

A 3-hour minimum rental is required, 4 hours on Saturday evenings and holidays. A guaranteed guest count is required 7 days prior to departure and the remaining balance is due 5 days prior to your event.

Special packages, starting at $24/guest, include your wedding ceremony performed by the captain, gourmet menu, champagne toast, customized wedding cake and a wedding coordinator's time. Yacht rental, beverage service, tax and gratuity are additional.

CANCELLATION POLICY: With 60 days' notice, 85% of the reservation deposit will be refunded; with less notice, the deposit will be forfeited.

AVAILABILITY: Anytime. No limits.

SERVICES/AMENITIES:

Restaurant Services: no
Catering: provided, no BYO
Kitchen Facilities: on board
Tables & Chairs: provided
Linens, Silver, etc.: provided
Restrooms: no wca
Dance Floor: yes
Bride's Dressing Area: yes

Parking: Pier 39 garage, validations available
Overnight Accommodations: yes, limited
Telephone: emergency cellular phone and radio
Outdoor Night Lighting: yes
Outdoor Cooking Facilities: no
Cleanup: provided
Other: complimentary wedding coordination

RESTRICTIONS:

Alcohol: provided, corkage $7/bottle
Smoking: outside only
Music: amplified ok

Wheelchair Access: no
Insurance: not required

THE GREEN ROOM

Veterans Building, Second Floor
San Francisco, CA 94102
(415) 621-6600 Elizabeth or Alberta
Reserve: 9–12 months in advance

The Green Room is actually green. But don't let that stop you from taking a healthy interest in this fabulous party facility. It's an outstanding and elegant place for a wedding reception. The Room has an incredibly high ivory and gold leaf ceiling, hardwood parquet floor, large pillars, mirrors and five stunning chandeliers adorning its interior. The Green Room opens onto a terra cotta-tiled loggia (balcony) which overlooks the enormous rotunda of City Hall. At night, from the loggia's vantage point, the view of the lighted City Hall is truly breathtaking.

CAPACITY: The room can accommodate 500 standing and 300 seated guests if there's no dancing. Dancing will reduce guest capacity.

FEES & DEPOSITS: To secure your date, a non-refundable $100 deposit is required plus a $200 refundable cleaning deposit. The rental fee is $525 plus the event manager's cost at $23.30/hour. Holidays are an additional $100. Fees include pre-function custodial service. Any other assistance, such as setup/breakdown attendant, security or custodial services, is additional.

AVAILABILITY: Anytime. If you rent this facility before 8am or after midnight, you will be charged for staff at time and a half.

SERVICES/AMENITIES:

Restaurant Services: no

Catering: BYO

Kitchen Facilities: minimal

Dance Floor: yes

Parking: nearby garage

Overnight Accommodations: no

Telephone: pay phone, lines CBA at extra cost

Tables & Chairs: provided, extra charge

Linens, Silver, etc.: BYO

Restrooms: wca

Outdoor Night Lighting: on loggia

Outdoor Cooking Facilities: no

Cleanup: caterer

Bride's Dressing Area: CBA

RESTRICTIONS:

Alcohol: BYO

Smoking: outside only

Music: amplified ok with restrictions

Wheelchair Access: no

Insurance: extra liability & damage required

Other: decorating restrictions

GREENS

Fort Mason, Building A
San Francisco, CA 94123
(415) 771-7955 Rick Jones
Reserve: 1–6 months in advance

Greens is a special restaurant, not just because it's located at Fort Mason, or because it's owned by a Zen Buddhist organization, or because it only serves gourmet vegetarian fare with flair. This place is special because the space makes you feel so good. Greens has enormous multi-paned windows extending the entire length of the restaurant. These windows have superb views of the Golden Gate Bridge and of the boat harbor which lies directly beyond the building. At sunset, the waning light reflected off the bridge and boats is a stunning sight to see. The interior of Greens is also exceptional, with really good original artwork, unusual carved wood seating and tables, plus a high, vaulted ceiling. The overall impression is light, airy and comfortable.

CAPACITY: Greens can accommodate 150 for a seated meal or 250 for a stand-up hors d'oeuvres reception. There's also a 30-person private dining room, great for rehearsal dinners.

FEES & DEPOSITS: A $250 non-refundable deposit is required to secure your event date. It is due when the event date is booked, and is credited to the final billing. Full meal service is provided. Rates vary according to group size: $50-60/person for a 50-person dinner; $30-40/person for 100 guests. These figures include space rental for 4 hours, labor, linens, flowers and candles. Gratuity and tax will be added to the final bill. Beyond 4 hours, there is a $200/hour fee.

AVAILABILITY: The private dining room is available everyday. Larger private parties restricted to Sundays from 5pm onwards and Mondays from 3pm onwards.

SERVICES/AMENITIES:

Restaurant Services: yes
Catering: provided, no BYO
Kitchen Facilities: n/a
Tables & Chairs: provided
Linens, Silver, etc.: provided
Restrooms: wca
Dance Floor: CBA, extra cost

Parking: large lot
Overnight Accommodations: no
Telephone: pay phone
Outdoor Night Lighting: access only
Outdoor Cooking Facilities: no
Cleanup: provided
Bride's Dressing Area: CBA

RESTRICTIONS:

Alcohol: provided, WBC only
Smoking: allowed
Music: amplified ok

Wheelchair Access: ramp
Insurance: not required

HAAS-LILIENTHAL HOUSE

2007 Franklin Street at Washington
San Francisco, CA 94109
(415) 441-3011 Events Coordinator
Reserve: 4 months in advance

The Haas-Lilienthal House is a stately gray Victorian located in Pacific Heights. It is one of the few houses that remains largely as it was when occupied by the Haas and Lilienthal families from 1886–1972. The house provides a unique and intimate environment for a wedding event. The main floor has 13-foot ceilings, two large parlors and formal dining room, foyer and hall. Downstairs, there's a ballroom for larger parties. The interior is very attractive, with subtle colors, oriental carpets, rich woodwork and turn-of-the-century furnishings. This architectural treasure is very comfortable and warm inside.

CAPACITY: The house can accommodate 200 guests for a standing reception; 80 seated in the ballroom or 50 seated on the main floor.

FEES & DEPOSITS: A $500 refundable deposit is required and is returned 30 days after the event. Fees range from $650–2,000 depending on the number of guests. The upper floor dressing room for the bride is an additional $300.

CANCELLATION POLICY: You must cancel 90 days prior to your party to receive a refund.

AVAILABILITY: Monday, Tuesday and Thursday until 10pm; Friday and Saturday until 11pm; Wednesday and Sunday 5pm–10pm.

SERVICES/AMENITIES:

Restaurant Services: no
Catering: BYO, select from list
Kitchen Facilities: moderate

Parking: on street, valet CBA
Overnight Accommodations: no
Telephone: emergency only

Tables & Chairs: most provided
Linens, Silver, etc.: BYO
Restrooms: no wca
Dance Floor: yes

RESTRICTIONS:
Alcohol: BYO, no red wine at standing events
Smoking: outside only
Music: amplified with restrictions

Outdoor Night Lighting: access only
Outdoor Cooking Facilities: BYO BBQ
Cleanup: caterer
Bride's Dressing Area: CBA

Wheelchair Access: no
Insurance: not required

HAMLIN MANSION

2120 Broadway
San Francisco, CA 94115
(415) 331-0544
Reserve: 6–12 months in advance

The Hamlin Mansion is an impressive structure inside and out. The interior features the elegant and spacious Foyer and the two-story Great Hall, complete with ornate oak columns, herringbone hardwood floors and crowned by a richly detailed leaded glass skylight. The magnificent staircase, backed on the landing by a huge leaded glass window, is perfect for presenting the bride. The Main Dining Room has a striking black marble and gold fireplace and great views of the Bay. With Italian hand-laid mosaic tile on its floor and walls plus lovely leaded Tiffany-style skylights, the Solarium is a jewel of old-fashioned craftsmanship. Upstairs are several rooms with sensational ornate plaster ceilings, painted detailing and fireplaces. Use the downstairs rooms or setup bar and tables on the upstairs balcony. With classic lines and plenty of rich detailing, the Mansion makes a wonderful place for an upscale, more traditional wedding.

CAPACITY: The Mansion can hold up to 200 seated guests or 350 for a standing reception.

FEES & DEPOSITS: A non-refundable $500 security deposit is required when the contract is signed. The rental fees vary according to day of week and guest count. Fees are payable 2 months prior to the event. Valet service runs $400–1,000 and a security guard is about $150/event.

AVAILABILITY: Sunday–Thursday to 10pm, Friday–Saturday to 11:30pm.

SERVICES/AMENITIES:
Restaurant Services: no
Catering: provided, no BYO
Kitchen Facilities: n/a
Tables & Chairs: provided
Linens, Silver, etc.: caterer
Restrooms: wca
Dance Floor: yes
Bride's Dressing Area: yes

Parking: valet
Overnight Accommodations: no
Telephone: pay phone
Outdoor Night Lighting: access only
Outdoor Cooking Facilities: no
Cleanup: caterer
Other: baby grand piano

RESTRICTIONS:

Alcohol: BYO
Smoking: allowed
Music: amplified with volume limit

Wheelchair Access: limited, elevator
Insurance: recommended
Other: decorations restricted, no rice

HERBST AND FESTIVAL PAVILIONS

Fort Mason Center
San Francisco, CA 94123
(415) 441-5706 Director of Sales
Reserve: 3 months–2 years in advance

Celebrations, ceremonies and receptions all come alive in these waterfront spaces located on historic covered piers. The Festival Pavilion has an extraordinary 50,000 square feet of clear-span space, which includes a mezzanine cafe/bar with great views of the Bay and Golden Gate Bridge. The Herbst Pavilion has 30,000 square feet of open space and offers the same flexible and highly unique surroundings. Both facilities have recently undergone extensive renovations and have white interiors, stunning glass entries, stainless steel food preparation areas and tiled restrooms. If you've got a large crowd, the Pavilions can handle it.

CAPACITY: Festival Pavilion up to 5,000; Herbst Pavilion up to 3,000 people.

FEES & DEPOSITS: A $2,000–3,000 portion of the rental fee reserves your date. A $2,000–3,000 refundable security deposit is also required. The rental fee is $3,500–5,000/day, depending on the type of event and Pavilion selected. The balance of the rental fee and security deposit are due 30 days prior to the event. If food and/or drink is served on site, there is a $1.00/person catering fee. Inquire about rental rates for non-profit organizations.

CANCELLATION POLICY: Call for cancellation policy.

AVAILABILITY: Year-round, everyday 8am–midnight.

SERVICES/AMENITIES:

Restaurant Services: no
Catering: BYO
Kitchen Facilities: large food prep area
Tables & Chairs: limited numbers
Linens, Silver, etc.: BYO
Restrooms: wca
Cleanup: renter provides

Parking: Fort Mason Center lot & Marina Green
Overnight Accommodations: no
Telephone: pay phone, private lines for clients
Outdoor Night Lighting: access only
Outdoor Cooking Facilities: BYO BBQ (permit req'd)
Dance Floor: BYO
Bride's Dressing Area: CBA

RESTRICTIONS:

Alcohol: BYO
Smoking: allowed
Music: amplified ok

Wheelchair Access: yes
Insurance: required

HORNBLOWER DINING YACHTS

Berkeley and San Francisco
(415) 394-8900 ext. 6
Reserve: see each vessel below

Hornblower Dining Yachts offers a wide range of vessels for hire, from sleek yachts to a replica of a turn-of-the-century coastal steamer. You'll travel in style with standard amenities that include white linens, flowers, china and silver service. All vessels are fully enclosed and carpeted. Hornblower staff can help you order everything from invitations and favors to balloons, flowers and entertainment. Also note that remote pickups and drop-offs can be arranged at many locations for a modest additional charge. For winter and early spring parties, Hornblower offers a 'good weather' guarantee that applies to rentals made between November 1st and March 31st.

FEES & DEPOSITS: The deposit amount varies depending on which vessel you select (see below). Wedding packages range from $49 per guest for a 3-hour brunch cruise to $84 per person for a 4-hour dinner cruise. A 15–20% gratuity and tax are additional. Hornblower's Charter Coordinators are available to customize your wedding, offering a multitude of special services.

AVAILABILITY: Year-round, anytime.

CAPTAIN HORNBLOWER & ADMIRAL HORNBLOWER
These two vessels are similar in design, including full galley, 2 decks, parquet dance floor, bar and sound systems. **Reserve:** 1 week–1 year in advance.

CAPACITY: Each yacht can accommodate 60 for a seated function and 75 standing.

DEPOSITS: A $1,000 deposit is due 7–10 days after setting a tentative date. The final balance is due 5 working days prior to your cruise.

CANCELLATION POLICY: You must cancel 60 days prior to the event or forfeit the deposit. If the date can be rebooked, it will be refunded.

COMMODORE HORNBLOWER
A gracious, custom-built motor yacht which offers 2 decks, all-wood interiors, parquet dance floor, 2 bars, full galley and sound system. **Reserve:** 2 weeks–1 year in advance.

CAPACITY: This vessel can carry up to 130 for a seated affair or 150 for a standing reception.

DEPOSITS: A $2,000 deposit is due after setting a tentative date. The final balance is due 5 working days prior to your cruise.

CANCELLATION POLICY: You must cancel 90 days prior to your event or forfeit the deposit. If the date can be rebooked, it will be refunded.

EMPRESS HORNBLOWER
This 100-foot vessel offers 2 large indoor decks, 1 large outdoor deck, 2 parquet dance floors, 3 bars, full

galley and sound system. **Reserve:** 2 weeks–1 year in advance.

CAPACITY: 500 for a standing reception or 270 for a seated meal. You may also charter a single deck for a smaller group.

DEPOSITS: A $2,000–3,000 deposit is due 7–10 days after setting a tentative date. The final balance is due 5 working days prior to your cruise.

CANCELLATION POLICY: You must cancel 120 days prior to the event or forfeit the deposit. If the date can be rebooked, your deposit will be refunded.

CALIFORNIA HORNBLOWER
Patterned after a classic steamer of the early 1900s, this large vessel has 3 decks, 3 dining salons, 3 parquet dance floors, 3 bars, full galley, sound system and expansive sun deck. **Reserve:** 1–12 months in advance.

CAPACITY: This vessel can accommodate 1,000 for cocktails or stand-up buffet and 800 for a seated meal. You can also charter a single deck for smaller groups. The capacity would then range from 100–900.

DEPOSITS: A $1,000–5,000 deposit is due 7–10 days after setting a tentative date. The final balance is due 5 working days prior to your cruise.

CANCELLATION POLICY: You must cancel 120 days prior to the event or forfeit the deposit. If the date can be rebooked, your deposit will be refunded.

PAPAGALLO II
This sleek yacht features 2 decks, 2 salons, bar, full galley and a master suite with spa. She has an intimate living room feel with 2 staterooms on the lower deck. This yacht is available for overnight and extended cruises. **Reserve:** 2 weeks–1 year in advance.

CAPACITY: 24 guests for a seated meal and 50 for a standing reception. She can accommodate 6 for an overnight cruise.

DEPOSITS: A $1,000 deposit is due 7–10 days after setting a tentative date. The final balance is due 5 working days prior to your cruise.

CANCELLATION POLICY: You must cancel 60 days prior to your event or forfeit the deposit. If the date is rebooked, your deposit will be refunded.

SERVICES/AMENITIES FOR ALL VESSELS:
Restaurant Services: no
Catering: provided
Kitchen Facilities: n/a
Tables & Chairs: provided
Linens, Silver, etc.: provided
Restrooms: wca varies each vessel
Bride's Dressing Area: CBA

Parking: various locations
Dance Floor: provided, except Papagallo II
Overnight Accommodations: Papagallo only
Telephone: credit card phone on board
Outdoor Night Lighting: varies
Outdoor Cooking Facilities: no
Cleanup: provided

RESTRICTIONS:
Alcohol: provided, corkage $7/bottle
Smoking: allowed
Music: amplified ok

Wheelchair Access: varies/vessel
Insurance: not required

JULIUS' CASTLE

1541 Montgomery Street
San Francisco, CA 94133
(415) 362-3042
Reserve: 2 months in advance

Julius' Castle, located in the heart of North Beach, is situated high atop Telegraph Hill. Built in 1922 by Julius Roz, who used materials and craftsmen from the 1915 Panama-Pacific Exposition to design a restaurant to look like a 'medieval castle', it's an unusual place to hold a wedding reception. The restaurant's main attractions, besides the cuisine, are its unparalleled panoramic views of the Bay from interior windows and outdoor deck on the upper floor. This deck opens off of the second floor Penthouse Dining Room and is an exceptional spot for a ceremony and champagne toasts. You may rent the second floor or, with enough notice, the entire restaurant.

CAPACITY: The Penthouse Dining Room has seating capacity for 60 people; the Main Dining Room up to 100.

FEES & DEPOSITS: The deposit is approximately $1,000, depending on the size of your party. No rental fee is required. Food service costs range from hors d'oeuvres at $4–21/person to full meals at $35-75/person. Gratuity and taxes are additional.

AVAILABILITY: From noon to 1am, everyday.

SERVICES/AMENITIES:

Restaurant: yes
Catering: no BYO
Kitchen Facilities: n/a
Tables & Chairs: provided
Linens, Silver, etc.: provided
Restrooms: no wca
Dance Floor: limited

Parking: valet only
Overnight Accommodations: no
Telephone: pay phone
Outdoor Night Lighting: access only
Outdoor Cooking Facilities: no
Cleanup: provided
Bride's Dressing Area: yes

RESTRICTIONS:

Alcohol: provided
Smoking: allowed
Music: no amplified

Wheelchair Access: no
Insurance: not required

Need a caterer, cake maker, florist? The Service Directory starting on page 412 features the best in the business.

LASCAUX

248 Sutter Street
San Francisco, CA 94108
(415) 391-1555   Manager
Reserve: 30 days in advance

A descent into this subterranean restaurant evokes the beauty and mystery of the Lascaux caves in France. Subdued lighting casts a soft, warm blush throughout. Wall surfaces suggest a cave's interior—uneven, tactile, earthy. A large stone fireplace provides a glowing focal point. Another contributor to the restaurant's unique ambiance is a rotisserie for meat specialties. Adjacent to the dining area, it is completely visible to all patrons, actively including them in the cooking experience. It's not surprising that Lascaux won San Francisco Focus Magazine's "Best Restaurant Design Award" two years in a row. For small rehearsal dinners and receptions, Lascaux is a real gem.

CAPACITY: Partially rented, groups of 30-35 guests. The entire facility (which can seat 140) can be reserved for a private party by prior arrangement; food and beverage minimums apply.

FEES & DEPOSITS: A refundable deposit of 20% of the estimated food and beverage total is required when reservations are confirmed. The balance is due upon completion of the event. Luncheons range from $22-25/person, dinners $35-40/person; buffets can be arranged. Tax and 15% service charge are additional.

CANCELLATION POLICY: 72-hour advance notice is required for a refund.

AVAILABILITY: Year-round, everyday from 11:30am–11pm except for major holidays.

SERVICES/AMENITIES:

Restaurant: yes
Catering: provided
Kitchen Facilities: n/a
Tables & Chairs: provided
Linens, Silver, etc.: provided
Restrooms: wca
Dance Floor: no

Parking: valet $5/car, adjacent garage
Overnight Accommodations: no
Telephone: pay phone
Outdoor Night Lighting: access only
Outdoor Cooking Facilities: no
Cleanup: provided
Bride's Dressing Area: no

RESTRICTIONS:

Alcohol: provided, corkage $10/bottle
Smoking: designated areas
Music: no amplified

Wheelchair Access: yes, elevator
Insurance: not required

Prices and policies <u>do</u> change. Call each facility and confirm everything you read in Here Comes The Guide.

MacARTHUR PARK

607 Front Street
San Francisco, CA 94111
(415) 398-5700
Reserve: 3–6 months in advance

Housed in a pre-1906 brick warehouse—built when the area was the infamous Barbary Coast—MacArthur Park is located just blocks from the Financial District. The Main Dining Room is light and airy with 18-foot ceilings, skylights and a couple of towering indoor trees. The lower part of the room, called The Arcade, is frequently used for cocktails and hors d'oeuvres. It features brick arches and an expanse of tall windows that overlook the park across the street. The Aviary, once a roosting place for peacocks and other tropical birds, offers a private and soothing atmosphere for small rehearsal dinners. A skylight ceiling, terra cotta floor and brick walls hung with modern prints create warmth and intimacy. The adjacent Patio provides a unique sheltered setting for open-air events, particularly luncheons and cocktail receptions. Guests can enjoy the fresh air, protected from the elements by a canvas roof and banks of heaters. The West Room accommodates larger groups with wood-paneled walls featuring limited-edition American watercolors, windows that open out onto an ivy-covered courtyard and a large brick fireplace. Connected by French doors, these three rooms can be used individually or in combination. Blending rustic and sophisticated elements, MacArthur Park is a genial location for your wedding event.

CAPACITY:

	Seated	Standing		Seated	Standing
Arcade	50	90	West Room	75	125
Aviary	38	50	Main Dining Room	120	200
Bar Area	50	250	Entire Restaurant	280	500
Patio	25	50			

FEES & DEPOSITS: A $500 deposit is required at the time of booking. The balance is due the day of the event. Per person food costs are $15.50-26.75 for luncheons, and $19.50-32.50 for dinners. Tax and an 18% gratuity are additional.

CANCELLATION POLICY: The deposit is fully refundable with 2 weeks' notice.

AVAILABILITY: Weekends, or evenings Monday through Friday.

SERVICES/AMENITIES:

Restaurant Services: yes
Catering: provided, no BYO
Kitchen Facilities: n/a
Tables & Chairs: provided
Linens, Silver, etc.: provided
Restrooms: wca
Dance Floor: yes
Bride's Dressing Area: CBA

Parking: complimentary valet (dinners only), on street
Overnight Accommodations: no
Telephone: pay phone
Outdoor Night Lighting: access only
Outdoor Cooking Facilities: no
Cleanup: provided

RESTRICTIONS:

Alcohol: provided, corkage $10/bottle
Smoking: in private dining rooms only
Music: amplified ok if entire restaurant reserved

Wheelchair Access: yes, except Aviary
Insurance: not required

THE MANSIONS HOTEL

2220 Sacramento Street
San Francisco, CA 94115
(415) 929-9444
Reserve: 2–6 months in advance

Two adjoining historic homes combine to form The Mansions Hotel. Each features a different ambiance but both have fine art, fanciful sculpture and eclectic furniture. There is a billiard room, cabaret with stage and theatrical lighting, courtyard sculpture gardens with gazebo and several dining rooms. Featuring treasured antiques, fine art, stained-glass walls and panoramic murals, the Mansions Hotel is a unique spot for a great celebration.

CAPACITY: The Mansions can hold up to 150 for a standing reception or 90 for seated meals.

FEES & DEPOSITS: A refundable $650 deposit is required when a tentative date is set. 50% of estimated total food and beverage cost is due 10 working days prior to the event. The fee is $650 for a 4-hour minimum rental depending on day of the week. A $200/hour fee will be applied to any time over the agreed rental period. Catering is provided and food service rates start at $25/person for hors d'oeuvres, $50/person for seated meals. Saturday night a minimum of $4500 in food, alcohol and room rental is required. Gratuity 18% and tax are additional. The remaining balance is due on the event day.

AVAILABILITY: Ceremonies and receptions are usually held between 11am and 4pm on Saturdays, noon to 10pm on Sundays. Saturday night bookings are negotiable.

SERVICES/AMENITIES:

Restaurant Services: yes
Catering: provided, no BYO
Kitchen Facilities: n/a
Tables & Chairs: provided
Linens, Silver, etc.: provided
Restrooms: no wca
Dance Floor: yes
Bride's Dressing Area: CBA

Parking: Webster/Clay garage
Overnight Accommodations: 21 guestrooms
Telephone: pay phone
Outdoor Night Lighting: yes
Outdoor Cooking Facilities: no
Cleanup: provided
Other: 2 pianos, billiard room

RESTRICTIONS:

Alcohol: provided, corkage $10/bottle
Smoking: allowed
Music: amplified until 10pm

Wheelchair Access: no
Insurance: not required

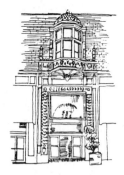

MARINES' MEMORIAL

609 Sutter Street
San Francisco, CA 94102
(415) 921-2689
Reserve: 4–6 months in advance

Marines' Memorial Club is a hidden jewel in the heart of downtown San Francisco. Although you need to find a sponsor to host an event here, almost anyone can find someone who has served in any branch of the U.S. military to act as a sponsor. Built in 1910 as a formal woman's club, it was transformed in 1946, as a memorial to marines who lost their lives in the Pacific during World War II. The non-profit Club has suites, restaurant, health club, indoor pool, library, museum and wonderful banquet rooms. Most people don't know that the Club has an exquisite, take-your-breath-away Crystal Ballroom that is available for grand receptions. Ornate chandeliers, detailed ceiling and wall paintings, raised stage plus a gleaming hardwood parquet floor all combine to form an exceptional venue for wedding receptions. The Regimental Room is also available for small receptions with vaulted, painted ceilings, marble fireplace and lots of wood detailing. The Heritage and Commandants Rooms are available for less formal weddings. And if you plan to hold your wedding here during June, July, January or February, they offer special rates. So if you're going to have a reception in the City, make sure you don't overlook this facility.

CAPACITY: 250 seated guests, maximum.

FEES & DEPOSITS: A $100–500 refundable deposit is required within 14 days of reserving a banquet room. There's no rental fee if you achieve a minimum guest count, however house catering is required. A guest count along with the estimated event total are required 7 days prior to the event—a final guest count 72 hours before. Seated luncheons and dinners run $13–24/person; hors d'oeuvres $4–10/person; buffets (min. 75 people) $17–25/person. All rates are subject to tax and 15% gratuity.

CANCELLATION POLICY: Your deposit is returned if you cancel at least 60 days prior to the event.

AVAILABILITY: Any day, from 7am–11pm. There are overtime charges for holidays.

SERVICES/AMENITIES:

Restaurant Services: yes
Catering: provided, no BYO
Kitchen Facilities: n/a
Tables & Chairs: provided
Linens, Silver, etc.: provided
Restrooms: wca
Dance Floor: yes
Other: full event coordination

Parking: nearby garage
Overnight Accommodations: 128 guestrooms
Telephone: pay and guest phones
Outdoor Night Lighting: access only
Outdoor Cooking Facilities: no
Bride's Dressing Area: CBA
Cleanup: provided

RESTRICTIONS:

Alcohol: provided, corkage $5/bottle
Smoking: designated areas
Music: amplified ok

Wheelchair Access: yes, elevator
Insurance: not required
Other: sponsor required

MARK MONROE PRODUCTIONS

449 Powell Street
San Francisco, CA 94102
(415) 928-7359
Reserve : 1–12 months in advance

Don't let the nondescript entryway on Powell Street deter you. Take the elevator to the third floor, where you'll find yourself in a completely captivating Italian villa. Rose-entwined lattices make their way up the walls; windows, balconies and lush countryside surround you. And the amazing thing is, all these wonderful details are illusions, painted by a very clever artist. Not everything is trompe l'oeil, however. The Concession Room has real trees, a softly weathered black and white tile floor and tall windows overlooking the central courtyard. Serve cocktails and hors d'oeuvres here, and have your guests flow into any of the three other spaces that circle the courtyard. The Main Ballroom, with its exceptionally high ceiling, hardwood floor and large stage is well suited for receptions with dining and dancing. The Salon Room has a smaller stage, a 20-foot coffered ceiling and original turn-of-the-century chandeliers. Brushed terra-cotta-colored walls, ochre wainscotting and tall windows that open out onto Powell Street give this room an earthy elegance, perfect for ceremonies or small receptions. The Sutter Street Room derives its romantic ambiance from coral-hued walls and flowing drapes. It's a lovely setting for an intimate rehearsal dinner. And last but not least, the courtyard itself is a great little place to relax. When the weather's fine, guests can bask in the afternoon sun or stargaze at night. Looking for a unique spot? This place veers well off the beaten path and is still conveniently located near Union Square.

CAPACITY: The facility can accommodate 30–300 guests, depending on the spaces reserved.

FEES & DEPOSITS: Rental rates start at $500. A deposit in the amount of the rental rate and a security deposit based on the space rented is required at the time of booking. The balance of the anticipated total cost is due 2 weeks prior to the event. Call for current catering rates.

CANCELLATION POLICY: The circumstances of the cancellation dictate the amount of refund.

AVAILABILITY: Year-round, everyday.

SERVICES/AMENITIES:
Restaurant Services: no
Catering: provided
Kitchen Facilities: n/a
Tables & Chairs: some provided
Linens, Silver, etc.: provided
Restrooms: wca
Dance Floor: yes
Other: event coordination

Parking: nearby inexpensive garages, on street
Overnight Accommodations: CBA
Telephone: pay phone, house phone
Outdoor Night Lighting: courtyard only
Outdoor Cooking Facilities: no
Cleanup: provided
Bride's Dressing Area: yes

RESTRICTIONS:
Alcohol: provided
Smoking: designated areas
Insurance: required

Wheelchair Access: yes
Music: amplified ok

MISS PEARL'S JAM HOUSE

601 Eddy Street
San Francisco, CA 94109
(415) 775-5267
Reserve: 2 weeks in advance

Paradise in the Tenderloin? It exists in the form of Miss Pearl's Jam House. This place vibrates with color: brilliant paintings hang everywhere, and the coral hues of a Caribbean sunset cover an entire wall. Chairs in the Main Dining Room are purple and straw; in the Sun Room they're covered with zebra stripes. The drama intensifies in the Bar, with its yellow floor, black ceiling and giant fish tank. Ceiling fans waft delectable smells throughout, and the half hull of a sailboat suspended over the Main Dining Room bar clinches the tropical feel. Right outside you can have your ceremony—next to the pool or in the sculpture garden. Terra cotta planters with palms and flowers add splashes of color around the poolside patio. People often have hors d'oeuvres and cocktails outdoors, followed by a sit-down dinner inside. By special arrangement you can even go swimming! And if you need to stay over, Miss Pearl's just happens to be located in the Phoenix Hotel, favorite hangout for touring rock stars and other celebs. Upbeat, funky, and just plain fun, Miss Pearl's is something completely different.

CAPACITY:	*Seated*	*Standing*		*Seated*	*Standing*
Restaurant & poolside	400	800	Bar	50	120
Restaurant	150	250	Poolside tented	40	75
Sun Room	40	—	Poolside open	250	550

FEES & DEPOSITS: A deposit in the amount of half of the estimated total charges is required one month in advance, and the balance is due three days prior to the event. There is no security or cleaning deposit. Food and beverage costs run $7-15/person for hors d'oeuvres, $12-20 for lunch and $15-35 for a sit-down or buffet dinner. Meals include house wine and beer. Tax and a 15% gratuity are additional.

CANCELLATION POLICY: All deposits are non-refundable.

AVAILABILITY: Year-round, daily except New Year's Day, 4th of July, Thanksgiving and Christmas.

SERVICES/AMENITIES:

Restaurant Services: yes
Catering: provided
Kitchen Facilities: n/a
Tables & Chairs: provided
Linens, Silver, etc.: provided
Restrooms: wca
Dance Floor: yes

Parking: on street, valet CBA Thurs-Sat
Overnight Accommodations: yes
Telephone: pay phone, guest phones
Outdoor Night Lighting: yes
Outdoor Cooking Facilities: no
Cleanup: provided
Bride's Dressing Area: yes

RESTRICTIONS:

Alcohol: provided, corkage $7/bottle
Smoking: allowed
Music: amplified ok

Wheelchair Access: yes
Insurance: not required

THE MIYAKO HOTEL

1625 Post Street
San Francisco, CA 94115
(415) 922-3200
Reserve for Events: 6–12 months in advance

Japantown's Miyako Hotel reflects an interesting blend of Japanese and California cultures. The Imperial Ballroom, with its Oriental art and soft beige tones, is an elegant, formal space for large wedding receptions. A custom-designed carpet adds vibrance, taking its rich blue and coral tones from antique obi sashes. More relaxed in style, the Sakura Ballroom can also host smaller receptions. Its Japanese ambiance is enhanced by a shoji panel coffered ceiling and a floor-to-ceiling view of the Summer Garden. Intimate receptions are often held in the Spring Room, a serene space with cool tones and a garden vista. For a visual treat, have your rehearsal dinner in Elka, the Hotel's unique restaurant. Painted in striking colors, it features art, sculptures and lighting fixtures created by local artisans. Whether you're planning an intimate or large wedding, The Miyako Hotel's multilingual staff and emphasis on service will make it a success.

CAPACITY:

	Seated	*Standing*
Imperial Ballroom*	250-500	300-600
Sakura Ballroom*	60-300	75-400
Spring Room	60-100	75-150

* These rooms can be sectioned

FEES & DEPOSITS: A $500 deposit is due at the time of booking. It is applied to the final payment due 72 hours prior to the event. Per person food costs not including wine are $15-23 for lunch and $25-36 for dinner. Tax and a 16% gratuity are additional.

CANCELLATION POLICY: The deposit will be refunded in full with 3 months' notice.

AVAILABILITY: Year-round, anytime.

SERVICES/AMENITIES:

Restaurant Services: yes
Catering: provided, no BYO
Kitchen Facilities: n/a
Tables & Chairs: provided
Linens, Silver, etc.: provided
Restrooms: wca
Dance Floor: yes
Other: wedding coordination, piano, stage

Parking: Valet, on street, lot
Overnight Accommodations: 218 guestrooms
Telephone: pay phones, guest phones
Outdoor Night Lighting: access only
Outdoor Cooking Facilities: no
Cleanup: provided
Bride's Dressing Area: yes

RESTRICTIONS:

Alcohol: provided, corkage $6.50+/bottle
Smoking: allowed
Music: amplified ok

Wheelchair Access: yes
Insurance: not required

NIMITZ CONFERENCE CENTER

410 Palm Ave., Bldg. 140
Treasure Island-90
San Francisco, CA 94130
(415) 395-5151
Reserve: 1–18 months in advance

The Conference Center offers a variety of reception spaces to those who have a sponsor (Military person on active duty, retired or a reservist). The largest is the Grand Ballroom, featuring a vaulted beamed ceiling, chandeliers, a hardwood dance floor and a 32-foot stage. A forest green carpet and light peach walls create a fresh ambiance. At the entrance to the Grand Ballroom, the 30-foot L-Bar runs the entire length of the Foyer, ending at a glass wall that overlooks the tennis courts. Comfortable chairs and contemporary art make this a more casual space. The Garden Ballroom has a view of surrounding lawns, and a huge skylight and floor-to-ceiling windows flood the room with light. This space is ideal for conferences or parties. The adjacent Garden Foyer is a wonderful pre-function area, often used for cocktails and hors d'oeuvres. Three skylights and a glass wall keep this room bright and airy, too. For smaller receptions or rehearsal dinners, the Treasure Room is a rustic, homey dining room. Part of the old Nimitz house, it has a vaulted ceiling, a large working fireplace and subdued evening lighting. During warm weather, the Patio Room provides a lovely spot for intimate dining. Its doors open out onto a terrace, overlooking a landscaped lawn. Whatever area you choose, the Conference Center will set it up any way you like, and insure that your event goes smoothly.

CAPACITY:

Area	Seated	Standing	Area	Seated	Standing
Grand Ballroom	389	500	Treasure Room	60	100
Garden Room	200	350	Captain's Lounge	20	40
L-Bar	60	100	Patio Room	50	100

FEES & DEPOSITS: A non-refundable deposit is required at the time of booking (25% of the total estimated cost for the Grand Ballroom and Garden Ballroom, $75 for smaller rooms). The estimated balance and a final guest count are due one week prior to the event. There is a $200 setup fee for conferences and receptions, which may be waived with meal service. Overtime hours are available after 11pm for an additional charge. Per person rates: dinners/buffets $10–30, hors d'oeuvres trays $35–200. Any menu can be customized, no tax is required, and the service charge is 15%.

CANCELLATION POLICY: Deposits and pre-payment are non-refundable.

AVAILABILITY: Year-round, everyday from 11am–4pm and 6pm–11pm.

SERVICES/AMENITIES:

Restaurant Services: no
Catering: provided
Kitchen Facilities: n/a
Tables & Chairs: provided
Linens, Silver, etc.: provided

Parking: large lot
Overnight Accommodations: no
Telephone: pay phone
Outdoor Night Lighting: yes
Outdoor Cooking Facilities: CBA

Restrooms: wca

Dance Floor: yes

RESTRICTIONS:

Alcohol: provided

Smoking: allowed

Music: amplified ok

Cleanup: provided

Bride's Dressing Area: yes

Wheelchair Access: yes

Insurance: not required

Other: votive candles only

OLD FEDERAL RESERVE BANK BUILDING

400 Sansome Street
San Francisco, CA 94111
(415) 392-1234 Catering
Reserve: 3–6 months in advance

We always get asked about mansions in San Francisco, and to tell you the truth, there are not many which can accommodate large wedding receptions indoors. Although the Old Federal Reserve Bank Building is not a mansion, it comes close to the kind of stately, elegant and understated grandeur you'd expect from a palatial estate. And it can handle quite a crowd. Originally part of the lobby of the 1924 Federal Reserve Bank, the structure has been fully restored and is included in the National Register of Historic Places. The Old Federal Reserve serves as a fine example of San Francisco's banking 'temple' tradition and the government's penchant for monumental classical architecture of that era. Inside, you'll find one of the most dramatic staircases we've ever seen. If you'd like to make a theatrical entrance, try descending the bronze and marble double stair which starts from two separate places and curves seamlessly onto the gleaming marble floor below. Everywhere you look, you'll see French and Italian marble (or a close facsimile). Expertly painted faux marbling has transformed the two rows of twenty-five foot tall Ionic columns that flank the room into "rock-solid" architectural elements. Entry doors are solid bronze. Drawing your eyes to the awe-inspiring thirty-four foot ceiling overhead are two bronze chandeliers, originals (designed by the architect) from the 1920s. All in all, if you have an extended guest list and are searching for a grand location in the City, you couldn't ask for a better spot.

CAPACITY: The Old Federal Reserve can hold 150–400 seated or 600 for a standing reception.

FEES & DEPOSITS: The rental fee is $1,800 weekdays, $2,500 on weekends. The fee may be waived depending upon the size of the event and the selection of caterer. A deposit, also based on event size, is due when the space is booked. The balance of all fees is due 14 days prior to the event.

CANCELLATION POLICY: With less than 60 days' notice, 50% of deposit is refunded; with 60–90 days' notice, 75% of deposit is returned; with more than 90 days' notice, the deposit is returned in full.

AVAILABILITY: Year-round, daily from 5pm–2am. For day use, it's by special arrangement.

SERVICES/AMENITIES:

Restaurant Services: no

Parking: adjacent garage, discounted on weekdays,

Dance Floor: CBA
Catering: select from preferred list
Restrooms: wca
Kitchen Facilities: no
Tables & Chairs: caterer
Linens, Silver, etc.: caterer
Bride's Dressing Area: CBA

RESTRICTIONS:
Alcohol: provided, corkage W $10/bottle
Music: amplified ok
Smoking: outside only

complimentary on weekends
Overnight Accommodations: 360 guestrooms at
Park Hyatt San Francisco including 37 suites
Telephone: pay phones
Outdoor Night Lighting: access only
Outdoor Cooking Facilities: no
Cleanup: provided

Wheelchair Access: yes
Insurance: not required

THE PACIFIC SPIRIT
Pacific Marine Yacht Charters

Berthed at Pier 39, East Basin
San Francisco, CA 94133
(415) 788-9100
Reserve: 1–9 months in advance

The Pacific Spirit is an 83-foot classic Broward Yacht with two enclosed decks and a full open flybridge. It features a comfortably appointed main salon with wet bar and an adjoining aft salon with a teak wood dance floor. Below deck are three intimate lounge salons, one appropriate for a bride's dressing room. Professional service and award-winning cuisine will make your wedding celebration an exceptional experience.

CAPACITY: The Pacific Spirit can accommodate up to 90 guests, weather permitting. Formal seating is available for up to 35 guests.

FEES & DEPOSITS: A $1,000 deposit is required to reserve your date and half the food and beverage cost is due 30 days prior to your event.

	Weekdays (before 6pm)	*Weekdays (after 6pm)*	*Weekends/Holidays*
Yacht rental rates	$350/hr	$375/hr	$450/hr
Groups of 20 guests or less	325/hr	350/hr	375/hr

A 3-hour minimum rental is required, 4 hours on Saturday evenings and holidays. A guaranteed guest count is required 7 days prior to departure and the remaining balance is due 5 days prior to your event.

Special packages, starting at $24/guest, include your wedding ceremony performed by the captain, gourmet menu, champagne toast, customized wedding cake and a wedding coordinator's time. Yacht rental, beverage service, tax and gratuity are additional.

CANCELLATION POLICY: With 60 days' notice, 85% of the reservation deposit will be refunded; with less notice, the deposit will be forfeited.

AVAILABILITY: Any time, no limits.

SERVICES/AMENITIES:

Restaurant Services: no
Catering: provided, no BYO
Kitchen Facilities: n/a
Tables & Chairs: provided
Linens, Silver, etc.: provided
Restrooms: 3, no wca
Dance Floor: yes
Bride's Dressing Area: yes

Parking: Pier 39 garage, validations available
Overnight Accommodations: no
Telephone: emergency cellular and radio
Outdoor Night Lighting: yes
Outdoor Cooking Facilities: no
Cleanup: provided
Other: complimentary wedding coordination

RESTRICTIONS:

Alcohol: provided, corkage $7/bottle
Smoking: aft enclosed salon
Music: amplified ok

Wheelchair Access: no
Insurance: not required

THE PALACE OF FINE ARTS

Lyon at Marina Boulevard
San Francisco, CA
(415) 666-7035 Recreation & Parks
Reserve: 1–12 months in advance

Designed by architect Bernard Maybeck for the Panama-Pacific Exposition of 1915, the Palace of Fine Arts is a magnificent San Francisco landmark and one of the most glorious spots you can imagine for an outdoor ceremony. Located in the Marina District, the picturesque shaded lagoon, ducks and swans, landscaped island and spraying fountain offer an exceptional setting for a reception. Seated functions are possible under the grand and impressive classic Roman rotunda. Your guests can roam anywhere around the lagoon's perimeter; the entire setting is idyllic and highly romantic. Although this is a public park space, you are allowed to rope off an area for your celebration or hire security personnel. Given the low fees for use of this spectacular park, we'd say this is a real find.

CAPACITY: The rotunda and park can accommodate 300–500 guests.

FEES & DEPOSITS: A 10% non-refundable deposit of the total fee is due 5 working days from the time you make your reservation. The rental fee for 2 hours is $225, and for each hour over that, the fee is $35/ hour. Any remaining fees are required 30 days prior to your event.

AVAILABILITY: Daily, from 9am to dusk.

SERVICES/AMENITIES:

Restaurant Services: no
Catering: BYO
Kitchen Facilities: no
Tables & Chairs: BYO
Overnight Accommodations: no

Linens, Silver, etc.: BYO
Restrooms: adjacent to Exploratorium
Dance Floor: no
Parking: on street
Outdoor Cooking Facilities: no

Telephone: pay phone
Outdoor Night Lighting: access only

RESTRICTIONS:
Alcohol: BYO
Smoking: allowed
Music: no amplified

Cleanup: caterer
Bride's Dressing Area: no

Wheelchair Access: yes
Insurance: sometimes required

PALIO D'ASTI

640 Sacramento Street
San Francisco, CA 94111
(415) 395-9800
Reserve: 2 weeks–12 months in advance

Named after a medieval bare-back horse race that's held annually in the Northern Italian city of Asti, Palio d'Asti is a contemporary restaurant with old-world roots. Built in 1990, it was chosen "best dressed" by Restaurant Design Magazine the following year. Their choice was well justified—this sleek Milano styled trattoria is a visual delight. Steam rises from the open kitchen where chefs prepare dozens of delicacies. You can witness the speed-production of fresh pasta, savor a pizza cooked to perfection in their wood-burning oven, or sample antipasti from a specially designed cart brought to your table. Everything here is made on the premises, using the best imported products as well as fresh items from local farms and ranches. Weathered concrete columns, unique lighting fixtures and festive banners create a colorful interior. Have your prenuptial dinner or family get-together in the completely private San Pietro Room or semi-private San Secondo Room, and give your eyes, nose and tastebuds a treat.

CAPACITY:

	Seated	Standing
San Pietro Room	50	75
San Secondo Room	50	75
Entire Restaurant	250	300

FEES & DEPOSITS: A non-refundable $200 deposit is required when booking a private dining room. If you reserve the entire restaurant, there is a $6,000 minimum, with 50% of the anticipated total required when reservations are confirmed. A guaranteed guest count is required 48 hours prior to the event. The balance is due 15 days after receipt of invoice. Luncheons start at $22.50/person, dinners at $35. Tax and a 20% gratuity are additional.

CANCELLATION POLICY: The deposit is not refundable.

AVAILABILITY: Monday–Saturday, flexible hours. Special events may be arranged on Sundays.

SERVICES/AMENITIES:
Restaurant Services: yes
Catering: provided, no BYO
Kitchen Facilities: n/a

Parking: valet ($4/car), inexpensive garages
Overnight Accommodations: CBA
Telephone: pay phone

Tables & Chairs: provided
Linens, Silver, etc.: provided
Restrooms: wca
Dance Floor: CBA

RESTRICTIONS:
Alcohol: provided, corkage $10/bottle
Smoking: designated areas
Music: amplified ok if reserve entire restaurant

Outdoor Night Lighting: access only
Outdoor Cooking Facilities: no
Cleanup: provided
Bride's Dressing Area: no

Wheelchair Access: yes
Insurance: not required

PAN PACIFIC HOTEL

500 Post St.
San Francisco, CA 94102
(415) 771-8600
Reserve: 9–18 months in advance

Elegant. Sophisticated. Tasteful. The Pan Pacific is all of these and then some. World-renowned architect, John Portman, has successfully blended Asian and American elements, warm colors and graceful design themes in this 21-story architectural gem. Eye-pleasing arches abound, from the exterior windows to interior entranceways. A Portuguese rose marble is used for flooring and columns throughout, and Oriental antiques and art lend a timelessness to an otherwise contemporary structure. The Executive Center, with its own dining area and staff, offers the seclusion of a private club for candlelit rehearsal dinners. The second floor is the Olympic Ballroom level, with a spacious foyer and four auxiliary rooms. Depending on the size of your reception, you can use these spaces in any combination, as the rooms flow conveniently into one another. The foyer is lovely with its marble floor and brilliant cut glass columns. The Ballroom features four enormous brass and crystal chandeliers, and a rear wall of beveled glass panels that let in natural light and add sparkle to the room. All of the rooms have the Hotel's custom teal, rose and mauve heather carpet, rose banquet chairs, and blush-colored walls. Upstairs on the third floor is the main lobby, including The Bar and conversation areas anchored by two imposing rectangular fireplaces. The focal point of the room is a bronze sculpture entitled "Joie de Danse," four fluid, larger-than-life dancers circling round a marble fountain. This area can be used for cocktails and hors d'oeuvres. Take the elevator to the 21st-floor Terrace Room where smaller receptions are often held. Wrap-around windows offer spectacular views—especially at sunset, when the light glowing off thousands of high-rise windows can take your breath away. A coffered ceiling, rosewood bar, and arched fireplaces create a comfortable ambiance. From the Terrace Room, guests can stroll into the Solarium, an open-air brick patio that also provides a delightful spot for ceremonies. The Penthouse, which is only a few steps away, can extend your reception space, host an intimate reception by itself, or simply offer one of the most luxurious overnight stays in San Francisco. More like a gracious home than a hotel suite, it features two bedrooms, custom designed furniture, a baby grand piano and a terrific view. And unlike most hotels, the Pan Pacific has a staff to guest ratio of 1 to 1, making service its top priority. What more could you ask for?

CAPACITY:	*Seated*	*Standing*		*Seated*	*Standing*
Olympic Ballroom	75–360	100–500	Executive Center	30–90	35–150
(can be sectioned)			The Terrace	52-120	175
Prefunction Foyer	180	300	Terrace Solarium	30-50	50
The Bar	100	50–300	Penthouse	10	80

FEES & DEPOSITS: A non-refundable $750–1,000 deposit is required 30 days after booking to secure your date, and the balance is due on the day of the event. A ceremony fee is additional. There is no rental fee for over 50 guests. Per person food costs range from $30–80 for lunch and $40–120 for dinner. Beverage, tax and an 18% gratuity are extra.

CANCELLATION POLICY: With less than 90 days notice, a cancellation fee in the amount of 50% of the anticipated revenue will be charged.

AVAILABILITY: Year-round except Christmas and New Year's Day.

SERVICES/AMENITIES:

Restaurant Services: yes
Catering: provided, no BYO
Kitchen Facilities: n/a
Tables & Chairs: provided
Linens, Silver, etc.: provided
Restrooms: wca
Dance Floor: yes
Other: wedding coordination

Parking: valet and nearby lots
Overnight Accommodations: 330 guestrooms
Telephone: pay phones, guest phones, house phones
Outdoor Night Lighting: Terrace Solarium only
Outdoor Cooking Facilities: no
Cleanup: provided

RESTRICTIONS:

Alcohol: provided, corkage $7–10/bottle
Smoking: allowed
Insurance: not required

Wheelchair Access: yes
Music: amplified ok
Other: live music in the Terrace Room ends at 11pm

PARK HYATT
SAN FRANCISCO

333 Battery Street
San Francisco, CA 94111
(415) 392-1234 Catering
Reserve: 3–6 months in advance

The Park Hyatt is a different kind of hotel. Understated and upscale, the Hotel provides an environment conducive to elegant affairs. It not only has a tasteful interior, but the Park Hyatt's professional staff is one of the best we've encountered. From the doorman to the catering manager, each hotel employee offers the kind of friendly, impeccable service that is rare in today's world. No matter what type of function you have here, you'll be able to relax and enjoy it knowing that this hostelry bends over backwards to provide a worry-free experience. Receptions or prenuptial dinners are held in the Park Grill or on Level Two. For brides who'd like to make a dramatic entry, you can arrive at either level via a spiral staircase. Level Two has an exclusive club-like atmosphere. Its decor is subdued and sumptuous: warm and elegant throughout, rich polished wood, translucent onyx fixtures, detailed ceiling and black baby grand piano are additional accoutrements. The Park Grill, a popular restaurant with a strong culinary as well as visual appeal, can host receptions or rehearsal meals. This is a top notch eatery, with lounge alcoves and a beautiful bar. For outdoor entertaining, the adjacent patio can be dressed up with black tables, white linens and large umbrellas. A sophisticated place with flawless style and service, the Park Hyatt actually delivers what most other places just talk about.

CAPACITY: Level 2 can accommodate 8–200 guests; the Park Grill holds up to 150 guests.

FEES & DEPOSITS: A deposit of 10% of the total estimated food and beverage bill is due at the time of booking. The balance is due 2 weeks prior to the event.

CANCELLATION POLICY: With 30 days' notice, your deposit will be refunded.

AVAILABILITY: Year-round, daily from 6am–2am.

SERVICES/AMENITIES:

Restaurant Services: yes
Dance Floor: yes
Restrooms: wca
Catering: provided
Kitchen Facilities: n/a
Tables & Chairs: provided
Linens, Silver, etc.: provided
Bride's Dressing Area: yes

Parking: adjacent garage, discounted weekdays, complimentary on weekends
Overnight Accommodations: 360 guestrooms, including 37 suites
Cleanup: provided
Telephone: pay phones
Outdoor Night Lighting: access only
Outdoor Cooking Facilities: no

RESTRICTIONS:

Alcohol: provided, corkage $10/bottle
Smoking: allowed
Music: amplified ok

Wheelchair Access: yes
Insurance: not required

PORTICO

246 McAllister Street
San Francisco, CA 94102
(415) 861-2939
Reserve: 2 weeks in advance

It's hard to believe that this hideaway restaurant was a carriage house complete with horse and buggy until 1990. A subterranean cafe in its current incarnation, Portico provides a cozy, Mediterranean ambiance for small wedding receptions. When you step down into the restaurant, your eye is immediately drawn to the lush garden window at the end of the room. Artfully lit at night, it's a dramatic focal point. Fields of tall grasses are painted on the walls, giving the impression of surrounding countryside. Dried manzanita branches poised over tables enhance the sensation of being outdoors. And the tables themselves are works of art: each one is a hand-painted abstract fresco in rich earth tones. Upstairs, the foyer and bar serve as a great staging area for cocktails and hors d'oeuvres. Tall arched windows, sunkissed walls and the hint of a balcony take you to...southern Italy, perhaps? Copper-topped tables and unique upholstered adirondacks make for some unusual seating. And those wonderful painted tables in the bar appear to glow at night, thanks to special track lighting. This blending of antique and contemporary elements works well, making the Portico Restaurant a charming and relaxed spot for prenuptial dinners or receptions.

CAPACITY: The restaurant can seat 100 guests or 150 for a standing reception; the bar 30 seated, 50 standing.

FEES & DEPOSITS: A deposit in the amount of half of the estimated total charges is required one month in advance, and the balance is due three days prior to the event. There is no security or cleaning deposit. Food and beverage costs run $7–15 for hors d'oeuvres, $12–20 for lunch and $15–35 for a sit-down or buffet dinner. Meals include house wine and beer. Tax and a 15% gratuity are additional.

CANCELLATION POLICY: All deposits are non-refundable.

AVAILABILITY: Year-round, everyday except New Year's Day, July 4th, Thanksgiving and Christmas.

SERVICES/AMENITIES:

Restaurant Services: yes
Catering: provided
Kitchen Facilities: n/a
Tables & Chairs: provided
Linens, Silver, etc.: provided
Restrooms: not wca
Dance Floor: yes

Parking: on street, valet CBA
Overnight Accommodations: yes
Telephone: pay phones, guest phones
Outdoor Night Lighting: access only
Outdoor Cooking Facilities: no
Cleanup: provided
Bride's Dressing Area: yes

RESTRICTIONS:

Alcohol: WCB
Smoking: allowed
Music: acoustic only

Wheelchair Access: bar only
Insurance: not required

THE QUEEN ANNE

1590 Sutter Street
San Francisco, CA
(415) 441-2828
Reserve: 4–6 months in advance

Built in 1890 by a Comstock silver king, this landmark building is now a popular, 49-room bed and breakfast hotel. The Queen Anne still has old world charm. It is handsomely furnished with English antiques that set off the oak paneling and inlaid floors. A grand staircase enables the bride to make a picture-perfect entry into the Parlor for the ceremony, after which, the bridal party retires to the Salon for the reception. The small patio located off the garden can also accommodate seated guests.

CAPACITY: The Hotel can serve 85 guests for a seated meal and up to 125 for a standing reception.

FEES & DEPOSITS: A $375 non-refundable security deposit is payable when you reserve your date. It will be applied towards the total charge. The rental fee for a reception is $950 which includes 5 hours of valet parking. If you or your party stay overnight, special rates apply. There is also a group rate available if multiple overnight accommodations are requested, minimum 10 rooms. Food service is provided, your choice of two preferred caterers.

AVAILABILITY: Any day, any time up to 11pm.

SERVICES/AMENITIES:

Restaurant Services: no
Catering: in-house caterer provided
Kitchen Facilities: n/a
Tables & Chairs: provided
Linens, Silver, etc.: caterer
Restrooms: wca
Dance Floor: CBA, extra charge

Parking: valet recommended
Overnight Accommodations: 49 guestrooms
Telephone: pay phone
Outdoor Night Lighting: yes
Outdoor Cooking Facilities: no
Bride's Dressing Area: CBA
Cleanup: caterer

RESTRICTIONS:

Alcohol: BYO, corkage $3-4/bottle
Smoking: allowed
Music: amplified until 10pm

Wheelchair Access: yes
Insurance: not required

ROCK & BOWL

1855 Haight Street
San Francisco, CA 94117
(415) 826-BOWL
Reserve: 3–12 months in advance

This is one of those places you just have to experience. By day, it's a mild-mannered bowling alley. By night (Friday and Saturday, that is) it becomes the infamous, raucous and outrageous Rock & Bowl. TV monitors over each lane run nonstop rock videos long into the night. Music blasts from overhead speakers, making every cell in your body vibrate with heretofore unknown energy. And—people actually bowl! Wedding celebrations here are nothing if not unique. Reserve a bunch of lanes, bring in some swell food and knock down those pins! Dancing is ok, talking loud is ok (and often required), and looking cool is de rigeur. Just be careful where you toss that bouquet—you might knock down somebody else's pins.

CAPACITY: This facility can hold 300 guests (4 is the minimum for a group reservation). With over 60 guests, you can reserve the entire facility.

FEES & DEPOSITS: The deposit for 3 or more lanes is $2/person. To reserve the entire facility, the deposit is 33% of the $1000–2500 rental fee, which varies with the day, time and league bowling schedules. Deposits are refundable and due when the reservation is confirmed. Fees include bowling lanes, shoes, balls and use of pool tables.

CANCELLATION POLICY: If lanes can be rebooked, the deposit is refunded.

AVAILABILITY: Year-round, everyday from 10am–2am except Christmas day.

SERVICES/AMENITIES:

Restaurant Services: snack bar
Catering: BYO
Kitchen Facilities: CBA
Tables & Chairs: some provided
Linens, Silver, etc.: BYO
Restrooms: no wca
Dance Floor: bowling areas

Parking: street, Kezar Stadium lot
Overnight Accommodations: no
Telephone: pay phones
Outdoor Night Lighting: access only
Outdoor Cooking Facilities: BYO
Cleanup: renter or provided, extra charge
Bride's Dressing Area: CBA

RESTRICTIONS:

Alcohol: provided, no BYO
Smoking: allowed
Music: amplified ok

Wheelchair Access: yes
Insurance: not required

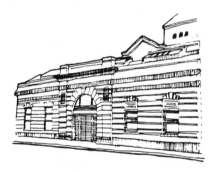

ROCOCO SHOWPLACE

165 Tenth Street
San Francisco, CA 94103
(415) 552-5600 Kate
Reserve: 1–6 months in advance

Rococo's ranks high on our list. Its ample space, uptempo decor and tremendous flexibility make it a perfect place for celebrating. Rococo is housed in an historic, south-of-Market building which was rebuilt after the 1906 earthquake. The entry is an attractive mix of old brick wall and modern glass and the interior looks much like an art gallery, with lofty ceilings and skylights. Original brick archways blend with modern plasterwork to form two comfortable rooms where small groups can gather for intimate chats. The main event room, Rococo Showplace, is a fantastic party space—one of the best we've seen. The interior walls are brick. Natural, ambient light filters in through a large skylight running the entire length of the unfinished wood ceiling. Paved in white marble with black detail along the border, the floor is a visual treat. In Rococo Showplace, you'll find faux colonnades, a massive white marble bar and an enormous old iron door above which hangs a terrific modern frieze of Trojan soldiers on horseback. Behind one balcony is a room with a pool table where guests can sharpen their cues or watch the activities below. The decor changes frequently—depending on which paintings are featured, the kind of events held and the whims of the owners. We think Rococo is a superb, one-of-a-kind event space. If you've got a sizeable party, don't worry. It can accommodate large groups with lots of panache.

CAPACITY: 350 for a standing reception; 140 seated guests.

FEES & DEPOSITS: Rococo's entire space rents for $1,500 for day use, and $2,600 for evening use. For evening use, a $700 non-refundable deposit is due when reservations are booked (this is the maximum deposit required).

AVAILABILITY: Year-round, seven days a week, including holidays.

SERVICES/AMENITIES:

Restaurant Services: no
Catering: preferred list, flexible
Kitchen Facilities: limited
Tables & Chairs: provided
Linens, Silver, etc.: BYO
Restrooms: wca
Bride's Dressing Area: CBA
Dance Floor: yes

Parking: street, nearby lot
Overnight Accommodations: no
Telephone: pay phone
Outdoor Night Lighting: access only
Outdoor Cooking Facilities: no
Cleanup: provided
Other: event planning

RESTRICTIONS:

Alcohol: BYO
Smoking: designated areas
Music: amplified within reason

Wheelchair Access: yes
Insurance: extra liability required

THE ROTUNDA
At Neiman Marcus

150 Stockton Street
San Francisco, CA 94108
(415) 362-4777
Reserve: 2–48 weeks in advance

The Rotunda at Neiman Marcus is famous for good reason. Located on the top floor, it has seating in the round beneath an extraordinary stained glass dome. The skylight is really a painting in glass—a sea theme with Neptune presiding. Constructed of 2,600 pieces of clear, rust and variegated green glass, the "ceiling" bathes diners in a warm glow. Every table here has a view of Union Square through a curved wall of glass descending four stories down to street level. Decorated in muted colors, much of the seating is arranged in tiered, private banquettes. Also well known for its San Francisco 'taste tour,' the restaurant creates numerous buffet tables decorated in themes of famous San Francisco spots such as Chinatown, Fisherman's Wharf, the Mission, North Beach and Japantown. Each table, of course, serves a theme-related food. Equally popular are NM's formal seated dinners which set the tone for a more upscale, elegant reception.

CAPACITY: The entire Rotunda can hold 350 for a reception or 200 seated guests.

FEES & DEPOSITS: A refundable deposit of 50% of the total estimated food and beverage cost is due when the contract is submitted. There is no rental fee with food service. The balance is due the day of the event. Per person rates: hors d'oeuvres $2–5, dinners start at $40, buffets at $18. Tax and 18% gratuity are additional. For you Neiman Marcus cardholders, note that you can make payment using your NM card to gain *Incircle* points.

CANCELLATION POLICY: With 2 weeks' notice, the deposit is refunded.

AVAILABILITY: Year-round, everyday from 6pm–midnight.

SERVICES/AMENITIES:

Restaurant Services: yes

Catering: provided, no BYO

Kitchen Facilities: n/a

Tables & Chairs: provided

Linens, Silver, etc.: provided

Restrooms: wca

Dance Floor: yes

Parking: Union Square garage

Overnight Accommodations: no

Telephone: pay phone

Outdoor Night Lighting: access only

Outdoor Cooking Facilities: no

Cleanup: provided

Bride's Dressing Area: yes

RESTRICTIONS:

Alcohol: provided, corkage $6/bottle

Smoking: allowed

Music: amplified ok

Wheelchair Access: yes

Insurance: not required

SAILING SHIP DOLF REMPP

Pier 42-44 on the Embarcadero,
South of Market St.
San Francisco, CA 94107
(415) 777-5771 or **(415) 543-4024** Camille Barnes
Reserve: 1–8 weeks in advance

This impressive, 100-year-old 3-masted schooner combines all the advantages of being 'out to sea' without any of the disadvantages. Because the vessel rests in an earthquake-proof concrete cradle at the southwest end of San Francisco's waterfront, guests will not miss the boat if late, can leave at will, and can enjoy the salt air, the sights and sounds of being on the water while remaining motionless. The Sailing Ship Dolph Rempp was built in 1884 as a trading vessel in the Baltic Sea, and has had an illustrious career. Jules Verne was aboard for exploratory journeys and used the schooner as inspiration for his novels. It was also a rum-runner, pleasure craft and a World War I supply carrier (used for espionage!). You and your guests will feel like stars in your own movie production when you board the Sailing Ship since it was, in fact, featured in more than 100 Hollywood films. It now combines its rich history with elegant dining and fabulous views of the City, Bay Bridge and the colorful South Beach Harbor Marina.

CAPACITY: 800 people can be accommodated for a stand-up reception, up to 165 for a sit-down meal on one level and 400 for a buffet dinner or luncheon on combined levels. Outdoor tents on the front deck and canopies on the back deck can be erected for an additional 200 or more guests.

FEES & DEPOSITS: A negotiable fee is due 1 month before your event to secure the date and cover the security deposit. A rental fee/person is required, based on the guest count. Food service is provided. Cocktail hors d'oeuvres run $5–14.50/person, luncheons or dinners are $20–50/person. Sales tax and 18% gratuity are applied to the final bill.

CANCELLATION POLICY: Normally, 3 months' notice is allowed unless you have booked during the holiday season, in which case, 4 months' notice is required.

AVAILABILITY: 7 days a week, including major holidays.

SERVICES/AMENITIES:

Restaurant Services: yes
Catering: provided, if BYO, extra charge
Kitchen Facilities: fully equipped
Tables & Chairs: provided
Linens, Silver, etc.: provided
Restrooms: no wca
Dance Floor: yes

Parking: on street
Overnight Accommodations: no
Telephone: pay phone
Outdoor Night Lighting: yes
Outdoor Cooking Facilities: BBQ CBA
Cleanup: provided
Bride's Dressing Area: yes

RESTRICTIONS:

Alcohol: provided
Smoking: allowed
Music: amplified ok

Wheelchair Access: yes
Insurance: not required

SAN FRANCISCO MARITIME MUSEUM

San Francisco Maritime National Historic Park
900 Beach Street at the foot of Polk
(415) 929-0202 Daria Booth
Reserve: 1–2 months in advance

Across from Ghirardelli Square, in the heart of Aquatic Park, stands the Maritime Museum. It houses hundreds of artifacts, photographs and documents of West Coast seafaring history. The building was cleverly designed to resemble a cruise ship, even down to the nautical looking air vents. The Museum is superb for an event because it is a marvel of Art Deco style, terrazzo floors, murals and chrome detailing. Loaded with marine artifacts and historic memorabilia, the main exhibit room is terrific. Adjacent to it is the Museum's open-air veranda featuring artifacts from old ships, a nineteen-foot sloop *The Mermaid*, Benny Buffano sculptures and 1930s Art Deco tile murals along the wall facing the Bay. From here the views towards the harbor and Alcatraz are unobstructed, and the water so close you can hear the waves lapping against the sand. Do yourself a favor and ask for a tour. This is a real find.

CAPACITY: For a standing reception, the building can hold 400 guests. For a seated function, 120 guests. For larger parties, you can rent the Bayview room in conjunction with the Museum.

FEES & DEPOSITS: A $1,500 security deposit is required. The deposit is usually returned 2 weeks after the event. A minimum of $900 is needed to rent the Museum. The total fee is based on the length of your event and the number of guests. Work out the fee details with the National Maritime Museum Association. The fee includes a National Park Ranger on duty during your event.

CANCELLATION POLICY: Deposits are refundable 21 days prior to your event.

AVAILABILITY: Year-round, 5pm–midnight.

SERVICES/AMENITIES:

Restaurant Services: no

Catering: BYO

Kitchen Facilities: minimal

Tables & Chairs: BYO

Linens, Silver, etc.: BYO

Restrooms: wca

Dance Floor: no

Parking: on street, nearby garage

Overnight Accommodations: no

Telephone: pay phone

Outdoor Night Lighting: access only

Outdoor Cooking Facilities: no

Cleanup: caterer or renter

Bride's Dressing Area: CBA

RESTRICTIONS:

Alcohol: BYO

Smoking: outside only

Music: amplified until 11pm

Wheelchair Access: yes

Insurance: required

SAN FRANCISCO MART
Grand Lobby and Mart Exchange

1355 Market Street
San Francisco, CA 94103
(415) 381-2311
Reserve: 1–12 months in advance

A walk into the restored San Francisco Mart Grand Lobby is a walk into an Art Deco wonderland. Dramatic and glamorous, the central rotunda sparkles with unexpected colors, textures and lighting. Nine structural columns clad in polished stainless steel overlaid with an intricate brass pattern support a ceiling ringed by concentric circles of incandescent and neon lights. A trip up the escalator to the mezzanine gives you an overview of the space below and a fuller appreciation of the terrazzo floors, laid out in a complex star pattern. Two large rectangular areas on either side of the rotunda can accommodate a reception with plenty of room for dancing. One of these areas ordinarily serves as an exhibition space, but it may be incorporated into your celebration. Up on the ninth floor, the Mart Exchange is a more intimate ballroom setting. Soft pastel hues create a warm ambiance while Art Deco chandeliers and wall sconces add distinction. Controlled lighting allows you to define the mood. A sleek, fully-appointed bar, professional kitchen and a baby grand piano are just a few of the amenities the Mart offers. Whether you have your reception in the unforgettable lobby or the elegant Mart Exchange, The San Francisco Mart will leave an indelible impression.

CAPACITY: Grand Lobby 500 seated, 800 standing. The Mart Exchange, 275 seated, up to 500 standing.

FEES & DEPOSITS: The Mart Exchange rents for $1,200. The Grand Lobby rental fee is based on the number of guests: $2,000 for up to 500, and $500 more for each additional 100 guests. The maximum fee is $3,500 for 800 guests. A refundable deposit of 50% of the rental fee is due when reservations are confirmed. A refundable $1,000 security and cleaning deposit, certificate of insurance plus the balance of the rental fees are required 10 days prior to the function. Extra security is occasionally required.

CANCELLATION POLICY: With 90 days' notice, full refund; with 60 days', a 50% refund. For December dates, no deposits are refunded. The security and cleaning deposit is usually refunded.

AVAILABILITY: Year-round, daily. Some weekday, daytime restrictions may apply to the Grand Lobby.

SERVICES/AMENITIES:

Restaurant Services: no
Catering: preferred list or BYO
Kitchen Facilities: prep only
Tables & Chairs: caterer or BYO
Linens, Silver, etc.: caterer or BYO
Restrooms: wca
Dance Floor: terrazzo floor
Bride's Dressing Area: CBA

Parking: on-site, secured garage extra charge, behind building, free
Overnight Accommodations: no
Telephone: pay phones
Outdoor Night Lighting: no
Outdoor Cooking Facilities: no
Cleanup: caterer and Mart

RESTRICTIONS:

Alcohol: provided or BYO
Smoking: allowed
Music: amplified ok

Wheelchair Access: yes
Insurance: certificate required
Other: no open flames

THE SAN FRANCISCO SPIRIT
Pacific Marine Yacht Charters

Berthed at Pier 39, East Basin
San Francisco, CA 94133
(415) 788-9100
Reserve: 1–9 months in advance

In June 1991, Pacific Marine Yacht Charters christened their luxurious, 150-foot custom-built flagship, the San Francisco Spirit, making it the fourth member of its elegant fleet. Warm neutral tones, plush furnishings and tasteful appointments in glass, brass, marble and stone provide a sophisticated backdrop for a dream wedding. Two spacious dance floors, three bars, central sound system, grand staircase and attractive interior are just some of the amenities this yacht has to offer. Add Pacific Marine's impeccable service and award-winning cuisine, and you have an exceptional choice for entertaining on the bay.

CAPACITY: The San Francisco Spirit can accommodate up to 700 guests for receptions. Formal seating is available for 300 in the Main Salon, 180 in the Upper Salon and 30 in the VIP Lounge.

FEES & DEPOSITS: For the entire vessel, a $4,000 deposit is required when you reserve your date; for half the vessel, $3,000. Half of the food and beverage cost is due 30 days prior to your event.

	Weekdays (before 6pm)	*Weekdays (after 6pm)*	*Weekends/Holidays*
Full boat rental fees are:	$1,800/hr	$2,200/hr	$2,700/hr
Half boat rental fees are:	1,000/hr	1,200/hr	1,500/hr

A 3-hour minimum rental is required, 4 hours on Saturday evenings and holidays. A guaranteed guest count is required 7 days prior to departure and the remaining balance is due 5 days prior to your event.

Special packages, starting at $24/guest, include your wedding ceremony performed by the Captain, gourmet menu, champagne toast, customized wedding cake and a wedding coordinator. Yacht rental, beverage service, tax and gratuity are additional.

CANCELLATION POLICY: With 90 days' notice, 85% of the reservation deposit will be refunded; with less notice, the deposit will be forfeited.

AVAILABILITY: Any time, no limits.

SERVICES/AMENITIES:

Restaurant Services: no
Catering: provided, no BYO
Kitchen Facilities: on board
Tables & Chairs: provided
Linens, Silver, etc.: provided
Restrooms: 1 wca
Dance Floor: yes
Bride's Dressing Area: yes

Parking: Pier 39 garage, validations available
Overnight Accommodations: no
Telephone: emergency cellular phone & radio
Outdoor Night Lighting: yes
Outdoor Cooking Facilities: no
Cleanup: provided
Other: complimentary wedding coordination, podium & microphone

RESTRICTIONS:

Alcohol: provided, corkage fee $7/bottle
Smoking: outside only
Music: amplified ok

Wheelchair Access: yes
Insurance: not required

SHARON ARTS CENTER AND CARROUSEL

Golden Gate Park
San Francisco, CA 94117
(415) 666-7035
Reserve: 3–12 months in advance

The Sharon Arts Center is a stately, historic stone building that's located not too far from the bocci ball lanes. It was originally used as a "mother's" building for families visiting Golden Gate Park. Adjacent to the Carrousel, it has recently been renovated and features a large room with cathedral ceiling, chandeliers, wood paneling and French doors that open onto a balcony overlooking the park and children's play area.

The Herschel Spillman Carrousel, circa 1912–1914, was painstakingly restored from 1977–1984. Originally carved in upstate New York, it was housed in several parks on the West Coast before coming here where it continues to be one of Golden Gate Park's extraordinary highlights. It was also the main carrousel of the 1939 Exposition World's Fair on Treasure Island. A Gebruder band organ made in Germany in the 1920s provides lively musical accompaniment. Do something really different! Stop the spinning and take your vows aboard the Carrousel or rent it as wonderful entertainment for your guests—young and old alike. Tents can be set up in front of the Carrousel for large outdoor receptions. The Carrousel is available only in the evenings after 5pm, when it's not open to the public.

CAPACITY: The Sharon Center can hold 80 seated or 100 standing. The Carrousel can accommodate 70 seated on the fanciful animals!

FEES & DEPOSITS: 10% of all fees are required as a deposit to secure your date. 30 days prior to your event, the balance of the refundable security/cleaning deposit is required: Sharon Center $150; Carrousel $750. The deposit is normally returned after the event if the premises are clean and undamaged. The base rental fee for the Sharon Arts Center is 5 hours for $250. Each additional hour is $50. The Carrousel is $200-500 for 4 hours, with rates depending on staff availability. A private security guard is required for Carrousel use, usually $20/hour.

CANCELLATION POLICY: If you cancel 30 days prior to your event, you will receive 90% of your deposit; if you cancel less than 10 working days in advance, no refund.

AVAILABILITY: The Sharon Center: Saturdays 6pm–11pm; Sundays 10am–4pm and 5pm–11pm. The Carrousel: any day after 5pm.

SERVICES/AMENITIES:

Restaurant Services: no

Catering: BYO

Kitchen Facilities: ample

Tables & Chairs: provided

Linens, Silver, etc.: BYO

Restrooms: wca in Sharon Center

Dance Floor: yes

Parking: park lots

Overnight Accommodations: no

Telephone: pay phone

Outdoor Night Lighting: access only

Outdoor Cooking Facilities: no

Cleanup: caterer or renter

Bride's Dressing Area: CBA

RESTRICTIONS:

Alcohol: BYO

Smoking: no

Insurance: sometimes required

Wheelchair Access: yes

Music: amplified inside only, requires permit outside

Prices and policies <u>do</u> change. Call each facility and confirm everything you read in Here Comes The Guide.

SHERATON PALACE HOTEL

2 New Montgomery Street
San Francisco, CA 94105
(415) 392-8600
Reserve: 6–9 months in advance

There is nothing quite like the Sheraton Palace. Following a stunning multi-million dollar renovation, it has reclaimed its role as San Francisco's premier historic hotel. If you've dreamed of an elegant wedding in a royal setting, the Palace is the perfect location. You can host a bridal tea in the world renowned Garden Court, one of the most exquisite rooms we've ever seen. The magnificent domed ceiling of pale yellow leaded glass floods the restaurant with warm natural light, and the original crystal chandeliers add old-world sparkle. Wedding ceremonies are often held in the Ralston Room, which served as The Men's Grille at the turn of the century. Reminiscent of a Gothic cathedral, this room soothes with its cream, gold and jewel tones. For large wedding receptions, the Grand Ballroom lives up to its name. English classical in style, its charm comes from unique lace plasterwork, and shimmering chandeliers decorated with carved crystal pears and apples. The Gold Ballroom is the most popular reception site. Once the Hotel's music room, it has the feel of a ballroom in a manor house. Tall draped windows highlight the intricate lattice plasterwork and gold leaf detailing throughout. An antique orchestra balcony, grand fireplace, and rich blue and gold carpet complete the lovely decor. For smaller ceremonies or receptions, the French Parlor features stained glass skylights, crystal chandeliers, marble fireplaces and a birds-eye view of the Garden Court ceiling that is guaranteed to take your breath away. And for a more contemporary space, the Sunset Court accommodates intimate gatherings and ceremonies beneath an arched glass dome. Grand and gorgeous, the Sheraton Palace Hotel is a place worth visiting even if you're not planning a wedding. Come and see for yourself why it's been a San Francisco landmark for over 100 years.

CAPACITY:

	Seated	Standing		Seated	Standing
Grand Ballroom	600	1000	French Parlor	100	150
Gold Ballroom	275	600	Sunset Court	300	600
Ralston Room	275	600			

FEES & DEPOSITS: A deposit in the amount of 10% of the estimated cost is required with the signed contract. The balance is due 48 hours prior to the event. There is a fee of $750–1,000 for ceremonies only, and no rental fee if the reception is held at the Hotel. Per person food service rates are: $25–35 for luncheons, $38–50 for dinners and $50–70 for buffets. Tax and a 17% service charge are additional.

CANCELLATION POLICY: To be discussed with the Hotel.

AVAILABILITY: Year-round, everyday.

SERVICES/AMENITIES:

Restaurant Services: yes
Catering: provided

Parking: valet CBA at a charge, or lot
Overnight Accommodations: yes

Kitchen Facilities: n/a
Tables & Chairs: provided
Linens, Silver, etc.: provided (specialty linens avail.)
Restrooms: wca
Dance Floor: yes

RESTRICTIONS:
Alcohol: provided, corkage $10/bottle
Smoking: allowed
Music: amplified ok

Telephone: pay phones
Outdoor Night Lighting: access only
Outdoor Cooking Facilities: no
Cleanup: provided
Bride's Dressing Area: yes

Wheelchair Access: yes
Insurance: provided by Hotel

THE SHERMAN HOUSE

2160 Green Street between Webster & Fillmore
San Francisco, CA 94123
(415) 563-3600
Reserve: 3 months in advance

This tastefully and artfully decorated house, originally built in 1876 by the founder of the Sherman/Clay Music Company, opened as a hotel 7 years ago and is rated one of the top ten hotels in the Zagat U.S. Hotel Survey. It's well known for its fine dining, providing an intimate atmosphere with impeccable service—just the right combination for an elegant wedding celebration. The Sherman House butlers escort guests into the house through a separate entry for private functions. Guests then move on to the music room featuring wood paneling, fireplace, leaded glass skylight, mirrors and a double staircase that descends into the room from an upper level gallery. The musicians' balcony, overlooking the music room, is a perfect spot for a harpist, guitarist or trio. The lush gardens in the back of the house are quite lovely, with a cobbled courtyard, gazebo and fountain. If you want a place that is really private, quiet and sophisticated, ask to see the Garden Suite. These quarters can be rented separately and come with private salon, bedroom, bath and two private gardens. The Sherman House staff offers personal, attentive service and will help you with flowers, cake or other party planning details.

CAPACITY: The house can accommodate up to 100 for an hors d'oeuvres reception, carried by silver tray butler service. Capacity for seated meals is 60.

FEES & DEPOSITS: A refundable deposit is required to secure your event date. The rental fee for use of the music room and gallery is $500–$2,000 depending on the number of guests, season and time of day. Use of the Garden Suite is $750. Food service costs range from hors d'oeuvres receptions $25-55/person to seated functions ranging from $55–80/person. Service charge of 20% and tax are added to the final bill. The final balance is due at least 30 days prior to your function.

CANCELLATION POLICY: Cancellation is required 30 days prior to your event to receive a refund and 45 days prior to your party during peak periods.

AVAILABILITY: Anytime. Guests must leave by 10pm during the week, 10:30pm on weekends.

SERVICES/AMENITIES:

Restaurant Services: yes
Catering: provided, no BYO
Kitchen Facilities: n/a
Tables & Chairs: provided
Linens, Silver, etc.: provided
Restrooms: wca
Bride's Dressing Area: CBA

Parking: valet CBA
Overnight Accommodations: 14 guestrooms
Telephone: house phone
Outdoor Night Lighting: access only
Outdoor Cooking Facilities: no
Cleanup: provided
Dance Floor: no

RESTRICTIONS:

Alcohol: provided, WBC only
Smoking: outside only
Music: no amplified

Wheelchair Access: yes
Insurance: not required

SHOWPLACE DESIGN CENTER

2 Henry Adams Street
San Francisco, CA 94103
(415) 864-1500
Reserve: 3–6 months in advance

Built in the early 1900s, this historic, versatile Cabaret encompasses an Italian piazza setting accented by natural teak wood furnishings. Floor-to-ceiling, multi-paned windows flood the reception area with natural light. State-of-the-art club sound and stage lighting create the mood. Guests can enjoy the festivities from the main dining area as well as the balcony level.

The Showplace Penthouse features spectacular views of the San Francisco skyline and the Bay Bridge from a glass-enclosed space and a rooftop terrace. Day or evening, it's perfect for receptions, dining and dancing.

CAPACITY, FEES & DEPOSITS:

Area	Seated	Reception	Rental Fees
Cabaret	250	500	$2,500*
Penthouse	up to 120	125	$850*

*The basic rental fee may vary depending on the specific details of your event.

A non-refundable deposit of 50% of the rental fee is required when the contract is submitted. The balance is due 30 days prior to the event. Fees include a house technician.

CANCELLATION POLICY: The fees and deposits can only be applied toward another event within a 90-day period.

AVAILABILITY: Year-round. The Cabaret Monday–Thursday after 3pm, Sunday from 8am; no Friday or Saturday nights. The Penthouse everyday from 8am.

SERVICES/AMENITIES:

Restaurant Services: no
Catering: in-house caterer or BYO w/approval, extra fee
Kitchen Facilities: minimal
Tables & Chairs: provided
Linens, Silver, etc.: BYO
Restrooms: wca Cabaret only
Dance Floor: yes

Parking: street, adjacent lot
Overnight Accommodations: no
Telephone: pay phones
Outdoor Night Lighting: access only
Outdoor Cooking Facilities: no
Cleanup: provided
Bride's Dressing Area: CBA
Other: event coordination, technician

RESTRICTIONS:

Alcohol: provided, no BYO
Smoking: allowed
Music: amplified ok

Wheelchair Access: limited
Insurance: certificate required

SPECTRUM GALLERY

511 Harrison Street
San Francisco, CA 94105
(415) 495-1111 Thomas Roedoc
Reserve: 2 weeks–2 years in advance

Designed and built by an event professional, this spacious fine art gallery has a 20-foot high wall of windows facing the entire downtown skyline. At night, the view sparkles with thousands of lights twinkling just four blocks away. Spectrum also offers almost every amenity you could want: a state-of-the-art lighting and dimming system that can pin-spot anything from dining tables to the wedding cake, a whisper-clear P/A system for music and toasts, a portable stage and dance floor, a private bride's dressing room, a 1,200-sq foot caterer's area, huge restrooms and abundant free parking nearby. Adaptable and adjustable, as few as 100 or as many as 400 can be seated comfortably, all in the same room. The museum-quality paintings and sculpture and the wide range of amenities create an environment that's unique, dramatic and truly memorable. Ceremonies are welcome, and Spectrum's experienced "hands-on" staff are always available to help with planning and coordination.

CAPACITY: This facility can hold 100–400 seated guests (with stage and dance floor), 150–650 guests for a standing reception.

FEES & DEPOSITS: A non-refundable deposit of 50% of the rental fee is due when reservations are confirmed. The balance is due 90 days prior to your event. Rental rates are $2,750 for Saturday evenings, $1,375 for daytime events Monday–Saturday, and $1,750 for Sundays. A refundable $1,000 cleaning/damage deposit is due 10 days prior to your function. Rates during December are higher.

CANCELLATION POLICY: The deposits, other than the cleaning/damage deposit, are non-refundable. If the date can be rebooked, most of the deposit will be returned.

AVAILABILITY: Year-round, everyday from 8am–2am.

SERVICES/AMENITIES:

Restaurant Services: no
Catering: any insured caterer
Kitchen Facilities: moderate
Tables & Chairs: provided
Linens, Silver, etc.: BYO
Restrooms: wca
Dance Floor: yes
Parking: abundant on-street

Overnight Accommodations: no
Telephone: pay phones
Outdoor Night Lighting: access only
Outdoor Cooking Facilities: no
Cleanup: caterer and Spectrum
Other: stage, riser, projection screen
Special: lighting/dimming and sound
Bride's Dressing Area: yes

RESTRICTIONS:

Alcohol: provided
Smoking: allowed
Music: amplified ok

Wheelchair Access: yes
Insurance: required, available

SPLENDIDO

Four Embarcadero Center
Promenade Level
San Francisco, CA 94111
(415) 986-3222
Reserve: 1–6 months in advance

Walk through the 200-year-old Spanish olivewood doors and you're in for a big surprise. This restaurant draws you into a fantastic world where no matter where you look, an uncanny mix of Mediterranean architectures surrounds you. Over the foyer is a circular, hand-chiseled stone dome. Nearby, Moorish arches blend into rustic French stone walls; Italian hand-painted tiles complement a Spanish wrought iron banister. The handcrafted, one-ton pewter bar was flown from Portugal in ten sections, along with its builder, to ensure problem-free reassembly. Stone archways and columns, constructed of rubble collected from ancient ruins, form intimate dining areas. Hand-painted wormwood cabinetry, massive, hand-hewn beams and warm hues of teal, gray, rose and muted peach create an earthy quality throughout. Unusual and fanciful light fixtures suggest octopi and Greek jugs. In the center of the restaurant, a massive European bread oven made of stone and brick stands on display. Overhead, the ceiling areas vary, from grapevine stakes and willow branches to vaulted brick and fabric canopies. For guests who like to watch food being artfully prepared, Splendido offers an exhibition kitchen, with open grill and wood-burning pizza oven. Outdoors, the restaurant has a large, permanent, cream-colored canopy and granite-topped bar for al fresco functions. Warmed by heaters and captivated by the view, you may forget you're in San Francisco and think you're relaxing on the tranquil Mediterranean.

CAPACITY: Indoors, 24 seated guests in a separated area; Outdoor Patio, 75 seated guests or 150–200 for a standing reception. On Sunday or Monday night, the entire restaurant can be reserved for up to 150–200 seated guests.

FEES & DEPOSITS: For groups of 20 or more guests, a $200 deposit is required within a few days of booking. A guaranteed guest count is required 72 hours in advance. For parties of 10 or more, a special large party menu is available with prices ranging from $20–45/person for cocktail parties and seated luncheons. Dinners run $30–50/person. Approximately 50%–75% of the anticipated food and beverage total is due 1 week prior to the event. Alcoholic beverages, tax and 15% service charge are additional. Customized cakes can be prepared with 3 days' notice from the Splendido bakery. Non-Splendido cakes are subject to a $2.50/plate fee.

CANCELLATION POLICY: With less than 5 days' notice, the deposit is forfeited.

AVAILABILITY: Year-round, everyday. Closed July 4th, Christmas, New Years, Thanksgiving and Labor days.

SERVICES/AMENITIES:

Restaurant Services: yes
Dance Floor: no
Catering: provided, no BYO
Kitchen Facilities: n/a
Tables & Chairs: provided
Linens, Silver, etc.: provided
Restrooms: wca
Bride's Dressing Area: no

Parking: Embarcadero garages, after 5pm free with validation
Overnight Accommodations: no
Telephone: pay phone
Outdoor Night Lighting: yes
Outdoor Cooking Facilities: no
Cleanup: provided

RESTRICTIONS:

Alcohol: provided, corkage $10/bottle
Smoking: designated areas
Music: moderate amplified outside, indoors only if entire restaurant rented

Wheelchair Access: yes
Insurance: not required

Prices and policies do change. Call each facility and confirm everything you read in Here Comes The Guide.

SQUARE ONE

190 Pacific at Front Street
San Francisco, CA 94111
(415) 788-1110
Reserve: 2–4 months in advance

Often rated as one of the top ten restaurants in the US, Square One consistently delivers a sublime culinary experience. In keeping with its name, this San Francisco eatery makes almost everything from scratch (even ice cream and pickles!), using seasonal foods and fresh local produce. Bread and dessert aficionados will feel they've gone to heaven. The menu, an eclectic mix of robust and sensual international dishes, changes daily. Not only is the food splendid, but the far-ranging wine list has won five prestigious awards. The main dining room is contemporary and appealing, but for those who want to savor the essence of Square One, the Private Dining Room is where to go. Artist Carlo Marchiori has transformed two dimensional walls into an intimate Italian garden, replete with topiary, song birds and misty Tuscan landscape. You don't have to worry about a thing—restaurant staff will cheerfully handle all the arrangements and with enough notice, they'll customize any menu. And, master sommelier Peter Granoff will help you choose the perfect wine to accompany your meal. At Square One, wine and dine your family and friends while enjoying views of Walton Park. If you've ever wondered how to make a small reception, rehearsal luncheon or dinner really special, wonder no more. This place is run by people who love to cook for people who love to eat, and they do it with a warmth and friendliness that will make you want to come back for more.

CAPACITY: The Private Dining Room seats up to 45 guests.

FEES & DEPOSITS: To reserve the Private Dining Room, a $600 deposit is required for dinners, $300 for luncheons. Any menu can be customized. Dinners run $45–60; alcohol, tax and service charge are additional. The balance is payable on completion of the event. The average luncheon is $400, dinners $600 Sunday–Thursday, Friday and Saturday $1,000 depending on number of guests. Flowers, cakes and other services can be arranged with advance notice.

CANCELLATION POLICY: With 1 week's notice, the deposit is refunded.

AVAILABILITY: Year-round from 11:30am to midnight. Luncheons Monday–Friday only, dinners daily.

SERVICES/AMENITIES:

Restaurant Services: yes
Catering: provided
Kitchen Facilities: n/a
Tables & Chairs: provided
Linens, Silver, etc.: provided
Restrooms: wca
Dance Floor: no
Other: award-winning wine cellar

Parking: valet at night & adjacent garages
Overnight Accommodations: no
Telephone: pay phones
Outdoor Night Lighting: access only
Outdoor Cooking Facilities: no
Cleanup: provided
Bride's Dressing Area: no

RESTRICTIONS:

Alcohol: provided, corkage $10/bottle
Smoking: allowed
Music: no

Wheelchair Access: yes
Insurance: not required

SS JEREMIAH O'BRIEN

Fort Mason
San Francisco, CA 94123
(415) 441-3101 Marci Hooper
Reserve: 1–6 months in advance

This is America's last unaltered Liberty Ship. Out of more than 2,700 nearly identical ships, the Jeremiah O'Brien is the only known Liberty Ship that is in original and full operating condition! Preserved as a National Historic Landmark, the 441-foot long ship is now docked at Fort Mason and is available for Bay charter cruises, tours and special events. The forward gun tub and deck are great places to hold ceremonies because the views of Alcatraz, Angel Island and Aquatic Park are sensational. This is a wonderful spot to tie the knot, and there is an additional bonus. During events, the ship's staff is available to give highly interesting tours of the multiple decks and machine rooms.

CAPACITY: 300 standing guests or 210 for seated functions.

FEES & DEPOSITS: A $125 cleaning deposit is required. There's a flat rental fee of $65–250 (depending on which space is reserved) plus an additional $3/person.

CANCELLATION POLICY: A 10-day advance notice is required for a full refund.

AVAILABILITY: 9:30am to midnight. No events on New Year's, Christmas, Easter or Thanksgiving holidays.

SERVICES/AMENITIES:

Restaurant Services: no
Catering: BYO
Kitchen Facilities: no
Tables & Chairs: provided
Linens, Silver, etc.: BYO
Restrooms: no wca
Dance Floor: yes

Parking: large lot
Overnight Accommodations: no
Telephone: office phone
Outdoor Night Lighting: yes
Outdoor Cooking Facilities: no
Cleanup: caterer
Bride's Dressing Area: captain's quarters

RESTRICTIONS:

Alcohol: BYO
Smoking: outside preferred
Music: amplified until 11:30pm

Wheelchair Access: no
Insurance: sometimes required
Other: gangway entry steep & narrow

THE STANFORD COURT

905 California Street
San Francisco, CA 94108
(415) 989-3500
Reserve: 1 week–12 months in advance

Conveniently located atop prestigious Nob Hill, this historic five-star hotel will transport you to an earlier era of gracious service and refined luxury. Enter through the elegant carriage courtyard, covered by a dramatic, Tiffany-style stained glass dome. The lobby evokes the 19th-century splendor of Nob Hill with Baccarat chandeliers, fine French antiques and wood paneling. Carrara marble floors, Oriental carpets, original artwork and collectibles such as an 1806 grandfather clock once owned by Napoleon add to the richness of the decor. For special parties, the International Terrace just off the lobby offers a unique setting overlooking San Francisco's only cable car crossing and the downtown skyline. The award-winning Fournou's Ovens restaurant features four private dining rooms ideal for prenuptial dinners. Receptions are often held in the Stanford Ballroom, sparkling with Baccarat chandeliers originally from Paris' Grand Hotel, or the India Suite, decorated with hand-painted murals depicting romantic scenes from India circa 1810. Three elegant rooms featuring burlwood paneling and crystal chandeliers are available for more intimate gatherings.

CAPACITY:

Room	Reception	Seated
Stanford Ballroom	800	550
India Suite	275	200
Telegraph Hill Room	40	30
Russian Hill	50	40
Nob Hill	90	70
Fournou's Ovens Private Rooms (4)	—	10–24
International Terrace	150	80

FEES & DEPOSITS: An advance non-refundable deposit is payable when reservations are confirmed. The estimated food and beverage total and final guest count are due 3 days prior to the event. Per person rates: luncheons start at $22, dinners $32, buffets $32–46 and hors d'oeuvres $10. Tax and a 15% gratuity are additional.

CANCELLATION POLICY: If the space(s) can be rebooked, the deposit will be refunded.

AVAILABILITY: Year-round, everyday, any time.

SERVICES/AMENITIES:

Restaurant Services: yes
Catering: provided, no BYO
Kitchen Facilities: n/a
Tables & Chairs: provided
Overnight Accommodations: 400 guestrooms
Telephone: pay phones

Linens, Silver, etc.: provided
Restrooms: wca
Dance Floor: yes
Parking: valet
Outdoor Cooking Facilities: no
Cleanup: provided

Outdoor Night Lighting: access only
Bride's Dressing Area: yes

RESTRICTIONS:
Alcohol: provided, no BYO
Smoking: designated areas
Music: amplified w/approval

Other: event coordination, piano

Wheelchair Access: yes
Insurance: sometimes required
Other: no open flames

THE ST. FRANCIS HOTEL

335 Powell Street, Union Square
San Francisco, CA 94102
(415) 774-0126 Catering Manager
Reserve: 1 day–9 months in advance

Named The Westin St. Francis in 1982, this famous San Francisco landmark has been the hotel of choice for internationally prominent guests since 1904. From royalty to presidents and society notables to Hollywood stars, The St. Francis has offered first-class dining and lodging for almost 100 years. This stately, 12-story building facing Union Square was one of the few structures to survive the 1906 earthquake. Considerably damaged by fire, it was quickly refurbished using California's most skilled artists and craftsmen to recreate the ornate and opulent interior, and many innovations were added to make it the most sophisticated hotel of its time. Marble Corinthian columns, paneled ceilings with gold leaf trim and crystal chandeliers are highlights of the newly restored Powell Street Lobby. A grand and impressive place, The St. Francis is more than qualified to host your wedding celebration.

CAPACITY: The St. Francis has 26 rooms that can accommodate events. Here are a few:

Room	Seated	Reception
Grand Ballroom	1,000	1500
Colonial Room	340	400
California Ballroom	450	600
4 Elizabethan Rooms (ea)	100–110	120–130
St. Francis Suite (3 sections)	100	100–200
Oz, Victor's, St. Francis Grill	*By Special Arrangement*	

FEES & DEPOSITS: A refundable $500–1,000 deposit is required when you confirm your reservation and the estimated event total is due 1 week prior to the function. Deposits and fees vary with guest count, type of function and room(s) rented. Any remaining balance is invoiced, payable 30 days following the function. If food service is provided, rental fees are reduced. Per person rates: luncheons $23–50, dinners $34–70, hors d'oeuvres start at $10 and buffets range from $27–65. Tax and an 18% service charge are added to the final bill. If your party is staying here, ask for special room rates.

AVAILABILITY: Year-round, everyday, any time up to 2am.

SERVICES/AMENITIES:

Restaurant Services: yes
Catering: provided, no BYO
Kitchen Facilities: n/a
Tables & Chairs: provided
Linens, Silver, etc.: provided
Restrooms: wca
Dance Floor: yes
Parking: hotel garage or adjacent lots

Overnight Accommodations: 1,200 guestrooms
Telephone: pay phone
Outdoor Night Lighting: access only
Outdoor Cooking Facilities: no
Cleanup: provided
Other: event coordination, grand piano
Bride's Dressing Area: complimentary guestroom
Special: theme party coordination

RESTRICTIONS:

Alcohol: provided, WB corkage $12/bottle
Smoking: allowed
Music: amplified ok

Wheelchair Access: yes
Insurance: not required

ST. PAULUS CHURCH

950 Gough Street
San Francisco, CA 94102
(415) 673-8088
Reserve: 6–12 months in advance

Often referred to as the "Wedding Cake Church" because of its ornate exterior detailing, St. Paulus Church has been a part of San Francisco's history for a century. With its soaring spires, triple arched portal and elegant rose window, St. Paulus is reminiscent of the Gothic cathedrals of Europe. Ceremonies are held in the Sanctuary, a vaulting chapel featuring wood shingled walls, carved wooden bannisters and an imposing German pipe organ. During the day, sunlight streams through tall, stained-glass windows, making them glow with exceptional brilliance. Downstairs, the Reception Hall is an unpretentious space for informal receptions. A high ceiling, creamy white walls and arched windows create a light, airy ambiance. Ficus trees in planters add a dash of greenery, and a stage is available for impromptu toasts. During the 1906 quake, St. Paulus was within seconds of being dynamited to create a fire break. A frantic pastor begged firemen to try a hydrant on the corner, despite the fact that almost all water mains were broken. Much to the astonishment of everyone, the hydrant worked and the church was saved. Divine intervention? Maybe. Get married here and who knows—the church's good luck might rub off on you.

CAPACITY: The Sanctuary can seat up to 750; the Reception Hall can hold 250 seated, 450 standing.

FEES & DEPOSITS: A $500 fee covering a four-hour period is required at the time of booking to reserve either the Sanctuary or the Hall (to reserve both, the fee is $1,000). Additional time costs $50/hour, and must be arranged in advance. All fees must be paid two weeks prior to the wedding. The wedding party is responsible for removing any items they bring in; St. Paulus will clean the facility.

CANCELLATION POLICY: With 90 days notice, all but $50 will be refunded. With 89-30 days notice, 50% of payments will be refunded. No refunds will be made if cancellation occurs less than 30 days from the wedding date.

AVAILABILITY: The Sanctuary is available for non-denominational ceremonies Saturdays at 11am or 3pm, and Sundays at 2pm. The Reception Hall can be reserved anytime.

SERVICES/AMENITIES:

Restaurant Services: no

Catering: provided or BYO with approval

Kitchen Facilities: CBA for fee

Tables & Chairs: provided

Linens, Silver, etc.: caterer or BYO

Restrooms: wca

Dance Floor: Reception Hall only

Parking: on street, Opera Plaza

Overnight Accommodations: no

Telephone: pay phone

Outdoor Night Lighting: no

Outdoor Cooking Facilities: no

Cleanup: renter and St. Paulus

Bride's Dressing Area: yes

RESTRICTIONS:

Alcohol: wine and beer ok, liquor license may be required for mixed drinks

Smoking: not allowed

Music: amplified ok

Wheelchair Access: CBA

Insurance: not required

Other: decorations restricted; no bird seed, rice, confetti etc; no food or drink in the Sanctuary

SWEDENBORGIAN CHURCH

2107 Lyon Street at Washington
San Francisco, CA 94115
(415) 346-6466
Reserve: 1 month in advance

This church is listed because of its size, intimacy and architectural importance. Built in 1895, in Pacific Heights, by a coterie of artists, architects and spiritual seekers, the historic chapel is rustic and charming in the Arts and Crafts tradition. There's a huge brick fireplace in the chapel and with lit candles, the interior is exceptionally beautiful and serene. Floors, walls and ceilings are wood and the overhead arching beams are good sized madrone tree trunks. In lieu of conventional pews, hand-made maple chairs are provided. Adjacent to the chapel is a more modern house with garden room, living and dining rooms used for receptions. A quiet and pretty garden with small pool, trees, benches and flowers that provide year-round color is in front of the house. Traditional, contemporary and interfaith ceremonies are offered with weddings scheduled usually 2 hours apart. Reception space is limited, so the reception facilities are available only after the last wedding of the day on Saturday and Sunday. If you're willing to get married on a weekday there's much greater flexibility.

CAPACITY: The chapel can seat 115 (standing room to 150); the house, up to 60 guests for sit down dinners and to 100 for stand-up affairs.

FEES & DEPOSITS: A $100 deposit is required to secure your wedding date and time. For receptions, a refundable security deposit of $250 is required. A donation of $700 is required for Saturday and Sunday wedding ceremonies. Weekday weddings with fewer than 20 guests will cost $350, and with over 20, $550. The rental fee for the reception area is $250/hour, not including setup and cleanup time. Full payment is due 1 month before the wedding. The donation includes a minister's services, staff musician, the assistance of a wedding hostess, 2 floral arrangements, bridal dressing room and use of the garden for wedding photos.

CANCELLATION POLICY: Full refunds are given (less the deposit) with 30 days' advance notification. With less than 30 days, 50% refund less the deposit.

AVAILABILITY: Saturday receptions are possible only after the 7pm wedding; Sundays, after the 4pm wedding. Weekday receptions can be scheduled by arrangement. Guests must vacate the premises by 11pm.

SERVICES/AMENITIES:

Restaurant Services: no
Catering: BYO
Restaurant Services: no
Kitchen Facilities: modest
Tables & Chairs: provided
Linens, Silver, etc.: BYO
Restrooms: no wca
Bride's Dressing Area: yes

Dance Floor: yes, small receptions only
Parking: on street
Overnight Accommodations: no
Telephone: house phone
Outdoor Night Lighting: access only
Outdoor Cooking Facilities: no
Cleanup: caterer

RESTRICTIONS:

Alcohol: BYO WBC
Smoking: outside only
Music: no amplified

Wheelchair Access: no
Insurance: not required
Other: no rice or seeds

THE TROCADERO
Sigmund Stern Grove Clubhouse

19th Ave. and Sloat Blvd.
San Francisco, CA 94116
(415) 666-7035 Recreation & Parks
Reserve: 1–12 months in advance

In the middle of Stern Grove, approached from a lovely entry drive flanked by eucalyptus and stone walls, sits The Trocadero Clubhouse. This turn-of-the-century, two-story Victorian is available for special events and features a spacious veranda, river rock fireplace, hardwood floors, old fashioned bar and fully equipped industrial kitchen. Adjacent park amenities include a pond, redwood grove, bridge, meadow, outdoor stone fireplaces and picnic tables. In Stern Grove, you can ignore the fact that you're in urban San Francisco; this is an oasis in the heart of the City.

CAPACITY: The Trocadero can hold up to 150 guests for a standing reception and 125 for seated meals. The outdoor picnic area can accommodate 1,000 with seating for 100–150 guests.

FEES & DEPOSITS: The fees and a refundable cleaning/security deposit of $150 are due 30 days prior to your event. The rental fee is $300 for a 6-hour function on weekdays. From 5pm Friday to 11pm Sunday and holidays, the fee is $400. An outdoor ceremony costs an extra $100.

CANCELLATION POLICY: If you cancel 30 days prior to your event, you will receive 90% of your deposit; if less than 10 working days in advance, no refund.

AVAILABILITY: Rental times are 10am–4pm and 5–11pm in 6-hour blocks any day of the week. Extended hours 9–10am and 11am–1pm can be arranged with advance notice.

SERVICES/AMENITIES:

Restaurant Services: no

Catering: BYO

Kitchen Facilities: moderate

Tables & Chairs: provided

Linens, Silver, etc.: BYO

Restrooms: wca

Dance Floor: yes

Bride's Dressing Area: CBA

Parking: 50–75 cars

Overnight Accommodations: no

Telephone: distant pay phone

Outdoor Night Lighting: yes

Outdoor Cooking Facilities: stone fireplaces

Cleanup: caterer

Other: wooded area and gardens nearby

RESTRICTIONS:

Alcohol: BYO

Smoking: allowed

Music: amplified until 11pm

Wheelchair Access: yes

Insurance: not required

Need a caterer, cake maker, florist? The Service Directory starting on page 412 features the best in the business.

THE WATTIS ROOM
At Davies Symphony Hall

201 Van Ness Avenue
San Francisco, CA 94102
(415) 552-4089
Reserve: 1–6 months in advance

Most folks don't know that The Wattis Room, a private club for major donors in Davies Symphony Hall, is available for social events. Well, luckily for us, it is. This is a space tucked away on the first floor, approached through the main doors on Grove Street. As you enter The Wattis Room, you'll notice the large art pieces on the walls, rotating exhibits from the San Francisco Museum of Art. The lighting is subdued and the Room's decor is sophisticated and understated. From prenuptial dinners to formal seated receptions, this location is versatile enough to handle any type of crowd.

CAPACITY: The Wattis Room can hold 100 seated guests or 200 guests for a reception.

FEES & DEPOSITS: No deposit is required. The $450 rental fee covers a 4-hour block. Rental includes a symphony staff member, flowers, piano and custodial services. Any time over 4 hours costs $100/ hour. Food service is provided. Buffets range $15–25/person, luncheons start at $15/person, dinners at $20/person and hors d'oeuvres start at $6/person. Staff, table service equipment, tax and a 20% production charge are additional.

AVAILABILITY: Year-round, any day, any time. Dates in June, July, August and Christmas holidays are more available because the Symphony is in recess. Overtime will be charged for functions past midnight.

SERVICES/AMENITIES:
Restaurant Services: no
Catering: in-house caterer, Creative Catering, has first right of refusal
Kitchen Facilities: fully equipped
Tables & Chairs: some provided
Linens, Silver, etc.: provided, extra fee
Dance Floor: CBA

Parking: Grove & Franklin garage
Overnight Accommodations: no
Telephone: pay phone
Outdoor Night Lighting: access only
Outdoor Cooking Facilities: no
Cleanup: provided
Bride's Dressing Area: restroom

RESTRICTIONS:
Alcohol: provided, corkage $3.50–5/bottle corkage negotiable
Smoking: allowed
Music: amplified ok

Wheelchair Access: yes
Insurance: not required
Other: no red wine at standing functions, votive candles only

Half Moon Bay

DOUGLAS BEACH HOUSE

Miramar Beach
Half Moon Bay, CA 94018
(415) 726-4143
Reserve: 1 week in advance

You can't get much closer to the ocean than this. On a secluded stretch of coast just north of Half Moon Bay lies the Douglas Beach House, otherwise known as The Bach Dancing and Dynamite Society and famous for its concerts. It's actually a rambling complex of a house with recital/music hall, decks and dining rooms. The proprietor, Pete Douglas is well known for his jazz and classical programs presented regularly on Sundays. Saturdays and weekdays are set aside for private parties. The decor has been described as "comfy-funky in that rustic Northern California style of hanging ferns, dark wood and stained glass." The multiple decks and ocean vistas make this a great place to have a prenuptial gathering or an out-of-the-ordinary wedding.

CAPACITY: The dining area can hold 95 guests for seated meals. The entire facility can accommodate up to 150.

FEES & DEPOSITS: For social events, a non-refundable deposit of 50% of the total estimated rental fee is due on confirmation. The rental fee is $800–1,200, depending on the date, time and number of guests.

CANCELLATION POLICY: Fees will be refunded only if the space can be rebooked on the event date.

AVAILABILITY: Year-round. Parties are scheduled for Saturdays 2pm–7pm, or 3pm–8pm; and occasional Friday nights may be scheduled, if available.

SERVICES/AMENITIES:

Restaurant Services: no
Catering: BYO
Kitchen Facilities: ample
Tables & Chairs: provided
Linens, Silver, etc.: BYO
Restrooms: no wca
Dance Floor: yes

Parking: parking lot
Overnight Accommodations: no
Telephone: pay phone
Outdoor Night Lighting: yes
Outdoor Cooking Facilities: BYO
Cleanup: provided
Bride's Dressing Area: yes

RESTRICTIONS:

Alcohol: BYO, no kegs
Smoking: allowed
Music: amplified ok

Wheelchair Access: limited
Insurance: not required

MILL ROSE INN

615 Mill Street
Half Moon Bay, CA 94019
(415) 726-9794
Reserve: 8–12 months in advance

The Mill Rose Inn is an outstanding location for a wedding in an English country garden setting. And, if you want to honeymoon here, it offers suites with fireplaces, double whirlpool tubs and canopy beds. With its gingerbread detailing, dormers and bay window alcoves overlooking the garden, this venue offers a first-rate experience. Framed by a sensational floral palette with hundreds of roses in bloom, the gardens and courtyards offer intimate spaces for outdoor wedding receptions. The flagstone courtyard behind the Inn is sheltered by a handsome maple and embraced by multi-color flowers. There's also a rose-covered gazebo and a cascading fountain. Inside, every room is appealing, many with excellent floral arrangements. The dining room is light and fresh, with rose carpets, a fireplace and decorative wallpaper. The parlor is warm and inviting, with lots of color and appointments that express attention to detail. The library is a small jewel-of-a-room that features a beautifully painted fireplace and window alcove overlooking the blooms outside. In addition to being a lovely place, there's another reason why the Mill Rose Inn is so popular—once a bride has registered, all she has to do is relax while the Inn takes care of all the details.

CAPACITY: This facility can accommodate 125 guests, which includes both gardens and interconnecting banquet room.

FEES & DEPOSITS: The full rental fee is required as a deposit to reserve your date. A $2,500 wedding package includes full event planning and coordination, 8-hour rental for ceremony and reception, table setup and cleanup, total floral decoration and complimentary room for honeymoon and champagne breakfast. A mini 2-hour wedding package is available midweek for 10–20 guests starting at $750 which includes setup, cleanup and some decorations. Cake, served hors d'oeuvres and beverage start at $25/person plus tax.

CANCELLATION POLICY: The deposit will only be refunded if the space can be rebooked on your event date.

AVAILABILITY: Year-round, any day from 11am to 7pm.

SERVICES/AMENITIES:

Restaurant Services: no
Catering: BYO or select from preferred list
Kitchen Facilities: ample
Tables & Chairs: provided
Linens, Silver, etc.: some provided
Restrooms: no wca
Bride's Dressing Area: yes
Special: event coordination, floral arrangements, piano

Dance Floor: garden patio
Parking: on and off street
Overnight Accommodations: 6 guestrooms
Telephone: house & guest phones
Outdoor Night Lighting: yes
Cleanup: provided
Outdoor Cooking Facilities: BBQs

RESTRICTIONS:

Alcohol: BYO
Smoking: outside only
Music: amplified ok

Wheelchair Access: limited
Insurance: recommended
Other: no bird seed or rice

Montara

MONTARA GARDENS

496 6th Street
Montara, CA 94037
(415) 728-7442 or **(415) 355-9750**
Reserve: 6–10 months in advance

For those of you who don't know where Montara is, it's right on the ocean, about eight miles north of Half Moon Bay. This small, coastal town is quiet and peaceful. Montara Gardens, formerly Montara Grammar School, is a designated historic landmark and is a handsome example of early 1900 Mission Revival architecture. Although there are several interior spaces for small to medium-sized receptions, (including an oak-floored auditorium) it's the outdoor spaces that make Montara Gardens such a delightful spot for weddings. Outside, you can smell the fresh air and occasionally feel ocean breezes. There are several wood lath redwood gazebos set in two very pretty garden courtyards. One is large enough to hold a sizable wedding party underneath its canopy. Each flower-filled courtyard is beautifully landscaped and well-maintained. Both are sheltered by enormous cypress trees, making them warm and comfortable even on chilly days. During the ceremony or reception, guests are treated to spectacular views of the nearby ocean, which can be glimpsed through openings in the foliage.

CAPACITY: 150 seated guests or 150 for a standing reception.

FEES & DEPOSITS: A non-refundable deposit of 20% of the rental fee is payable upon reservation; the balance is due 2 weeks prior to the event. The rental fee varies depending on guest count. The fees below are for a 5-hour function. For less time, subtract $100/hour, ie. 4-hours use at 100 guests would total $1,150, 3-hours use would total $1,050.

Number of Guests	50	80	90	100	120	150
Fee	$950	$1,050	$1,150	$1,250	$1,350	$1,450

AVAILABILITY: Year-round, Saturdays only from 11:30am–5:30pm.

SERVICES/AMENITIES:

Restaurant Services: no
Catering: BYO

Parking: medium sized lot
Overnight Accommodations: no

Kitchen Facilities: moderate
Tables & Chairs: provided
Linens, Silver, etc.: BYO
Restrooms: wca
Dance Floor: yes

RESTRICTIONS:
Alcohol: BYO, WBC only
Smoking: outside only
Music: amplified inside only

Telephone: no
Outdoor Night Lighting: access only
Outdoor Cooking Facilities: no
Cleanup: caterer, some provided
Bride's Dressing Area: yes

Wheelchair Access: yes
Insurance: certificate required
Other: no rice or birdseed

POINT MONTARA LIGHTHOUSE

16th Street at Highway 1
Montara, CA 94037
(415) 728-7177
Reserve: 6–9 months in advance

Time may actually have stopped here. Twenty-five miles from San Francisco off Highway 1, the picturesque Point Montara Lighthouse occupies a phenomenal location right above the ocean. Built here because several ships ran aground at Point Montara in the 1860s, the light house started as a fog station in 1875. In 1900, a red oil lantern was added and a fresnel lens followed. In 1928 the lighthouse took its present form. Now a youth hostel operated by a non-profit group, the lighthouse and an appealing mix of modern and restored turn-of-the-century buildings provide an unusual environment. Much of it is similar to a village right out of the 1880s. In between the old lighthouse and the largest Victorian structure, is a lush rectangular lawn dotted by venerable cypress trees and surrounded by a white picket fence. Pollyanna would be right at home here. This is a place where romantic, old fashioned weddings are appropriate. Ceremonies are held on the lawn or at the ocean's edge. Views of the rugged coastline are magnetic, and November through April, migrating whales can be spotted from shore. If you'd like a glimpse of the past century, this garden setting will take you back.

CAPACITY: Maximum 60 guests for a seated or standing function.

FEES & DEPOSITS: The total rental fee is due at the time of booking, and a refundable $100 cleaning/damage deposit is due 30 days prior to the event. The rental fee is $5/person, with a minimum of $150.

CANCELLATION POLICY: With 30 days' notice, the deposit is refunded.

AVAILABILITY: Year-round. Daily 10am–4pm. There is an additional $25 charge for major holidays.

SERVICES/AMENITIES:
Restaurant Services: no
Catering: BYO
Kitchen Facilities: fully equipped

Parking: large lot
Overnight Accommodations: 13 guestrooms, space for 30 guests

Tables & Chairs: provided
Linens, Silver, etc.: BYO
Restrooms: wca
Dance Floor: CBA inside
Bride's Dressing Area: yes

Telephone: pay phone
Outdoor Night Lighting: access only
Outdoor Cooking Facilities: BYO or BBQ CBA
Cleanup: caterer or renter

RESTRICTIONS:
Alcohol: BYO BWC only
Smoking: outside only
Music: amplified ok

Wheelchair Access: yes
Insurance: sometimes required
Other: no pets

San Gregorio

RANCHO SAN GREGORIO

5086 La Honda Road/Highway 84
San Gregoio, CA 94074
(415) 747-0810
Reserve: 6 months in advance

Five miles inland from San Gregorio Beach is a sun-drenched, fifteen-acre ranch with a Spanish mission-style home. Now a bed and breakfast, this country retreat was built in 1971 by the present owners, Bud and Lee Raynor. These gracious and helpful hosts extend everyone a warm welcome, offer lots of creative input and spend considerable time coordinating all the details. For your wedding, their home becomes yours for the day. Sunny decks and patios, a lush lawn with gazebo, an informal barbecue area and a sweet-smelling apple orchard provide a variety of locations for ceremonies and receptions. You can dress these areas up for a formal function, go casual or have a theme party wedding. There's enough room to play badminton, volleyball, horseshoes or lawn croquet. All guestrooms have access to the upper deck, which has a lovely view of nearby farmland and wooded hills. Framed by surrounding oaks, bays and pines, Rancho San Gregorio provides an environment where you can relax and breathe. If you're looking for an escape from the urban sprawl, you'll find it here.

CAPACITY: Rancho San Gregorio can accommodate up to 125 guests.

FEES & DEPOSITS: To secure your date, a $250 deposit, which is applied towards the rental fee, plus a refundable $250 damage/cleaning deposit are due when the contract is finalized. The rental balance is due 2 weeks before the event. The rental fee for use of the garden, barbecue area, gazebo, house and kitchen: under 75 guests $450, 76–100 guests $550, 101–125 guests $650. If your group is over 40 guests, rental of 4 guestrooms is required, each runs $80–135/night. For small groups under 40 guests, you can rent the garden and have use of the house for $100/hour without rental of guestrooms. The Barn or barbecue area can be rented for $150. The damage/cleaning deposit(s) will be returned within 2 weeks of the function, minus any damages.

AVAILABILITY: Year-round. Large groups, weekends from 11am–9pm. Small groups under 40 guests, 11am–5pm, with a 4-hour minimum.

SERVICES/AMENITIES:

Restaurant Services: no
Catering: licensed caterer required
Kitchen Facilities: house kitchen
Tables & Chairs: BYO, some provided
Linens, Silver, etc.: BYO
Restrooms: no wca
Dance Floor: decks or patios
Other: wedding coordination

Parking: several lots
Overnight Accommodations: 4 guestrooms
Telephone: house phone
Outdoor Night Lighting: yes
Outdoor Cooking Facilities: yes
Cleanup: caterer or renter
Bride's Dressing Area: CBA, separate charge if rooms not rented

RESTRICTIONS:

Alcohol: BYO
Smoking: outside decks only
Music: amplified ok

Wheelchair Access: limited
Insurance: may be required, CBA, extra fee
Other: no pets, children must be supervised

Belvedere

CHINA CABIN

54 Beach Road
Belvedere, CA
(415) 435-2251 Beverly Bastian
(415) 435-1853 Landmarks Society
Reserve: 10 days in advance

In 1866, the Pacific Steamship Company commissioned W.M.Webb to construct a sidewheel steamer. Unfortunately, with a wood hull, the ship was destined for a short career and was burned for scrap metal in 1886. The China Cabin, the First Class social salon, was removed intact from the ship and set on pilings in the Belvedere Cove. The Cabin consists of a large room and two small staterooms. Its plain exterior belies the ornate and regal appointments inside. This place is impressive. The walls and domed ceiling are panels of elaborately carved wood that have been painted a crisp white and highlighted with gold leaf. Along the sides of the Cabin are a series of small, delicately etched-glass windows; handsome crystal chandeliers hang at each end of the room. The Cabin also has decks on three sides that have wonderful views of the San Francisco skyline and of the colorful boats berthed at the nearby yacht harbor. The China Cabin offers a glimpse of old world elegance and attention to detail; the result is a rich, sophisticated appearance that makes this a very unique setting for a special wedding event.

CAPACITY: The Cabin can hold up to 55 standing or 48 seated guests. The outdoor deck allows for 65 guests during summer months.

FEES & DEPOSITS: A $100 deposit is required when you make your reservation and a $250 refundable damage deposit is also required. The rental fee is $520 for a 5-hour minimum rental block and $100 for each additional hour. The total fee is due 30 days prior to your party.

CANCELLATION POLICY: Should you cancel 30 days before the event, your deposit will be refunded, less a $50 administrative fee.

AVAILABILITY: Any day, anytime until midnight except Wednesday and Sunday afternoons from April through October.

SERVICES/AMENITIES:

Restaurant Services: no
Catering: BYO, must be approved
Kitchen Facilities: no
Tables & Chairs: chairs available
Linens, Silver, etc.: available
Restrooms: wca
Dance Floor: yes

Parking: CBA
Overnight Accommodations: no
Telephone: house phone
Outdoor Night Lighting: deck only
Outdoor Cooking Facilities: no
Cleanup: caterer
Bride's Dressing Area: CBA

RESTRICTIONS:

Alcohol: BYO
Smoking: not allowed indoors or on deck
Music: no amplified

Wheelchair Access: yes
Insurance: proof of personal liability coverage
Other: decorations restricted; no rice, seeds, grains, petals or confetti

Fairfax

DEER PARK VILLA

367 Bolinas Road
Fairfax, CA 94930
(415) 456-8084
Reserve: 1–6 months in advance

The Villa is nestled among 4 acres of redwoods, oaks and lush hydrangeas. This homey Italian restaurant is supported by a very professional catering and restaurant staff with plenty of experience hosting wedding parties. The facility includes a front garden with outdoor dance area, bar, covered and heated patio, towering redwood trees and a small Japanese pagoda and foot bridge. The main dining area is decorated in muted pinks and dark mint green with windows on three sides; adjacent to the dining area is a full bar. The split level, back deck is intimate and surrounded by dense greenery. Operated by the Ghiringhelli family since 1937, the Deer Park Villa is a Marin County dining and banquet tradition.

CAPACITY: The Redwood Grove holds up to 300 guests; the Redwood Deck and adjoining indoor room, 125. The Villa can accommodate up to 225, but can be partitioned so that smaller groups have privacy.

FEES & DEPOSITS: A $450–675 non-refundable deposit secures your reservation and is applied towards the total fee. The Redwood Grove rental is $675 for groups up to 150; for larger groups add $1/additional guest to the rental fee. The fee for the Redwood Deck with an adjoining indoor room is $450. During fall and winter the entire Villa indoor space rents for $675. When wedding ceremonies require setup, an additional $1.50/person charge is applied to the fee. When dancing takes place indoors, add $75 for dance floor setup. Per person in-house catering rates: hors d'oeuvres receptions start at $16.50, buffets at $19–23 and seated meals at $20. Bar charges range from $5/person for champagne only to $7/person for full bar services. Sales tax and a 17% gratuity will be applied to the total food and bar service bill, excluding rental fees. Note that there is also a "Celebration Day Special", a package with special rates for receptions.

AVAILABILITY: Any day, anytime.

SERVICES/AMENITIES:

Restaurant Services: yes

Parking: large lot

Catering: provided, no BYO
Kitchen Facilities: n/a
Tables & Chairs: provided
Linens, Silver, etc.: provided
Restrooms: wca limited
Dance Floor: yes

Overnight Accommodations: no
Telephone: pay phone
Outdoor Night Lighting: yes
Outdoor Cooking Facilities: BBQs
Cleanup: provided
Bride's Dressing Area: yes

RESTRICTIONS:

Alcohol: provided, W&C corkage $5.50/bottle
Smoking: allowed
Music: restricted: amplified outdoors until 8pm, indoors amplified until 1am

Wheelchair Access: yes
Insurance: not required

Larkspur

THE LARK CREEK INN

234 Magnolia Avenue
Larkspur, CA 94939
(415) 924-1602 or **924-7766** Banquet Manager
Reserve: 2–12 months in advance

The Lark Creek Inn, one of the most popular restaurants in the Bay Area, is a delightful place for a wedding or reception. Built in 1888, this former Victorian country home is nestled in a grove of redwoods, next to a flowing creek. Sunlight filters through trees and windows, warming the tables in the main dining room. Overhead, an enormous skylight creates an open, airy ambiance. Muted colors, rich wood paneling and rotating original art complete the tasteful interior. The garden patio is perfect for a romantic outdoor ceremony, and the formal front garden with fountain provides a lovely backdrop for photographs. The Lark Creek Inn has received national acclaim as well as local restaurant awards, and we have found the food here to be some of the best we've ever tasted. Note that the banquet manager is available to coordinate all aspects of your party planning. Add that to the outstanding ambiance and you'll understand why your wedding celebration here will receive rave reviews. The Lark Creek Inn rates high on our list.

CAPACITY, FEES & DEPOSITS:

Area	Reception	Seated	Rental Fees/Event
Private Dining Room	—	32	$ 50
Garden	100	60	100
Sun Porch	65	44	100
Sun Porch & Garden	150	100	100
Entire Restaurant	250	200	500

The entire restaurant can be reserved on Saturdays between 11am and 4pm. Other time frames are available by special arrangement. The minimum food and beverage cost is $6,000. The minimum food and beverage requirement for the private dining room is $600 at lunch or brunch, and $1,000 at dinner. Minimums for the private dining room in the month of December are $750 at lunch and $1,500 at dinner. The minimum food and beverage requirements for the patio and sun porch vary depending on the day of the week. A deposit of 50% of the food and beverage minimum is due when reservations are confirmed. The balance is due the day of the function. Tax and an 18% gratuity are additional.

CANCELLATION POLICY: 50% of the deposit is refundable with 30 days' written notice.

AVAILABILITY: Year-round, everyday, anytime. Closed Christmas eve and day, and New Year's day.

SERVICES/AMENITIES:

Restaurant Services: yes

Catering: provided, no BYO

Kitchen Facilities: n/a

Tables & Chairs: provided

Linens, Silver, etc.: provided

Restrooms: wca

Dance Floor: yes

Bride's Dressing Area: CBA

Parking: large lot

Overnight Accommodations: no

Telephone: pay phone

Outdoor Night Lighting: yes

Outdoor Cooking Facilities: BBQs

Cleanup: provided

Other: in-house pastry chef

RESTRICTIONS:

Alcohol: provided, corkage $10/bottle

Smoking: bar and patio only

Music: amplified w/approval

Wheelchair Access: yes

Insurance: not required

Mill Valley

THE MILL VALLEY OUTDOOR ART CLUB

1 West Blithedale
Mill Valley, CA
(415) 383-2582
Reserve: 12 months in advance

The Outdoor Art Club, located in downtown Mill Valley, is one of Marin's favorite event spots. You enter through a wooden arch into a restful garden patio that immediately removes you from the bustle of every-day life. Centered in the large patio is a sprawling grand oak that provides a canopy, allowing dappled light to filter through. The flowers and other landscaping add to the serenity of this outdoor space. The clubhouse, designed in 1904 by Bernard Maybeck, displays his trademark peaked roof line. Inside, the main hall is spacious and majestic with a very high ceiling of dark exposed beams. Windows across the south side lighten the room and can be opened to admit breezes. There's a large stage at one end of the clubhouse for a dance band and a smaller room, running the full length of the clubhouse, which is perfect for a lavish buffet. There's no question why the Outdoor Art Club is so popular—this is a great place.

CAPACITY: The facility can hold up to 200 standing or 120 seated guests. The Sun Room holds an additional 40 seated guests.

FEES & DEPOSITS: A refundable deposit of 50% of the rental fee is required to reserve a date. A security deposit of $500 is also required and is refunded after the keys are returned. The Club's rental fee is $1,200. The remaining 50% is due 10 days before your function.

CANCELLATION POLICY: The deposit is refunded only if the date can be rebooked.

AVAILABILITY: Weekends 8am–1am. Weekdays are negotiable.

SERVICES/AMENITIES:

Restaurant Services: no

Catering: BYO

Kitchen Facilities: ample

Tables & Chairs: most provided

Linens, Silver, etc.: some provided

Restrooms: wca

Dance Floor: yes

Bride's Dressing Area: yes

Parking: street only

Overnight Accommodations: no

Telephone: pay phone

Outdoor Night Lighting: yes

Outdoor Cooking Facilities: no

Cleanup: caterer

Other: caretaker provided

RESTRICTIONS:

Alcohol: BYO

Smoking: allowed

Music: amplified until midnight, indoors only

Wheelchair Access: yes

Insurance: not required

Need a caterer, cake maker, florist? The Service Directory starting on page 412 features the best in the business.

MOUNTAIN HOME INN

810 Panoramic Highway
Mill Valley, CA 94941
(415) 381-9000
Reserve: 1–6 months in advance

Perched on the eastern slope of Mt. Tamalpais is a modern wooden structure with spectacular views of Marin, San Francisco Bay and Mt. Diablo. The decor in the main dining room is simple, but elegant. Furnishings and rugs are in muted pastels and a large stone fireplace enhances a feeling of cozy intimacy. The Mountain Home Inn also features a bar area which is light and airy with high ceilings adorned with natural redwood tree trunks. Nearby is a large deck that takes full advantage of the panoramic views below. An additional dining room downstairs uses mirrors to draw the light through double glass doors off the neighboring deck. For a redwood tree and blue sky ceremony, try the Honeymoon Suite's deck, which is conveniently located near the downstairs dining area.

CAPACITY:	*Area*	*Season*	*Standing*	*Seated*
	Upper & Lower Floor and Deck	March–Oct	110	40–110
	Upper & Lower Floor	Oct–March	80	80
	Lower Floor	—	40	35

FEES & DEPOSITS: A non-refundable deposit in the amount of your rental fee is required to secure your date. The Upper & Lower Floor rental rate is $1,500. The Lower Floor rental fee is $250. The rate for each of the 10 guestrooms ranges from $112–178/night. Food service is provided. Food costs run $20/person for hors d'oeuvres or light meals, $25–35/person for buffets and seated meals. Bar service, sales tax and 15% gratuity are added to the final bill. The Honeymoon Suite is $178/night.

AVAILABILITY: Everyday, from 11:30am–4pm and 5:30–11pm.

SERVICES/AMENITIES:

Restaurant Services: yes
Catering: provided, no BYO
Kitchen Facilities: n/a
Tables & Chairs: provided
Linens, Silver, etc.: provided
Restrooms: wca
Dance Floor: yes

Parking: easy evenings, difficult weekend days
Overnight Accommodations: 10 guestrooms
Telephone: pay phone
Outdoor Night Lighting: yes
Outdoor Cooking Facilities: no
Cleanup: provided
Bride's Dressing Area: CBA, extra charge

RESTRICTIONS:

Alcohol: provided, WBC only, corkage $8/bottle
Wheelchair Access: yes
Smoking: allowed

Music: amplified until 11pm
Insurance: not required

Ross

MARIN ART AND GARDEN CENTER
Caroline Livermore Room

30 Sir Francis Drake Blvd.
Ross, CA 94957
(415) 454-1301
Reserve: 1–2 months in advance

The Caroline Livermore Room is located in a rustic building set way back into the lovely ten acres of the Marin Art and Garden Center. Just off Sir Francis Drake Blvd. in Ross, this special indoor-outdoor space is perfectly suited for wedding events. The indoor space has a large party room with multiple glass doors opening out onto the deck and stone patio. The adjacent outdoor gravel and paved areas are surrounded by large trees and flowers which provide spots of color. This facility, a favorite among Marin residents because of its park-like setting, attracts groups from all over the Bay Area.

CAPACITY: This facility can accommodate 225 standing or 130 seated guests. In combination with the outdoor areas, it can hold up to 500 guests.

FEES & DEPOSITS: For special events, a $300 non-refundable deposit is required to secure your date and fees vary depending on season and guest count. Fees must be received 10 days prior to your event.

Number of Guests	Winter Fee	Spring/Summer Fee
50-75	$550	$650
75-300	—	850
301-400	—	1,000
401–500	—	1,200

AVAILABILITY: Year-round. Wintertime indoor functions: Friday eves, Saturday and Sunday until 11pm. Spring/Summer outdoor events: weekends until dusk.

SERVICES/AMENITIES:

Restaurant Services: no
Catering: BYO, must be licensed
Kitchen Facilities: ample
Tables & Chairs: provided
Linens, Silver, etc.: caterer
Restrooms: wca
Dance Floor: yes
Bride's Dressing Area: yes

Parking: large lot
Overnight Accommodations: no
Telephone: pay phone
Outdoor Night Lighting: yes
Outdoor Cooking Facilities: no
Cleanup: caterer
Other: security guard

RESTRICTIONS:

Alcohol: BYO, caterer must serve
Smoking: allowed
Music: inside only

Wheelchair Access: yes
Insurance: liability required
Other: no rice, birdseed only

MARIN ART AND GARDEN CENTER
Ross Garden Restaurant

30 Sir Francis Drake Blvd.
Ross, CA 94957
(415) 457-2151
Reserve: 2 weeks–6 months in advance

Within the Marin Art and Garden Center located in lovely residential Ross, is the Ross Garden Restaurant. Parties may take place indoors or on the spacious patio which has umbrella-shaded tables for balmy al fresco dining. Converted from a 1930s home and set off from the rest of the garden complex, the restaurant derives its secluded, woodsy ambiance from the surrounding canopy of trees and the adjacent ten acres of beautiful gardens, where you can have your private ceremony. Consequently, it's a wonderful place for a relaxed, comfortable outdoor function, especially during spring, summer and fall. In wintertime, enjoy the fireplace indoors.

CAPACITY: The restaurant and garden patio can accommodate 150 guests spring through fall. The private dining room can hold 75 guests year-round.

FEES & DEPOSITS: The $500 rental fee is the deposit required to secure your date for a 4-hour function. Limited overtime is available for an extra fee. Other fees include a security guard fee of $75 for outdoor functions and $75 for use of the ceremony site and dressing room. Hors d'oeuvres run $18/person. The Elegant Buffet is $20/person; the Grand Buffet, $21/person. Tax and 15% gratuity are additional. The event balance is payable by the end of the function.

CANCELLATION POLICY: The deposit is non-refundable unless the space can be rebooked.

AVAILABILITY: For outdoor functions, weekdays, 4pm to dusk; Saturdays and Sundays, anytime to dusk. Indoor events after 4pm everyday. The restaurant is closed two weeks over the Christmas holiday.

SERVICES/AMENITIES:
Restaurant Services: yes
Catering: provided, no BYO
Kitchen Facilities: n/a
Tables & Chairs: provided
Linens, Silver, etc.: provided
Restrooms: wca
Dance Floor: patio
Other: special events director

Parking: large, shared lot
Overnight Accommodations: no
Telephone: pay phone
Outdoor Night Lighting: no
Outdoor Cooking Facilities: no
Cleanup: provided
Bride's Dressing Area: yes

RESTRICTIONS:
Alcohol: provided, WBC only, corkage $7/bottle
Smoking: allowed
Music: amplified restricted

Wheelchair Access: ramp
Insurance: not required

San Rafael

DOMINICAN COLLEGE

50 Acacia Avenue
San Rafael, CA 94901
(415) 485-3228
Reserve: 6–12 months in advance

This facility is situated in a quiet residential area of San Rafael, on an 80-acre wooded campus developed at the turn of the century. For an outdoor affair, the Anne Hathaway Garden provides a lovely lawn, ringed with roses and other annuals, which can be equipped with a dance floor or decorated with night lighting. Housed in a modern building nearby, the Shield and Creekside Rooms offer spaces for smaller parties. Also located on campus is Meadowlands, a grand, three-story Victorian structure that has been meticulously maintained. Broad steps lead up to a sunny veranda, and the massive front door seems a threshold into another era. Spacious and inviting, the interior entry hall and dining room feature polished wood paneling and patterned ceilings. Downstairs you'll see the dance hall and stage alcove lit by brilliant sunlight coming through stained glass windows. The Meadowlands can accommodate a very large group by offering variety—the veranda and grounds for sun, the main floor for quiet dining and conversation and the downstairs for lively dancing.

CAPACITY, FEES & DEPOSITS: The full rental fee is the deposit required to secure your date.

Area	Standing	Seated	Rental Fee
Meadowlands	250	150	$800
Anne Hathaway Garden	200+	100	220
Shield Room	500	300	650–750
Creekside Room	100	50–75	220–380

CANCELLATION POLICY: With 90 days' notice, you'll receive a full refund.

AVAILABILITY: Meadowlands: Mid-May to mid-June. Anne Hathaway Garden: weekends only. The Creekside Room is available anytime; however, the Shield Room has restricted hours.

SERVICES/AMENITIES:

Restaurant Services: no

Catering: select from preferred list

Telephone: pay phone

Kitchen Facilities: varies

Tables & Chairs: some provided

Linens, Silver, etc.: through caterer

Restrooms: wca

Dance Floor: yes or CBA

Parking: large lot, on street

Overnight Accommodations: summer only

Outdoor Night Lighting: CBA

Outdoor Cooking Facilities: BBQ CBA

Cleanup: caterer

Bride's Dressing Area: CBA

Other: baby grand piano

RESTRICTIONS:

Alcohol: BYO, permit required
Smoking: allowed
Music: Shield Room only

Wheelchair Access: mostly yes
Insurance: certificate required
Other: no ceremonies

FALKIRK MANSION

1408 Mission Street
San Rafael, CA 94901
(415) 485-3328
Reserve: 3–5 months in advance

Magnificent oaks and colorful magnolias frame the historic Falkirk Mansion, a lovely Queen Anne Victorian built in 1888, nestled on eleven acres in the heart of San Rafael. You can take your vows on the sprawling lawns outdoors or inside Falkirk. Spacious foyer, parlor and dining room lend themselves beautifully to wedding receptions. The interior's redwood paneling, ornate mantelpieces, shiny hardwood floors and elegant wall coverings are noteworthy. The dining area has a huge fireplace and floor-to-ceiling stained glass windows overlooking the deck. Curving around two sides of the Mansion is a wide veranda, great for dancing and casual dining, bordered by colorfully planted flower boxes. Located on the hill above City Hall, this century-old Victorian mansion has a charm and intimacy along with a central location to be found nowhere else in Marin.

CAPACITY: October–April, standing capacity is 85; seated capacity 50–60 guests. April–October, the house and veranda up to 125 guests.

FEES & DEPOSITS: A non-refundable deposit of 50% of the rental fee is required to reserve your date. Weekends, from October 15–April 15, there is a $90/hour rental fee for a 6-hour minimum block; $135/hour overtime. From April 16–October 14, the fee is $115/hour for a 6-hour minimum (weekends only); $165/hour overtime. A refundable $500 security deposit and any remaining balance are payable 45 days in advance of your event. Weekday rates vary; call for more information.

AVAILABILITY: Year-round. Saturdays from 1pm–11pm, Sundays all day. Weedays 9am–11pm by arrangement.

SERVICES/AMENITIES:

Restaurant Services: no
Catering: select from approved list
Kitchen Facilities: minimal
Tables & Chairs: CBA, extra charge for chairs
Linens, Silver, etc.: BYO
Restrooms: wca
Dance Floor: yes

Parking: large lot
Overnight Accommodations: no
Telephone: pay phone
Outdoor Night Lighting: CBA
Outdoor Cooking Facilities: no
Cleanup: caterer
Bride's Dressing Area: yes, extra charge

RESTRICTIONS:

Alcohol: BYO
Smoking: outside only
Music: amplified to 90 decibels

Wheelchair Access: yes
Insurance: extra liability required
Other: no candles, decorations restricted

FORTY TWENTY CIVIC CENTER DRIVE
The Event Center

4020 Civic Center Dr.
San Rafael, CA 94903
(415) 507-1000
Reserve: 1–3 months in advance

The Marin Association of Realtors now offers a new site for Marin wedding celebrations. Four rooms in their new facilities have been completely remodeled for events. These spaces are clean, light and, a novelty in this county, air conditioned. The decor is uncluttered and contemporary. The larger space, designed in shades of gray, has a movable stage, a large dance floor, recessed lighting and wall-to-wall carpeting. This attractive room is flexible, breaking down into three different-sized spaces, depending on your guest count. Windows lining the west-facing wall look out onto a small, landscaped side yard. In the corner of the building is the Garden Room. This space, with its high tongue-in-groove ceiling, wood rafters and pleasantly patterned gray ceramic tile floors, has a more open feel. Afternoon light streams in through large windows and glass doors that lead to a well-landscaped patio area surrounded by high stucco walls. The facility also has a nice dressing room set up for brides. Overall, this is a clean, well-lighted place for wedding receptions, with ample space, great kitchen facilities and a friendly, accommodating staff.

CAPACITY: Indoors, 300 seated guests; 500 for a standing reception. The Garden Room and adjoining patio can each accommodate 75 seated.

FEES & DEPOSITS: A refundable $200 deposit, which is applied towards the rental fee, is required to secure your date. The fee is $700 for the entire facility for 4 hours; $100/hour for each additional hour. A refundable $200 damage/cleaning deposit is payable, along with the rental fee, at least 30 days prior to the function.

CANCELLATION POLICY: With 30 days' notice, the deposit is returned.

AVAILABILITY: Year-round, any day, anytime.

SERVICES/AMENITIES:

Restaurant Services: no
Catering: BYO
Kitchen Facilities: ample
Tables & Chairs: provided
Linens, Silver, etc.: BYO

Parking: large lot
Overnight Accommodations: no
Telephone: pay phone
Outdoor Night Lighting: no
Outdoor Cooking Facilities: no

Restrooms: wca
Bride's Dressing Area: yes

RESTRICTIONS:
Alcohol: BYO, licensed server
Smoking: outside only
Insurance: proof of liability

Cleanup: renter or caterer
Dance Floor: yes

Wheelchair Access: yes
Music: amplified ok
Other: decorations restricted

FOSTER HALL
At Marin Academy

1600 Mission Avenue
San Rafael, CA 94901
(415) 258-9211   Debra
Reserve: 3–6 months in advance

Rejoice. If you've despaired of finding a site for over 200 guests in Marin, here is a new spot that can handle both ceremonies and sizable receptions. Set back from Mission Avenue by a large circular lawn and drive, stately neoclassic Foster Hall is now available for private functions. This historic building on the Marin Academy campus has a combination of spaces for seated receptions. You can set up a wedding arch and take your vows on the lawn in front of Foster Hall. Afterward, guests can repair to the two-story structure for celebrations. A long veranda with tables and umbrellas is great for outdoor functions, and several sets of French doors connect the veranda to interior rooms. The entry hall has a unique, geometric parquet floor and features a grand staircase with a handsome bannister railing. The color scheme indoors is in eye-pleasing tan and cream, and each event space has multi-paned windows overlooking landscaped grounds. Although unadorned, Foster Hall has some fine architectural details that make it a great spot for receptions. When this building is "dressed up", it can look positively sensational.

CAPACITY: Foster Hall can hold up to 250 seated guests, 500 guests for a standing reception. The front lawn can seat 200 for a ceremony.

FEES & DEPOSITS: A $250 deposit, which is applied towards the rental fee, is required when you book this facility. The rental fee is $250 for the largest event space or $450 for the entire building. A $500 refundable security/cleaning deposit plus 90% of the anticipated food and beverage total is due 1 week prior to the event. The balance is due the day of the event. Tax and a 15% service charge are additional. Food service is provided by All Seasons Party Productions who will customize any menu depending on your needs and budget.

CANCELLATION POLICY: With 90 days' notice, your deposit will be refunded.

AVAILABILITY: Year-round. Evenings from 5pm–2am, Saturday and Sunday anytime until 2am. June 10 through September 3, anytime.

SERVICES/AMENITIES:

Restaurant Services: no
Catering: provided, no BYO
Kitchen Facilities: n/a
Tables & Chairs: provided
Linens, Silver, etc.: provided
Restrooms: wca
Dance Floor: yes

Parking: ample
Overnight Accommodations: no
Telephone: pay phone
Outdoor Night Lighting: yes
Outdoor Cooking Facilities: CBA
Cleanup: provided
Bride's Dressing Area: yes

RESTRICTIONS:

Alcohol: provided, corkage $5/bottle
Smoking: outside only
Music: amplified ok indoors

Wheelchair Access: yes
Insurance: not required

MARIN BEACH AND TENNIS CLUB

250 Point San Pedro Road
San Rafael, CA 94901
(415) 258-9211
Reserve: 1–2 months in advance

Set on the water's edge, this small post and beam wood structure overlooks the Bay, the colorful boats berthed nearby and the Club's own athletic facilities. From the Marin Beach and Tennis Club's wide decks, which encircle the entire second floor, you can see San Francisco, all three bridges and Marin's waterfront. Parties and receptions are held in the Club Room, upstairs. Contemporary in style, it's been recently refurbished with new furnishings, paint and carpet. Floor-to-ceiling glass windows and doors keep it bright and airy during the day. At night, you can see the glittering lights from afar. A wood-burning fireplace warms the room on cool, winter evenings, and during the rest of the year, the decks are perfect for relaxing, sipping champagne and conversing with friends. Outdoors, you can seat guests around the pool, which has fabulous views of the Bay, or you can tent the adjacent tennis courts for much larger functions.

CAPACITY: The Club Room holds 60–75 for a seated function or 100–125 for a standing reception. During summer months, 175 standing guests. If you tent a tennis court, it can hold up to 250 seated, 500 standing guests.

FEES & DEPOSITS: A refundable $250 security/cleaning deposit and a $250 rental fee are due when reservations are made. 90% of the estimated catering total is due 7 days before the event. The balance is due at the conclusion of the event. Per person rates start at $15 for buffets and $20 for seated dinners. Tax, beverage and 15% service charge are additional. Please call for costs regarding tennis court tenting.

CANCELLATION POLICY: With 30 days' notice, the deposit and rental fee will be refunded.

AVAILABILITY: Year-round, everyday from 4pm–1am. Earlier hours by special arrangement.

SERVICES/AMENITIES:

Restaurant Services: no

Catering: provided

Kitchen Facilities: n/a

Tables & Chairs: some provided, some CBA

Linens, Silver, etc.: CBA

Restrooms: no wca

Bride's Dressing Area: yes

Other: event coordination

Parking: ample

Overnight Accommodations: no

Telephone: emergency only

Outdoor Night Lighting: access only

Outdoor Cooking Facilities: BBQ

Cleanup: renter or caterer

Dance Floor: yes

RESTRICTIONS:

Alcohol: provided, corkage $4/bottle

Smoking: allowed

Insurance: required

Wheelchair Access: no

Music: amplified ok

SAN RAFAEL
IMPROVEMENT CLUB

Corner of 5th and H Streets
San Rafael, CA 94901
(415) 459-9955
Reserve: 2 weeks–6 months in advance

The San Rafael Improvement Club is one of the few structures remaining from the 1914 San Francisco Pan Pacific Exhibition. The building, designed by William B. Faville, was brought over to San Rafael in 1915 and purchased by the Improvement Club. It's now an historic landmark, ensconced in a small garden setting with an adjacent brick patio. Its interior is sophisticated and attractive, accented with scalloped pillars, large windows and a sculpted ceiling. Light and airy, this facility is great for parties of any kind.

CAPACITY: The Club can hold up to 160 for a buffet or 125 seated guests.

FEES & DEPOSITS: A $200 refundable security deposit is required to reserve a date. On weekends, the rental fee is $350. The rental fee for luncheons during the week is $225, evening events $275. The final rental balance is due 10 days prior to the event along with an insurance certificate.

CANCELLATION POLICY: The deposit for weekend events is fully refundable with 60 days' notice October–April, 90 days' notice May–September.

AVAILABILITY: Weekends, 10am–midnight. During the week, 8am–midnight. Thursdays and Fridays from 10am–5pm are not available for bookings.

SERVICES/AMENITIES:

Restaurant Services: no

Parking: lot and street

Catering: BYO
Kitchen Facilities: minimal
Tables & Chairs: provided
Linens, Silver, etc.: BYO
Restrooms: wca
Dance Floor: yes

RESTRICTIONS:
Alcohol: BYO
Smoking: not allowed
Music: amplified until 10pm

Overnight Accommodations: no
Telephone: pay phone
Outdoor Night Lighting: yes
Outdoor Cooking Facilities: no
Cleanup: caterer
Bride's Dressing Area: yes

Wheelchair Access: yes
Insurance: liability required
Other: decorations restricted, no candles

Sausalito

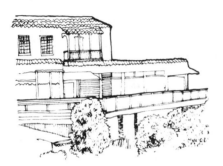

THE ALTA MIRA

125 Bulkley Avenue
Sausalito, CA 94965
(415) 332-1350
Reserve: 2 weeks–6 months in advance

The Alta Mira is one of Marin's oldest and most renowned hotels. The property was originally the residence of Thomas Jackson, who later converted his villa into a hotel. After the original structure was lost in a fire, Jackson's son rebuilt the Alta Mira as a Spanish-style villa. The main dining room has a huge deck, reminiscent of the Riviera with its round tables and bright umbrellas. The deck also has one of the most spectacular panoramic views of the San Francisco skyline, Sausalito Harbor and Angel Island. It's understandably a very popular spot for private gatherings. The main dining area is relaxed but elegant, highlighted with leaded glass mirrors and floral designs. A private dining room called the Fiesta Room has high ceilings, chandeliers and a gorgeous fireplace with hand-painted tiles displaying a country garden. Large mirrors extend the open, sunny feeling of this beautiful room and the adjoining deck has a lovely view of the San Francisco skyline. Outdoors, the Garden Terrace, with its surrounding flowers and bay view, provides a romantic setting for ceremonies and receptions. Rooms at the hotel are available, including a suite in an adjacent Victorian house that includes sitting room, kitchen and deck.

CAPACITY: The Annex Dining Room and Deck can hold 200 standing guests and 150 seated. There is a 130-guest minimum requirement for this space. The Fiesta Room can accommodate 110 for a buffet and 100 seated guests, with a 35-guest minimum. The Outdoor Patio seats 150, and the Garden Terrace accommodates 150 seated and 200 standing.

FEES & DEPOSITS: For special events, a $500 refundable deposit is required to reserve a date and is applied towards the food and beverage bill. For a luncheon or dinner, there is no rental fee. 50% of the anticipated total is due 30 days prior to your function and the balance is due the day of the event. Food service is provided. Hors d'oeuvres/receptions average $35–45/person and seated meals $30–45/person, including bar service. Tax and 15% gratuity will be added to the final bill.

CANCELLATION POLICY: If you give notice 6 months in advance, your deposit will be returned.

AVAILABILITY: The Annex and Deck are available Saturdays, 2:30pm–6:30pm, and Sundays, 5pm–10pm. The Fiesta Room is available anytime during the week, noon–5pm and 6:30pm–11pm Saturday, and 4pm–10pm Sunday. The Garden Terrace is available in conjunction with one of the other event spaces for a $300 fee.

SERVICES/AMENITIES:

Restaurant Services: yes

Catering: provided, no BYO

Kitchen Facilities: n/a

Tables & Chairs: provided

Linens, Silver, etc.: provided

Restrooms: limited wca

Dance Floor: yes

Bride's Dressing Area: CBA

Parking: valet CBA, on street

Overnight Accommodations: 29 guestrooms

Telephone: pay phone

Outdoor Night Lighting: patio only

Outdoor Cooking Facilities: no

Cleanup: provided

Special: event planning services

RESTRICTIONS:

Alcohol: provided, corkage $10/bottle

Smoking: allowed

Music: no amplified

Wheelchair Access: limited, entry CBA

Insurance: sometimes required

CASA MADRONA HOTEL AND RESTAURANT

801 Bridgeway
Sausalito, CA 94965
(415) 322-0311 or **(415) 332-0350**
Reserve: 1–12 months in advance

Located in the hills of Sausalito, Casa Madrona Hotel and Restaurant are a haven of comfort and retreat. Built in 1885, the original Victorian mansion has been expanded to include three cottages and the New Casa—sixteen uniquely decorated rooms set into the hillside. The result is a grand establishment that offers a variety of services and settings. Casa Madrona Restaurant has a dramatic, glass-enclosed terrace, with retractable sliding glass roof and walls that create an open, outdoor feeling. It is situated high on a hill and has spectacular views. Below the Restaurant is a 1300 square foot outdoor tiled terrace. Views of Angel and Belvedere Islands, Sausalito Harbor, the Bay Bridge and San Francisco skyline are unsurpassed. Villa Madrona Suite is a unique location for smaller receptions. Its three verandas overlook the San Francisco Bay, and two private terraces and a fireplace add to the homey atmosphere. This room, like all others, shows meticulous attention to detail.

CAPACITY:	*Seated*	*Standing*	*Facility Fee*	*5-Hour Availability*
Restaurant	100	140	$850	12–5pm or 5–10pm*
Villa Madrona Suite	26	60	300	3–10pm
Lower Terrace**	40	120	100	open

* call for more information on evening receptions   *** for ceremonies*

FEES & DEPOSITS: A $750 deposit is required when you make reservations, 80% of the anticipated event total (including the deposit) is due 1 month prior to the event, and the balance is payable on the day of the event. The average per person food cost including beverage is $40 (the beverage charge is based on consumption). Reduced rates are offered November through February.

CANCELLATION POLICY: Your deposit will be refunded in full with at least 120 days' written notice.

AVAILABILITY: Year-round, everyday.

SERVICES/AMENITIES:

Restaurant Services: yes
Catering: provided, no BYO
Kitchen Facilities: n/a
Tables & Chairs: provided
Linens, Silver, etc.: provided
Restrooms: no wca
Dance Floor: yes

Parking: lot, valet for overnight hotel guests only
Overnight Accommodations: 34 rooms
Telephone: pay phone, house phone, guest phones
Outdoor Night Lighting: access only
Outdoor Cooking Facilities: no
Cleanup: provided
Bride's Dressing Area: yes

RESTRICTIONS:

Alcohol: provided, corkage $10/bottle
Smoking: in designated areas
Music: amplified ok

Wheelchair Access: no
Insurance: not required

Need a caterer, cake maker, florist? The Service Directory starting on page 412 features the best in the business.

SAUSALITO WOMAN'S CLUB

120 Central Ave.
Sausalito, CA 94965
(415) 332-0354
Reserve: 2–6 months in advance

This Sausalito landmark is a classic, craftsman-style Julia Morgan building nestled in the hills overlooking the Bay. Since its dedication as a woman's club in 1918, it has been a preferred place for weddings and receptions through the years. The structure is clad in brown shingles and is designed with simple and understated detailing. The large auditorium room has a stage, original fixtures, hardwood floor and large paned windows, perfect for receptions. Multiple doors open onto a small brick patio sheltered by mature oaks. The landscaping is well-maintained and the canopy of trees surrounding the Woman's Club filters glimpses of the Bay beyond. Unpretentious yet stately, this structure fits into the hillside landscape perfectly. It's a bit hard to find, but worth the exploratory trip into the always interesting and visually stimulating Sausalito hills.

CAPACITY: The Club can hold 125–150 for weddings, 150–175 for a sit-down meal; 200 for auditorium-style activities.

FEES & DEPOSITS: For weekend events, a refundable $500 deposit is due when the rental contract is submitted. The rental fee is $825 for 48 hours for Friday, Saturday and Sunday. For weekday events the deposit is $275 and the rental fee is $300 for 12 hours. The rental balance is due 10 days prior to the function.

CANCELLATION POLICY: The deposit is refunded with 6 months' notice.

AVAILABILITY: Year-round, everyday until midnight except Thursdays.

SERVICES/AMENITIES:

Restaurant Services: no

Catering: BYO

Kitchen Facilities: setup only

Tables & Chairs: provided

Linens, Silver, etc.: BYO

Restrooms: wca

Dance Floor: yes

Parking: street, shuttle encouraged

Overnight Accommodations: no

Telephone: house phone

Outdoor Night Lighting: no

Outdoor Cooking Facilities: no

Cleanup: caterer or renter

Bride's Dressing Area: yes

RESTRICTIONS:

Alcohol: BYO

Smoking: outside only

Music: acoustical only, until 10pm

Wheelchair Access: limited

Insurance: certificate required

Other: decorations restricted

Stinson Beach

STINSON BEACH 'CREEKSIDE' COMMUNITY CENTER & CHURCH

32 Belvedere Ave.
Stinson Beach, CA 94970
(415) 868-1444
Reserve: 2–6 months in advance

Looking for a special spot near the ocean? Here's one you'd never know about unless you went looking for it. Situated alongside a meandering creek and in front of coastal foothills is the Stinson Beach Community Center and Church. Sitting next to each other, they are on a quiet, residential side street away from the bustle of town activities. The Community Center is a modest one-story, with a sloping shake roof and a wide porch. In spring, the oaks in front of the building are covered with long, delicate white flowers which hang in such profusion, you can hardly see the Center's entry. Inside is a large, open space with a vaulted wood beam ceiling, hardwood floor, working stone fireplace and large windows overlooking a creekside patio. For receptions, the outdoor area is lovely. The patio borders the creek (actually the confluence of two bubbling creeks) and makes a delightful space for al fresco dining. An added feature is a huge maple tree which creates a shaded, leafy canopy overhead. For ceremonies, the Church is just a step away and a minister is also available. Both Center and Church offer a casual, warm and friendly environment for weddings and receptions.

CAPACITY:	_Area_	_Seated_	_Standing/Reception_
	Community Center	150	300
	Center with Patio Space	200	400
	Community Church	110	—

FEES & DEPOSITS: For special events, a partially refundable $175 security/cleaning deposit is required 60 days prior to the function. The rental fee is $450 plus $100 for full use of the kitchen, payable 1 week in advance of the event. The fee covers a block from 7am–1am. The Church rents for $100/day.

CANCELLATION POLICY: The deposit is refundable. If you cancel, 50% of the rental fees will be returned.

AVAILABILITY: Year-round, everyday from 7am–1am except 1 week in mid July.

SERVICES/AMENITIES:

Restaurant Services: no
Catering: BYO
Kitchen Facilities: new, fully equipped

Parking: Center's pkg area & on street
Overnight Accommodations: no
Telephone: emergency only

Tables & Chairs: some provided
Linens, Silver, etc.: some provided
Restrooms: wca
Dance Floor: yes
Other: some event coordination, grand piano, minister

RESTRICTIONS:
Alcohol: BYO
Smoking: outside only
Insurance: certificate required

Outdoor Night Lighting: access only
Outdoor Cooking Facilities: BBQ
Cleanup: caterer or renter
Bride's Dressing Area: yes

Wheelchair Access: yes
Music: amplified ok

Tiburon

CORINTHIAN YACHT CLUB

End of Main Street
Tiburon, CA 94920
(415) 435-4771
Reserve: 2–12 months in advance

Reminiscent of a ship captain's parlor, the Corinthian Yacht Club Ballroom is a spacious room that is popular for receptions, business luncheons and banquets. It features wood paneling with hardwood floors plus high ceilings which are draped with nautical flags and lit by two chandeliers made from wooden ship wheels. There is an enormous stone fireplace, above which soars a majestic bronze eagle. Adjacent is a glass-enclosed solarium with a fantastic view of the Tiburon Harbor and San Francisco Bay. When there's a full moon, this panoramic view is absolutely breathtaking (not to mention romantic). Downstairs, the newly remodeled main dining room is also available for parties. The neighboring deck overlooks the picturesque marina and has a similar, sensational view of the harbor and Bay.

CAPACITY: The Ballroom can accommodate up to 400 guests. The Main Dining Room can hold up to 135.

FEES & DEPOSITS: A refundable deposit (ranging from $800–1800 depending on the space and date booked) is applied towards the total cost and is required at the time of booking. The rental fee for the Ballroom starts at $800 and can exceed $2,000, depending on the day of rental. The Dining Room fee varies between $4.50 and 6.50/person. These fees are for a 5-hour maximum rental. 80% of the anticipated total is due two weeks prior to the event, and the balance is payable at the conclusion of the event.

Food service is provided. For wedding receptions, per person prices range from $20 to $45. A $400 minimum for bar service is required; an open bar usually costs $14–20/person. Tax and 17% gratuity are added to the final bill. Note that rental discounts of up to 50% are available Monday–Friday for events.

CANCELLATION POLICY: With 90 days' advance notice in writing, you will receive a full refund. Less than 90 days, the deposit is forfeited.

AVAILABILITY: The Ballroom is available everyday from 7am–midnight. The Dining Room, Monday–Thursday, from 7am–midnight.

SERVICES/AMENITIES:

Restaurant Services: yes
Catering: provided, no BYO
Kitchen Facilities: n/a
Tables & Chairs: provided
Linens, Silver, etc.: provided
Restrooms: limited wca downstairs
Dance Floor: yes
Other: church setup ok

Parking: public lot nearby
Overnight Accommodations: no
Telephone: pay phone
Outdoor Night Lighting: yes
Outdoor Cooking Facilities: no
Cleanup: provided
Bride's Dressing Area: limited

RESTRICTIONS:

Alcohol: provided, BYO possible
Smoking: on decks only
Music: amplified restricted

Wheelchair Access: downstairs only
Insurance: not required
Other: security required

GUAYMAS

5 Main Street
Tiburon, CA 94920
(415) 435-6300
Reserve: 2–4 weeks in advance

Guaymas features authentic regional Mexican cuisine in a truly spectacular location. Set at the edge of the Tiburon Harbor, the restaurant has a sweeping view of the Marin hills and San Francisco, as well as the local boats docked a stone's throw from the dining room. The restaurant has a festive ambiance: vibrantly colored hand-cut paper flags hang from wooden beams and flutter in the breeze; displays of tropical fruit and whimsical Mexican artwork decorate walls and counters. Rough hewn chairs and tables covered with sun gold tablecloths and pink napkins add zest. And in winter, a huge adobe fireplace warms the semi-private area in the Main Dining Room. The real attraction, however, is the Arriba (upstairs) Deck—a glorious place for a prenuptial dinner or reception. Bordered by sky and water, this patio is open to sun, stars and sea breezes. Geranium-filled planters provide color and greenery, and a wind shield and heaters keep guests comfortable. The Private Dining Room is perfect for smaller rehearsal dinners. It overlooks the deck and features a large decorative fireplace, and glass doors which reveal the same wonderful vistas shared by the rest of the restaurant. It's easy to understand why people come from all over to dine and celebrate at Guaymas.

CAPACITY:

Area	Seated	Standing
Main Dining Room	55	—
Private Dining Room	28	40
Arriba Deck	100	150

FEES & DEPOSITS: Rental fees are $100 for the Private Dining Room and $500 for the Arriba Deck. A deposit may be required to hold your date. The rental fee and deposit are due at the time of booking. Per person food service costs are: $15–24 for luncheons, $18–30 for dinners and $15–25 for buffets. Beverages, tax and a 16% gratuity are additional.

CANCELLATION POLICY: The rental fee and deposit are refundable with 2 weeks notice.

AVAILABILITY: Everyday except Christmas and Thanksgiving.

SERVICES/AMENITIES:

Restaurant Services: yes
Catering: provided, no BYO
Kitchen Facilities: n/a
Tables & Chairs: provided
Linens, Silver, etc.: provided
Restrooms: wca
Dance Floor: no

Parking: validated M–F, 11:30am–4pm
Overnight Accommodations: no
Telephone: pay phone
Outdoor Night Lighting: deck only
Outdoor Cooking Facilities: no
Cleanup: provided

RESTRICTIONS:

Alcohol: provided, $8/bottle corkage, WC
Music: allowed with restrictions
Insurance: not required

Wheelchair Access: main dining level only
Smoking: allowed

THE LYFORD HOUSE

376 Greenwood Beach Road
Tiburon, CA 94920
(415) 388-2524
Reserve: 6–12 months in advance

Perhaps inspired by their 1876 visit to the Philadelphia Centennial Exposition, Benjamin and Hilarita Lyford built their Victorian home in Tiburon shortly afterwards. Lyford's interior boasts a circular staircase and bannister of African mahogany. The two downstairs rooms are graced with antiques, chandeliers and historic photographs while the upstairs has a dressing room and restroom for bridal party use. The highly-detailed yellow house is distinctive, with a unique tower and ornate finials of carved urns, floral trim and clusters of flowers. A large brick terrace facing the Bay is encircled by a low, wrought iron fence and enchanting flower garden. Lyford House's best feature is the magnificent view of San Francisco Bay and Belvedere Island.

CAPACITY: The House plus outdoor terrace can hold up to 125 guests.

FEES & DEPOSITS: A non-refundable $400 deposit is required to hold your reservation. A $200 security deposit is due 60 days prior to your party. For both indoor and outdoor use of the facility from 9am–5pm or 11am–7pm, the fee is $900. Overtime will be charged at $100/hour.

CANCELLATION POLICY: If you give 3 months' notice and the date can be rebooked, your deposit will be partially refunded.

AVAILABILITY: Saturdays and Sundays, May 1st–October 15th, 9am–5pm or 11–7pm.

SERVICES/AMENITIES:

Restaurant Services: no
Catering: select from list
Kitchen Facilities: minimal
Tables & Chairs: some provided
Linens, Silver, etc.: BYO
Restrooms: wca
Dance Floor: no

Parking: on s treet
Overnight Accommodations: no
Telephone: emergency only
Outdoor Night Lighting: no
Outdoor Cooking Facilities: no
Cleanup: caterer
Bride's Dressing Area: yes

RESTRICTIONS:

Alcohol: BYO, WBC only
Smoking: outside only
Music: no amplified

Wheelchair Access: yes
Insurance: not required
Other: decorations restricted

OLD ST. HILARY'S

Esperanza Road via Beach Road
Tiburon, CA 94920
(415) 435-1853 Landmarks Society
Reserve: 1–6 months in advance

If you'd like to have your ceremony in a very special place, reserve Old St. Hilary's in Tiburon. This is a simple deconsecrated chapel (built in 1888)—one of the few examples of "carpenter's Gothic" style in California to survive in its original condition. It's situated atop a knoll overlooking the Tiburon hills, Angel Island and the Golden Gate. The site is protected as a rare wildflower preserve. The small white clapboard building with high peaked roof has interior walls of natural redwood, a ceiling of Douglas fir, oak pews and is lit with replicas of the original oil-burning chandeliers. The only original stained-glass window, above the door, depicts St. Hilary, patron saint of scholars; the other side windows are Gothic arches of amber glass. Take your vows in an uncluttered space that embraces you with a sense of peace and tranquility.

CAPACITY: Total occupancy, 125. Oak pews are stationary. No standing room.

FEES & DEPOSITS: To reserve Old St. Hilary's, a $100 deposit is required. The rental fee is $520, which includes rehearsal, setup and ceremony time. A refundable security deposit is $250. All fees are payable 45 days prior to the ceremony.

CANCELLATION POLICY: With 45 days' notice, there is a full refund, less a $50 administrative fee.

AVAILABILITY: Year-round, any day or evening, except Wednesday and Sunday afternoons from April through October.

SERVICES/AMENITIES:

Restaurant Services: no
Catering: not allowed
Kitchen Facilities: n/a
Tables & Chairs: stationary oak pews
Linens, Silver, etc.: n/a
Restrooms: no wca
Bride's Dressing Area: yes
Dance Floor: no dancing

Parking: limited to 5 cars, shuttle required
Overnight Accommodations: no
Telephone: house phone
Outdoor Night Lighting: access only
Outdoor Cooking Facilities: no
Cleanup: renter
Other: piano and organ available

RESTRICTIONS:

Alcohol: not allowed
Smoking: no smoking indoors nor outdoors
Music: acoustical inside only

Wheelchair Access: yes
Insurance: proof of personal liability coverage
Other: no food/beverages indoors nor outdoors, no rice, seeds, grains nor confetti

Bodega Bay

BAY HILL MANSION

3919 Bay Hill Road
Bodega Bay, CA 94923
(800) 526-5927 or **(707) 875-3577**
Reserve: 2–3 months in advance

This contemporary Queen Anne Victorian bed and breakfast sits up high, overlooking a sweeping panorama of Bodega Bay, its sand dunes and marinas. The main rooms are spacious and inviting, warmed by abundant natural light, comfortable furniture and a lovely fireplace. Marble and hardwood floors, high ceilings and soft colors create an elegant interior. All of the guestrooms have ocean views and fresh flowers from the surrounding hills. Whether you're planning a small ceremony or reception, the Bay Hill Mansion will provide a serene and intimate setting.

CAPACITY: The facility has a maximum capacity of 50.

FEES & DEPOSITS: The entire facility must be reserved, and a $500 deposit is due at the time of booking. The balance is due on arrival. In-house catering runs from $15 to $30 per person.

CANCELLATION POLICY: A full refund will be given with 1 month's notice. With less than a month's notice, the deposit is forfeit unless the inn is rebooked.

AVAILABILITY: Year-round, everyday.

SERVICES/AMENITIES:
Restaurant Services: no
Catering: provided or BYO
Kitchen Facilities: ample
Tables & Chairs: provided to 48
Linens, Silver, etc.: provided to 48
Restrooms: wca
Dance Floor: living room or deck
Bride's Dressing Area: yes

Parking: off street
Overnight Accommodations: 6 guestrooms
Telephone: common area
Outdoor Night Lighting: yes
Outdoor Cooking Facilities: yes, extra fee
Cleanup: caterer
Special Services: massage room
Other: full wedding coordination, in-house cakes

RESTRICTIONS:
Alcohol: corkage $50 for all wine service
Smoking: outside or designated areas only
Music: approval required

Wheelchair Access: limited
Insurance: not required

Cazadero

TIMBERHILL RANCH

35755 Hauser Bridge Road
Cazadero, CA 95421
(707) 847-3258
Reserve: 4–6 months in advance

Timberhill Ranch is a little like Shangri-la—a place steeped in beauty and harmony, far removed from the rest of the world. Set on a sunlit ridge, surrounded by high meadows and towering redwoods, Timberhill is an oasis of tranquility, perfect for small ceremonies or receptions. The Main Lodge provides an intimate yet open space for private celebrations. Floor-to-ceiling windows and skylights bring the outdoors in and the warmth of a parquet floor, wood and stone fireplace, exposed beams and comfortable seating invite wedding guests to relax and stay a while. Fifteen private cottages work a similar magic: each has its own fireplace, private deck and tiled bath and is fragrant with scents of cedar and fresh flowers. Add tennis courts, a swimming pool, a jacuzzi and exceptional cuisine and you have a resort that is, perhaps, the ultimate escape.

CAPACITY: The Dining Room and Main Room in the Lodge can accommodate 40 people. This number is negotiable depending on the function.

FEES & DEPOSITS: Use of the facility is only available to overnight guests. Rates for accommodations are $350 per couple/double occupancy on weekends, and $296 per couple/double occupancy on weekdays. Fees include breakfast and dinner. There are special policies for holidays. A one night deposit is required at the time of booking and the balance is due 45 days prior to arrival.

CANCELLATION POLICY: With 30 days' written notice, a full refund less a 5% processing fee is given. With less notice, a full refund less a 10% processing fee is given only if the accommodations are rebooked.

AVAILABILITY: Everyday except 2 weeks in January.

SERVICES/AMENITIES:

Restaurant Services: yes
Catering: provided, no BYO
Kitchen Facilities: n/a
Tables & Chairs: provided
Linens, Silver, etc.: provided
Restrooms: wca
Dance Floor: CBA

Parking: off street
Overnight Accommodations: 15 cottages
Telephone: house phone
Outdoor Night Lighting: minimal
Outdoor Cooking Facilities: no
Cleanup: provided
Bride's Dressing Area: guestroom

RESTRICTIONS:

Alcohol: BW provided, BYO in cottages only
Smoking: designated areas only
Insurance: not required

Wheelchair Access: limited
Music: with approval

Fort Bragg

MENDOCINO COAST BOTANICAL GARDENS

18220 N. Highway 1
Fort Bragg, CA 95437
(707) 964-4352
Reserve: 2–3 months in advance

It's hard to believe that a garden as spectacular as this exists a mere 500 feet from the highway. When you walk through the entrance, a seemingly endless landscape of colorful and varied plants unfolds before you. Meandering paths take you past plant species from all over the world—the Mediterranean, South Africa, Australia and more! Nestled between the pine forest and the main garden is the Meadow Lawn, a lovely, semi-private clearing surrounded by trees, bushes and flowers. On a sunny day the setting is just right for a small reception or an intimate ceremony. With 47 acres of garden and pine forest to explore, this is a one-of-a-kind event location.

CAPACITY: The Meadow Lawn accommodates 30.

FEES & DEPOSITS: Fees for ceremonies and receptions are in flux. Call for current rates.

CANCELLATION POLICY: A full refund will be given with 30 days' notice.

AVAILABILITY: Everyday except Thanksgiving, Christmas, and the second Saturday in September. Hours are 9am–5pm, March–October; 9am–4pm, November–February. The rainy season is mid-October through mid-March.

SERVICES/AMENITIES:

Restaurant Services: yes
Catering: BYO
Kitchen Facilities: no
Tables & Chairs: BYO
Linens, Silver, etc.: BYO
Restrooms: wca
Dance Floor: no

Parking: lot
Overnight Accommodations: no
Telephone: pay phone
Outdoor Night Lighting: no
Outdoor Cooking Facilities: no
Cleanup: renter or caterer
Bride's Dressing Area: no

RESTRICTIONS:

Alcohol: BYO
Smoking: designated areas only
Music: no power available

Wheelchair Access: yes
Insurance: required
Other: no vehicle access to site; 500-foot walk from lot

SHORELINE PROPERTIES

18300 Old Coast Highway
Fort Bragg, CA 95437
(707) 964-1444 or **(800) 942-8288**
Reserve: 2–3 months in advance

If you have ever wanted to experience the ocean as part of your wedding event, Shoreline Properties has what you have been looking for. Most of their homes are less than 100 feet from the water's edge! Each home is unique and the majority have decks, barbecues, hot tubs, fireplaces and panoramic views of the coast. Your wedding group of family and friends can rent one or more homes (usually just a short walk from one another) depending on the size of the group. The Mendocino coast offers unlimited quiet, privacy and salt air along with a wide variety of activities: hiking, horseback riding, fishing, canoeing and of course, whale watching. Whether you're planning a relaxed ceremony out on the cliffs or an overnight reception retreat, Shoreline Properties can arrange facilities to meet all your special needs.

CAPACITY: There are approximately 25 properties which range in capacity from 2–15 guests.

FEES & DEPOSITS: Houses rent for $110–275/night with significant discounts for week-long stays. A deposit is due within 10 days of contract receipt. The balance along with bed tax, cleaning fee and refundable security deposit are due at least 3 weeks prior to arrival. Call for exact fees.

CANCELLATION POLICY: A full refund is given within 7 days of making the reservation. With 2 weeks' notice prior to the event date, the charge is 50% of all rental fees. With less than 2 weeks' notice, no refund.

AVAILABILITY: Everyday.

SERVICES/AMENITIES:

Restaurant Services: no
Catering: BYO
Kitchen Facilities: adequate
Tables & Chairs: provided
Linens, Silver, etc.: provided
Restrooms: some wca
Dance Floor: no
Cleanup: caterer

Parking: off street
Overnight Accommodations: yes, varies
Telephone: house phone
Outdoor Night Lighting: varies
Outdoor Cooking Facilities: yes
Cleanup: provided
Bride's Dressing Area: CBA
Special: full event coordination

RESTRICTIONS:

Alcohol: BYO
Smoking: designated areas only
Wheelchair Access: yes
Music: with approval

Insurance: required
Other: children under 12, smoking & pets allowed in some homes, not in others

Jenner

MURPHY'S JENNER INN

10400 Coast Highway 1
Jenner, CA 95450
(707) 865-2377
Reserve: 3–6 months in advance

Jenner by the Sea is surrounded by fifteen miles of sandy beaches, the ocean and hundreds of acres of state park. And, if you're planning a small ceremony or reception, the Inn can address all your needs. It's conveniently located right off of the coastal highway, has its own restaurant and offers a variety of overnight accommodations. The Salon, with fireplace, antiques and cut flowers, has a Victorian coastal charm, suitable for wedding parties. The Solarium, an attractive, fully landscaped 2,000 square foot greenhouse with spectacular views of the coast, is also available. Note that the Inn is an ideal location for a romantic honeymoon featuring numerous guestrooms and cottages that have hot tubs, fireplaces and ocean views.

CAPACITY: The Salon holds up to 45 guests; the Solarium, up to 90 guests.

FEES & DEPOSITS: A deposit of 50% of the rental fee is due when reservations are confirmed and the balance is payable the day of the event. The Salon rents for $100/hour up to $300. The Solarium fee is $200–300 depending on guest count. Catering fees run approximately $15–25/person for hors d'oeuvres, seated dinners or buffets. The wedding coordination fee is 20% of the reception cost. For overnight stays, rooms are available. Call for specific rates.

CANCELLATION POLICY: A full refund is given with 45 days' notice. With less notice, the refund depends on whether the spaces can be rebooked.

AVAILABILITY: Everyday.

SERVICES/AMENITIES:
Restaurant Services: yes
Catering: provided or BYO if entire inn rented
Kitchen Facilities: ample
Tables & Chairs: provided
Linens, Silver, etc.: provided
Restrooms: no wca
Dance Floor: yes
Other: interdenominational minister, wedding coordination

Parking: on and off street
Overnight Accommodations: 11 rooms, several rental homes
Telephone: pay phone
Outdoor Night Lighting: CBA for fee
Outdoor Cooking Facilities: CBA for fee
Cleanup: caterer
Bride's Dressing Area: in solarium

RESTRICTIONS:
Alcohol: provided, corkage $5/bottle
Smoking: outside only
Music: no restrictions if entire inn rented

Wheelchair Access: limited
Insurance: not required

Little River

INN AT SCHOOLHOUSE CREEK

7051 N. Highway 1
Little River, CA 95456
(707) 937-5525 Linda Wilson
Reserve: 2–6 months in advance

Once part of a large coastal ranch, the Inn has offered lodging to visitors since the 1930s. Quaint cottages built at the turn of the century are surrounded by tall cypress trees and gardens. White picket fences add old-fashioned charm. Most of the rooms and cottages have ocean views and fireplaces. The main inn building, known as the old Ledford home, was built in 1862 and offers an intimate and romantic space for small weddings and receptions. Redwood walls and ceilings, wide-plank fir floors, a brick fireplace and baby grand piano create a warm, homey ambiance. The dining room has views of the sea and the adjacent forest. Wedding ceremonies can be performed on the grounds amidst the gardens, in the meadow with the forest as backdrop or indoors by the fireplace.

CAPACITY: The Inn's main building accommodates 50 standing or 20 seated guests; outdoors, an additional 50 guests. Maximum overnight capacity is 36 guests.

FEES & DEPOSITS: A deposit of one night's stay is due at the time of booking and the balance is due on arrival. Use of the main building for ceremonies or receptions usually requires rental of the entire Inn. Fees vary depending on the use of the facilities and whether food is included with the event. Per person catering costs run about $7–20 for lunch and $15–25 for dinner.

CANCELLATION POLICY: A full refund less a $10 cancellation fee is given for cancellations with more than 3 days' notice; 30 days' notice is required if the entire Inn is reserved. Refunds will be made if rooms are rebooked.

AVAILABILITY: Everyday.

SERVICES/AMENITIES:

Restaurant Services: yes
Catering: provided or BYO licensed
Kitchen Facilities: ample
Tables & Chairs: provided
Linens, Silver, etc.: provided
Restrooms: no wca
Dance Floor: no

Parking: off street
Overnight Accommodations: 6 cottages, 7 rooms
Telephone: house phone
Outdoor Night Lighting: no
Outdoor Cooking Facilities: no
Cleanup: provided
Bride's Dressing Area: yes

RESTRICTIONS:

Alcohol: provided, BWC only
Smoking: designated areas only
Music: amplified ok if entire inn rented

Wheelchair Access: no
Insurance: not required

RACHEL'S INN

8200 N. Highway 1
Little River, CA 95456
(707) 937-0088 Rachel Binah
Reserve: 3 months in advance

The first thing you notice when you drive up to the Inn is the old-fashioned garden. Rachel has a way with flowers—they blossom wildly, creating a tapestry of color all around the grounds. Inside, the Inn is fresh and tasteful. The fireplace in the dining room, piano in the parlor and newly-cut flowers everywhere are the kinds of touches that make guests feel right at home. The space in the Inn is also very flexible and can be arranged to accommodate any of your special event needs.

CAPACITY: The facility accommodates 30 seated or 125 standing guests. The Inn can hold up to 24 overnight guests.

FEES & DEPOSITS: Wedding celebrations require a 2-night booking of the entire Inn. A deposit for one night's lodging ($1,170-1,290 depending on guest count) and a 20% deposit for catering are due when reservations are confirmed. Catering starts at $25/person. The balance of all fees is due upon departure.

CANCELLATION POLICY: A full refund is given with 1 month's notice or more. Otherwise a refund is only given if the rooms are rebooked.

AVAILABILITY: Everyday.

SERVICES/AMENITIES:

Restaurant Services: no
Catering: provided, no BYO
Kitchen Facilities: n/a
Tables & Chairs: provided
Linens, Silver, etc.: provided
Restrooms: wca
Dance Floor: no
Other: wedding coordination

Parking: off street
Overnight Accommodations: 9 guestrooms
Telephone: house phone
Outdoor Night Lighting: yes
Outdoor Cooking Facilities: no
Cleanup: provided for a fee
Bride's Dressing Area: guestroom

RESTRICTIONS:

Alcohol: provided, corkage $5/bottle
Smoking: allowed
Music: no amplified

Wheelchair Access: 1st floor only
Insurance: not required

Mendocino

AMES LODGE

42287 Little Lake Road
Mendocino, CA 95460
(707) 937-0811
Reserve: 1–2 months in advance

Located in a secluded forest near Mendocino, this casual, comfortable, family-run lodge is a unique facility for small, private wedding parties. Guests can relax in the main room with its fireplace, stereo, library and piano or gather on the sundeck beneath surrounding redwoods. Nearby trails meander through redwood and pygmy forests or to the river. Only minutes from town and the coast, Ames Lodge provides privacy and intimacy in a truly rustic setting.

CAPACITY: This facility can accommodate day groups of up to 30 guests, overnight up to 18 guests.

FEES & DEPOSITS: You must rent the entire facility. A 2-night deposit for all 7 rooms ($660) is due when reservations are confirmed. The balance is due on arrival. Partial day use rates are $100/day, available in conjunction with overnight use only.

CANCELLATION POLICY: A full refund will be given with 1 month's notice. A sliding fee is imposed on short-notice cancellations.

AVAILABILITY: Everyday except for occasional closures.

SERVICES/AMENITIES:

Restaurant Services: no
Catering: BYO, vegetarian only
Kitchen Facilities: ample
Tables & Chairs: provided
Linens, Silver, etc.: provided
Restrooms: wca
Dance Floor: no

Parking: off street
Overnight Accommodations: 7 guestrooms
Telephone: house phone
Outdoor Night Lighting: limited
Outdoor Cooking Facilities: no
Cleanup: provided except for kitchen
Bride's Dressing Area: guestroom

RESTRICTIONS:

Alcohol: BYO BW, hard alcohol discouraged
Smoking: outside only
Music: no amplified

Wheelchair Access: no
Insurance: not required
Other: no pets, no meat

Need a caterer, cake maker, florist? The Service Directory starting on page 412 features the best in the business.

MENDOCINO HOTEL

45080 Main St.
Mendocino, CA 95460
(800) 548-0513 or **(707) 937-0511**
Reserve: 6–12 months in advance

The Mendocino Hotel occupies a select spot on the village's Main Street—directly overlooking the rugged Mendocino coast. Built in 1878, the hotel was recently remodeled. While the original Victorian style is maintained, with antiques, rich wood detailing and stained glass, guests will appreciate the Hotel's many modern amenities. In the main Hotel, the Garden Room is an unusual place to hold a ceremony or small reception. Once an outdoor patio, it is now enclosed by a translucent ceiling which lets in plenty of light. Plants abound, increasing the sensation of being outside. And the Mendocino Hotel's location couldn't be better—visitors not only have the ocean right across the street, but the entire town with its shops, galleries and distinctive architecture! Also note that the staff aims to please. The Hotel offers a complimentary lunch with site inspection to any couple planning their reception here.

CAPACITY: About 50–80 guests is ideal for wedding functions, although the Hotel can accommodate more. The Garden Room seats 110, maximum.

FEES & DEPOSITS: The Garden Room's fee varies, call for current rates. Catered luncheons run $8–15/person, dinners $15–30/person, hors d'oeuvres start at $5/person and buffets can be arranged. 50% of the estimated cost is due 30 days prior to the event and the balance is due upon departure.

CANCELLATION POLICY: The cancellation policy depends on the number of rooms reserved.

AVAILABILITY: Year-round, everyday.

SERVICES/AMENITIES:

Restaurant Services: yes
Catering: provided, no BYO
Kitchen Facilities: n/a
Tables & Chairs: provided
Linens, Silver, etc.: provided
Restrooms: wca
Dance Floor: yes

Parking: on and off street
Overnight Accommodations: 51 guestrooms
Telephone: guest phones
Outdoor Night Lighting: limited
Outdoor Cooking Facilities: no
Cleanup: provided
Bride's Dressing Area: guestroom

RESTRICTIONS:

Alcohol: provided, no BYO
Smoking: not in Garden Room
Music: with approval

Wheelchair Access: yes
Insurance: not required
Other: wedding coordination

Monte Rio

HUCKLEBERRY SPRINGS

8105 Old Beedle Rd.
Monte Rio, CA 95462
(800) 822-2683 or **(707) 865-2683**
Reserve: 1–12 months in advance

Above the Russian River is Huckleberry Springs, an unusual country inn with accommodations for the entire wedding party or for just the honeymoon couple. With its fresh, regional cuisine and natural hot springs, this retreat facility with five cabins gives guests the advantages of the French auberge and the Japanese ryokan. Located on 56 heavily wooded acres, the inn enjoys spectacular views of the surrounding hills. The main lodge is comfortable and airy, with lots of light from windows and skylights. A new Solarium dining addition is also available for receptions. Ceremonies often take place outdoors, in the redwood groves nearby or on the water garden deck, which also has wonderful vistas. Each cabin is unique in design, but all offer privacy, wood stoves and the soothing, restful feeling that comes from communing in the forest. Huckleberry Springs can arrange rehearsal dinners, formal seated meals and/or wedding buffets, all in-house.

CAPACITY: The facility accommodates 65 guests, maximum.

FEES & DEPOSITS: Day use of the facility and grounds is for a minimum of 4-1/2 hours. For groups under 25, the rate is $450 and for groups of 25–65 (max.) the rate is $550. Additional time is charged at $25 per 15 minutes. Cottages are available at a 10% discount if booked 30 days in advance. A 50% deposit is required at the time of booking, and the balance is due 7 days prior to the event. Catering costs $11–19/person, depending on the menu selection.

CANCELLATION POLICY: Special events require 30 days' notice for a full refund.

AVAILABILITY: Open Wednesday–Sunday; closed Monday & Tuesday. Closed January and February.

SERVICES/AMENITIES:
Restaurant Services: no
Catering: provided, BYO for fee
Kitchen Facilities: ample
Tables & Chairs: provided
Linens, Silver, etc.: provided or BYO
Restrooms: wca, main building only
Dance Floor: pool area or deck

Parking: off street
Overnight Accommodations: 5 cabins
Telephone: house phone
Outdoor Night Lighting: limited
Outdoor Cooking Facilities: BBQ
Cleanup: caterer
Bride's Dressing Area: yes

RESTRICTIONS:
Alcohol: BW provided, no BYO
Smoking: outside only
Music: amplified ok

Wheelchair Access: limited
Insurance: required for day use
Other: no pets

Atherton

HOLBROOK PALMER PARK

150 Watkins Avenue
Atherton, CA 94027
(415) 688-6534
Reserve: 12 months in advance

Holbrook Palmer Park is what's left of an old estate, complete with historic buildings, mature oak trees and an 1870 water tower. Located on Watkins Avenue between El Camino and Middlefield Road, the park consists of 22 acres of open space in exclusive, residential Atherton. The main house rests in the center of the property and has wide, gracious steps that lead from the main reception room down to a spacious patio framed by large trees. The patio and steps are perfect for an outdoor ceremony or seated reception. Nearby is the Jennings Pavilion, a modern structure which can accommodate large events and bands. Outside the Pavilion is another patio which is appropriate for outdoor seated functions. Additionally, the 1896 Carriage House is available for special parties and weddings. Although you might think that a facility in Atherton would require formality, just the opposite is true. The house and Pavilion both lend themselves to outdoor functions on warm days and the feeling here is one of relaxed informality.

CAPACITY: The Main House, with outdoor seating, can accommodate 100 guests; the Jennings Pavilion holds 250 guests including outside seating; the Carriage House seats 85 guests.

FEES & DEPOSITS: A $250 refundable security/damage deposit is required when reservations are made.

Wedding Guests	Resident Fee*	Non-Resident Fee*
1–100	$700	$1,000
101–200	1,200	1,500
201–250	1,600	1,900

Resident refers to a resident of Atherton.

The use fee is required 1 month before the event. Fees are based on a 7-hour use period; 1–2 hours for setup, 4–5 hours for the event, 1 hour for cleanup. For events exceeding 7 hours, a charge of $50/hour charge will apply. Additional hours must be arranged in advance.

CANCELLATION POLICY: With 6 months' notice, the deposit is refunded; with 4–6 months' notice, $200; and 2–3 months' notice, $175 is refunded.

AVAILABILITY: Saturdays 10am–5pm or 5pm–midnight, including setup and cleanup. Sundays, only one event which must end by 9pm. Cleanup must be completed by 10pm.

SERVICES/AMENITIES:

Restaurant Services: no

Catering: BYO or provided

Parking: several lots

Overnight Accommodations: no

Kitchen Facilities: yes
Tables & Chairs: provided
Linens, Silver, etc.: BYO
Restrooms: wca in Pavilion only
Dance Floor: CBA

RESTRICTIONS:
Alcohol: BYO
Smoking: outside only
Music: amplified inside only

Telephone: pay phones
Outdoor Night Lighting: yes
Outdoor Cooking Facilities: BYO
Cleanup: caterer
Bride's & Groom's Dressing Areas: yes

Wheelchair Access: yes
Insurance: included in fees

Belmont

RALSTON HALL

1500 Ralston Avenue
Belmont, CA 94002
(415) 508-3501 ext. 501
Reserve: 12 months in advance

Ralston Hall is a stunning Victorian mansion, completed in 1867 by William Chapman Ralston, founder of the Bank of California. Ralston purchased the land in 1864, and modified the original Italian villa with touches of Steamboat Gothic and Victorian details to create a lavish and opulent estate. The exterior of this three-story mansion is meticulously maintained. The front doors have delicately etched glass panes. Inside, Ralston Hall is an outstanding example of a bygone era. The first floor consists of a large ballroom, several parlors, dining rooms and a sun porch. Each room is decorated with beautiful antiques, stunning crystal chandeliers and elegant oriental rugs. The ballroom is particularly sensational. The patterned hardwood floors are encircled by mirrored walls. Three delicate chandeliers hang gracefully from the huge skylight. At the far end of the ballroom is a large bay window with a curving green moiré bench seat and regal, matching draperies. Musicians can set up in a ballroom alcove without interfering with the grandeur and flow of the ballroom floor. The spacious dining rooms were decorated with an attention to detail that is mind-boggling by today's standards. Because of Ralston Hall's size and layout, you can choose from a variety of setups that include the entire first floor or the West or East wings. This facility is a special and outstanding location for an elegant, sophisticated and memorable wedding.

CAPACITY: The entire facility can accommodate 250 guests. The East Wing, 150 seated guests and the West Wing, 100 guests with partial seating.

FEES & DEPOSITS: A $500 refundable deposit is required when you make reservations. For an 8-hour function:, the rental fees are: the entire first floor $3,600, the East Wing $3,100, the West Wing $1,700. Fees include a security person and 2 hours for setup, 1 hour for cleanup.

CANCELLATION POLICY: If you cancel 120 days prior to your party, your deposit minus a $50 administration fee is refunded.

AVAILABILITY: Ralston Hall is open for events everyday 9am–1am, except Thanksgiving Day, December 24–25th, December 31st and January 1st.

SERVICES/AMENITIES:

Restaurant Services: no

Catering: BYO from approved list

Kitchen Facilities: moderate

Tables & Chairs: CBA, extra charge

Linens, Silver, etc.: BYO

Restrooms: wca

Dance Floor: yes except for West Wing

Bride's Dressing Area: CBA

Parking: ample

Overnight Accommodations: no

Telephone: local calls only

Outdoor Night Lighting: no

Outdoor Cooking Facilities: BBQ

Cleanup: caterer

Other: security available

RESTRICTIONS:

Alcohol: BYO

Smoking: not permitted

Music: amplified ok

Wheelchair Access: limited

Insurance: extra liability required

Other: candles not permitted

Burlingame

KOHL MANSION

2750 Adeline Drive
Burlingame, CA 94010
(415) 591-7422
Reserve: 12 months in advance

Commissioned by C. Frederick Kohl and his wife in 1912, the Kohl Mansion was built on 40 acres of oak woodlands in Burlingame. Kohl, heir to a shipping fortune, loved to entertain and created this grand estate to include manor house, tennis court, pool, greenhouses, rose garden, large carriage house and 150,000- gallon reservoir. The elegant rosebrick Tudor mansion is again available for parties and has many spectacular rooms for events. The wood-paneled Library, with large granite fireplace, bookcases and graceful French doors opening to a center courtyard, ends in a Gothic bay window, which catches the light filtered through the oaks on the lawns outside. The sizeable Great Hall, a copy of the Arlington Tudor Hall in Essex, England, was built for music and entertaining. It has very high ceilings, plus its oak paneling and walnut floors create a fine acoustical setting for music. A lighter twin of the Library, the spacious and airy Dining Room has delicate, pristine white plaster relief on the walls and ceiling. This marvelous dining environment is complete with views of oaks and lawns from bay windows. Guests can roam outdoors, surrounded by a courtyard combination of green lawns, red brick bordered by aggregate and a large terrace. The Kohl Mansion is a perfect facility for those who want a sumptuous wedding in a grand style.

CAPACITY: Indoors, the Mansion can hold 450 standing or 250 seated guests. The indoor facilities plus outdoor tents can hold up to 600 for a reception or 400 seated guests.

FEES & DEPOSITS:

	Saturday and Sunday				*Friday*		
	Guests	Oct–Mar	Apr–Sept		Guests	Oct–Mar	Apr–Sept
Use of the entire house:	80–100	$2,700	$3,000		80–100	$2,400	$2,600
	100–150	2,900	3,200		—	—	—
	151–250	3,400	3,600		150–250	3,000	3,200
	251–350	4,000	4,200		251–350	3,600	3,800
Great Hall & Clock Hall	—	—	—		100–150	2,600	2,800

A $500 security deposit is due when you reserve your date. The final balance is due 30 days in advance of the party. There is also a $12/table setup charge, a $100 fee for rehearsal and $100 fee for use of the baby grand piano. The rental fee for tents is about $1,200, depending on the size.

CANCELLATION POLICY: The deposit, minus $50, will be refunded only if the date can be rebooked.

AVAILABILITY: From Sept–June, parties can be held after 4pm on Fridays and anytime on Saturday and Sunday. June through mid-August, everyday, anytime.

SERVICES/AMENITIES:

Restaurant Services: no
Catering: BYO, select from list
Kitchen Facilities: ample
Tables & Chairs: provided
Linens, Silver, etc.: BYO
Restrooms: wca
Dance Floor: yes

Parking: lot or on street
Overnight Accommodations: no
Telephone: pay phone
Outdoor Night Lighting: limited
Outdoor Cooking Facilities: BBQ
Cleanup: caterer
Other: baby grand piano

RESTRICTIONS:

Alcohol: BYO, bartender required
Smoking: outside only
Music: amplified inside until 10pm

Wheelchair Access: yes
Insurance: certificate required

Hillsborough

THE CROCKER MANSION

6565 Skyline Boulevard
Hillsborough, CA 94010
(415) 348-2272
Reserve: 6–12 months in advance

The Crocker Mansion, a palatial estate designed by the architect of San Francisco's Opera House and City Hall, was built for W.W. Crocker in the 1930s. The large white facade and arches create an atmosphere of permanence and stability. Guests are ushered into the Mansion through impressive wood double doors into a round foyer and second set of double doors leading into the Ballroom. The Ballroom, complete with lofty arched glass doors and fireplace with mantel, is light and airy. A baby grand piano is available for wedding functions. The room has a wide stone balcony with sensational views of the adjacent property which is landscaped with orange and olive trees. The building is bordered by impeccably kept gardens and a serene woodland running 35 acres along Hillsborough's Skyline Ridge. Several areas are especially well suited for outdoor weddings: the wide lawns joined by a winding fieldstone stairway and a cloistered courtyard are graced by manicured hedges and bright flowers. The Italian Renaissance-style mansion, now a private school for children, is a beautiful and versatile event setting for large or small celebrations.

CAPACITY: In summer, the Mansion can accommodate 300 guests using both indoor and outdoor spaces. In winter, 100–150 guests, depending on use.

DONATION: The minimum donation is $2,500 and includes use of the Mansion for one 8-hour event.

AVAILABILITY: Saturday and Sunday only.

SERVICES/AMENITIES:

Restaurant Services: no
Catering: BYO, select from preferred list
Kitchen Facilities: moderate
Tables & Chairs: provided for 150 guests
Linens, Silver, etc.: caterer
Restrooms: no wca
Dance Floor: yes
Bride's Dressing Area: yes

Parking: large lot
Overnight Accommodations: no
Telephone: pay phone
Outdoor Night Lighting: limited
Outdoor Cooking Facilities: CBA
Cleanup: caterer
Other: baby grand piano

RESTRICTIONS:

Alcohol: BYO, service by caterer only
Smoking: outside only
Music: amplified inside, acoustical outside

Wheelchair Access: limited
Insurance: required
Other: no seeds, rice

Menlo Park

ALLIED ARTS GUILD RESTAURANT

75 Arbor Road at Cambridge
Menlo Park, CA 94025
(415) 324-2588
Reserve: 3–12 months in advance

Enclosed by a low adobe wall, the Allied Arts Guild complex of arts and crafts shops and historic structures is hidden away in a quiet, residential neighborhood not far from the Stanford campus. In 1929, Mr. and Mrs. Garfield Merner bought three and a half acres of what was once the vast Rancho de las Pulgas, a Spanish land grant dating back to the 1700s, and developed it into a crafts guild similar to those in Europe. The site retains the original Hispanic ambiance of white adobe walls, red tile roofs and patio courtyards. The grounds are nicely landscaped and meticulously maintained. Wedding receptions are held in the restaurant, which is also of Spanish colonial design. Guests will enjoy strolling in the relaxed setting of the Guild's beautiful gardens, fountains and Spanish objects d'art.

CAPACITY: A minimum of 100 guests is required for buffets and luncheon receptions. Between May 1st and September 30th, the guest maximum is 155; in October the maximum is 100. For hors d'oeuvres receptions, the maximum is 200 guests.

FEES & DEPOSITS: The rental fee is required as a deposit when reservations are confirmed. For receptions, the fee is $500, for ceremonies and receptions the fee is $750. There will be additional charges for special rental requests. Food service for buffets, hors d'oeuvres or seated receptions starts at $21/person. Non-alcoholic beverages only. Sparkling cider service runs $1.25/person. Note that the Restaurant is operated by the Palo Alto Auxiliary solely for the benefit of the Lucile Salter Packard Children's Hospital at Stanford.

CANCELLATION POLICY: With 6 weeks' notice, the rental fees are refundable.

AVAILABILITY: Receptions January 2–October 31st from 11am–4:30pm. No parties on holiday weekends.

SERVICES/AMENITIES:

Restaurant Services: yes
Catering: provided
Kitchen Facilities: n/a
Tables & Chairs: provided
Linens, Silver, etc.: provided
Restrooms: wca available nearby
Dance Floor: yes

Parking: large lots, on street
Overnight Accommodations: no
Telephone: pay phone
Outside Night Lighting: no
Outdoor Cooking Facilities: no
Cleanup: provided
Bride's Dressing Area: yes

Other: wedding coordination, flowers

RESTRICTIONS:

Alcohol: not allowed

Smoking: outside only

Music: amplified within reason

Wheelchair Access: yes

Insurance: not required

LATHAM HOPKINS GATEHOUSE

555 Ravenswood
Menlo Park, CA 94025
(415) 858-3470
Reserve: 3–6 months in advance

The Gatehouse is a Victorian structure that has been tastefully restored to its former splendor. This facility is rather small, and lends itself to more intimate gatherings. With mansard roof and decorative Victorian shingling, the Gatehouse is an attractive reminder of days gone by. The main entrance for functions is at the back of the house, where a circular lawn is ringed by large oaks. Beyond the small lawn is a much larger lawn backdrop, separating the Gatehouse from City Offices. At the lawn's edge is an old-fashioned fountain supported by two Mermen (as opposed to Mermaids), with water spouting out of the mouths of fanciful turtles and lion-like animals. The Gatehouse has a medium-sized wood deck with stairs gracefully cascading down to the lawn. (This is a splendid place for a ceremony.) Its interior is decorated with understated floral wallpaper and attractive appointments. The dining room, living room and kitchen are available for functions. Even though the Latham Hopkins Gatehouse can accommodate only very small parties, it has considerable charm and appeal.

CAPACITY: In the winter, the Gatehouse can accommodate 44 guests including 15 seated. In the summer, the facility can hold up to 100 total for a standing buffet with 45 seated guests using the patio area.

FEES & DEPOSITS: The total rental fee is required as a refundable deposit: $400 cleaning/security deposit plus the $60–72/hour rental fee multiplied by the number of hours anticipated. The cleaning/security deposit is usually returned 2–3 weeks after your event. The rental fee is $60/hour for Menlo Park residents and $72/hour for nonresidents. This fee includes a staff person for your function and applies to a 3-hour block minimum.

CANCELLATION POLICY: If you give more than 2 weeks' notice, the total deposit is refunded less $25.

AVAILABILITY: Monday–Friday 1pm–10pm; Saturday and Sunday, all day to 8pm.

SERVICES/AMENITIES:

Restaurant Services: no

Catering: BYO

Kitchen Facilities: minimal

Parking: on street, lot

Overnight Accommodations: no

Telephone: no

Tables & Chairs: BYO
Linens, Silver, etc.: BYO
Restrooms: no wca
Dance Floor: no

RESTRICTIONS:
Alcohol: BYO, WBC only
Smoking: outside only
Music: no amplified

Outside Night Lighting: limited
Outdoor Cooking Facilities: BBQ
Cleanup: caterer
Bride's Dressing Area: yes

Wheelchair Access: no
Insurance: not required

STANFORD PARK HOTEL

100 El Camino Real
Menlo Park, CA 94025
(415) 322-1234   Rita Hubner
Reserve: 3–12 months in advance

The Stanford Park Hotel, a 1992 Mobil 4-Star property, offers several choice spaces for your celebration. Inside the brass entry doors is a softly lit lobby with an immense brick fireplace and oak staircase. Just past the lobby is a beautiful inner courtyard with old world ambiance that we enthusiastically recommend for outdoor ceremonies and receptions. Although the Stanford Park is located on busy El Camino Real, its tranquil courtyard is completely insulated from the noise of traffic and urban bustle. It is beautifully landscaped, with lots of multi-colored flowers, good-sized trees and handsome, stone benches. The upper courtyard is separated from the larger, lower courtyard by a vine-covered brick wall. Ceremonies are held in the upper level, next to which is a prefunction area from which bridal processionals begin. Permanently seated on a bench in the upper area is a full bronze statue of Benjamin Franklin, a guest at every wedding here. The lovely walkway is bordered by blooming flowers. Free-standing beige canvas umbrellas are available to shade wedding guests in the lower courtyard. Inside the Hotel, the Atherton and Menlo Rooms are popular spaces for small indoor ceremonies, receptions and dinner parties. These pleasant spaces are all designed in a classic style with a contemporary touch. They have high vaulted ceilings, soft muted colors and are furnished with pieces designed specifically for the Stanford Park. And for honeymooners and their guests who'd like to stay overnight, we like the fact that very special room rates are offered to the wedding party.

CAPACITY, FEES & DEPOSITS:

Area	*Seated*	*Standing*	*Reception Fee*	*Ceremony Fee*
Menlo Room	64	80	$100	$400
Atherton Room	64	80	100	400
Woodside Room	130	180	300	n/a
			(includes Foyer)	
The Courtyard	250	250	500	n/a
(Upper & Lower)				
Upper Courtyard Ceremony	150	—	—	400

A non-refundable deposit of $750 is required when reservations are confirmed. 80% of the estimated event total is due 2 weeks prior to the event with the balance payable by the end of the function. For anytime over 4-1/2 hours there will be $100/hour charge. Ceremonies cost $400 for setup. Food service is provided. Per person rates: buffets begin at $35 per person and include champagne toast, cake cutting fee and ice carving. Dinners begin at $30 per person and include champagne toast and cake cutting. Tax and a 17% gratuity are additional.

AVAILABILITY: Year-round, everyday from 9am–midnight. The Courtyard is available May–September, 9am–9pm.

SERVICES/AMENITIES:

Restaurant Services: yes

Catering: provided, no BYO

Kitchen Facilities: n/a

Tables & Chairs: provided

Linens, Silver, etc.: provided

Restrooms: wca

Bride's Dressing Area: yes

Other: wedding coordination

Parking: large lot

Overnight Accommodations: 162 guestrooms

Telephone: pay phones

Outdoor Night Lighting: yes

Outdoor Cooking Facilities: no

Cleanup: provided

Dance Floor: yes, Woodside room

RESTRICTIONS:

Alcohol: provided, corkage $15/bottle, $30/magnum

Smoking: designated areas

Insurance: not required

Wheelchair Access: yes

Music: amplified within reason

Other: no birdseed or rice

Mountain View

RENGSTORFF HOUSE

Shoreline at Mountain View
Mountain View, CA 94039
(415) 903-6088 Events coordinator
Reserve: 3–12 months in advance

Some old homes have such character, historic interest and charm, that concerned citizens rescue them from the wrecking ball at the last minute. Such is the case with Rengstorff House, an Italianate-style Victorian that has received a new lease on life from the City of Mountain View. Purchased by the City, the house was relocated to its current site and completely renovated. A circular walkway leads to the cream-colored home with its widow's walk and green-trimmed windows. The surrounding yard has been well-landscaped. To one side is a pretty brick patio surrounded by hedges and perennials and handsome park benches. An expansive green lawn extending beyond the patio is bordered by a white picket fence; beyond is a fifty-acre saltwater lake. Inside the Rengstorff House there are three front parlors and a dining area downstairs available for your celebration. Each has wainscotted walls, polished oak floors, carved marble fireplaces and stunning Bradbury & Bradbury period reproduction wallpapers. The home has Eastlake furnishings, mixed with some beautiful antique pieces donated by local residents. Original paintings by John Rengstorff decorate the walls. The dining room, running the width of the house, has a brick fireplace with marble hearth, wood wainscoting, walls in burgundy and gold, lovely large Persian rugs on the hardwood floor and two large antique dining tables with matching burgundy upholstered chairs. An elegant rehearsal dinner could be staged here. Although it is situated in an urban environment, the Rengstorff House affords its guests the privacy of the country. It is a sweet location for an afternoon wedding with garden reception.

CAPACITY: Indoors 24 seated guests; 60 for a standing reception. Indoors and outdoors combined, 85 guests maximum.

FEES & DEPOSITS: A refundable deposit of 50% of rental fee is required when reservations are confirmed. The balance plus a $500 refundable security deposit are due 30 days prior to the event. The rental fee Monday–Friday is $300 for a 3-hour minimum, with $100 for each additional hour. Weekend rates: $375 for a 3-hour minimum, with $125 for each additional hour. For a full 8-hour day, the rate is $850.

CANCELLATION POLICY: With 60 days' notice, deposits are refunded, less a $50 fee.

AVAILABILITY: Year-round. Open daily except for Sunday, Tuesday or Wednesday 11am–5pm, when the House is open for public tours.

SERVICES/AMENITIES:

Restaurant Services: no

Catering: BYO

Kitchen Facilities: fully equipped

Tables & Chairs: BYO

Linens, Silver, etc.: BYO

Restrooms: wca

Bride's Dressing Area: yes

Other: wedding referrals

Parking: large lot and special lot

Overnight Accommodations: no

Telephone: pay phone

Outdoor Night Lighting: yes

Outdoor Cooking Facilities: no

Cleanup: renter or caterer

Dance Floor: terraces

RESTRICTIONS:

Alcohol: BYO, BWC only

Smoking: outside only

Insurance: liability required

Wheelchair Access: yes

Music: acoustic only

Other: no red wine, no rice

Need a caterer, cake maker, florist? The Service Directory starting on page 412 features the best in the business.

Palo Alto

THE ELIZABETH F. GAMBLE GARDEN CENTER

1431 Waverley Street
Palo Alto, CA 94301
(415) 329-1356   Patricia Polhemus
Reserve: 1–12 months in advance

The Elizabeth F. Gamble Garden Center is one of the most perfect garden ceremony/reception sites we've seen. Miss Gamble willed the home and its grounds to the City of Palo Alto, which acquired the estate in 1985. The estate is now run by a community horticulture foundation. The main house is a 1902 Colonial/Georgian Revival-style structure built in a lovely, older residential area of Palo Alto. Inside, a dining room, living room and library are available for indoor receptions. Each room has been carefully restored using colorful, turn-of-the-century reproduction wallpapers. Dark, natural wood wainscoting has been returned to its original splendor and there are graceful, molded ceilings and nicely finished oak floors throughout. Each room has its own fireplace. A set of large doors in the Library opens onto a brick porch that leads down to the first of many beautifully landscaped spaces. Behind the main house is the Tea House, constructed in 1948. This small outbuilding has a full kitchen and a brick fireplace. Glass doors along the length of the house open onto a brick patio. Next to the Tea House is the Carriage House, which also has a separate kitchen area adjacent to its large main room. Three large doors open out onto yet another brick patio. As lovely as the buildings are, our favorite parts of this site are the formal and informal gardens—the cumulative work of a full-time horticulturist and 300 volunteers. Each separately landscaped area feels like a private, secret garden: the rose garden with its 100 species of roses, the wisteria garden, the clock golf circle, Victorian grotto—separately or combined—provide elegant settings for small wedding ceremonies and receptions. The Center has succeeded in creating a place of serenity and beauty. We recommend it highly.

CAPACITY: 75-guest maximum.

FEES & DEPOSITS: A $50 non-refundable deposit is required when reservations are confirmed. The rental fee for an 8-hour block of time is $800. The full amount and a $300 cleaning/damage deposit are due 60 days prior to the date reserved. The damage/cleaning deposit is generally refunded within one week following your event.

CANCELLATION POLICY: With 60 days' notice, half the rental fee and security deposit will be refunded.

AVAILABILITY: Year-round, everyday, 9am–10pm.

SERVICES/AMENITIES:

Restaurant Services: no   *Parking:* lot

Catering: BYO
Kitchen Facilities: yes
Tables & Chairs: BYO
Linens, Silver, etc.: BYO
Restrooms: wca
Bride's Dressing Area: yes
Other: piano available for $20 fee

RESTRICTIONS:

Alcohol: BYO WCB
no beer kegs or red wine in main house
Smoking: not allowed
Insurance: required if alcohol served

Overnight Accommodations: no
Telephone: house phone
Outdoor Night Lighting: yes
Outdoor Cooking Facilities: BYO BBQ
Cleanup: renter and/or caterer
Dance Floor: yes

Wheelchair Access: yes
Music: no amplified,
no recorded music
Other: all activities must end at 10pm, no rice or birdseed

GARDEN COURT HOTEL

520 Cowper Street
Palo Alto, CA 94301
(800) 824-9028 or **(415) 322-9000**
Reserve: 4–12 months in advance

Designed as a re-creation of a European village square, this four-story hotel looks more like something you'd see in a Tuscan town than in bustling downtown Palo Alto. Yet it offers one of the few spots on the Peninsula where you can host your wedding and reception and house all your guests at the same location. The Garden Court Hotel provides a warm Mediterranean ambiance combined with modern facilities and top-notch service. All is visually appealing: dark green and white trim contrast against terra cotta-colored walls, potted planters are filled to the brim with colorful annuals and perennials. Built in the shape of a square, the structure encloses an inviting interior courtyard. Guests can relax in the warm sun, sip champagne or sample hors d'oeuvres before repairing to the expansive Courtyard Ballroom for a seated meal. Just like in an Italian village, a multitude of balconies allow guests to watch and enjoy the activities from above. Additional rooms, which can accommodate receptions on the Garden Court's second floor, come with terraces and feature huge, arched windows. One of the benefits of having your celebration here is that the in-house caterer is Il Fornaio, a restaurant renowned for its Northern Italian cuisine. If that weren't enough, an additional plus is that if you have your reception at the Garden Court, you'll be offered a complimentary guestroom for the wedding couple, complete with fireplace or jacuzzi, flower bouquet, champagne and continental breakfast. What more could you ask for?

CAPACITY:	*Room*	*Seated*	*Standing*	*With Dancing*
	Grove Ballroom	175	200	150
	Terrace Room	50	80	—
	Courtyard Ballroom	250	300	225

FEES & DEPOSITS: A $500 non-refundable deposit is due within 2 weeks of booking, which is applied to the event balance. The estimated total is due 2 weeks prior to the event, and any remaining balance is due 30 days after of the event. The rental fee for the Grove Room is $250 Sunday–Friday and Saturday during the day, and $500 Saturday evening. The rental fee for the courtyard is $500. There is no rental fee for the Terrace Room, however there is a guaranteed 30-guest minimum. Meals run $25-35 per person; beverages, tax and 17% service charge are additional. Optional security and coat room attendants are additional.

AVAILABILITY:

	Weekday	*Saturday*	*Sunday*
Terrace Room or Grove Ballroom	6pm–midnight	11:30am–4:30pm 6pm–midnight	10am–midnight
Courtyard Ballroom (any 5 hours)	n/a	10am–8pm	10am–8pm

SERVICES/AMENITIES:

Restaurant Services: yes
Catering: provided, no BYO
Kitchen Facilities: n/a
Tables & Chairs: provided
Linens, Silver, etc.: provided
Restrooms: wca
Dance Floor: yes
Other: complimentary guestroom when event has 75 or more guests

Parking: valet, large lot
Overnight Accommodations: 61 guestrooms
Telephone: pay phones
Outdoor Night Lighting: access only
Outdoor Cooking Facilities: no
Cleanup: provided
Bride's Dressing Area: CBA, extra fee

RESTRICTIONS:

Alcohol: provided, corkage $10/bottle, WC only
Smoking: designated areas
Music: amplified ok

Wheelchair Access: yes
Insurance: not required
Other: no birdseed or rice

MacARTHUR PARK

27 University Ave.
Palo Alto, CA 94301
(415) 321-9990
Reserve: 3–12 months in advance

Although a popular restaurant, MacArthur Park's biggest secret is that it's also a great venue for wedding receptions and intimate rehearsal dinners. The landmark building which houses MacArthur Park was designed in 1918 by renowned architect Julia Morgan, and originally served as a recreation facility for World War I troops. The structure's simple yet handsome design was dictated by a rock-bottom YWCA budget ($1800), and is a fine example of Morgan's ability to combine craftsman style with utilitarian needs. The main dining room has a vaulted ceiling with exposed wood trusses and beams. Details include several balconies and two large brick fireplaces situated at either end of the room. The decor is subdued. Black chairs contrast against white linens; attractive framed artwork graces board and batten walls. Rooms are painted in rich, soothing café au lait colors. The small, but very attractive private dining rooms feature the same warm tones and wall treatments as the main dining room and are well suited for rehearsal dinners. Several sets of French windows are framed by long drapes, gathered and held back by brass knobs. For outdoor functions, take a peek at the enclosed courtyard. An aggregate patio supports white chairs and matching linen-covered tables. Striped fabric shades guests from the sun and heat lamps take the chill off during cooler months or during evening affairs.

CAPACITY: The main dining room holds up to 222 seated guests; with balconies, the total indoor capacity rises to 270. The patio courtyard 90 seated guests or 120 for a standing reception. Lofts hold up to 25 guests, each.

FEES & DEPOSITS: Up to 100 guests, the rental fee is $500; over 100 guests, $750. The rental fee serves as a deposit, and is due when you book reservations. Food service is provided. Seated functions, including food, beverages tax and gratuity run $40–50/person.

CANCELLATION POLICY: With 90 days' notice, your rental deposit is returned less a $100 administration fee.

AVAILABILITY: The entire restaurant is available only on Saturdays from 9am–4:30pm. Private parties in separate spaces are held Sunday–Friday from 11:30am–2am, Saturday from 5pm–2am.

SERVICES/AMENITIES:

Restaurant Services: yes
Catering: provided, no BYO
Kitchen Facilities: n/a
Tables & Chairs: provided
Linens, Silver, etc.: provided
Restrooms: wca
Dance Floor: CBA
Other: some flowers, event coordinator

Parking: valet available, large lot
Overnight Accommodations: no
Telephone: pay phone
Outdoor Night Lighting: yes
Outdoor Cooking Facilities: yes
Cleanup: provided
Bride's Dressing Area: yes

RESTRICTIONS:

Alcohol: provided, corkage $7–10/bottle
Smoking: outside only
Music: amplified ok

Wheelchair Access: yes
Insurance: not required

STANFORD BARN

Corner of Welch and Quarry Roads
Palo Alto, CA 94304
(415) 322-4341
Reserve: 1–12 months in advance

This landmark building has just become the newest spot for wedding receptions on the Peninsula. Built by Leland Stanford in 1888, it's had a long and illustrious past as a working winery, dairy barn and cattlemen's association headquarters. A handsome, three-story brick structure shaded by mature palms and softened by ivy clinging to its walls, it now houses offices, the California Cafe and attractive retail shops. One of the last reminders of a time when Stanford was really a farm, the Barn is a survivor of a bygone era. It stayed intact through the 1906 quake and luckily avoided the wrecking ball during the urban encroachments of the 40s, 50s and 60s. And even though the Stanford Shopping Center, Hospital and University have mushroomed around it, the Barn still stands, its exterior virtually unchanged since it was built. The southwest portion of the ground floor and adjacent wind-protected courtyard are available for wedding events. The main interior room is brightened by French windows, several of which overlook the patio. Dark green shutters and window trim complement the terra cotta color of old bricks walls, and a fifteen-foot ceiling is supported by three wood posts which punctuate an otherwise open and uncluttered space. One set of doors opens onto a landscaped courtyard, perfect for seated ceremonies, outdoor receptions or champagne and hors d'oeuvres. A nearby lawn can also be used for ceremonies. This combination of spaces is the answer for couples who beg us for the perfect Peninsula location: a garden spot with an interior space that can handle a large group when the weather proves uncooperative.

CAPACITY: Inside, up to 200 seated guests, 275 standing. In combination with the courtyard, up to 290 seated, 350 standing guests.

FEES & DEPOSITS: A deposit in the amount of half the rental fee is required to secure your date. The rental fee balance plus a $500 refundable cleaning/security deposit are due 7 days prior to the event. The rental fee for 8-hours use, including setup and cleanup, ranges from $1,000–$2,000, depending on day of week and guest count.

CANCELLATION POLICY: With 30 days' notice the deposit will be returned.

AVAILABILITY: Year-round, daily from 8am–2am.

SERVICES/AMENITIES:

Restaurant Services: CBA
Catering: CBA or BYO
Kitchen Facilities: set up only
Tables & Chairs: CBA or BYO
Linens, Silver, etc.: BYO
Restrooms: wca
Dance Floor: CBA or courtyard

Parking: large lot
Overnight Accommodations: no
Telephone: pay phones
Outdoor Night Lighting: yes
Outdoor Cooking Facilities CBA
Cleanup: caterer or CBA
Bride's Dressing Area: no

RESTRICTIONS:
Alcohol: CBA or BYO
Smoking: outside only
Music: amplified ok

Wheelchair Access: yes
Insurance: not required

Portola Valley

LADERA OAKS

3249 Alpine Road
Portola Valley, CA 94028
(415) 854-3101 Annie
Reserve: 1–12 months in advance

Located off Alpine Road in Portola Valley, the Ladera Oaks' shingled clubhouse and beautifully landscaped grounds provide a really pleasant spot for weddings and receptions. The building's exterior is covered with vines and the courtyard garden between clubhouse and pools has an extremely attractive interior garden, with two-tiered lawn areas surrounded by oak trees, flowering annuals and perennials. Outdoor cermonies are usually held on the steps of the raised brick patio in front of the trellis. The clubhouse Ballroom offers a sizeable space for indoor dining, with hardwood floors and large picture windows overlooking the garden. An adjoining Lounge can be used in conjunction with the Ballroom or separately for smaller gatherings. Private and quiet, this is a great location for indoor/outdoor celebrations.

CAPACITY: The Ballroom can seat 100–150 guests in the daytime, 180 in the evening and, in combination with the garden, 350. Alone, the Courtyard Garden can accommodate 200 seated guests. The Lounge can hold up to 35 seated.

FEES & DEPOSITS: To make a reservation, a partially refundable $500 deposit is required. A 4-hour time block is usually provided for wedding receptions with 2 additional hours for preparation and 1 hour for cleanup.

	Month	*Hours Available*	*Fee*
Mon–Thurs	year-round	7am–6pm	$6/guest ($300 min)
		6pm–10pm	$6/guest ($500 min)
Friday	year-round	7am–6pm	$6/guest ($300 min)
	Jan, Feb, Nov	6pm–1am	$9/guest ($900 min)
	Mar–October	6pm–1am	$9/guest ($1,000 min)
	December	6pm–1am	$9/guest ($1,200 min)
Saturday	Jan, Feb, Nov	7am–1am	$9/guest ($900 min)
	Mar–October	7am–5pm	$9/guest ($1,350 min)
		5pm–7pm	$9/guest ($2,000 min)

	Month	Hours Available	Fee
	December	7am–4pm	$9/guest ($900 min)
	December	4pm–1am	$9/guest ($1,200 min)
Sunday	Jan, Feb, Nov, Dec	7am–10pm	$9/guest ($900 min)
	Mar & Oct	7am–10pm	$9/guest ($1,350 min)
	April–Oct	—	not available

CANCELLATION POLICY: If you cancel within 5 days of making the reservation, 50% of your deposit will be refunded. Thereafter, 50% of the deposit will be refunded only if your date can be rebooked.

AVAILABILITY: Monday–Thursday, 6pm–10pm. Fridays 6pm–1am and Saturdays 7am–1am. Occasional Sundays are available. Call for specific dates and times.

SERVICES/AMENITIES:

Restaurant Services: no

Catering: BYO

Kitchen Facilities: ample

Tables & Chairs: provided

Linens, Silver, etc.: BYO

Restrooms: wca

Dance Floor: yes

Parking: large lots, limited weekdays

Overnight Accommodations: no

Telephone: pay phone

Outdoor Night Lighting: yes

Outdoor Cooking Facilities: BBQ

Cleanup: caterer and club staff

RESTRICTIONS:

Alcohol: BYO

Smoking: allowed

Music: amplified inside only

Wheelchair Access: yes

Insurance: not required

THOMAS FOGARTY WINERY AND VINEYARDS

19501 Skyline Blvd.
Portola Valley, CA 94028
(415) 851-1946
Reserve: 2–12 months in advance

If we were to rate facilities on a scale from 1 to 10, the Fogarty Winery would be deemed a 10! Located off Skyline Boulevard, this has got to be one of the best places we've seen for ceremonies and receptions. Commanding an extraordinary view of the Bay and Peninsula, the Winery sits high on a ridge in a quiet, vineyard setting. A small, lovely pond with circling swans and vineyards all around greet you as you drive in. At the top of the ridge is a large lawn, beautifully landscaped around the perimeter—a perfect spot for an outdoor reception. The building steps down the hill, and is designed with incredible attention to detail, with stone fireplaces, fine woodwork, skylights and lots of decks. The Tasting Room is light and airy, arranged with custom-built 'barrel' tables, handcrafted leather chairs, wood burning stove and full kitchen. In the restroom, there's even a bluegreen slate and stone bath tub! The Hill House is at the lower level. It has a semi-enclosed deck, stone fireplace, wine bar and professional kitchen. This is an exceptionally pleasant environment for a wedding celebration, with wood parquet floors, comfortable seating and windows overlooking the adjacent vineyard and distant Bay. The Tasting Room and Hill House both reflect the ambiance of the surrounding environment with taste and sophistication. We can't recommend it more highly.

CAPACITY: Hill House 200 seated guests, maximum. The Tasting Room and lawn can accommodate 125 guests.

FEES & DEPOSITS: A non-refundable deposit of 50% of the rental fee is due when reservations are confirmed. The balance is payable 4 months prior to your function.

Area	Months	8 hours
Total Facility	April–Nov	$3,250
Tasting Room & Lawn	April–Nov	2,500
Total Facility	Dec–Mar	2,000
Tasting Room & Lawn	Dec–Mar	1,500

AVAILABILITY: Year-round, weekends until 9pm. Closed Thanksgiving, Christmas Day and January 1st.

SERVICES/AMENITIES:

Restaurant Services: no

Catering: must select from preferred list

Kitchen Facilities: fully equipped

Tables & Chairs: some provided

Linens, Silver, etc.: BYO

Restrooms: no wca

Dance Floor: inside Hill House

Parking: large lots or valet

Overnight Accommodations: no

Telephone: pay phone

Outdoor Night Lighting: yes

Outdoor Cooking Facilities: CBA

Cleanup: caterer

Other: audio-visual equipment, event coordination

Special: wine tasting

Bride's Dressing Area: yes

RESTRICTIONS:

Alcohol: WC provided, no BYO

Smoking: outside only

Music: must select band from preferred list

Wheelchair Access: no

Insurance: certificate required

Prices and policies <u>do</u> change. Call each facility and confirm everything you read in Here Comes The Guide.

Redwood City

HOTEL SOFITEL
At Redwood Shores

223 Twin Dolphin Drive
Redwood City, CA 94065
(415) 598-9000
Reserve: 6–12 months in advance

The Hotel Sofitel is special because, unlike most large hotels, this one conveys a sense of warmth and intimacy. It has friendly and experienced staff that make you feel right at home. The Hotel offers lots of reception choices—the author's favorite is Baccarat, a sophisticated restaurant on the premises which overlooks the water. With floor to ceiling bay windows, Baccarat is light and warm. This is a small, intimate space where you can eat at square tables instead of typical six foot rounds. Colors are soft and muted, in creams, pale teals and greens. At one end of the restaurant is the Crystal Room, named for the brilliant Baccarat chandelier suspended from the ceiling. When the etched glass doors are closed, this is a private dining room. Open them and voila, another room for a buffet setup, bar or head table. The small marble-floored foyer leading into Baccarat is perfect for a gift table or guest book signing. Adjacent to Baccarat is La Terrasse, an appealing two-tiered area with great views of the water and the Hotel pool and patio. La Terrasse's floor is sensational—a geometrical woven pattern of black, tan and rose colored rectangles of polished marble. You can elect to have your ceremony here or serve cocktails, champagne and hors d'oeuvres before moving elsewhere for a seated meal. For the adventurous, the outdoor pool and patio can be tented for receptions. If your guest list is large, don't worry. Hotel Sofitel's 6,200 square foot Grand Ballroom can accommodate a sizable crowd. Guests will enter through the impressive marble-floored Hotel Lobby, and head to the Ballroom foyer for prefunction champagne and hors d'oeuvres. Inside, the Grand Ballroom can be left whole or divided in half, depending on the size of your party. All is designed in pastels—soft peach with silver and teal accents. For smaller receptions, wedding showers or rehearsal dinners, use the Grand Salon. To help you relax after the big event, Hotel Sofitel offers a complimentary room for the bride and groom and special group rates for your out-of-town guests.

CAPACITY:	*Room*	*Seated*	*Standing*
	Half Grand Ballroom	180	325
	Grand Ballroom	450	700
	Baccarat Dining Room	85	—
	Pool & Patio Tented	200	400
	La Terrasse	—	150
	Grand Salon	70	125

FEES & DEPOSITS: A non-refundable deposit is due 2 weeks after booking your event. Full payment of the estimated balance is due 5 working days before the function. Any remaining balance is due at the conclusion of your reception. Several wedding packages are available: Bordeaux $48.50/person; Burgundy $63/person and Champagne $79/person. A guaranteed guest count is required 72 hours in advance. A service charge of 17% and tax will apply to the total food and beverage bill. Non-Sofitel wedding cakes can be brought for an additional serving charge of $1.75/person.

CANCELLATION POLICY: With less than 30 days' notice, you will forfeit 75% of the estimated cost of your event.

AVAILABILITY: Weddings in the Grand Ballroom are held 11am–4:30pm or 6pm–1am. If no other receptions are scheduled on the day you have yours, the time frame becomes very flexible. All wedding functions must fit into a 6-hour block. The Baccarat Dining Room is available Saturdays 11–4:30pm and on Sunday evenings from 4pm–midnight. Events elsewhere can be scheduled as available.

SERVICES/AMENITIES:

Restaurant Services: yes
Catering: provided
Kitchen Facilities: n/a
Tables & Chairs: provided
Linens, Silver, etc.: provided
Restrooms: wca
Dance Floor: provided
Other: full wedding coordination

Parking: large lot, valet
Overnight Accommodations: 326 guestrooms
Telephone: pay phones
Outdoor Night Lighting: no
Outdoor Cooking Facilities: no
Cleanup: provided
Bride's Dressing Area: yes

RESTRICTIONS:

Alcohol: provided, corkage $12/bottle
Smoking: designated areas
Music: amplified ok

Wheelchair Access: yes
Insurance: not required
Other: no rice or birdseed

PACIFIC ATHLETIC CLUB
at Redwood Shores

200 Redwood Shores Parkway
Redwood City, CA 94065
(415) 593-9100
Reserve: 4-12 months in advance

You know you're almost there once you see the distinctive, green copper pyramid-shaped roofs of a new 7-acre complex of event spaces, restaurant, pools and athletic courts. Enter the foyer and step onto the tan mosaic flagstone floor. The space soars to thirty-five feet, with huge Douglas fir poles supporting a an enormous skylights. Wedding guests are led to the lounge and reception areas, the latter, an octagon-shaped room with an unusual two-tone floor of Brazilian walnut and cherry hardwoods. There are several mirrored arches, one of which cleverly pushes back to provide a place for a band. Hors d'oeuvres and cocktails are served here before an event, and after a seated meal elsewhere, guests often return to dance. The adjacent Main Dining Room is a large, light-filled room with a sizable skylight and two walls of floor-to-ceiling glass. The other two walls feature pastel-colored landscapes. Four large Douglas fir poles that match those in the foyer, support a very high, vaulted ceiling. Attached to these poles are multi-tiered pinpoint fixtures, making evening functions sparkle. Tables are dressed with crisp white linens overlapping chintz fabric prints. Beyond the glass walls and doors is the garden courtyard, lushly planted and landscaped to accommodate outdoor ceremonies. Nearby is a large pergola, tennis court and croquet lawn. If you'd like to have just an outdoor function on the patio, it can be screened off from the pool; lawn functions can be tented. This is a must-see location for receptions. Be prepared to be impressed—we think that the Pacific Athletic Club is the best new event site on the Peninsula.

CAPACITY:	*Area*	*Seated*	*Standing*	*Area*	*Seated*	*Standing*
	Dining Room	250	600	Outdoor Patio	200	500
	Lounge & Reception	—	250	Lawn Area	600	1,000
	Ceremony Courtyard	75	150			

FEES & DEPOSITS: A $1,000 non-refundable deposit is required to secure your date. The room rental fee is $800-1,500 depending on the day of week reserved, and covers a 5-hour block of time. Half the anticipated food and beverage cost is payable 30 days in advance and the balance, along with a confirmed guest count, are due 72 hours prior to the function. Seated meals start at $21.50/person, not including hors d'oeuvres or beverages. Tax and an 18% service charge are additional. Coat check service is $100 extra.

AVAILABILITY: Year-round, daily. The only time the Dining Room is not available for private functions is Monday-Friday from 11:30am–2pm.

SERVICES/AMENITIES:

Restaurant Services: yes
Catering: provided
Kitchen Facilities: n/a
Tables & Chairs: provided
Linens, Silver, etc.: provided
Restrooms: wca
Dance Floor: yes
Other: full event coordination

Parking: valet available, large lot
Overnight Accommodations: no
Telephone: pay phones
Outdoor Night Lighting: yes
Outdoor Cooking Facilities: yes
Cleanup: provided
Bride's Dressing Area: CBA

RESTRICTIONS:

Alcohol: provided, corkage available
Smoking: designated areas
Music: amplified ok

Wheelchair Access: yes
Insurance: not required
Other: no birdseed, rice or helium balloons

Woodside

GREEN GABLES

Address withheld
Woodside, CA
(415) 952-1110
Reserve: 1–12 months in advance

Green Gables is one of the most exclusive and one of the loveliest private estates we've seen. This 1912 country estate was built by Green and Green, famous architects from the turn of the century who had a talent for fitting man-made elements into the natural environment without destroying it. The property is sizable, with ancient oaks, native grasses and an undisturbed California landscape surrounding an enclave of formal terraced lawns, gardens and pools. All has been designed to take advantage of the panorama of the Woodside hills and spectacular views of the coastal range beyond. When you arrive, you'll come up a series of steps to the mansion's lovely brick terrace, which can be set up with umbrella-shaded tables for champagne and hors d'oeuvres. Very large seated receptions, with or without tents, can be held on the sloping lawns. Guests can wander through the garden, enjoying the colorful profusion of annuals and perennials which contrast nicely against the darker greens of background trees. Standing at one edge of the lawn, you'll be in for a surprise. Look down to an unbelievably beautiful green rectangular reflecting pool which is surrounded by walls and archways of multi-colored stone. Narrow lawns and clay pots filled with white flowers are laid out on either side of the reflecting pool, creating a feeling of order and symmetry while just beyond these man-made features, is an untouched natural landscape of flowering trees, oaks and bays. To be sure, weddings here are the stuff that dreams are made of.

CAPACITY: 1,200 guests, maximum.

FEES & DEPOSITS: A security deposit of $1,000 is payable when reservations are made. The rental fee is $5,000. Half of the rental fee is due 60 days in advance and the balance is payable 1 week prior to the event. Event planning and design can be provided. Any menu or service can be customized for your party. Estimates for catering and other services are developed on a per function basis depending on your budget. The security deposit is usually refunded if the site is left in good condition.

AVAILABILITY: Green Gables is normally available September through May or June. Only one event per day is scheduled.

SERVICES/AMENITIES:

Restaurant Services: no
Catering: provided, no BYO
Kitchen Facilities: n/a
Tables & Chairs: provided by caterer
Linens, Silver, etc.: provided by caterer

Parking: valet CBA, private lot
Overnight Accommodations: no
Telephone: emergency only
Outdoor Night Lighting: CBA
Outdoor Cooking Facilities: CBA

Restrooms: wca
Dance Floor: CBA

RESTRICTIONS:
Alcohol: provided, no BYO
Smoking: outside only
Music: amplified ok

Cleanup: provided by caterer
Bride's Dressing Area: yes

Wheelchair Access: yes
Insurance: required
Other: no birdseed or rice

PULGAS WATER TEMPLE

Canada Drive
Woodside, CA
(415) 872-5900   Joe Naras or Jack O'Shea
Reserve: 6–12 months in advance

Pulgas Water Temple is a lovely, albeit campy, neoclassic remnant of the 30s. Located on Canada Road just off Highway 280, it is situated in San Francisco Water Department's watershed lands, just east of the upper Crystal Springs Reservoir. Here the vegetation is lush and the stillness is broken only by the local songbirds. As you proceed from the parking area along a short wooded path, you come to a large, open field. The setting evokes images of dancing wood nymphs trailing diaphanous scarves, or a Maxfield Parish print. The Temple itself, situated at one end of the field, is a classic Roman style structure, open at the top to the sky. A flight of circular steps leads up to a central array of high columns that surround a large central well. Inside the well is an aqua-tiled area where water, transported from the Hetch Hetchy reservoir, rushes in with a low roar. For outdoor ceremonies only, this is a sensational and dramatic setting. In front of the Temple is a huge reflecting pool flanked on each side by a row of junipers and, at the opposite end, a set of circular stairs leads to a small garden. Isadora Duncan would have felt very much at home here. This is *the* spot in which to have your rites performed (particularly if you have a penchant for the pagan).

CAPACITY: 150 guests

FEES & DEPOSITS: A non-refundable $150 rental fee, which covers a 2-hour period, is payable within two weeks of written confirmation from the water department.

AVAILABILITY: April through October, everyday except for the 1st and 3rd Sundays of each month.

SERVICES/AMENITIES:
Restaurant Services: no
Catering: n/a
Kitchen Facilities: n/a
Tables & Chairs: BYO
Linens, Silver, etc.: BYO
Restrooms: wca
Bride's Dressing Area: no

Parking: lot for 50 cars
Overnight Accommodations: no
Telephone: no
Outdoor Night Lighting: no
Outdoor Cooking Facilities: no
Cleanup: renter
Dance Floor: no

RESTRICTIONS:

Alcohol: not allowed
Smoking: not allowed
Insurance: not required

Wheelchair Access: yes
Music: no amplified
Other: permit required from the San Francisco Water Dept., ceremonies only

Need a caterer, cake maker, florist? The Service Directory starting on page 412 features the best in the business.

Benicia

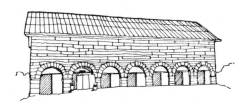

CAMEL BARN MUSEUM

2024 Camel Road
Benicia, CA 94510
(707) 745-5435
Reserve: 1–12 months in advance

Once a military storehouse, the building acquired some distinction in 1864 when 35 camels were housed there pending auction. They stayed for approximately 6 weeks, during which time folks started referring to the place as the Camel Barn. Needless to say, the name stuck. Today, the museum is housed upstairs and celebrations take place on the first floor. The building's interior is cool, with 22"-thick sandstone walls. Down the center of the first floor are a series of graceful arches which support the upper level, and arched windows along the length of one side let in some natural light. White and unadorned, the room lends itself to decoration. Way off the beaten path, the Camel Barn Museum is an interesting and little known part of Benicia's history.

CAPACITY: The Camel Barn can accommodate 154 for banquets, 330 for standing reception.

FEES & DEPOSITS: The rental fee is $400. A refundable deposit of $100 is due when reservations are confirmed and is applied towards the fee. A $200 damage/cleaning deposit plus the rental balance is due 3 weeks before the function.

CANCELLATION POLICY: With 14 days' notice, the deposit will be returned.

AVAILABILITY: Year-round, everyday 8am–1am.

SERVICES/AMENITIES:

Restaurant Services: no
Catering: BYO
Kitchen Facilities: moderate
Tables & Chairs: provided
Linens, Silver, etc.: BYO
Restrooms: wca
Dance Floor: wood floor
Bride's Dressing Area: no

Parking: large lot
Overnight Accommodations: no
Telephone: restricted, emergencies only
Outdoor Night Lighting: access only
Outdoor Cooking Facilities: yes, needs prior approval
Cleanup: caterer or renter
Other: raised platforms

RESTRICTIONS:

Alcohol: BYO, license required
Smoking: outside only
Music: amplified ok

Wheelchair Access: yes
Insurance: not required

CAPTAIN WALSH HOUSE

235 East L Street
Benicia, CA 94510
(707) 747-5653
Reserve: 3–6 months in advance

This is a rare find—a classic Carpenter's Gothic Cottage. Purchased as a derelict relic in 1989, the house has undergone a complete renovation. Selected out of a catalog by General Vallejo in the mid-1800s, it was built in Boston, dismantled, packed in crates and sent around Cape Horn to be finally erected across from Benicia City Hall in 1849. The first occupant was General Vallejo's daughter Epifinia. The second, and most notable occupants were Captain John and Eleanor Walsh. They and their descendants occupied the house through the 1960s. Now revived, the house sports a warm, pale taupe color; its white trim highlights the classic Gothic detailing around the roof edge. Landscaping has been selected so that green and white predominate, except for the multi-colored rose garden in the rear. Under the shade of a large pine, the front drive turns into a quartzite patio, perfect for outdoor receptions and ceremonies. Get ready for a surprise. Although the house exterior is subdued, the architect-designed interior is a fanciful, eclectic blend of old and new. Softwood floors have been painted a glossy white with black faux marble diamonds. The entry foyer features mauve, bird's-eye maple veneer which complements cool gray walls. Mirrors with gold gilt molding, antiques and a stately stair with curved bannister and shining wood treads invite guests in for a closer look. The Grand Parlor has numerous details that capture the eye. Drapes are artistically hung over windows with tie backs, tassels and braids in gold, raspberry and green. Ceiling medallions and rosettes, marble fireplace and gold harp all add to the high level of detail. The adjacent Small Parlor has received similar attention, with Regency-style furniture and panels featuring Gothic Carpenter's wallpaper. No matter where you look, you'll notice custom-designed and hand-painted elements: yellow walls with gray stripes, faux-finished surfaces, gold accents and trim. Epifinia's Room upstairs is the honeymoon suite, complete with claw foot tub and gold plated faucets. The owners deserve a pat on the back for taking on two years of intense, back-breaking work. Their home, the Captain Walsh House, reflects a labor of love.

CAPACITY: Inside, 40 seated guests; 100 for a standing reception. With outdoor spaces, 175 guests maximum.

FEES & DEPOSITS: A non-refundable deposit of $250 is due when reservations are confirmed and a $400 refundable security/cleaning deposit is payable when you send in your contract. The event balance is due 3 weeks prior to the event. The rental fee for 4 hours is $750–1500 based on guest count and day of week. Extra hours are $100/hour.

AVAILABILITY: Year-round, everyday from 10am–10pm.

SERVICES/AMENITIES:

Restaurant Services: no
Catering: preferred list only
Kitchen Facilities: ample
Tables & Chairs: caterer or CBA, extra fee

Dance Floor: outside only
Parking: street
Overnight Accommodations: 4 guestrooms
Outdoor Night Lighting: yes

Linens, Silver, etc.: caterer or CBA, extra fee
Restrooms: wca
Bride's Dressing Area: CBA
Other: wedding coordination & referrals, harpist avail.

Outdoor Cooking Facilities: BBQ CBA
Telephone: house phone
Cleanup: caterer

RESTRICTIONS:

Alcohol: BYO or CBA
Smoking: outside only
Music: amplified restricted, none after 10pm

Wheelchair Access: yes
Insurance: certificate required
Other: no open flames, red wine, rice or confetti indoors

FISCHER-HANLON HOUSE

135 West G. Street
Benicia, CA 94510
(707) 745-3385
Reserve: 2 months in advance

This lovely old Federal-style house is located in the center of historic Benicia, next door to the Capital. Filled with period artifacts and antiques, the house is off limits except for the parlor, which is available for small ceremonies. Outside, the rear brick patio and gardens serve as a setting for festivities. Surrounded by a wide variety of trees, bushes and a garden, the patio has a secluded, intimate quality. Even on warm days, the nearby water cools the local breezes and guests can wander leisurely along the brick paths through the gardens.

CAPACITY: The parlor is limited to a maximum of 20 people; the grounds 100 standing guests or 50 seated.

FEES & DEPOSITS: There is a $25 refundable cleaning deposit due at the time of booking. The parlor and upstairs changing room rent for $50 each. There is a minimum $50 fee for the use of the garden, with an additonal charge of $2 per person over 25 people.

AVAILABILITY: Weekdays 9am–9pm. Weekends, the parlor is unavailable noon–4pm during public tours. However, the gardens are still available.

SERVICES/AMENITIES:

Restaurant Services: no
Catering: BYO
Kitchen Facilities: no
Tables & Chairs: some chairs provided
Linens, Silver, etc.: BYO
Restrooms: no wca
Dance Floor: BYO
Bride's Dressing Area: yes

Parking: on street, limited
Overnight Accommodations: no
Telephone: no
Outdoor Night Lighting: access only
Outdoor Cooking Facilities: no
Cleanup: caterer
Other: vintage carriage CBA

RESTRICTIONS:

Alcohol: BYO
Smoking: outside only
Music: amplified ok, low volume

Wheelchair Access: no
Insurance: not required

Berkeley

THE BANCROFT CLUB

2680 Bancroft Way
Berkeley, CA 94704
(510) 549-1000
Reserve: 2–6 months in advance

Here's a new discovery! The Bancroft Club, located across the street from the University of California and next door to the University Art Museum, is now open to the public for the first time since it was built in 1928. Originally the home of the College Women's Club, it was designed by Walter Steilberg (an associate of Julia Morgan) and is currently a National Register landmark building. An absolute must see is the Club's one-of-a-kind event space. Immediately to the right of the foyer is a large room with three parts, featuring floor-to-ceiling woodwork, Mediterranean detailing, leaded stained glass windows and hardwood floors. The raised stage is suitable for musicians while the recessed middle could be transformed into an intimate dance floor. The other end could be set up for wining and dining. The room is large and the space extremely flexible—you could probably arrange your party in a multitude of ways and still have it work beautifully. The Bancroft Club has recently undergone restoration and it's now perfect for a warm, comfortable reception. This is a small boutique hotel, ideal for housing out-of-town relatives and friends—a real find. If you are looking for an indoor wedding site that is distinctive, has warmth and imparts a sense of history, the Bancroft Club is a wonderful choice.

CAPACITY: The Bancroft Club can hold up to 250 seated guests; 350 for a standing reception.

FEES & DEPOSITS: To secure your date, a deposit in the amount of the rental fee is payable when the contract is submitted. The deposit is applied towards the event total. A refundable $500 security/cleaning deposit is also required. The rental fee averages $400 and varies depending on season and day of week. Half the fee is payable 60 days prior; the balance due 2 weeks before the event.

CANCELLATION POLICY: With 90 days' notice, your deposit will be refunded.

AVAILABILITY: Year-round, everyday beginning Summer 1993.

SERVICES/AMENITIES:

Restaurant Services: yes
Catering: provided, no BYO
Kitchen Facilities: n/a
Tables & Chairs: provided

Overnight Accommodations: 22 guestrooms
Telephone: pay phones
Outdoor Night Lighting: CBA
Outdoor Cooking Facilities: no

Linens, Silver, etc.: provided
Restrooms: wca
Dance Floor: yes
Bride's Dressing Area: CBA

RESTRICTIONS:
Alcohol: provided, corkage fee if BYO
Smoking: not allowed
Music: amplified restricted

Cleanup: provided
Other: event coordinator
Parking: adjacent lot or valet CBA

Wheelchair Access: yes
Insurance: sometimes required
Other: decorations restricted, no rice, birdseed or confetti

BERKELEY CITY CLUB

2315 Durant Avenue
Berkeley, CA 94704
(510) 848-7800
Reserve: 3–6 months in advance

The Berkeley City Club is a sensational landmark building, located just one block from the U.C. Berkeley campus. It's a private social club, designed in 1927 by Julia Morgan in a Venetian-Mediterranean style with inner landscaped courtyards and fountains. The Club includes a 75-foot swimming pool, dining room, bar lounges, conference and reception rooms, many of which are available for celebrations. Throughout, the detailing and craftsmanship are impressive. The Drawing and Patio Rooms are large, gracious rooms with beamed ceilings, fireplaces, wall tapestries, tile floors, oriental carpets and sizeable leaded glass windows. The Ballroom is a large, spacious theater-like space with stage, parquet floor and leaded glass windows. A wonderful outdoor spot on a warm day for a party, the Terrace is an appealing reception area that has a terra cotta-colored canopy overhead. Berkeley campus and downtown life bustles all around the City Club, yet it remains a quiet, old-world haven of comfort.

CAPACITY, FEES & DEPOSITS: A $500 non-refundable deposit is required when the reservations are confirmed and is applied toward the rental fee.

Room	Ceremony	Reception	Seated	Fees
Drawing Room	130	80	60	$200
Patio Room	60	30	20	200
Drawing Rm, Patio & Courtyard	—	125 total	—	500
Courtyard	60	30	25	100
Loggia Court	—	—	12	50–75
Ballroom	300	275	250	300
Venetian Room	—	50	—	100
Ballroom & Venetian Rooms	—	325 total	300	400
The Terrace	150	120	100	200
Julia Morgan Room *(for rehearsal dinners)*	—	—	40	100

All fees cover a 4-hour rental period. An additional flat fee of $500 is applied to Sunday and holiday-weekend events. The balance and a final guest count are due 10 days prior to the function. For a separate bar setup, there's a $100 bartender fee. Food service is provided. Per person rates are: hors d'oeuvres buffet $18, seated luncheons $9.50–15.50, dinner buffets $23–27, luncheon buffets $14–18 and seated dinners by arrangement. If your group would like to stay overnight, bed and breakfast rates will apply. Call for more information.

AVAILABILITY: Year-round, everyday from 6am–10pm; extra hours can be arranged. Closed Christmas and Thanksgiving.

SERVICES/AMENITIES:

Restaurant Services: yes
Catering: provided, no BYO
Kitchen Facilities: n/a
Tables & Chairs: provided
Linens, Silver, etc.: provided
Restrooms: wca
Dance Floor: yes
Parking: $4/car if reserved City Club spaces, lots nearby, street

Overnight Accommodations: 20 guestrooms
Telephone: pay and guest phones
Outdoor Night Lighting: yes
Outdoor Cooking Facilities: no
Cleanup: provided
Other: reception coordinator
Special: candelabras
Bride's Dressing Area: yes

RESTRICTIONS:

Alcohol: provided, no BYO
Smoking: designated areas
Music: amplified ok

Wheelchair Access: yes
Insurance: sometimes required
Other: security sometimes required

BERKELEY CONFERENCE CENTER

2105 Bancroft Way
Berkeley, CA 94704
(510) 848-3957
Reserve: 1–2 months in advance

Don't let the modest, understated entry on Bancroft fool you. The Berkeley Conference Center has remarkable facilities for special events. Housed in an historic, 4-story landmark building, the Center has over 11,000 sq. ft. of meeting and banquet space. Built in 1905 as a Masonic Temple, this building has an amazing assortment of highly detailed, classically beautiful spaces great for small parties or big receptions. The Ballroom is magnificent. This is an enormous and elegant room with high ceilings, diffused lighting and a color palette that is superb. The Carleton and Haste Rooms are also large, with lots of wood moulding and high ceilings. The Board Room is at the top, featuring bay views out of a long wall of windows. This is a medium-sized room, equipped with a small bar, which can handle small receptions for 50. Throughout, the facility maintains a high standard of excellence, not only in the decor, but in the high level of staff support. This location is an unexpected and delightful surprise.

CAPACITY:

Room	Seated	Standing	Room	Seated	Standing
Grand Ballroom	220	350	Haste	160	275
Carleton	150	250	Board Room	60	125
Bancroft	60	75	Ashby	40	40
Evans	40	30	Channing	40	30

FEES & DEPOSITS :

Room	4-hour fee	8-hour fee	Room	4-hour fee	8-hour fee
Grand Ballroom	$400	$800	Haste	$200	$400
Carleton	200	400	Board Room	150	250
Bancroft	125	200	Ashby	100	150
Evans	80	120	Channing	80	120

A deposit equal to the room rental is required to secure the date. Half of the estimated food and beverage balance is due 2 months prior to the event, the remaining balance due 2 weeks before the event. For extended hours, there are additional fees.

CANCELLATION POLICY: For events, 60 days' notice is required for a refund.

AVAILABILITY: Year-round, everyday from 6am to midnight.

SERVICES/AMENITIES:

Restaurant Services: no
Catering: provided, no BYO
Kitchen Facilities: n/a
Tables & Chairs: provided
Linens, Silver, etc.: provided
Restrooms: mostly wca
Dance Floor: yes
Bride's Dressing Area: no

Parking: lot nearby
Overnight Accommodations: Shattuck Hotel
Telephone: pay phone
Outdoor Night Lighting: access only
Outdoor Cooking Facilities: no
Cleanup: provided
Other: full event planning and coordination

RESTRICTIONS:

Alcohol: provided, corkage $6/bottle
Smoking: restricted
Music: amplified ok

Wheelchair Access: mostly yes
Insurance: not required
Other: security guards sometimes required

Need a caterer, cake maker, florist? The Service Directory starting on page 412 features the best in the business.

BERKELEY ROSE GARDEN

Euclid Avenue at Eunice
Berkeley, CA 94708
(510) 644-6530   Recreation Department
Reserve: 3–4 months in advance

This is one of the best rose gardens we've ever seen—public or private. What makes this one so special is its Bay-view location up in the Berkely Hills and the site's physical layout. Situated in an old quarry about a mile uphill from the University, the garden's profusely blooming roses are planted on steep terraces which are made of grey stone, each hand-set by WPA workers in the early 1930s. Above the level sections are numerous trellises and pergolas, all draped with intertwining multi-colored roses. From the top along Euclid Avenue there is a breathtaking view of the Bay, framed by trees and roses. And, as you descend into the garden, you're completely surrounded by the smells and colors of hundreds of varieties. The City of Berkeley does a remarkable job of maintaining this park and receives plenty of help from a volunteer organization. Since it's a public park, there is no exclusive rental allowed. If you're a budget-minded person looking for an outdoor ceremony spot that is truly outstanding, come April through July and take a look at the spectacular show. Receptions would not be appropriate here.

CAPACITY: The garden can accommodate up to 150 easily.

FEES & DEPOSITS : The rental fee is $253 for 4 hours and $32/hour for each additional hour.
AVAILABILITY: Year-round, daytime only. April–June are the best months.

SERVICES/AMENITIES:
Restrooms: wca
Kitchen Facilities: no
Cleanup: renter

Parking: on street
Telephone: pay phone on street

RESTRICTIONS:
Alcohol: not allowed (not enforced)
Smoking: allowed
Music: permit required

Wheelchair Access: limited
Insurance: not required
Other: auto access limited

BRAZILIAN ROOM

Tilden Park
Berkeley, CA 94708
(510) 540-0220 Jeri Honderd
Reserve: 2–12 months in advance

Once a part of the 1939 Golden Gate Exposition on Treasure Island, the Brazilian Room was presented as a gift to the East Bay Regional Park District by the country of Brazil. The original interior hardwood paneling and parquet flooring were kept intact, while a new exterior of local rock and timber was constructed to permanently house the room. Natural light flows through the floor-to-ceiling leaded glass windows that run the length of the room on both sides and a huge stone fireplace gives the space an added charm and warmth. Outside, the large flagstone patio overlooks a sloping lawn and the adjacent botanical garden. Located in Tilden Park, nestled high in the Berkeley Hills above UC Berkeley, the serene, pastoral surroundings offer an environment free from noise and distraction. It's no surprise that the Brazilian Room has become one of the most popular wedding sites in the East Bay.

CAPACITY: The Main Room holds 225 standing guests, 150 seated.

FEES, DEPOSITS & AVAILABILITY: A $250 non-refundable reservation deposit wil be required at the time of booking. This deposit will become the refundable cleaning/damage deposit after your event takes place, as long as all the terms of the contract are met.

Weekend Rates (min. 5 hours)	*Fee*	*Timeframes*
Saturday, Sunday, holidays	$575	9am–4pm or 5pm–12am
Friday evening	575	6–12am
Additional hours	100/hr	
Weekday Rates (min. 3 hours)		
Monday, Wednesday, Thursday	150	8am–midnight
Friday day (any 3-hour block)	150	8am–4pm
Each additional weekday hour costs $50		
Special all day rate	200	8am–4pm
Seasonal Sunday Rates (min. 6 hours)		
November through April, any 6-hour block	675	9am–midnight
Each additional hour	75	

The fee balance is due 90 days prior to the event. Optional services are available for a fee. If using a non-preferred caterer, add $75. For non-residents of Alameda and Contra Costa counties, add $100 on weekends and holidays only. Caterers must be licensed and have insurance.

CANCELLATION POLICY: The reservation deposit will be forfeited if you cancel. Any money paid for room rental will also be non-refundable.

SERVICES/AMENITIES:

Restaurant Services: no
Catering: provided or BYO, must be licensed
Kitchen Facilities: ample
Tables & Chairs: some provided
Linens, Silver, etc.: BYO
Restrooms: wca
Dance Floor: yes

Parking: lot
Overnight Accommodations: no
Telephone: pay phone
Outdoor Night Lighting: yes
Outdoor Cooking Facilities: yes
Cleanup: caterer
Bride's Dressing Area: yes

RESTRICTIONS:

Alcohol: BYO. WCB only, kegs of beer restricted
 to patio and kitchen
Smoking: outside only
Music: amplified inside only

Wheelchair Access: yes
Insurance: extra liability required
Other: decorations restricted

HILLSIDE CLUB

2286 Cedar Street
Berkeley, CA 94709
(510) 848-3227
Reserve: 1 month in advance

The Hillside Club was founded by a group of Berkeley citizens who wished to protect the hills of their town from "unsightly grading and the building of unsuitable and disfiguring houses." The original 1906 Club building was designed by renowned architect Bernard Maybeck. Destroyed in the great fire of 1923, it was redesigned by Maybeck's partner, John White, and rebuilt that year. Its style is that of an English Tudor hall, featuring a high wood-beamed ceiling and massive fireplace. Afternoon light traverses the tall, multi-paned windows, warming the dark wood interior. Recitals often make use of the stage, piano and newly improved lighting system. The hardwood floor is perfect for dancing. An integral part of Berkeley's history, the Hillside Club is a warm, friendly place to host your event.

CAPACITY: The Club accommodates 200 standing or 150 seated.

FEES & DEPOSITS: $150 or 50% of the fee, whichever is larger, is due at the time of booking. Weekdays and evenings (except Friday evening) the facility rents for $200. Friday evening, Saturday or Sunday it rents for $300. The balance of the fee is due a week before the event. The basic rental is for a 4-hour block of time. For each hour over 4 hours, there is a $40 charge. There are additional fees for use of certain items.

CANCELLATION POLICY: Cancellations are handled on an individual basis.

AVAILABILITY: Until 11pm everyday.

SERVICES/AMENITIES:

Restaurant Services: no

Parking: on street

Catering: BYO
Kitchen Facilities: yes
Tables & Chairs: provided
Linens, Silver, etc.: BYO
Restrooms: no wca
Dance Floor: yes
Bride's Dressing Area: yes

RESTRICTIONS:
Alcohol: BYO, BWC only
Smoking: not allowed
Music: amplified ok

Overnight Accommodations: no
Telephone: no
Outdoor Night Lighting: access only
Outdoor Cooking Facilities: no
Cleanup: caterer or renter
Other: sound system, movie screen, piano

Wheelchair Access: no
Insurance: not required
Other: no confetti or rice

Concord

CENTRE CONCORD

5298 Clayton Road
Concord, CA 94521
(510) 671-3466
Reserve: 9–12 months in advance

The best kept secret in this neck-of-woods is Centre Concord. Hidden in the back of the Clayton Faire Shopping Center, it's a bit hard to find, but you'll be well rewarded if you need a place for a large reception. The building has been totally remodeled, with subtle and attractive decor. Its most outstanding feature is the Ballroom. Easy on the eyes, the room's colors are neutral grays, with a rose carpet and teal-green accents. The walls are covered with fabric, and even the ceiling has a soft, textured appearance. But the minute you hit the light switch, it's showtime—multiple sets of chandeliers glitter and sparkle, setting an upscale tone. The room is bright when fully lit, and quite glamourous when the lights are dimmed. Each section of lights can be individually controlled. This is a large room, but because it can be divided into three sections, small groups won't be overwhelmed. If you are looking for something a bit grand, this is a must-see location.

CAPACITY: The Ballroom can accommodate a maximum of 400 guests.

FEES & DEPOSITS: The rental fee for the Ballroom, Friday night–Sunday, is $100/hour (non-residents $120/hour) for 4-hours, minimum. Half the anticipated rental fee, plus a non-refundable setup/cleanup fee, is required to secure your date. The setup/cleanup fee is $300 for the entire ballroom, 2/3 the space $225, 1/3 the space $180. The balance of the rental fee and any additional fees are due 2 weeks prior to the event. Dance floor and portable risers are extra. A $500 refundable security deposit is required 2 weeks in advance along with another $500 security deposit if you use the Centre's kitchen.

CANCELLATION POLICY: With more than 60 days' notice, you will receive a full refund of the rental deposit, minus a $5 service charge. The security deposit is only refunded if the room(s) are left in good condition.

AVAILABILITY: Year-round, everyday. The Centre is open weekends until 2am, weekdays until 11pm.

SERVICES/AMENITIES:

Restaurant Services: no

Catering: BYO

Kitchen Facilities: fully equipped industrial

Tables & Chairs: provided

Linens, Silver, etc.: BYO, table skirts available

Restrooms: wca

Dance Floor: yes, extra fee

Parking: community lot

Overnight Accommodations: no

Telephone: pay phone

Outdoor Night Lighting: no

Outdoor Cooking Facilities: no

Cleanup: caterer or renter

Bride's Dressing Area: CBA

RESTRICTIONS:

Alcohol: BYO

Smoking: outside only

Music: amplified ok

Wheelchair Access: yes

Insurance: sometimes required

Crockett

CROCKETT COMMUNITY CENTER

850 Pomona
Crockett, CA 94525
(510) 787-2414
Reserve: 1–12 months in advance

Looking at the modest, rustic wooden exterior of the Center, one is surprised by the spacious vaulted auditorium inside, which can accommodate a large reception. Designed by San Francisco architect William Crim for the C&H Sugar Company, the building is constructed on a grand scale, featuring a post and beam style ceiling, hardwood floor, an enormous (and functional) stone fireplace, a monumental bar and a stage. In addition to the main hall, there is one smaller room with kitchenette that can be rented separately. A park area is also available for outdoor activities.

CAPACITY: The Main Hall accommodates 350–400 people. The other room can handle 50 people, maximum.

FEES & DEPOSITS: A $200 cleaning and damage deposit is required for all rentals.

Auditorium including park area (10-hour rental): $315 residents, $565 non-residents. This includes $6.50/

hour for in-house security. For rentals over 10 hours, add $25/hour for overtime. For rentals under 10 hours, the rate is $55/hour.

Kitchen facilities: Add $50 to above rates for use of large kitchen.

Multi-purpose Room (4-hour rental): Room and kitchenette rental is $50 (includes security). Add $50 for use of large kitchen. For rentals over 4 hours, add $12.50/hour for overtime.

Park and Restroom facilities: $50

CANCELLATION POLICY: Cancellations must be submitted in writing. Refund of the fee's rental portion will be returned to the renter upon receipt of written notice of cancellation. Refund of the total deposit is based upon the following time frame: 30 days' notice, 75% refund; 14-29 days' notice, 50% refund; less than 14 days, forfeiture of entire deposit.

AVAILABILITY: All year, 8am–2am.

SERVICES/AMENITIES:

Restaurant Service: no
Catering: BYO
Kitchen Facilities: ample
Tables & Chairs: provided
Linens, Silver, etc.: BYO
Restrooms: wca
Dance Floor: yes
Bride's Dressing Area: yes

Parking: on street
Overnight Accommodations: no
Telephone: pay phone
Outdoor Night Lighting: access only
Outdoor Cooking Facilities: yes
Cleanup: caterer and renter, or provided for a fee
Other: podium, sound system

RESTRICTIONS:

Alcohol: BYO
Smoking: not allowed
Music: amplified ok

Wheelchair Access: yes
Insurance: not required
Other: decorations restricted

Need a caterer, cake maker, florist? The Service Directory starting on page 412 features the best in the business.

Danville

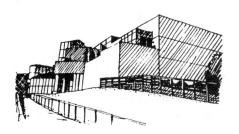

BEHRING AUTO MUSEUM & U.C. BERKELEY MUSEUM OF ART, SCIENCE AND CULTURE

Blackhawk Plaza Circle
Danville, CA 94506
(510) 736-2280
Reserve: 3–6 months in advance

The U.C. Berkeley Museum and Behring Auto Museum are exciting places for private events. The Behring Museum is a study in glass, granite and stainless steel. Overlooking Blackhawk Plaza, this multi-million dollar museum showcases rare, classic automobiles in elegant, sumptuous surroundings. The lobby is awesome with its soaring skylights and dusty rose Italian marble floors and walls. The juxtaposition of metal and stone with soft rich colors creates a vivid impression. As the sun sets through the tinted glass facade, the entire space is bathed in a warm, hazy glow. The dining room presents a striking contrast: black from its granite floor to unadorned ceiling. Vintage car galleries border the dining area and can be illuminated or rendered invisible by a network of computerized lights. Here guests are dazzled by colorful fender curves, gleaming metal and sparkling chrome. The new U.C. Museum of Art, Science and Culture is a handsome and stately structure located adjacent to the Behring Museum. Designed along classical lines and presented in terra cotta colors, this is the crowning touch to an already impressive mercantile center, Blackhawk Plaza. Although functions are not set up in this museum, guests can roam through the exhibits during dining and dancing festivities at the Behring Museum. Whether you come here to savor Ken Behring's ultra-modern vision or you simply like the idea of a private celebration amidst classic cars and a showcase of living history, prehistory and scientific discovery, the Museums at Blackhawk will make your wedding unforgettable.

CAPACITY: The Dining Room in the Behring Museum accommodates up to 500 seated guests. For more than 300 guests, additional fees may be required for a special dining room setup. The Lobby holds 600 standing.

FEES & DEPOSITS: The Museums rent space only. All services are provided by others.

Security/Maintenance Fees			*Rental Fees*		
Reception Only	2hrs	$280	Reception Only	2hrs	$500
(Over 100 Guests, $40 per each 50 guests)			Each Additional Hour	—	150
Reception & Seated Dinner	2hrs	520	Reception & Dinner	2hrs	1,000
Reception, Seated Dinner & Dancing	2hrs	650	Reception, Dinner & Dancing	2hrs	1,500

A non-refundable deposit of 50% of the total maintenance and rental fees is due when reservations are confirmed; the balance is due the day of the event. A $1000 refundable security deposit is due 30 days prior to the event. Caterers must be selected from a preferred list.

CANCELLATION POLICY: The security deposit will be refunded if you cancel 30 days in advance of your function.

AVAILABILITY: Tuesdays–Sundays 6:30pm–12:30am. Private parties can only be arranged when museums are closed to the public and there are no conflicting activities.

SERVICES/AMENITIES:

Restaurant Services: no
Catering: preferred list only
Kitchen Facilities: no
Tables & Chairs: caterer
Linens, Silver, etc.: caterer
Restrooms: wca
Dance Floor: granite foyer

Parking: large lots
Overnight Accommodations: no
Telephone: pay phone
Outdoor Night Lighting: yes
Outdoor Cooking Facilities: no
Cleanup: caterer
Bride's Dressing Area: no

RESTRICTIONS:

Alcohol: through licensed caterer,
Wheelchair Access: yes
Smoking: outside only

Music: amplified limited
Insurance: certificate required

EL RIO

Danville, CA
Address withheld to maintain privacy.
(510) 837-0777
Reserve: 1–6 months in advance

This is a very large, private residence available for ceremonies and receptions. With over 8,000 square feet of living space and a sizeable garden, it offers flexibility and a variety of event spaces. El Rio has 7 bedrooms, 8 baths, a wet bar, French doors, new hardwood floors, fireplaces and a large, well-equipped kitchen. Outdoors are a heated pool with poolhouse, a sunken conversation pit and expansive courtyard. Even the poolhouse has 2 bathrooms and a bar. If you would like to have your wedding in a very private location in the East Bay, and need accommodations for up to 14 guests, this is the place. In addition, any service you can dream of, from maid service and entertainment to flowers and catering, can be provided by the house management.

CAPACITY: Indoors 150 seated or 200 standing guests; outdoors 150 seated or 600 standing guests.

FEES & DEPOSITS: A non-refundable deposit of 100% of the rental fee is due when the contract is signed. A refundable cleaning and security deposit will be required, and will be returned within 2 weeks following the event. The rental fee for a 4-hour minimum period is $100/hour.

CANCELLATION POLICY: The cleaning/security deposit is refundable as per the rental contract.

AVAILABILITY: Year-round, everyday from 9am.

SERVICES/AMENITIES:

Restaurant Services: no
Catering: provided or BYO
Kitchen Facilities: ample
Tables & Chairs: BYO or CBA
Linens, Silver, etc.: BYO or CBA
Restrooms: no wca
Bride's Dressing Area: CBA
Special: event coordination

Dance Floor: yes
Parking: valet required, extra charge
Overnight Accommodations: 7 guestrooms
Telephone: house phone, extra charge
Outdoor Night Lighting: yes
Outdoor Cooking Facilities: BBQs
Cleanup: caterer or provided, extra charge

RESTRICTIONS:

Alcohol: BYO or CBA
Smoking: outside only
Music: amplified with approval

Wheelchair Access: yes
Insurance: extra liability required
Other: decorations require approval

THE VICTORIAN AND THE EXECUTIVE ESTATE

Danville, CA
Addresses withheld to maintain privacy.
(510) 837-0777
Reserve: 1–6 months in advance

These two sizeable homes occupy the same parcel, yet are separated by considerable open space, including a tennis court. The first house you encounter is a remodeled white Victorian with cream walls and carpets, hardwood floors, fireplaces, sunken tubs and 7 bedrooms. In the backyard garden, you'll find a spa and heated pool. Receptions can take place either outdoors around the pool or inside. The interior rooms are large, making it a very flexible event site. The second residence, The Executive Estate, is a recently built 6,600 square foot home with state-of-the-art kitchen and baths. The kitchen in this house is very sophisticated, with gray granite and white cabinets. The bathrooms all feature raised marble tubs and other elegant amenities. The interior is light and airy, with a multitude of windows overlooking the hillsides beyond. There are many rooms in this enormous house, some of which connect to form large event spaces. Both houses provide guest accommodations for those who'd like to spend the night. And for those who need assistance planning a wedding, the staff is able to coordinate catering, limousines, entertainment and maid/valet services.

CAPACITY: The Victorian's indoor capacity is 75 seated or 125 for a standing reception. Outdoor capacity is 200 standing guests; add 500 to that figure if you use the tennis court. Indoors, The Executive Estate can hold up to 80 seated guests or 150 for a standing reception. Using its terraces, you can plan for an additional 50 seated people.

FEES & DEPOSITS: A non-refundable deposit of 100% of the rental fee is due when the contract is signed. A refundable cleaning/security deposit is also required and will be returned within 2 weeks following the event. The Victorian's rental fee for a 4-hour minimum is $200/hour. The Executive

Estate's rental fee is $300/hour. Overnight stays can be arranged for both places; call for rates.

CANCELLATION POLICY: The cleaning and security deposit is refundable if you cancel.

AVAILABILITY: Year-round, everyday from 9am.

SERVICES/AMENITIES:

Restaurant Services: no

Catering: provided or BYO

Kitchen Facilities: ample

Tables & Chairs: BYO or CBA

Linens, Silver, etc.: BYO or CBA

Restrooms: no wca, both residences

Bride's Dressing Area: CBA

Special: event coordination, heated pool, spa, tennis court

Parking: valet required, extra charge

Overnight Accommodations: 7 guestrooms w/private baths each residence

Telephone: house phone, extra charge

Outdoor Night Lighting: yes

Outdoor Cooking Facilities: BBQs

Cleanup: caterer or provided, extra fee

Dance Floor: CBA

RESTRICTIONS:

Alcohol: BYO or CBA

Smoking: outside only

Music: amplified inside only with approval

Wheelchair Access: no

Insurance: extra liability required

Other: decorations restricted

Fremont

ARDENWOOD HISTORIC PRESERVE

34600 Ardenwood Blvd.
Fremont, CA 94555
(510) 462-1400 Reservations Office
Reserve: 3–12 months in advance

Ardenwood is a 205-acre working farm, established during the last half of the 19th century. Here, you can travel back in time—draft horses still pull wagons, ladies wear Victorian dresses and the land still grows the kinds of crops it did 100 years ago. Guests can stroll through the beautiful gardens that surround the Patterson Mansion, the impressive focal point of Ardenwood. An expansive lawn, complete with a white, Victorian-style gazebo, provides a wonderful area for weddings and receptions. Here you are enveloped by the peace and quiet of the country, and civilization seems a million miles away.

CAPACITY: The Poolside area accommodates up to 200 guests, and the Gazebo 500.

FEES & DEPOSITS: Non-refundable reservation deposits: for a ceremony $300; reception $350; ceremony plus reception $400. Rental rates are as follows.

	Fee	*Hours*
Ceremony	$550	2 hours
Reception only	550–850	4-1/2 hours
Ceremony & reception	725–1,025	5-1/2 hours
Rehearsal	50	1 hour TBA
Each additonal half hour	100	

Catering fees run $11–30/person for food, and $3.25–5.25 for beverage packages. The balance of all fees is due one week before the event.

AVAILABILITY: Ardenwood is available from 9am–11pm Thursday–Sunday, April 1st to November 1st.

SERVICES/AMENITIES:

Restaurant Services: no
Catering: provided
Kitchen Facilities: n/a
Tables & Chairs: provided
Linens, Silver, etc.: provided
Restrooms: wca
Dance Floor: yes
Bride's Dressing Area: yes

Parking: ample lots
Overnight Accommodations: no
Telephone: pay phone
Outdoor Night Lighting: yes
Outdoor Cooking Facilities: BBQs
Cleanup: caterer
Other: horse-drawn carriage CBA, complete event serices

RESTRICTIONS:

Alcohol: WBC provided
Smoking: allowed
Music: amplified after 4:30pm only

Wheelchair Access: yes
Insurance: not required
Other: park open to public from 10am to 4:30pm

THE PALMDALE ESTATE

159 Washington Blvd.
Fremont, CA 94539
(510) 651-8908
Reserve: 2–12 months in advance

The Palmdale Estate is an unexpected jewel in Fremont. Towering palm trees, lakes, rose gardens and expansive lawns grace this 23-acre estate. And now, there's even a gazebo for al fresco ceremonies. Best House (built by Mrs. Best) is a white, brown-trimmed Tudor-style home. Built in 1915, it features a large ballroom with burgundy drapes, hardwood floors and murals on the walls and ceilings. The Music room is decorated in gold leaf and has artwork everywhere you look. French doors, chandeliers, hardwood and marble floors make this an attractive and special spot to take your vows and have a wedding reception.

CAPACITY: The gardens can hold 1,000 guests for a reception and Best House can hold 150 seated indoors and, combined with outdoor spaces, up to 500 guests.

FEES & DEPOSITS: To rent the house and garden, a $250 refundable security deposit is due when the rental agreement is submitted. Rental fees are as follows:

	Fees	*Timeframe*
Weekend	$1500/8 hours	8am–1am*
Weekday	$500/8 hours or $100/hour	9am–5pm
Weekday Evenings	$150/hour	5pm–midnight

CANCELLATION POLICY: The security deposit is forfeited if you cancel.

AVAILABILITY: Year-round, everyday except Easter and Christmas. *On Saturdays between April and October, there are 2 time periods for receptions: 9am–5pm and 5:30pm–1am.

SERVICES/AMENITIES:

Restaurant Services: no
Catering: BYO
Kitchen Facilities: minimal
Tables & Chairs: provided to 150 guests
Linens, Silver, etc.: CBA
Restrooms: wca
Dance Floor: Ballroom
Bride's Dressing Area: yes

Parking: large lot
Overnight Accommodations: no
Telephone: lounge phone
Outdoor Night Lighting: CBA
Outdoor Cooking Facilities: BBQ
Cleanup: CBA
Other: event coordination

RESTRICTIONS:

Alcohol: BYO WCB only, hard alcohol restricted
Smoking: outside only
Music: amplified within limits

Wheelchair Access: yes
Insurance: not required

SHINN GARDENS

1251 Peralta
Fremont, CA 94536
(510) 791-4340 Leisure Services
Reserve: 6 months in advance

The Shinn historic house and garden turns out to be a surprisingly quiet and serene oasis in the heart of Fremont. Built in 1876 by James and Lucy Shinn, who founded a pioneer nursery business in the East Bay, the Shinn residence is a lovely, restored Victorian ranch house set in four and a half acres of lawns and gardens. Several rose-covered trellises cover the house exterior and in front of the house is an expansive lawn studded with large, century-old trees. Of special interest is a little Japanese garden adjacent to the house. Inside this garden, featuring meticulously manicured shrubs and rare trees, is a wisteria-draped trellis structure with bench seat that makes an attractive ceremony spot. This site is an historic treasure. If you're in the market for a romantic, old-world location in the East Bay, give the Shinn historic garden serious consideration.

CAPACITY: The garden can accommodate 200 guests.

DEPOSIT: A refundable cleaning/damage deposit of $150 and use fees are required to reserve your date. In addition, you must complete a use application. A park ranger is assigned during functions.

CANCELLATION POLICY: 90% of the use fee will be refunded if written notice is given 30 days in advance; a 70% refund for 29–11 days advance notice. If weather does not permit an outdoor party, the deposit will be refunded in full, and the City will retain 10% of the use fee. Allow four weeks for a refund.

FEES & DEPOSITS:	*Fees*	*Resident**	*Non-Resident*
	3-Hour Minimum Use	$190	$285
	Additional Hourly Rate	60	80
	8-Hour Block	385	550

*Bride, groom or parent must be a Fremont resident for "resident" status.

AVAILABILITY: Everyday from 8am to dusk, April through September.

SERVICES/AMENITIES:
Restaurant Services: no
Catering: BYO
Kitchen Facilities: no
Tables & Chairs: 150 chairs, 5 tables provided
Linens, Silver, etc.: BYO
Restrooms: wca
Dance Floor: tennis court

Parking: 40 spaces
Overnight Accommodations: no
Telephone: no
Outdoor Night Lighting: access only
Outdoor Cooking Facilities: BYO
Cleanup: caterer
Bride's Dressing Area: yes

RESTRICTIONS:
Alcohol: BYO, WCB only
Smoking: outside only
Music: no bands, DJ ok
Wheelchair Access: yes

Insurance: sometimes required
Other: no portable dance floors, decorations restricted, no rice

VALLEJO ADOBE
HISTORICAL PARK

36501 Niles Blvd.
Fremont, CA 94537
(510) 791-4340 Leisure Services
Reserve: 6 months in advance

If you've always dreamed of getting married in truly rustic surroundings, the Vallejo Adobe may be the perfect place for you. Built in 1843, practically everything in this building is hand-made: its 3-foot thick walls of mud and straw brick, the heavy redwood door at the entrance, and the wooden beams and rafters supporting the structure. Even the replacement tile roof was specially designed and hand constructed. The interior is graced only by a round fireplace in one corner. Outside, the sun filters through redwood and eucalyptus trees onto an expanse of lawn, and it's so quiet you can hear birds chattering and the rustling of leaves.

CAPACITY: The facility accommodates 49 guests inside and 100 total.

FEES & DEPOSITS: A refundable $150 security/cleaning deposit is due at the time of booking. A completed use application must also be submitted.

CANCELLATION POLICY: A refund will be made if the renter gives written notice of cancellation at least 11 days prior to the date reserved. If you cancel 30 or more days in advance, use fees will be refunded less 10%; 11–29 days, less 30%; 10 days or less, no refund. Allow four weeks for refund.

FEES:	*Fees*	*Resident**	*Non-Resident*
	3-Hour Minimum Use	$190	$285
	Additional Hourly Rate	60	80
	8-Hour Block	385	550

* Bride, groom or parent must be a Fremont resident.

AVAILABILITY: Everyday, 8am to dusk, April through September.

SERVICES/AMENITIES:

Restaurant Services: no
Catering: BYO
Kitchen Facilities: no
Tables & Chairs: 100 chairs, 4 tables provided
Linens, Silver, etc.: BYO
Restrooms: no wca
Dance Floor: no
Bride's Dressing Area: yes

Parking: lot
Overnight Accommodations: no
Telephone: at nursery if open, or attending ranger has radio
Outdoor Night Lighting: CBA
Outdoor Cooking Facilities: BYO
Cleanup: caterer

RESTRICTIONS:

Alcohol: BYO WCB only, hard alcohol restricted
Smoking: outside only
Music: amplified within limits

Wheelchair Access: yes
Insurance: sometimes required

Lafayette

LAFAYETTE PARK HOTEL

3287 Mt. Diablo Blvd.
Lafayette, CA 94549
(510) 283-3700 or (800) 368-2468
Reserve: 3–12 months in advance

The Lafayette Park is truly a different kind of hotel because comfort, ambiance and attentive service are the hallmarks here. The staff treats you like royalty, offering a level of service rarely found in hotel environments nowadays. You'll have no difficulty locating it—the distinctive Norman French architecture, with dormers, French windows, green shutters and peaked roofline, makes the Hotel a landmark in Lafayette. Designed around three European-style courtyards, it has spacious rooms for receptions. If you're interested in an outdoor party or ceremony, the interior Fountain Courtyard is especially lovely. Here you'll find ivy-trellised urns which support flowering trees and multi-colored flowers. Umbrella-shaded tables encircle a hand-carved Italian limestone fountain, which provides a wonderful background for wedding photos. If you'd like the option of an indoor/outdoor reception, tall French doors lead to interior rooms. For more private, intimate gatherings, try the second floor Wishing Well Courtyard, which has an imported stone wishing well as the centerpiece. With an 18th century imported marble mantel, wood burning fireplace, oak floors and tasteful furnishings, the Diderot Library makes a perfect venue for rehearsal dinners or bridal showers. All meals in the Library, created by the hotel's award-winning chef, are served on china and crystal. As if this weren't enough, the Hotel offers a complimentary fireplace room for the honeymoon couple and special overnight rates for your wedding guests.

CAPACITY:

Room	Reception	Banquet	Room	Reception	Banquet
Independence Hall	220	175	Fountain Courtyard	300	150
George Washington Room	130	100	Independence Hall		
Benjamin Franklin Room	50	42	with Courtyard	500	280
Diderot Library	30	20	Wishing Well Courtyard	100	50-60

FEES & DEPOSITS: An $875 non-refundable deposit is required to reserve your date. The Hotel's $875 wedding package (min. 100 guests) includes butler service, champagne and hors d'oeuvres, beverages, linens, centerpieces, fireplace guestroom and use of Independence Hall and Courtyard. Special wedding menus range from $32.50–45/person. Tax and service charges are additional. The balance is due 2 weeks prior to your event.

SERVICES/AMENITIES:

Restaurant Services: yes

Catering: provided

Kitchen Facilities: n/a

Tables & Chairs: provided

Linens, Silver, etc.: provided

Restrooms: wca

Dance Floor: yes

Other: wedding coordination

Parking: lot and valet

Overnight Accommodations: 139 guestrooms

Telephone: pay phones

Outdoor Night Lighting: yes

Outdoor Cooking Facilities: CBA

Cleanup: provided

Bride's Dressing Area: complimentary

RESTRICTIONS:

Alcohol: provided, corkage $10/bottle

Smoking: outdoors only

Music: amplified within limits

Wheelchair Access: yes

Insurance: not required

Livermore

CONCANNON WINERY

4590 Tesla Road
Livermore, CA 94550
(510) 447-3760
Reserve: 3–6 months in advance

An arch with the Concannon name on it welcomes you to this historic family winery. Surrounded by acres of vineyards, Concannon offers multiple options for ceremonies and receptions, so ask for the full tour. When you arrive, the first area you'll see is the lawn area in front of the winery, shaded by large trees and bordered by roses and vineyards. There's a pretty gazebo here, perfect for formal vows or a reception. Nearby is a vine-covered arbor with carriage lamps, with adjoining lawn area for receptions or ceremonies. Stand underneath the arbor and look up. Overhead is a ceiling of intertwined grape vines with grapes dangling delicately through the greenery. Sunlight filters through to the herringbone brick arbor floor. At one end, an archway provides a dramatic entry for the bride, who can step into the arbor for a ceremony underneath the canopy of foliage. In cooler months the arbor can be covered by a custom-made tent, creating an area for indoor/outdoor receptions. Through the archway is a lovely green lawn, next to which sits an arch with climbing roses. Not too far away is the Concannon home, an old-fashioned white Victorian farmhouse, with a wisteria-covered veranda. In front of the house is a heart-shaped lawn, ringed by pines. It's completely shaded and can be used for ceremonies. The Tasting Room has a warm feel, with both brick and redwood walls. In winter, the old fashioned wood-burning fireplace is aglow and for color, local art is displayed on the walls, with shows rotating every month. For evening dining or dancing, the Tasting Room Courtyard is wind-protected and intimate. Here guests can sit at candlelit tables or dance without worrying about an evening chill.

CAPACITY:

Area	Seated	Standing	Area	Seated	Standing
Arbor	150	200	Heart-Shaped Lawn	75	100
Arbor Lawn	150	300	Trellis Archway Garden	50	100
Tasting Room and Ctyard	80	160	Gazebo Lawn	300	450
La Pergola	500	750			

FEES & DEPOSITS: A refundable security deposit of $350 is required to reserve your reception or ceremony date. The security deposit is refundable 1 week after the event. The rental fee for receptions is $12/person and is due 2 weeks prior to the event; a ceremony fee is an additional $100. If you only have a ceremony here, the rental fee is $300. The fee includes setup, tables, chairs, glassware, valet parking, 1-hour rehearsal and wine service staff. Wine may be purchased at a case discount. Horse and carriage rental can be arranged for $150; dance floor for $250.

CANCELLATION POLICY: With 90 days' notice, the deposit will be refunded less 20%.

AVAILABILITY: Everyday, year-round. Outdoors from 10am–midnight; Tasting Room 6pm–midnight. Closed Thanksgiving, Easter and Christmas.

SERVICES/AMENITIES:

Restaurant Services: no
Catering: preferred list
Kitchen Facilities: minimal
Tables & Chairs: provided
Linens, Silver, etc.: by caterer
Restrooms: wca
Dance Floor: tasting room or courtyard
Other: event coordination

Parking: valet available
Overnight Accommodations: no
Telephone: house phone
Outdoor Night Lighting: yes
Outdoor Cooking Facilities: BBQ
Cleanup: by caterer
Bride's Dressing Area: yes

RESTRICTIONS:

Alcohol: provided, no BYO
Smoking: outside only
Music: amplified ok

Wheelchair Access: yes
Insurance: not required
Other: no birdseed or rice

RAVENSWOOD
Historic Site

2647 Arroyo Road
Livermore, CA 94550
(510) 373-5700 Park District Office
Reserve: 3–12 months in advance

Ravenswood is one of those places you want to explore the minute you see it. A pepper tree-lined driveway draws your eye straight up to the two houses set far back from the main road. The Cottage House, built in 1885, looks out over a lovely little garden. As you walk toward the main house, the fragrance of roses accompanies you. A Queen Anne Victorian, the larger house on the estate has real old-fashioned charm. A comfortable wrap-around veranda encourages lazy afternoon socializing, and the palm-ringed front lawn is a perfect spot for an al fresco repast. Inside, high ceilings, a fireplace, hardwood floors and simple decor make you feel right at home. Behind both houses is grassy area with a gazebo. Surrounded by a dozen trees, it rests in dappled shade, completing a picture of country serenity.

CAPACITY: The Main House can hold 150 seated, 71 standing; the grounds up to 150 seated, 150 standing; Billard Room up to 75 seated, 50 standing.

FEES & DEPOSITS : A $50 rental deposit is required to secure a date. The balance of the rental fee and a $150 cleaning deposit are due 30 days prior to the event. The rental fee is $480 for Livermore residents, and $720 for non-residents. There is also an additional liquor permit charge.

CANCELLATION POLICY: If the event is cancelled three months or more prior to the event, 50% of the rental deposit is returned. If you cancel within 3 months of the event, the deposit will be forfeited. For either period, any prepaid rental charges in excess of the facility rental deposit are refunded. With less than one month's notice, only the cleaning deposit is returned.

AVAILABILITY: Everyday 8am–9pm, except Tuesdays.

SERVICES/AMENITIES:

Restaurant Services: no
Catering: BYO
Kitchen Facilities: moderate
Tables & Chairs: some provided
Linens, Silver, etc.: BYO
Restrooms: wca
Dance Floor: yes
Bride's Dressing Area: yes

Parking: lot
Overnight Accommodations: no
Telephone: restricted use
Outdoor Night Lighting: access only
Outdoor Cooking Facilities: no
Cleanup: caterer and renter
Other: horse-drawn carriage allowed

RESTRICTIONS:

Alcohol: WCB only with license
Smoking: outside only
Music: no amplified music

Wheelchair Access: yes
Insurance: damage and liability required
Other: decorations restricted

TRI VALLEY
Aahmes Activity Center

170 Lindbergh Ave.
Livermore, CA 94550
(510) 294-8667
Reserve: 1–6 months in advance

This brand new facility has two things going for it. The first is that it can hold a really large crowd (up to 540 seated guests!) for a wedding and the second is that Beets Catering is the exclusive caterer/coordinator. We know of no other site in the tri valley area that offers this square footage indoors. Although the space is an unpretentious auditorium with stage and vaulted ceiling over an expansive linoleum floor, Beets can transform it into something special. Import a large, white lath gazebo to the center of the room and have your ceremony underneath. Lace the space with balloon arches or soften it up with greenery from a plant rental outfit. Whatever you want, whether it's budget-minded or sky's-the-limit, Beets can probably do it. We'd also like to point out that Beets does a fine job in the catering department, too. From gourmet, fancy finger foods to modest but tasty morsels for a gathering of six hundred, this caterer does a professional job. So if you've got a sizeable guest list, and Livermore is geographically well suited to your needs, call and ask for a tour.

CAPACITY: The facility accommodates 540 seated guests; 1,000 for a standing reception.

FEES & DEPOSITS : A deposit is required to hold your event date. The rental fee for Friday, Saturday or Sunday is $550. Rental includes a 5-hour period plus 2 hours for setup. The full rental fee and 50% of the estimated food total are due 60 days prior to the event. The balance is due 1 week prior to the function, with any remainder due the day of the event. Additional event staff are available. Call for hourly rates.

AVAILABILITY: Fridays and weekends 8am–midnight.

SERVICES/AMENITIES:

Restaurant Services: no
Catering: provided, no BYO
Kitchen Facilities: n/a
Tables & Chairs: provided
Linens, Silver, etc.: CBA
Restrooms: wca
Dance Floor: yes
Bride's Dressing Area: CBA

Parking: large lot
Overnight Accommodations: no
Telephone: pay phone
Outdoor Night Lighting: CBA
Outdoor Cooking Facilities: CBA
Cleanup: provided
Other: wedding coordination

RESTRICTIONS:

Alcohol: BYO
Smoking: outside & foyer only
Music: amplified ok

Wheelchair Access: yes
Insurance: certificate required

WENTE BROS.
ESTATE WINERY

5565 Tesla Road
Livermore, CA 94550
(510) 447-3603
Reserve: 6–12 months in advance

The Estate Winery is located in the scenic Livermore Valley wine country in a lovely vineyard setting. This 100-year-old winery has charm and a rustic ambiance perfect for weddings, receptions, leisurely brunches or evening dinners in the Estate Tasting Room or on the adjacent patio. During the summer, the patio is shaded by a canopy of fruitless mulberry trees offering protection from the sun.

CAPACITY: The banquet room holds up to 100 standing or 70 seated guests; the patio up to 500 standing or 250 seated guests.

FEES & DEPOSITS: A deposit of 50% of the estimated total is due when reservations are made. The remainder is due at the conclusion of the event. For receptions of up to 250 people, there is a $250 fee for the use of any part of the facility. For over 250 people, add $2 per person. For wedding ceremonies (which include a walk-through rehearsal and consultation) add $500. Per person catering costs run between $15–40 and do not include wine. Sales tax and a 17% gratuity are additional.

CANCELLATION POLICY: With 90 days' notice, the deposit minus $200 will be refunded. With less than 90 days' notice, the deposit is forfeited.

AVAILABILITY: The facility is available everyday from 10am–midnight.

SERVICES/AMENITIES:
Restaurant Services: no
Catering: provided, no BYO
Kitchen Facilities: n/a
Tables & Chairs: provided
Linens, Silver, etc.: provided
Outdoor Night Lighting: yes
Outdoor Cooking Facilities: no

Restrooms: wca
Dance Floor: CBA
Parking: lot
Overnight Accomodations: no
Telephone: pay phone
Cleanup: provided
Bride's Dressing Area: CBA

RESTRICTIONS:
Alcohol: provided, WC only
Smoking: outside only
Music: amplified ok

Wheelchair Access: yes
Insurance: not required

WENTE BROS. SPARKLING WINE CELLARS

5050 Arroyo Road
Livermore, CA 94550
(510) 447-3023
Reserve: 6–12 months in advance

Situated in a picturesque canyon at the southern end of the Livermore Valley, Wente Bros. Sparkling Wine Cellars is surrounded by vineyards, sycamore groves and rolling hills. The site offers wedding guests unparalleled vistas and an appealing, natural environment for ceremonies and receptions. The grounds also include a Visitor's Center, Conference Center and an award-winning, casually elegant restaurant serving top-notch cuisine. The white, Spanish-style stucco buildings are accented with tile roofs and floors, terra cotta pots full of flowering plants and acres of vineyards which convey a strong Mediterranean feeling. Shimmering white and green in the soothing afternoon sun, this winery is an oasis in the midst of our dry California hills.

CAPACITY:

Area	Standing	Seated	Area	Standing	Seated
Restaurant	200	185	Garden Area	—	700
Visitor's Center	200	170	Veranda Area Restaurant	—	75

FEES & DEPOSITS: A deposit of 50% of the estimated event total is due when the contract is submitted. The remainder is due 30 days prior to the event. If you have both the ceremony and reception here, the facility fee is $500 for a 5-hour time period. The facility fee for a ceremony only is $1,500. Hors d'oeuvres, buffets, seated luncheons and dinners can be arranged. Call for specific rates.

CANCELLATION POLICY: If you cancel 6 months in advance, the deposit minus $600 will be refunded. With less than 6 months' notice, the deposit will be forfeited unless Wente is able to rebook the event date.

AVAILABILITY: Year-round, everyday from 10am–11pm.

SERVICES/AMENITIES:

Restaurant Services: yes
Catering: provided
Kitchen Facilities: n/a
Tables & Chairs: provided
Linens, Silver, etc.: provided
Outdoor Night Lighting: yes
Outdoor Cooking Facilities: no
Bride's Dressing Area: yes

Restrooms: wca
Dance Floor: yes
Parking: lot
Overnight Accommodations: no
Telephone: pay phones
Cleanup: provided
Other: audio-visual equipment

RESTRICTIONS:

Alcohol: provided, WC only
Smoking: outside only
Music: amplified ok

Wheelchair Access: yes
Insurance: not required
Other: no birdseed or rice

Montclair

MONTCLAIR WOMAN'S CLUB

1650 Mountain Blvd.
Oakland, CA 94611
(510) 339-1832
Reserve: 2–12 months in advance

Although it was originally slated to be a men's club, the founding businessmen of Montclair Valley ran out of money early on and failed to realize their plans. A group of women took over, paid off the loan on the building and, 65 years later, it is still a woman's club. The Main Hall is simple and spacious with a stage, piano and hardwood floors. The Fireside Room, with its own bar, is often used for hors d'oeuvres and cocktails. A blazing fire keeps guests cozy in wintertime, and of special note are the Mayan tiles which form the fireplace's unusual facade. Outside, the lawn area in back is a pleasant spot for small ceremonies. Conveniently located, this unpretentious clubhouse is an affordable setting for large or small weddings.

CAPACITY: The Club accommodates 360 standing guests; 188 for seated functions. The Fireside Room holds 25 seated and 40 standing.

FEES & DEPOSITS: If you rent the entire facility, a combined security and cleaning deposit of $300 is due at the time of booking. It is refundable 30 days after the event. The rental fee is $600 and covers a 6-hour block. If you only want to reserve part of the Club, call for rates.

AVAILABILITY: The Club is available Friday, Saturday and Sunday.

SERVICES/AMENITIES:

Restaurant Services: no
Catering: BYO
Kitchen Facilities: moderate
Tables & Chairs: provided
Linens, Silver, etc.: BYO or CBA extra fee
Restrooms: no wca
Dance Floor: yes

Parking: off street and lot
Overnight Accommodations: no
Telephone: pay phone
Outdoor Night Lighting: yes
Outdoor Cooking Facilities: BYO
Cleanup: caterer
Bride's Dressing Area: yes

RESTRICTIONS:

Alcohol: BYO
Smoking: outside only
Music: amplified until 11:30

Wheelchair Access: yes
Insurance: not required

Moraga

HACIENDA DE LAS FLORES

2100 Donald Drive
Moraga, CA 94556
(510) 376-2520
Reserve: 2–12 months in advance

An authentic Spanish-style mansion, the Hacienda de las Flores sits on land that was once the hunting ground for Miwok Indians. The historic structure is painted white with blue trim, and is surrounded by park grounds. A large lawn spreads out behind the building, enhanced by blue spruce trees, weeping willows, palms and flowers. A circular flower bed and fountain in the middle of the patio serve as the focal point for receptions. Inside the building, hardwood floors, beamed ceilings, a fireplace and red leather furniture create a warm and inviting setting. Tranquil and secluded, the Hacienda is a favorite wedding spot in the Bay Area.

CAPACITY: The Hacienda accommodates 200 guests outdoors or 128 for a seated meal indoors. The Pavilion seats 40 inside and has an outdoor capacity of 100.

FEES & DEPOSITS: A security deposit is due at the time of booking and will be refunded within 30 days after the event, provided all conditions have been met. A $75 insurance premium is also required. Completed rental packet and final fees are due 60 days before the event. May–Oct there is a $125 surcharge.

	Residents*		Non Residents	
Friday	*Deposit*	*Fee*	*Deposit*	*Fee*
Hacienda	$475	$510	$475	$790
Pavilion	475	370	475	645
Hacienda & Pavilion	475	735	475	1205
Sat/Sun	*Deposit*	*Fee*	*Deposit*	*Fee*
Hacienda	$475	$765	$475	$1125
Pavilion	475	580	475	955
Hacienda & Pavilion	475	1,175	475	1,860

Bride, groom or parents are Moraga residents.

CANCELLATION POLICY: Cancellations must be made in writing. Special event deposit refunds will be made as follows: over 120 days' notice, 100% of deposit less a $50 bookkeeping fee; 90–120 days' notice, 50% returned.

AVAILABILITY: Friday, Saturday and Sunday (8 consecutive hours between 10am and 11pm).

SERVICES/AMENITIES:

Restaurant Services: no

Catering: BYO, must be licensed

Parking: on street and lot

Overnight Accommodations: no

Kitchen Facilities: ample
Tables & Chairs: provided
Linens, Silver, etc.: BYO
Restrooms: wca
Dance Floor: yes

RESTRICTIONS:
Alcohol: BYO, WCB only
Smoking: outside only
Music: no outdoor amplified music

Telephone: pay phone
Outdoor Night Lighting: access only
Outdoor Cooking Facilities: no
Cleanup: provided
Bride's Dressing Area: yes

Wheelchair Access: yes
Insurance: mandatory insurance premium
Other: decorations restricted, no birdseed, rice or mylar balloons

Oakland

ATHENIAN NILE CLUB

410 14th Street
Oakland, CA 94612
(510) 451-0693
Reserve: 2–6 months in advance

This location may be one of the best kept secrets in the East Bay. Operating for 110 years as a private club, the Athenian Nile Club is now available to the public for wedding receptions. Don't let the nondescript front door on 14th Street deter you. Once inside, you'll be ushered upstairs to the facility's light and airy Dining Room. The size of a small ballroom, it features a stage, hardwood dance floor and a thirty-foot ceiling. The decor is in grays, whites and burgundies, and comfortable, upholstered chairs contrast against crisp linens. Silver flatware, crystal and china are provided for all events. A working fireplace with decorative white mantle adds a homey touch, and soft lighting is cast by wall sconces around the room. If you've got a large crowd and you'd like to be close to downtown, come by for a site visit.

CAPACITY: The Dining Room can accommodate 250 seated, 350 guests for a standing reception. For smaller functions, the room can be split into 2 sections. For Saturday and Sunday events, a minimum of 100 guests is required.

FEES & DEPOSITS: A $250 non-refundable deposit applied toward the event total is required when reservations are confirmed. A final guest count is required 72 hours in advance. The food & beverage total is payable on the day of the event. Functions after 6pm require a security guard at $15/hour. Seated luncheons start at $15/person, dinners at $22/person and buffets at $20/person. Tax and a 15% service charge are additional. Bartenders cost $75 per 5-hour function.

CANCELLATION POLICY: The deposit is forfeit if you cancel at anytime.

AVAILABILITY: Year-round, everyday from 7am–2am.

SERVICES/AMENITIES:

Restaurant Services: no
Catering: provided
Kitchen Facilities: n/a
Tables & Chairs: provided
Linens, Silver, etc.: provided
Restrooms: no wca
Dance Floor: yes

Parking: valet
Overnight Accommodations: no
Telephone: house phone
Outdoor Night Lighting: no
Outdoor Cooking Facilities: no
Cleanup: provided
Bride's Dressing Area: yes

RESTRICTIONS:

Alcohol: provided, corkage $5–6/bottle
Smoking: allowed
Music: amplified ok

Wheelchair Access: yes
Insurance: not required

CAFE FONTEBELLA

1111 Broadway
Oakland, CA 946073
(510) 452-2500
Reserve: 3–12 months in advance

Talk about a sophisticated environment for a wedding reception. Clad in a stunning combination of granite and glass, Cafe Fontebella has heretofore been a secret favorite of this author. Hidden inside a glass-walled highrise in downtown Oakland, this facility occupies the ground floor of the American President's Companies Building. The Cafe, which bustles during the work week, is quiet and peaceful evenings and weekends, making it a great space for prenuptial dinners. It takes up a small portion of the total floor space and its decor reflects an Art Deco and craftsman influence with contemporary black tables and chairs and large, colorful paintings. The rest of the open space is divided between the spacious conservatory and the impressive lobby. Thirty-foot floor-to-ceiling glass panels on three sides allow abundant light to flood into the conservatory, and a contemporary sculpture exhibit, which is changed every four months, acts as a centerpiece. Adjacent is the grand lobby which has one of the most exquisite floors we've ever seen. High-polished granite, in geometric patterns of rose, black, tan and gray, is a design element that visually holds all the spaces together. Adding warmth are tasteful leather furniture and wood paneled walls, and nearby are several glass display cases holding large ship replicas, which can be moved if the need arises. Outside the conservatory's glass and chrome doors is a lovely landscaped courtyard with a raised lawn area, ringed by a granite benchseat. Large sculptures and granite stepping stones provide visual interest, and slabs of gray granite with polished surfaces form a patio. Tall trees surround the perimeter, enclosing the space. Off to one side is a nicely designed waterfall fountain, constructed of stone. The rush of water creates an inviting sound that eliminates the feeling you are in the heart of the city. If we had to rate Cafe Fontebella, we'd give it a ten. Both indoor and outdoor spaces combine to form one of the most elegant and understated event spaces we've seen.

CAPACITY: Cafe Fontebella can seat 75 guests. Including the conservatory and lobby, the entire ground floor can seat up to 275 or 1000 standing guests. A minimum party of 25 is required.

FEES & DEPOSITS: A $500 refundable cleaning/damage deposit is payable when reservations are confirmed. There's no fee for renting the Cafe, alone. The rental fee for the entire ground floor, including the Cafe space, is $750–2000 depending on day of week, guest count and services required. Food service is provided by Cafe Fontebella. Any menu can be customized and prices will vary accordingly. Tax and a 15% service charge are additional. Half of the total estimated event cost is payable 6 weeks prior to your function and the final half, plus a confirmed guest count, are due 1 week in advance. Any remaining balance is payable at the event's conclusion.

CANCELLATION POLICY: With 120 days' notice, your deposit will be refunded minus $100 administration fee. The deposit is non-refundable on major holidays or during the holiday season. If your date can be rebooked with comparable size party, your deposit will be refunded less a $100 fee.

AVAILABILITY: Year-round, everyday. Evenings from 6pm–midnight. Saturday and Sunday from 9am–1am.

SERVICES/AMENITIES:

Restaurant Services: yes
Catering: provided, no BYO
Kitchen Facilities: n/a
Tables & Chairs: provided for 75 guests or CBA
Linens, Silver, etc.: provided for 75 guests or CBA
Restrooms: wca
Dance Floor: yes
Other: event coordination, fresh flowers

Parking: adjacent garage for free
Overnight Accommodations: no
Telephone: pay phone
Outdoor Night Lighting: yes
Outdoor Cooking Facilities: no
Cleanup: provided
Bride's Dressing Area: CBA

RESTRICTIONS:

Alcohol: provided, corkage $8/bottle
Smoking: bar only
Music: amplified ok

Wheelchair Access: yes
Insurance: not required
Other: decorations restricted

Need a caterer, cake maker, florist? The Service Directory starting on page 412 features the best in the business.

CALIFORNIA BALLROOM

1736 Franklin Street
Oakland, CA 94612
(510) 834-7761
Reserve: 3–12 months in advance

The California Ballroom is just a few blocks from Lake Merritt in Oakland. Built in 1926 as the grand ballroom of the elegant old Leamington Hotel, it showcases a majestic 45-foot gold-leafed ceiling, a 500-square foot stage with curtain and spotlights, a 700-square foot dance floor—maybe the largest in the Bay Area. Although the Leamington no longer exists, its impressive Art Deco Ballroom is still going strong. Renovated in 1986, this landmark space is one of few locations in the East Bay that can seat over 300 for receptions. Large, original Art Deco lights are suspended from the soaring ceiling. Burgundy draperies and carpet contrast nicely with the cream-colored walls and gold detailing above the doors and mirrors. The stage is impressive, and can be used for the head table or to feature a band or DJ. Tables can be arranged around the hardwood dance floor which occupies the center of the room. The California Ballroom is a good choice if you've got a sizable guest list and would like to dance the night away.

CAPACITY: 300–350 for seated functions; 600 for a standing reception.

FEES & DEPOSITS: Half the rental fee is required when you book this facility. The balance is payable 90 days prior to the event. Any function beginning after dusk will require a security guard. Non-refundable rental fees are as follows:

	Saturday & Holidays	*Sunday–Friday*
8am–5pm	$600	$500
7pm–2am	800	500
Each additional hour after 2am	150	125
All day up to 12 hours	1,000	500

AVAILABILITY: Year-round, everyday until 2am. Saturday receptions can be held from 8am–5pm or 7pm–2am or you can rent the Ballroom all day, up to 12 hours.

SERVICES/AMENITIES:
Restaurant Services: no
Catering: BYO with approval
Kitchen Facilities: minimal
Tables & Chairs: provided
Linens, Silver, etc.: caterer or BYO
Restrooms: wca
Dance Floor: yes
Other: wet bar, on-site non-denominational minister

Parking: adjacent garages, private lot
Overnight Accommodations: no
Telephone: pay phone
Outdoor Night Lighting: access only
Outdoor Cooking Facilities: no
Cleanup: caterer or renter
Bride's Dressing Area: yes

RESTRICTIONS:
Alcohol: BYO
Smoking: outside only
Music: amplified allowed

Wheelchair Access: yes
Insurance: not required
Other: decorations restricted, no tacks, staples or tape

CAMRON-STANFORD HOUSE

1418 Lakeside Drive
Oakland, CA 94612
(510) 836-1976 Elizabeth Way
Reserve: 1–6 months in advance

Gracing the shore of Lake Merritt, the Camron-Stanford House is the last of the grand Victorian homes that once ringed the lake. Constructed in 1876, it derives its name from the Camrons who built it and the Stanfords who occupied it for the longest period. When the building was scheduled for demolition in the late 1960s, concerned citizens formed the Camron-Stanford House Preservation Association and spent the intervening years raising funds to return the home to its former splendor. Elaborate molding, authentic wallpaper and fabrics have all been recreated to match the originals as closely as possible. Rooms filled with period artifacts, antiques and photos take you back to the late 1800s. The only operational gas chandelier in Northern California is located here. Outside, an enormous rear veranda overlooks Lake Merritt. Receptions can take place in the house, on the veranda or on the expansive lawn that extends to the lake. An iron fence enclosing the site ensures privacy while allowing guests to appreciate the colorful tapestry of boats, birds and joggers that surrounds them.

CAPACITY: The facility accommodates 125 guests inside; 250 outside.

FEES & DEPOSITS: Half the rental fee and a refundable $50 cleaning deposit are due at the time of booking.

Area	*Fee*
Veranda, Hall, Dining Room, Kitchen (2 hours)	$ 325
Veranda, Hall, Dining Room, Kitchen (4 hours)	525
Additional time	100/hr.
Period Room (maximum 2 hours)	50/hr.

CANCELLATION POLICY: If less than 30 days' notice is given, 50% of the rental fee will be forfeited. The remainder of the fee and the cleaning deposit are usually returned.

AVAILABILITY: To 10pm weekdays, and to 11pm Saturdays.

SERVICES/AMENITIES:

Restaurant Services: no
Catering: BYO licensed
Kitchen Facilities: moderate
Tables & Chairs: BYO
Linens, Silver, etc.: BYO
Restrooms: wca
Dance Floor: CBA, extra fee
Bride's Dressing Area: CBA

Parking: on street, lot
Overnight Accommodations: no
Telephone: emergencies only
Outdoor Night Lighting: CBA
Outdoor Cooking Facilities: BYO
Cleanup: caterer
Other: Lake tour on Merritt Queen paddleboat CBA

RESTRICTIONS:

Alcohol: BYO

Insurance: proof required

Smoking: outside only
Music: amplified outside only
Wheelchair Access: limited

Other: decorations restricted, no candles, flame-heated chafing dishes, confetti

THE CLAREMONT RESORT, SPA & TENNIS CLUB

Ashby and Domingo Avenues
Oakland, CA 94623
(510) 843-3000 Jan Hagers
Reserve: 1–12 months in advance

The Claremont rises up from the Oakland/Berkeley Hills where it has been a Bay Area landmark for decades. The resort and spa offer an extensive range of services and amenities and numerous areas for receptions and ceremonies. This is a full-service facility with over 32,000 sq. ft. of event space. You can choose from among private rooms, balconies, trellised patios or lawns and gardens. The Claremont can cater a small cocktail party, a formal sit-down feast for hundreds, or anything in between. If you need help with any aspect of your event, the Claremont has the staff to assist you. So whether you want an affair on a grand scale or a small informal gathering of friends and family, the Claremont can accommodate your needs.

CAPACITY: Two of the ballrooms can accommodate 400 standing or 350 seated guests. Capacities for the 20 other available rooms vary.

FEES & DEPOSITS: For special events, a $500 non-refundable deposit, which is applied toward the fee, is due at the time of booking. 95% of the total estimated bill is due 5 days prior to the event, and the balance is due at the conclusion. The fee schedule is based on the room(s) selected and the number of guests attending.

AVAILABILITY: Any day between 6am and 1am.

SERVICES/AMENITIES:

Restaurant Services: yes
Catering: provided, no BYO
Kitchen Facilities: n/a
Tables & Chairs: provided
Linens, Silver, etc.: provided
Restrooms: wca
Dance Floor: yes
Parking: lot, valet

Overnight Accommodations: 239 guestrooms
Telephone: pay phone
Outdoor Night Lighting: access only
Outdoor Cooking Facilities: yes
Cleanup: provided
Special: spa, tennis courts, swimming pool
Other: event coordination
Bride's Dressing Area: cba

RESTRICTIONS:

Alcohol: provided
Smoking: allowed
Music: no music at poolside

Wheelchair Access: yes
Insurance: not required
Other: receptions held inside only

COMMODORE DINING CRUISES

Docked at Embarcadero Cove
Port of Oakland, CA
(510) 256-4000
Reserve: 1–12 months in advance

You'll have no problem locating Commodore Dining Cruises—its fleet of four white yachts is lined up in a row at the dock next to Quinn's Lighthouse in Port of Oakland's historic Embarcadero Cove. The largest, the flagship Jack London Commodore, holds 350 seated guests; Stockton, the smallest of the four, seats 72. Each vessel is well equipped and especially designed for entertaining on San Francisco Bay. Parquet dance floors, full galley, bars and even sleeping quarters are on board. During the cruise, weather permitting, canvas coverings can be rolled up for unobstructed views of San Francisco, Alameda and the bridges. Take a deep breath. Relax. Nothing beats a reception on the water. Guests can stroll about the decks or join the captain in the pilot house for a chat. If a church ceremony is not your style, have yours on the foredeck performed by the captain, or ashore in the Commodore's Gazebo. Another specialty of the house is the release of white doves—a treat guaranteed to thrill your guests. Enjoy the sea lions while gliding by Pier 39. Sail beneath the Bay Bridge or circle Treasure Island. Whether you come aboard for a rehearsal dinner, ceremony or reception, Commodore Dining Cruises will host your wedding event in a grand and gracious style without straining your pocketbook (offering a tremendous service at very competitive prices). Your guests will rave about the great time they had, and you'll have memories of salt water breezes and the excitement of getting married on the Bay.

CAPACITY:

Vessel	Seated	Standing	Vessel	Seated	Standing
Argo Commodore	50–60	100	Showtime Commodore	150	150
Commodore Stockton	72	86	Jack London Commodore	350	450

FEES & DEPOSITS: A $500–2,000 refundable deposit, which is applied toward the event total, is required to secure your date. The food and beverage balance is payable 2 weeks prior to the function. Fees run form $25–60/person, including yacht rental and food. Tax and gratuity are additional.

CANCELLATION POLICY: With 90 days' notice, the deposit will be refunded. With less notice, refunds will be given only if the yacht can be rebooked, minus a $200 rebooking fee.

AVAILABILITY: Year-round, anytime.

SERVICES/AMENITIES:

Restaurant Services: no
Catering: provided, BYO by arrangement
Kitchen Facilities: fully equipped
Tables & Chairs: provided
Linens, Silver, etc.: provided

Overnight Accommodations: Argo sleeps 32 guests
Telephone: ship to shore
Outdoor Night Lighting: access only
Outdoor Cooking Facilities: no
Cleanup: provided

Restrooms: no wca
Dance Floor: yes
Other: event coordination, decorations, homing doves, non-denominational ceremonies

RESTRICTIONS:
Alcohol: provided, BYO by arrangement
Smoking: some restrictions
Music: amplified ok

Parking: free parking, large lot
Bride's Dressing Area: yes

Wheelchair Access: yes
Insurance: not required

DUNSMUIR HOUSE

2960 Peralta Oaks Court
Oakland, CA 94605
(510) 562-0328
Reserve: 12 months in advance

Nestled in the East Bay foothills, the historic Dunsmuir House and Gardens offer a lovely and secluded setting featuring a turn-of-the-century white mansion and a 40-acre expanse of lawn and trees, evoking the serenity of a bygone era. The House was a romantic wedding gift from Alexander Dunsmuir to his bride on the occasion of their marriage in 1899. Its foyer offers a formal, softly lit space for ceremonies. The bride can make an impressive entrance as she descends the staircase, and a baby grand piano is always available to provide musical accompaniment. The Pond Area, with its weeping elms and delicate white gazebo, is the most popular site for ceremonies. Receptions are often held on its beautiful lawn with vistas of the Mansion and gardens. The Carriage House is a unique, rustic setting for indoor receptions. Its quaint seating nooks and mahogany paneling add an old-fashioned feel. Lit up with hundreds of twinkling lights and draped with evergreen garlands throughout, the Pavilion, with its large dance floor, is an especially lovely room for evening receptions. Built in the 1930s as a summer guest house, Dinkelspiel House has an English cottage ambiance. Six sets of glass French doors open out onto a patio, surrounded by huge pine trees and flowers. Inside, the knotty pine trim and fireplace make this a cozy place for a small wedding and/or reception. The grounds here are private, peaceful and beautiful throughout the year. This is one of the most exceptional sites in the Bay Area for a wedding celebration.

CAPACITY:	*Area*	*Standing*	*Seated*
	Mansion	80 (by special arrangement)	—
	Carriage House	200	100 or more
	Pavilion	300	200
	Pond area	300	300
	Meadow (partial use)	200–500	200–500
	Meadow (full use)	3,000	3,000
	Dinkelspiel House	60	60

FEES & DEPOSITS: A minimum refundable $500 deposit reserves your date. The balance of fees is due thirty days prior to the event. If you select a caterer not from the preferred list, there is a $300 charge. There is a wedding rehearsal charge of $50/hour. Use fees below are for a 6-hour time block and include use of some tables and chairs as well as setup and breakdown.

Wedding/Reception Locations	Use Fees			
	75 Guests	*100 Guests*	*150 Guests*	*200 Guests*
Mansion		*by special arrangement*		
Carriage House	$1,800	$1,950	$2,100	$2,250
Pavilion or	1,800	1,950	2,100	2,250
Meadow (partial use)				
Meadow (full use)		*by special arrangement*		
Pond Area	1,800	1,950	2,100	2,250
Dinkelspiel House	1,500	—	—	—

Any additional equipment must be rented through Dunsmuir House.

CANCELLATION POLICY: No refund will be given 72 hours after reservations are made.

AVAILABILITY: Any day, February–October.

SERVICES/AMENITIES:

Restaurant Services: no
Catering: select from preferred list
Kitchen Facilities: no
Tables & Chairs: limited
Linens, Silver, etc.: BYO
Restrooms: wca
Parking: on street, or $100/parking lot
Bride's Dressing Area: yes, $50/event

Dance Floor: Greenhouse only; lawn area CBA, extra fee
Overnight Accommodations: no
Telephone: pay phone
Outdoor Night Lighting: access only
Outdoor Cooking Facilities: CBA
Cleanup: provided
Other: mansion photos, $100/hour

RESTRICTIONS:

Alcohol: provided or BYO, BWC only
Smoking: outside only
Music: amplified ok

Wheelchair Access: yes
Insurance: may be required
Other: decorations limited, no rice

THE LAKE MERRITT HOTEL

1800 Madison Street at Lakeside
Oakland, CA 94612
(510) 832-2300
Reserve: 3–12 months in advance

Totally enclosed in twenty-foot floor-to-ceiling windows, the Lake Merritt Hotel's Terrace Room presents a spectacular panorama of Lake Merritt, Lakeside Park and the Oakland hills. At night, the lake glitters below, reflecting the Necklace of Lights gracing its perimeter. Recently, over $1.5 million was spent to turn the Hotel and restaurant into one of Oakland's premier entertainment sites. This classic, 1927 Art Deco landmark has been renovated with new furnishings, carpeting and soft colors throughout. During the day, the multi-level Terrace Room is bathed in light. In the evening, it has an intimate, almost cabaret feeling. Here you'll find a semi-circle hardwood dance floor, very good original watercolor paintings and a sizeable mural along one wall (circa 1927) depicting Lake Merritt before the Depression. Fresh flowers, a black baby grand piano and Art Deco fixtures are nice finishing touches. In addition to having a great location along the perimeter of Lake Merritt and a good restaurant in-house, the staff aims to please by offering highly personalized services, many of which can be specifically tailored to your wedding.

CAPACITY: The Terrace Room accommodates 275 standing or 225 guests for a seated affair.

FEES & DEPOSITS: A $500 non-refundable security deposit is required to reserve your date. 50% payment is required 1 month prior and the balance is due 2 weeks prior to your event. For events, the Terrace Room rental fee varies from complimentary to $1,000 based on the specifics of each function. In-house food and beverage service is provided. For full seated service including food and beverage, rates run approximately $35/person. Buffets start at $20/person; hors d'oeuvres start at $10/person. Sales tax and a 17% service charge are additional. Cake cutting costs $2/person.

AVAILABILITY: The Terrace Room is available everyday from noon to midnight.

SERVICES/AMENITIES:

Restaurant Services: yes
Catering: provided
Kitchen Facilities: n/a
Tables & Chairs: provided
Linens, Silver, etc.: provided
Restrooms: no wca
Dance Floor: yes
Bride's Dressing Area: CBA

Parking: on street, valet CBA
Overnight Accommodations: suites &
packages available
Telephone: pay phone
Outdoor Night Lighting: access only
Outdoor Cooking Facilities: no
Cleanup: provided
Special: full event coordination in-house

RESTRICTIONS:

Alcohol: provided, champagne corkage $4/bottle
Smoking: designated areas
Music: amplified restricted

Wheelchair Access: limited
Insurance: not required

MILLS COLLEGE CHAPEL

5000 MacArthur
Oakland, CA 94613
(510) 430-2145
Reserve: 6–8 months in advance

Located on the Mills College campus, the Chapel is a unique contemporary structure. It is built in the round, from selected redwoods, mahogany, fir, cedar and glass. The altar is in the center and to the side. A choir loft and pipe organ are well integrated into the Chapel's design. The surrounding greenery is visible from every point through the large windows, enhancing the effect of quiet intimacy. If you are looking for a lovely, indoor spot to take your vows, we suggest you take a look.

CAPACITY: The Chapel accommodates 175 seated guests.

FEES & DEPOSITS: The $350 deposit is the rental fee, due when reservations are confirmed.

CANCELLATION POLICY: There's a $75 administration charge for any cancellations.

AVAILABILITY: Year-round, any day.

SERVICES/AMENITIES:

Tables & Chairs: no
Restrooms: wca
Bride's Dressing area: yes

Parking: on street
Telephone: no
Cleanup: renter

RESTRICTIONS:

Alcohol: not allowed
Smoking: not allowed
Music: acoustical only

Insurance: not required
Wheelchair Access: yes
Other: no rice or birdseed, only tie-on decorations

MORCOM ROSE GARDEN

700 Jean Street
Oakland, CA
(510) 238-3187
Reserve: 11 months in advance

In season, the Rose Garden offers one of the most striking and fragrant wedding sites in the East Bay. The ascent to the Wedding Terrace is flanked by rows of multicolored roses. The Terrace itself is ringed with pine trees and overlooks a waterfall series of fountains that tumble down through a tapestry of rose bushes (unfortunately, since the drought and earthquake, the fountains are not operational). Even though the site is not far from downtown, the Garden seems miles away—a quiet and secluded haven.

CAPACITY: The Wedding Terrace holds up to 200 standing guests.

FEES & DEPOSITS: A refundable $200 deposit and a $150 rental fee is due when you confirm reservations.

CANCELLATION POLICY: With more than 31 days' notice, you will forfeit $75; with less, the entire rental fee will be forfeited.

AVAILABILITY: (The Garden will be closed from October 1992–October 1993 for renovation.) Normally open Mother's Day through October 31, 9am–8pm.

SERVICES/AMENITIES:

Parking: on street above garden

Telephone: no

Cleanup: renter

Tables & Chairs: few benches, chair rental CBA

Restrooms: no wca

Outdoor Night Lighting: access only

Bride's Dressing Area: no

RESTRICTIONS:

Alcohol: not allowed

Smoking: allowed

Music: acoustic only, no outlets

Wheelchair Access: very limited

Insurance: not required

Other: no food, beverages or rice

OAKLAND HILLS TENNIS CLUB

5475 Redwood Road
Oakland, CA 94619
(510) 531-3300
Reserve: 6–12 months in advance

Here's a new introduction with a killer view of the Bay. Set on ten acres atop the Oakland Hills, this facility is now hosting wedding receptions. Don't be deterred by the front door which says 'members only'. For those who have reserved the Club for functions after regular hours, this place is definitely open. The entry walk to the front door is shaded by old oaks and new landscaping. The swimming pool is on your right and the multiple tennis courts are below, on your left. Although you'll find the usual paraphernalia of a tennis club inside (sports clothing, equipment, lockers and the like), the building is new and nicely designed. For receptions, you'd use the west part of the building. The aerobics room, a large, uncluttered space with a shiny, oak hardwood floor, a vaulted wood-beamed ceiling, a wall of mirrors and wall-to-wall windows has a remarkable, unobstructed view of the Bay Area. For outdoor entertaining, the long deck running the length of the room can be arranged with tables, chairs and umbrellas. The Club's Cafe is next door, which is connected to the aerobics room by way of double doors. Both can be used simultaneously for larger receptions. We think the Club is a good choice if you're looking for a light and contemporary space for a prenuptial dinner, wedding ceremony or reception.

CAPACITY: 110 seated guests; 200 for a standing reception. Additional seating for 40 available on adjacent deck.

FEES & DEPOSITS: A $250 non-refundable security deposit reserves your date. The rental fee is $500 per event, due 30 days prior to the function. An extra $75/hour will be charged for any use of the facility after 10pm.

AVAILABILITY: Year-round, Friday, Saturday and Sunday after 4pm. Rentals prior to 4pm will only be considered during the Club's non-peak times.

SERVICES/AMENITIES:

Restaurant Services: yes

Catering: provided or BYO

Kitchen Facilities: fully equipped

Tables & Chairs: provided, extra charge

Linens, Silver, etc.: BYO or provided, extra charge

Restrooms: wca

Dance Floor: yes

Bride's Dressing Area: CBA

Parking: large parking lot

Overnight Accommodations: no

Telephone: pay phone

Outdoor Night Lighting: yes

Outdoor Cooking Facilities: CBA

Cleanup: provided and/or caterer

Other: some event coordination provided

RESTRICTIONS:

Alcohol: BYO, some restrictions

Smoking: outside only

Music: amplified volume restricted

Wheelchair Access: yes

Insurance: required

OLIVETO

5655 College Avenue
Oakland, CA 94618
(510) 547-5356
Reserve: 1 week–12 months in advance

A passion for Mediterranean cooking was the inspiration for this Northern Italian restaurant, situated on the second floor of the Rockridge Market Hall. Oliveto's main dining room is a fragrant, high-ceilinged space with tall windows that open out onto the street below. Sunset-colored stucco walls are reminiscent of Tuscany, and old Italian flower pots have been cleverly transformed into wall sconces. On the day we paid a visit, a vibrant display of fall leaves and flowers, framed by two enormous pumpkins, gave the room a colorful and festive ambiance. The open kitchen adds a bit of drama, and almost everything here is prepared from scratch, using plenty of fresh ingredients grown by local farmers, and organically raised beef, pork and duck. Have your rehearsal dinner in the Siena Room, a private space at the far end of the dining room. A wall of interior windows gives you a great view of the activities in the rest of the restaurant, while maintaining total privacy. Natural light, warm colors and its own floral arrangement makes this an inviting spot for a family get-together. Once considered a "mad project" by the owners' friends, Oliveto has become an East Bay favorite, creating imaginative and consistently delicious food.

CAPACITY: The Siena Room can accommodate 26 seated guests.

FEES & DEPOSITS: A deposit in the amount of $100 for dinner or $50 for lunch is required to confirm your reservation. The balance is due at the conclusion of the event. Lunches are $18.50/person, dinners range from $28.50–36.50/person depending on the number of courses. Tax and gratuity are included.

CANCELLATION POLICY: With 1 week's notice, the deposit is fully refunded.

AVAILABILITY: Monday–Friday for lunch, and every evening for dinner.

SERVICES/AMENITIES:

Restaurant Services: yes
Catering: provided, no BYO
Kitchen Facilities: n/a
Tables & Chairs: provided
Linens, Silver, etc.: provided
Restrooms: wca
Dance Floor: no

Parking: lot in back, on street
Overnight Accommodations: no
Telephone: pay phone
Outdoor Night Lighting: access only
Outdoor Cooking Facilities: no
Cleanup: provided

RESTRICTIONS:

Alcohol: provided, corkage $8/bottle
Smoking: not allowed
Music: not allowed

Wheelchair Access: yes
Insurance: not required

PIEMONTE OVEST

3909 Grand Avenue
Oakland, CA 94610
(510) 601-0500
Reserve: 1 week–12 months in advance

Piemonte Ovest serves up innovative Italian specialties in one of the most appealing restaurants in the East Bay. As you walk through the gentle arches in the entry, your eye is drawn to vivid flower arrangements, reflected in an enormous mirror behind the bar. The Main Dining Room has a wall of floor-to-ceiling windows and a softly draped skylight, both designed to follow the peaked contours of the roofline and admit lots of natural light. Warmth emanates from the beautifully painted walls, roughly brushed with ochre, pink, cream and pale yellow hues. These sunkissed tones also give the Back Room and upstairs Private Dining Room a special glow. Both spaces have plenty of windows and the Back Room overlooks Piemonte's garden courtyard. This two-level patio is a lovely spot for a rehearsal dinner on a balmy evening. It's enclosed by latticed fencing and an overhead trellis, and Magnolia, lemon and Japanese Maple trees grow through and around the wooden deck and brick areas. Impatiens and ferns create colorful clusters at the patio's edge. And on cooler evenings, a fire in the large brick oven takes the chill off. The restaurant is also an art gallery, with rotating exhibits in every room. Given its inviting ambiance and creative cuisine, it's no surprise that Piemonte has become a popular choice with Bay Area diners.

CAPACITY:

	Seated	Standing		Seated	Standing
Main Dining Room	28	—	Patio	55	70
Private Dining Room	55	70	Entire Restaurant	110	200
Back Room (semi-private)	18	—			

FEES & DEPOSITS: A non-refundable $100 is required when you reserve a private dining area. The entire restaurant can be reserved for a minimum of $5,000, with 50% of the anticipated total due at the time of booking. The balance in either case is payable at the conclusion of the event. Luncheons start at $13/person, dinners at $25. Beverage, tax and gratuity are additional.

CANCELLATION POLICY: The deposit is not refundable.

AVAILABILITY: The private dining areas are available Sunday–Thursday, 11am–midnight. Special events can be arranged Friday and Saturday.

SERVICES/AMENITIES:

Restaurant Services: yes
Catering: provided, no BYO
Kitchen Facilities: n/a
Tables & Chairs: provided
Linens, Silver, etc.: provided
Restrooms: no wca
Dance Floor: CBA

Parking: on street
Overnight Accommodations: no
Telephone: house phone
Outdoor Night Lighting: patio
Outdoor Cooking Facilities: no
Cleanup: provided
Bride's Dressing Area: CBA

RESTRICTIONS:

Alcohol: provided, corkage negotiable
Smoking: designated areas
Music: inside only if reserve entire rest.

Wheelchair Access: no
Insurance: not required

PRESERVATION PARK

660 & 668 13th St at Martin Luther King Jr. Way
Oakland, CA 94612
(510) 874-7580
Reserve: 1–6 months in advance

Occupying two blocks a heartbeat away from Oakland's City Center, Preservation Park is a recreation of a Victorian neighborhood where historic residences have been transformed back to their original splendor. Sixteen beautifully restored and colorfully painted Victorian homes have been relocated here, replicating a turn-of-the-century small-town setting, with period park benches, ornate wrought-iron fences and 19th century street lamps. A large, two-tiered fountain with the moon goddess Diana resting atop, acts as the Park's centerpiece. It is located in the center of a cul-de-sac, framed by manicured lawns and well-maintained landscaping. Two houses, in particular, are well-suited for special events. The Ginn House, circa 1890, features two delightful light and airy parlors which are reminiscent of an English country home. The Nile Club, circa 1911, is a craftsman-style building which has been connected to the Ginn house via a spacious hallway. Walk through and enter Nile Hall, which is a sensational space for a grand and elegant party. It has a soaring 30-foot high ceiling, skylights, multiple windows, stage plus theatrical lighting and sound system. This room is well designed, with soft colors, nice detailing and attractive appointments—and, enough room to please any couple with an extensive guest list. We think Preservation Park is an outstanding addition to the East Bay. This is a 'must see' facility.

CAPACITY:	Area	Standing	Seated		Area	Standing	Seated
	Ginn House	125	—		Nile Hall	250	140
	Large Parlor	105	50		Ginn & Nile	400	185
	Small Parlor	20	15				

FEES & DEPOSITS: A non-refundable $250 rental deposit, applied to the rental fee, is required to secure your date. The balance of the rental fee, together with a refundable cleaning/damage deposit, are payable 60 days prior to the event. The fee for Nile Hall is $800; for Nile Hall plus the Ginn House, $1175. For functions during the Christmas season, the non-refundable rental deposit is $500.

CANCELLATION POLICY: The rental deposit is not refundable. With less than 30 days' notice, the rental fee is forfeited.

AVAILABILITY: Year-round, everyday from 8am–1am.

SERVICES/AMENITIES:

Restaurant Services: no

Catering: provided, no BYO

Kitchen Facilities: set up only

Tables & Chairs: provided

Linens, Silver, etc.: provided by caterer

Restrooms: wca

Dance Floor: CBA

Parking: on street or City lot nearby

Overnight Accommodations: no

Telephone: pay phone

Outdoor Night Lighting: yes

Outdoor Cooking Facilities: no

Cleanup: caterer

Bride's Dressing Area: CBA

RESTRICTIONS:

Alcohol: provided, no BYO

Smoking: outside only

Music: amplified ok

Wheelchair Access: yes

Insurance: may be required

Need a caterer, cake maker, florist? The Service Directory starting on page 412 features the best in the business.

SAILBOAT HOUSE

568 Bellvue Ave. in Lakeside Park
Oakland, CA 94612
(510) 238-3187 Parks and Recreation Office
Reserve: 11 months in advance

Resting on the edge of Lake Merritt within Lakeside Park, the Sailboat House offers a wonderful view of the water. The large upstairs room that is available for parties and receptions is totally enclosed in glass and has an outdoor deck which runs the length of the lake side of the building. The atmosphere is especially light and airy during sunny afternoons, and at night the lakeside Necklace of Lights lends an added sparkle to events.

CAPACITY: The room accommodates 225 standing, 155 seated or 125 seated banquet style.

FEES & DEPOSITS: A refundable security deposit of $200 and the minimum rental fee are due when reservations are made. The facility rents for $50/hr between 9am–midnight; $60/hr between midnight–1am (Fri & Sat only) and $60/hr before 9am. There is a 4-hour minimum rental. Setup and teardown are available for $50 and $75, respectively. If champagne, beer or wine are served, there's an extra fee of $50; hard alcohol $75. Entry into Lakeside Park is $2/car.

CANCELLATION POLICY: With more than 31 days' notice, you forfeit $25, with less notice, $200 is forfeited.

AVAILABILITY: The facility is available from 8am–midnight Monday–Friday, and until 1am on Friday and Saturday nights.

SERVICES/AMENITIES:

Restaurant Services: no
Catering: BYO
Kitchen Facilities: moderate
Tables & Chairs: provided
Linens, Silver, etc.: BYO
Restrooms: wca
Dance Floor: yes
Bride's Dressing Area: no

Parking: lot ($2/car)
Overnight Accommodations: no
Telephone: pay phone
Outdoor Night Lighting: access only
Outdoor Cooking Facilities: no
Cleanup: whoever caters event, provided for $50 fee
Other: piano

RESTRICTIONS:

Alcohol: BYO (permit fee)
Smoking: outside only
Music: amplified ok

Wheelchair Access: yes
Insurance: usually not required

SCOTTISH RITE CENTER

1547 Lakeside Drive
Oakland, CA 94612
(510) 832-0819
Reserve: 3–6 months in advance

Although you might not pay too much attention to the rather nondescript facade of the Scottish Rite Center, once you're inside, it's an entirely different story. This historic building houses some of the most remarkable and impressive interior spaces we've ever seen. Constructed for the Masonic Order in 1927, it's just a stone's throw from Lake Merritt in Oakland. Here, you'll find a wide selection of differently designed small and large rooms. We were impressed by inlaid terrazzo and mosaic floors, walls of ornate design, soaring, hand-carved ceilings, grand staircases and period fixtures that create an old world ambiance. We were 'wowed' by two rooms in particular. The Grand Ballroom, on the first floor, is magnificent. Five chandeliers, suspended from an exquisite ceiling, light a 10,000 square foot hardwood floor. The twenty-eight foot vaulted ceiling is hand-painted mostly in golds, with highlights of greens, pinks and taupe. The decorative plaster friezes are delicate, almost lace-like as they curve down to meet the walls. The Ballroom has a refined elegance. On one side, a large, formally draped stage is perfect for a band—along the opposite wall, a balcony stretches the length of the room. Take the walnut-clad elevators to the top floor and step out into the auditorium foyer. This splendid space is the prefunction or waiting area for the Center's theater. It has its own loggia (balcony), overlooking Lake Merritt and has a remarkable ceiling. In fact the foyer, in its own right is so beautiful, it's hard to believe that what comes next could top it. Talk about a space that takes your breath away—this is a room you *must* see. The expansive theater is capped by a dome which rises eighty feet from the floor, partially supported by multiple Corinthian columns. Brass lamps, artfully suspended from the perimeter, provide a subtle glow. Curved theater seating in tiers is oriented towards the very large, professional stage. Heavy, burgundy velvet with gold and burgundy tie-backs, tassels and braids plus a hand-sewn canopy create a one and a half ton theater curtain that was, in 1927, the largest curtain outside of the Metropolitan Opera house in New York. Used for formal showings of film or videos, seminars, comedy competitions, fashion shows, talent competitions and theater productions, this auditorium is extraordinary. If you are looking for an East Bay location that can offer variety, distinction and a sense of grandness, we urge you to take a full tour of this facility. We think you'll be pleasantly surprised.

CAPACITY, FEES & DEPOSITS: A $200 non-refundable deposit is required when your date is confirmed. The rental fee plus a $250 refundable security/cleaning deposit are payable 30 days prior to your function. A stage electrician is an additional charge.

Area	*Seated*	*Standing*	*Fee*
Grand Ballroom	1,000	1,300	$1,000–1,300
Banquet Room	250–300	350	500–700
Auditorium/Theater	1,500	—	1,200–1,800

AVAILABILITY: Year-round, any day from 10am–midnight.

SERVICES/AMENITIES:

Restaurant Services: no
Catering: BYO or CBA
Kitchen Facilities: fully equipped
Tables & Chairs: provided
Linens, Silver, etc.: BYO
Restrooms: wca
Bride's Dressing Area: yes

Parking: private lot
Overnight Accommodations: no
Telephone: pay phone
Outdoor Night Lighting: access only
Outdoor Cooking Facilities: no
Cleanup: renter or caterer
Dance Floor: yes

RESTRICTIONS:

Alcohol: BYO
Smoking: designated areas
Music: amplified ok

Wheelchair Access: yes
Insurance: proof of liability required

SCOTT'S SEAFOOD RESTAURANT

#2 Broadway at Jack London Square
Oakland, CA 94607
(510) 444-5969 Catering
Reserve: 1 week in advance

Surprise! Scott's has great private facilities that are not part of their main dining room. Located on the Oakland Estuary, the Harbor View Rooms and Bay View Terrace have views of Alameda, San Francisco and passing ships. Recently developed, the Harbor View Rooms are sophisticated in color and decor, plus they have the advantage of multiple folding doors, which can be opened or closed to create a combination of spaces. Scott's can arrange these rooms to meet the needs of your special event. If you're looking for a waterfront location for your ceremony, wedding reception, rehearsal dinner or bridal shower—this is an unexpected find.

CAPACITY:

Room	Seated	Standing	Room	Seated	Standing
Harbor View A	80	120	Combined ABC	250	450
Harbor View B	60	80	Bay View/Terrace	45	75
Harbor View C	70	80			

FEES & DEPOSITS: A deposit of $500/room is required to secure your date. Per person prices: seated meals and buffets $20–30 and hors d'oeuvres $15–25. Tax and an 18% service charge are additional.

CANCELLATION POLICY: Deposits will be refunded only if the space(s) rented can be rebooked.

AVAILABILITY: Year-round, closed Christmas day. Everyday from 7am–2am. Saturday reception time frames: 11am–4pm and 6pm–12am.

SERVICES/AMENITIES:

Restaurant Services: yes
Catering: provided

Overnight Accommodations: no
Telephone: pay phone

Kitchen Facilities: n/a
Tables & Chairs: provided
Linens, Silver, etc.: provided
Restrooms: wca
Dance Floor: yes, extra charge
Bride's Dressing Area: no

RESTRICTIONS:
Alcohol: provided
Smoking: allowed
Music: amplified ok

Outdoor Night Lighting: yes
Outdoor Cooking Facilities: no
Cleanup: provided
Parking: valet or parking lot
Other: full event coordination, floral arrangements

Wheelchair Access: yes
Insurance: not required

SEQUOIA LODGE

2666 Mountain Blvd.
Oakland, CA
(510) 238-3187 Parks and Recreation Office
Reserve: 11 months in advance

Located among the trees at the base of the Oakland Hills, Sequoia Lodge has the feel of a mountain retreat. The interior features rustic wood paneling, a stone fireplace and a high pitched roof with a skylight. A sunken seating area in front of the fireplace gives guests an intimate spot for conversation and an outside deck area adds to the serene setting in the trees.

CAPACITY: The Lodge accommodates 150 standing, 100 seated or 80 seated guests at banquet tables.

FEES & DEPOSITS: A refundable security deposit of $200 and the minimum rental fee are due at the time of booking. The facility rents for $50/hr between 9am and midnight, $60/hr between midnight and 1am and before 9am. Minimum rental is 4 hours. If champagne, beer or wine are served, there's an extra $50 fee; hard alcohol $75. If needed, setup fee is $50 and teardown is $75.

CANCELLATION POLICY: With more than 31 days' notice, you forfeit $25; with less than 31 days' notice, $200 is forfeited.

AVAILABILITY: Monday–Thursday 3:30pm–midnight (9am–midnight during summer), Friday–Saturday 9am–1am, Sunday 9am to midnight.

SERVICES/AMENITIES:
Restaurant Services: no
Catering: BYO
Kitchen Facilities: ample
Tables & Chairs: provided
Linens, Silver, etc.: BYO
Restrooms: wca
Dance Floor: yes
Other: piano

Parking: on and off street, lot
Overnight Accommodations: no
Telephone: pay phone
Outdoor Night Lighting: yes
Outdoor Cooking Facilities: no
Cleanup: caterer or staff, extra fee
Bride's Dressing Area: restroom only

RESTRICTIONS:

Alcohol: BYO for $50–75 fee
Smoking: outside only
Music: amplified ok

Wheelchair Access: yes
Insurance: usually not required

Piedmont

PIEDMONT COMMUNITY CENTER

711 Highland Ave.
Piedmont, CA 94611
(510) 420-3081 Penny Robb
Reserve: 9–12 months in advance

Brick steps lead down to the Center, situated in a park setting. Mediterranean in style, the light taupe building with its tile roof and landscaped plaza is surrounded by redwoods and flowering cherry trees. Azaleas and camellias provide splashes of color near the round patio, and behind the building, a stream and more trees complete the circle of greenery. The Center's interior has recently undergone renovation and looks better than ever. This is a great party room, with high beamed ceiling, shining herringbone hardwood floors and chandeliers. Floor-to-ceiling windows allow lots of natural light and ensure that the feeling of the park carries over to your reception. This is a refined, nicely designed space, suitable for an elegant wedding. Reserve early—it's a popular spot.

CAPACITY: The Center accommodates 223 standing or 104 seated guests. The patio area holds 300 standing or 200 seated guests.

FEES & DEPOSITS: A security deposit of $300 is due two weeks after booking and is refundable four weeks after the event. For residents, the facility is rented in 6-hour blocks; the fee is $700. For non-residents, a 6-hour block is available for $1,200. These rates are for Friday, Saturday and Sunday. Payment is due 30 days prior to the event. For Monday–Thursday rates, please call for specifics.

CANCELLATION POLICY: If notification of cancellation is given 2 months prior to the event, half of the security deposit will be refunded. A full refund minus $30 will be given with 6 months' notice.

AVAILABILITY: The Center is available (one event per day) from 8am to midnight daily, with extensions possible if requested in writing 30 days in advance. The summer months are booked quickly.

SERVICES/AMENITIES:

Restaurant Services: no
Catering: BYO
Kitchen Facilities: minimal
Tables & Chairs: provided

Parking: on and off street
Overnight Accommodations: no
Telephone: pay phone
Outdoor Night Lighting: yes

Linens, Silver, etc.: BYO
Restrooms: wca
Dance Floor: yes

RESTRICTIONS:
Alcohol: BYO, must have controlled bar
Smoking: not allowed
Music: amplified ok

Outdoor Cooking Facilities: BYO
Cleanup: caterer or renter
Bride's Dressing Area: no

Wheelchair Access: yes
Insurance: included in weekend rates, you must provide for any weekday use

Pleasanton

CENTURY HOUSE

2401 Santa Rita Road
Pleasanton, CA 94566
(510) 484-8160
Reserve: 6–9 months in advance

Set far back from the main street, Century House is an unexpected sight. It's a white Victorian farmhouse with modest proportions and simple country detailing. The path leading up to the house is flanked by two expansive lawns and lined with blooming rose bushes. A decorative iron fence surrounds the site, enclosing a brick patio stretching the entire length of the house front. Like many homes built in the 1870s, this one has an oversized veranda, leaded glass panels in the front door and white latticework along the base of the building. Inside, the rooms are small but softly decorated in muted colors. On the south side of the house, a large brick patio and white gazebo shaded by Chinese elm trees provide a perfect setting for an outdoor ceremony. The Century House exudes an old-fashioned warmth that stirs memories of "the old days." Guests will feel that they've been transported out of suburban Pleasanton and into a different place and time altogether.

CAPACITY: October–April 50 guests; May–September 125 guests.

FEES & DEPOSITS: A $50 non-refundable deposit is required to secure your date with full payment due 4 weeks prior to the event. The rental fee is for 6 hours of use which includes setup and cleanup time.

	Resident		Non-Resident	
	Basic Fee	*Add. Hourly*	*Basic Fee*	*Add. Hourly*
up to 50 guests	$200	$25	$250	$35
51 to 125 guests	$250	$35	$300	$50

CANCELLATION POLICY: Cancellations must be made in writing at least 4 weeks prior to the date reserved and will incur a cancellation fee of $50. If less than 4 weeks' notice is given, the rental deposit and up to 50% of the rental fee will be forfeited.

AVAILABILITY: 10am to 10pm Friday and Saturday, 10am to 9pm Sunday through Thursday.

SERVICES/AMENITIES:

Restaurant Services: no

Catering: BYO

Kitchen Facilities: moderate

Tables & Chairs: some provided

Linens, Silver, etc.: BYO

Restrooms: wca

Dance Floor: limited

Parking: lot, on street

Overnight Accommodations: no

Telephone: pay phone

Outdoor Night Lighting: limited

Outdoor Cooking Facilities: not allowed

Cleanup: some provided, renter provides the rest

Bride's Dressing Area: yes

RESTRICTIONS:

Alcohol: BYO

Smoking: outside only

Music: no amplified, DJs or live music

Wheelchair Access: yes

Insurance: bodily injury and damage liability required

Other: decorations restricted, no rice or birdseed

THE PLEASANTON HOTEL

855 Main St.
Pleasanton, CA 94566
(510) 846-8112 or **(510) 846-8106**
Reserve: 6–12 months in advance

The Pleasanton Hotel sits in the center of Pleasanton's historic downtown. This 130-year-old building, flanked by stately magnolia and palm trees, is a turn–of–the–century Victorian with "gingerbread" detailing. The decor is vintage 1860s, with heavy window draping and colors in ivories, burgundies, forest greens and pastels. The recently redecorated interior boasts two large dining rooms and several adjacent smaller rooms, all of which can be connected via folding doors to accommodate large parties. There are numerous chandeliers, Tiffany lamps and Victorian appointments. On the magnolia-shaded patio outdoors, is a raised area great for outdoor wedding ceremonies, DJ's or bands. The patio includes a brick BBQ and outdoor bar as well as a bubbling fountain that completes the ambiance of this vintage setting.

CAPACITY: The Hotel can seat 300 guests inside, 100 on the patio.

FEES & DEPOSITS: A $250 non-refundable deposit is required to secure your date and a $500 non-refundable deposit is payable 60 days prior to your function. A $350 setup fee for ceremonies and receptions or a reception-only fee of $150 is required. Full meal service is provided. Luncheons range from $11–17/person and dinners from $15–22/person. Tax and 15% service charge will be applied to the final estimated bill, which is payable 30 days prior to the event.

CANCELLATION POLICY: The deposits are not refundable unless the space can be rebooked with a party of equal or larger size.

AVAILABILITY: Monday–Friday, anytime. Saturdays 11am–4pm and 6pm–11pm; Sunday 5pm–11pm.

SERVICES/AMENITIES:

Restaurant Services: yes
Catering: provided, no BYO
Kitchen Facilities: n/a
Tables & Chairs: provided
Linens, Silver, etc.: provided
Restrooms: wca
Parking: lot
Bride's Dressing Area: yes

Overnight Accommodations: no
Telephone: pay phone
Outdoor Night Lighting: yes
Outdoor Cooking Facilities: BBQ
Cleanup: provided
Dance Floor: yes
Other: wedding coordination

RESTRICTIONS:

Alcohol: provided, corkage $7.50/750 ml bottle
Smoking: allowed
Music: amplified ok

Wheelchair Access: yes
Insurance: not required
Other: no rice, birdseed

Point Richmond

EAST BROTHER
LIGHT STATION

San Francisco Bay, off Point San Pablo
(510) 233-2385
Reserve: 2–6 months in advance

A short but exhilarating boat ride takes you to the island. On this one-acre, sun-washed speck in the ocean sits the oldest operational lighthouse in or around San Francisco Bay. Constructed in 1873–74, the light station continues to preserve a little bit of maritime history. Gone are the telephone poles, cars, crowds and noise of the mainland. Here the only sounds come from seagulls, the sea and the foghorn. Small ceremonies are often held in the lighthouse tower balcony or on top of the island cistern. Receptions take place outdoors, and guests have a clear, unobstructed view of the San Francisco skyline and the coast of Marin. The main house, with its lace curtains, wooden floors and fireplaces, is relaxed and homey—a genuinely charming place for the honeymoon couple and a few friends to stay overnight. The innkeeper is also the chef, and a visit to her kitchen is a treat. When we were there, the afternoon sun was streaming in through the window onto two freshly baked pies. The fragrant warmth of the scene still lingers, and makes us want to pay the light station another visit.

CAPACITY: The island will accommodate a maximum of 250 people. The 4-bedroom guest house can accommodate up to 8 guests for an overnight stay.

FEES & DEPOSITS: A deposit in the amount of 25% of the estimated costs is required at the time of booking to secure your date. The balance is due within 30 days. Island fees range from $250–$2100 depending on the size of the group. A multi-course gourmet dinner with wines and a full hot breakfast can be added to the package for overnight guests. Fees for boat transportation, catering and all other services are extra and can be arranged by East Brother Light Station.

CANCELLATION POLICY: If cancellation is made 60 days prior to the event, a full refund will be made; between 30 and 60 days, a 90% refund is given. With less than 30 days notice, 90% of the deposit will be refunded only if the date can be rebooked.

AVAILABILITY: 11am to dusk Friday through Sunday.

SERVICES/AMENITIES:

Restaurant Services: no

Catering: provided or BYO

Kitchen Facilities: limited

Tables & Chairs: some provided

Linens, Silver, etc.: BYO

Restrooms: wca

Dance Floor: CBA

Parking: at yacht harbor

OvernightAccommodations: 4 guestrooms

Telephone: cellular for emergencies

Outdoor Night Lighting: yes

Outdoor Cooking Facilities: yes

Cleanup: caterer

Bride's Dressing Area: yes

RESTRICTIONS:

Alcohol: provided or BYO

Smoking: outside only

Music: amplified ok

Wheelchair Access: difficult

Insurance: not required

LINSLEY HALL

235 Washington Ave.
Point Richmond, CA 94801
(510) 235-7338   Donna Powers
Reserve: 3–6 months in advance

Linsley Hall, built in 1904 as a church, is now a distinctive, multi-use facility located in historic Point Richmond. With its vaulted ceiling, wood paneling and lovely original stained glass windows, the Chapel offers its guests turn-of-the-century warmth and dignity. The sanctuary's acoustics are so outstanding that it's rented quite often for concerts and recitals. Downstairs, the Reception Room has a custom-built oak bar and guests can flow out into the attractive flower garden which has shade trees, gazebo, brickwork and lawn. Evening weddings in the church are enhanced by candlelight, and daytime ceremonies are often performed in the gazebo outdoors.

CAPACITY: The Hall can hold up to 110 guests. The Reception Room holds 10–60 and the Garden 50.

FEES & DEPOSITS: A non-refundable deposit (25% of the rental fee) is due when reservations are made. For weddings, the rental fee is $900.

AVAILABILITY: All year, everyday from 9am to 7pm.

SERVICES/AMENITIES:

Restaurant Services: no
Catering: BYO
Kitchen Facilities: moderate
Tables & Chairs: most provided
Linens, Silver, etc.: BYO
Restrooms: no wca
Dance Floor: yes

Parking: on street
Overnight Accommodations: no
Telephone: local calls only
Outdoor Night Lighting: access only
Outdoor Cooking Facilities: yes
Cleanup: caterer
Bride's Dressing Area: yes

RESTRICTIONS:

Alcohol: BYO, WCB only
Smoking: outside only
Music: no amplified music outdoors

Wheelchair Access: limited
Insurance: not required

San Leandro

BEST HOUSE

1315 Clarke Street
San Leandro, CA 94577
(510) 351-0911
Reserve: 1–6 months in advance

This yellow Victorian is a bright spot in the city. The yard, where weddings and receptions are held, is shaded by a variety of trees, and the brick patio and low decks give guests plenty of room to unwind. A working water wheel and miniature street lamps add quaint touches to this quiet setting. Personalized service and a relaxed atmosphere make this facility terrific for private functions. Best House is also a bed and breakfast inn and wedding guests are welcome to stay the night.

CAPACITY: The grounds accommodate a maximum of 150 people.

FEES & DEPOSITS: A deposit of 50% of the rental fee is required to reserve your date. An additional $200 damage/cleaning deposit is due 30 days before your event and is refundable within 1 week of your event. The total rental fee is $850 for a 5-hour block of time and the remaining balance is due 30 days prior to the event.

CANCELLATION POLICY: With less than 30 days' notice, deposits are not refundable unless the date can be rebooked.

AVAILABILITY: Anytime between April and October. Reserve early for summer.

SERVICES/AMENITIES:

Restaurant Services: no
Catering: BYO, licensed only

Parking: lot and on street
Overnight Accommodations: 5 guestrooms

Kitchen Facilities: moderate
Tables & Chairs: some provided
Linens, Silver, etc.: BYO
Restrooms: wca in garden
Dance Floor: brick patio

RESTRICTIONS:
Alcohol: BYO, WCB only
Smoking: outside only
Music: amplified ok

Telephone: pay phone, emergencies only
Outdoor Night Lighting: yes
Outdoor Cooking Facilities: no
Cleanup: caterer
Bride's Dressing Area: yes

Wheelchair Access: outdoors only
Insurance: not required

San Pablo

ROCKEFELLER LODGE

2650 Market St.
San Pablo, CA 94806
(510) 235-7344
Reserve: 6–12 months in advance

Have you always wanted to do something a bit different for your wedding? Maybe have a Victorian theme in one room and French lace and balloons in another. Or maybe treat your guests to milk and cookies baked on the spot? Whatever your fantasy, the owner and staff of the Rockefeller Lodge love the challenge of making it a reality. And with its variety of rooms and outdoor areas, the Lodge can accommodate a wide range of creativity. Once a Japanese Buddhist Temple, the Rockefeller Lodge still offers a fragrant, woodsy serenity. The brown-shingled building derives its secluded feeling from the surrounding trees and quiet neighborhood. Winding brick paths and wisteria-covered arbors invite leisurely, relaxed strolls through the grounds. Outdoor ceremonies are often held in the gazebo or near the fish pond. The interior rooms are spacious, featuring hardwood floors, hand-hewn ceiling beams and a noteworthy fireplace constructed from burnt bricks from the 1906 earthquake.

CAPACITY: The Lodge and grounds accommodate 250 seated guests; the Lodge alone holds 150 seated, 250 for buffets. The entire site holds 500 total for a standing reception.

FEES & DEPOSITS: A deposit of $300–600 (depending on day of week) plus a $75 refundable security deposit are required to secure your date. The facility rents for $600 on Saturday day or evening, and $300 Sunday day or evening. There is no charge for use of the Lodge Monday-Friday. A 1-hour rehearsal can be arranged on Wednesday or Thursday evenings for $50. Per person catering charges start at $8 for a buffet with a minimum of 100 guests. Catering for 50 people, minimum, starts at $13.50/person. The usual range for a seated meal is $15–25/person. However, any menu can be customized for your party.

CANCELLATION POLICY: With 4 months' notice, a full refund minus a 20% bookkeeping charge is given. Less than 4 months, the deposit will be forfeited.

AVAILABILITY: Any day from noon–5pm and 6pm–11pm.

SERVICES/AMENITIES:

Restaurant Services: no
Catering: provided
Kitchen Facilities: n/a
Tables & Chairs: provided
Linens, Silver, etc.: provided
Restrooms: wca
Dance Floor: yes
Bride's Dressing Area: yes

Parking: 2 lots
Overnight Accommodations: no
Telephone: pay phone
Outdoor Night Lighting: yes
Outdoor Cooking Facilities: yes
Cleanup: provided
Other: full event planning

RESTRICTIONS:

Alcohol: provided; if BYO, $2.50/person service fee
Smoking: allowed
Music: amplified inside only, 4-piece band limit

Wheelchair Access: yes
Insurance: not required
Other: no rice or birdseed

San Ramon

MUDD'S RESTAURANT

10 Boardwalk
San Ramon, CA 94583
(510) 837-9387   Patty McCurdy
Reserve: 3–6 months in advance

Surrounded by 10 acres of open space and situated next to a two-acre garden, this restaurant is in a world of its own. Virginia Mudd, the restaurant's founder and namesake, had a vision—she wanted to combine the features of a peaceful, quiet rural setting with an urban-chic eating establishment. Luckily for us, she succeeded. Stroll among the acres of organic flowers, herbs and fruit trees. Bite an apple. Smell the lavender. There are vegetables galore, many of which find their way into Mudd's dishes. Under the shade of large oaks, elms and bay trees, the Fireside Deck and adjacent lawns form a nice spot for a ceremony. If it's a small party, you can repair to the Fireside Room for the reception. Or, you can try the Board Room, which is terrific for intimate receptions or rehearsal dinners. It also has its own private deck, surrounded by oaks. Larger groups can reserve the entire Mudd's dining room, an appealing combination of spaces with distinctive curved ceilings. It's a contemporary design with enough wood detailing and warmth to suggest a feeling of country. Windows are everywhere, in all sorts of shapes and sizes. Most provide guests with views of the garden tapestry—vivid colors and soft, subtle shades of green. For outdoor dining, several French doors open to patios, screened by overhead trellises. All in all, Mudd's is a rare find. If you are looking for the optimum wedding garden setting, yet would like the benefits of a full service restaurant, we suggest that you start your search here.

CAPACITY: Board Room, 20 seated; Fireside Room, 45 seated; Fireside Room & Deck, 60–70 for a standing reception; Main Dining Room, 150 seated.

FEES & DEPOSITS: There's a $750 fee to reserve the entire restaurant, a $350 charge for the Fireside Room, $100 for the Board Room if you have a reception there. Luncheons start at $8–15/person, dinners at $10–21/person and wedding buffets $15–25/person. Tax and a 15% service charge are additional. Payment in full is due by the end of the function.

AVAILABILITY: Main Dining Room and grounds are available Saturday from 11am to 5pm. Board Room and Fireside Room, anytime.

SERVICES/AMENITIES:

Restaurant Services: yes
Catering: provided
Kitchen Facilities: n/a
Tables & Chairs: provided
Linens, Silver, etc.: provided
Restrooms: wca
Dance Floor: in bar area
Other: event coordination, fresh flowers

Parking: large lot
Overnight Accommodations: no
Telephone: pay phone
Outdoor Night Lighting: no
Outdoor Cooking Facilities: no
Cleanup: provided
Bride's Dressing Area: yes

RESTRICTIONS:

Alcohol: provided, corkage $5/bottle
Smoking: outside only
Music: no amplified

Wheelchair Access: yes
Insurance: not required
Other: no birdseed or rice

SAN RAMON COMMUNITY CENTER

12501 Alcosta Blvd.
San Ramon, CA 94583
(510) 275-2300
Reserve: 1–12 months in advance

Normally, we don't include park and recreation buildings because they're pretty uninteresting. In this case, however, we'd like to introduce you to a sophisticated newcomer that offers spaces that compete with the best event sites. Built in 1989, this rose-colored granite and glass community center is outstanding. The building is surrounded by pools, fountains and lush landscaping. For ceremonies, there's even a rose garden. Inside, the Fountain Room is the most popular area for receptions. Curved, laminated beams radiate from a center point, creating a domed ceiling seventy feet high. In subtle plums and lavenders, this sizable room is equally suitable for black tie affairs or more casual parties. For smaller affairs, we like the Terrace Room and Gallery, which are rented as a duo. The cool, gray Terrace

Room can be used for intimate dinners while the semi-circular Gallery is for hors d'oeuvres and champagne receptions. The Gallery features different works of art each month. Its plum and lavender interior is warmed by light filtering through a forty-foot wall of windows overlooking a fountain courtyard. If you are looking for a site in this area, come take a look. We think that the San Ramon Community Center is a real find—the price and the ambiance are sure to please.

CAPACITY: The Fountain Room can seat 250 guests; 450 for a standing reception. The Terrace Room, which comes with the Gallery, can accommodate 80 seated, and 150 for a standing reception. The Rose Garden can hold 130 guests for ceremonies.

FEES & DEPOSITS: A $100–200 security deposit is due when you book the facility and a $100–200 security deposit is due 90 days prior to the event. The rental fee is payable 30 days prior to the event and ranges from $40–65/hour weekdays to $60-105/hour weekends depending on spaces rented and San Ramon residency. A 2-hour minimum required is required. San Ramon residents are charged a discounted rate.

CANCELLATION POLICY: With 60 days' notice, half the deposit and the full rental fee is refunded. With 30–60 days' notice, the full rental fee is returned. With less notice, half the rental fee is returned.

AVAILABILITY: Year-round, daily. Sunday–Thursday and holidays, 7am–11pm; Friday and Saturday 7am– 1am.

SERVICES/AMENITIES:

Restaurant Services: no

Catering: select from preferred list

Kitchen Facilities: fully equipped industrial

Tables & Chairs: provided

Linens, Silver, etc.: some available, extra fee

Restrooms: wca

Dance Floor: yes

Other: baby grand piano, extra fee

Parking: ample lot

Overnight Accommodations: no

Telephone: pay phone

Outdoor Night Lighting: yes

Outdoor Cooking Facilities: no

Cleanup: renter or caterer

Bride's Dressing Area: CBA, extra fee

RESTRICTIONS:

Alcohol: BYO

Smoking: outside only

Music: amplified inside only

Wheelchair Access: yes

Insurance: sometimes required

Other: decorating restrictions; no birdseed, rice or petals; red wine & punch discouraged

---

Prices and policies <u>do</u> change. Call each facility and confirm everything you read in Here Comes The Guide.

SAN RAMON SENIOR CENTER

San Ramon, CA 94583
(510) 275-2316
Reserve: 6–12 months in advance

While senior activities take priority, this contemporary building (completed in 1992) has something for everyone. We particularly like the Vista Grande Room—an upscale event space, well suited for wedding receptions. The floor is light oak, great for dancing, and the walls are painted in a neutral, dusky peach. A high, vaulted ceiling, recessed lighting and windows which provide views of rolling hills, add to its charm. The room's terrace, accessible through multiple doors, and the adjacent fully equipped commercial kitchen are additional attractions. Outdoors, the East Terrace is a peaceful courtyard, surrounded by a terraced, landscaped hillside, abloom with pink oleander and purple Mexican sage. You can arrange tables with umbrellas in this wind-protected area for luncheons, or just set up buffet tables for champagne and hors d'oeuvres. We think the San Ramon Senior Center is very attractive and, for those on a budget, very easy on the pocketbook.

CAPACITY:	*Area*	*Seated*	*Standing*	*Assembly*
	Vista Grande Room & Terrace	115	250	150
	Half Vista Grande	60	125	75
	East Terrace	30	75	50

FEES & DEPOSITS: A $100 security deposit is due when you book the facility and a $100 cleaning deposit is due 90 days prior to the event. The rental fee averaging $45–80/hour on weekends and $30–50/hour on weekdays (with a two-hour minimum rental charge) is payable 30 days prior to the event. San Ramon residents are charged a discounted rate. The Vista Grande Room can be partitioned in half, and may be rented as a half space. There is an additional fee to reserve the East Terrace.

CANCELLATION POLICY: With 60 days' notice, half the deposit and the full rental fee is refunded. With 30-60 days' notice, the rental fee is returned. With less notice, half the rental fee is returned.

AVAILABILITY: Year-round, daily. Sunday–Thursday and holidays, 7am–11pm; Friday and Saturday 7am–1am.

SERVICES/AMENITIES:

Restaurant Services: no
Catering: select from preferred list
Kitchen Facilities: fully equipped
Tables & Chairs: provided
Linens, Silver, etc.: some available, extra fee
Restrooms: wca
Dance Floor: yes
Other: baby grand piano, extra fee

Parking: ample lot
Overnight Accommodations: no
Telephone: pay phone
Outdoor Night Lighting: yes
Outdoor Cooking Facilities: BBQ, extra fee
Cleanup: renter or caterer
Bride's Dressing Area: CBA, extra fee

RESTRICTIONS:

Alcohol: BYO
Smoking: outside only
Music: amplified inside only

Wheelchair Access: yes
Insurance: sometimes required
Other: decorating restrictions; no birdseed, confetti, rice, glitter or petals; red wine & punch discouraged

Sunol

ELLISTON VINEYARDS

463 Kilkare Road
Sunol, CA 94586
(510) 862-2377
Reserve: 1–12 months in advance

Tucked in a sheltered valley between the Pleasanton and Sunol ridges, amongst acres of vineyards, is the 1890 Victorian estate of Gold Rush pioneer, Henry Hiram Ellis. This is an exceptional spot for both receptions and garden ceremonies. Elliston Vineyard's landmark Mansion, constructed of thick sandstone from nearby Niles Canyon, has graceful stone arches over windows and entrances designed in a Romanesque style. The Mansion has a dressing room for brides that has original furnishings brought from around the Horn. Especially nice are the Mansion's Drawing Room, a favorite spot for formal photographs or small wedding ceremonies, and the Dining Room, which can accommodate seated prenuptial dinners. A picture-perfect rose garden with lawn and arbor make a beautiful setting for an outdoor wedding. The adjacent Carriage House has been remodeled. Inside, the Terrace Room, with expansive glass windows and doors, opens out to a secluded deck, furnished with white umbrella-shaded tables and a Victorian gazebo large enough for a bridal table of sixteen. Although close to civilization, it seems like you're a million miles away. The quiet, country atmosphere makes a nice contribution to any wedding celebration. When you want to get away, but not go very far, this is the spot.

CAPACITY: The Terrace Room and adjoining deck can seat 240 guests. The Mansion may be reserved for rehearsal dinners or ceremonies up to 24 guests. The rose garden lawn can seat 250 guests for a ceremony.

FEES & DEPOSITS: A refundable $500 deposit is required when reservations are confirmed. The minimum cost for functions Monday–Friday is $4,000, Saturday $6,000 and Sunday $5,000, which includes meals, rental fees and beverages. 50% of the estimated cost is due 2 months prior to your function, 25% 1 month prior and the balance, with a confirmed guest count, 2 weeks prior to the event. Additional staff charges may apply for seated functions.

CANCELLATION POLICY: With 6 months' notice, the deposit less a 25% service charge, is refunded.

AVAILABILITY: Year-round. Monday through Saturday until 10pm, Sunday until 6pm.

SERVICES/AMENITIES:

Restaurant Services: no
Catering: provided, no BYO
Kitchen Facilities: n/a
Tables & Chairs: provided
Linens, Silver, etc.: provided
Restrooms: wca
Dance Floor: yes
Bride's Dressing Area: yes

Parking: large lot, parking attendants
Overnight Accommodations: no
Telephone: office phone
Outdoor Night Lighting: yes
Outdoor Cooking Facilities: no
Cleanup: provided
Other: event planning

RESTRICTIONS:

Alcohol: WC provided, corkage $5/bottle
Smoking: outside only
Music: amplified inside only

Wheelchair Access: yes
Insurance: not required
Other: no rice, birdseed or confetti

Vallejo

FOLEY CULTURAL CENTER
Dan Foley Park

East end of N. Camino Alto
Vallejo, CA 94589
(707) 648-4630 Eileen Brown
Reserve: 6–11 months in advance

This community park has a multipurpose auditorium, and several smaller rooms are available for private parties. The auditorium, known as The Lake Room, overlooks the large, man-made Chabot Lake. Hexagonal in shape, it has a high beamed ceiling and a wall of windows with a view. The interior is light and airy and is designed for a wide variety of uses. Outside, a wide deck runs along one side of the building, providing relaxed, breezy seating right off the lake. The whole facility is situated inside a lovely 65-acre park, making a nice setting for gatherings of friends and family.

CAPACITY: The Lake Room can hold up to 500 seated, 600 standing guests. The Vista Room can hold up to 50 seated, 75 standing.

FEES & DEPOSITS: A $100 deposit, applied toward the rental fee, is due when the use permit is submitted. The balance and a $100 cleaning/damage deposit is payable 60 days prior to the event. The rental for private parties is approximately $525/10 hours.

CANCELLATION POLICY: If you cancel, 10% of the total fees and charges will be forfeited; with 30 days' notice or less, 50% will be forfeited.

AVAILABILITY: Year-round, Friday–Sunday from 10:30am–2am; Monday–Thursday, only if there is a cancellation in a regularly scheduled program. Closed most major holidays.

SERVICES/AMENITIES:

Restaurant Services: no
Catering: BYO
Kitchen Facilities: fully equipped
Tables & Chairs: provided
Linens, Silver, etc.: BYO
Restrooms: wca
Dance Floor: yes
Bride's Dressing Area: no

Parking: large lots
Overnight Accommodations: no
Telephone: pay phone
Outdoor Night Lighting: access only
Outdoor Cooking Facilities: in adjacent park
Cleanup: renter or CBA, extra fee
Other: stage, setup service, pianos, PA system

RESTRICTIONS:

Alcohol: BYO, sales need permit, surcharge $25
Smoking: designated areas
Music: amplified ok

Wheelchair Access: yes
Insurance: not required
Other: security required

Walnut Creek

SCOTT'S GARDENS

1719 Bonanza Street
Walnut Creek, CA 94596
(510) 934-0598
Reserve: 2–6 months in advance

Take note! If you are looking for an exceptional East Bay outdoor wedding spot, you must see this facility. Scott's Gardens is a site that could be aptly described as an urban oasis. Situated in the heart of Walnut Creek's retail district, Scott's has spared no cost to transform a small hillside into a brick-walled, multi-terraced courtyard garden with a conservatory cover. Under the expansive canopy of a four-hundred-year-old oak tree (the site's centerpiece) you'll find handsome amenities such as designer wood benches, large heat lamps and sizeable, self-standing umbrellas, in addition to lush landscaping. Of special interest are a green lattice aviary, several fountains and an antique water wheel. Observe the details here. All of the terraces are paved with slate and even the outdoor bar and indoor dressing room feature marble counters. The latter is absolutely the best bride's dressing room we've ever seen—with floor to ceiling mirrors, armoire and well-lit makeup area. At the topmost terrace, you'll find a back stairway leading to Scott's restaurant, where there's another outdoor patio for evening rehearsal dinners and small weekend receptions. Inside the restaurant, additional private and semi-private rooms are available for parties.

CAPACITY: The Garden can accommodate a maximum of 200 seated guests, 300 for a standing reception.

FEES & DEPOSITS: A non-refundable deposit of $1,000 is due when the event date is booked. The rental fee is $500 Sunday–Thursday and $1,000 Friday and Saturday for blocks between 10am–4pm or 6pm–1am. Rental includes tables, chairs, linens, silverware, setup and cleanup. Hors d'oeuvres receptions start at $20/person, buffets start at $22/person, seated luncheons or dinners range from $20–30/person. Tax and an 18% service fee will be applied to the final bill. Normally, 80% of the estimated food and beverage total is due 72 hours prior to the event. The remaining portion is payable at the conclusion of the event. Coffee and cake cutting runs $2.50/person.

CANCELLATION POLICY: Your deposit is not refundable unless the date is rebooked.

AVAILABILITY: Any day, from 10am–4pm and 6pm–12am.

SERVICES/AMENITIES:

Restaurant Services: yes
Catering: provided, no BYO
Kitchen Facilities: n/a
Tables & Chairs: provided
Linens, Silver, etc.: provided
Restrooms: wca
Bride's Dressing Area: yes
Cleanup: provided

Dance Floor: yes
Parking: complimentary valet
Overnight Accommodations: no
Telephone: pay phone
Outdoor Night Lighting: yes
Outdoor Cooking Facilities: CBA
Special: full-service event coordination, flowers, wedding cakes, entertainment

RESTRICTIONS:

Alcohol: provided, no BYO
Smoking: outside only
Music: DJ or small combos

Wheelchair Access: yes
Insurance: not required

SHADELANDS RANCH and Historical Museum

2660 Ygnacio Valley Road
Walnut Creek, CA 94598
(510) 935-7871
Reserve: 1 week–12 months in advance

Shadelands is a 1903 colonial revival-style home that exists today in virtually its turn-of-the-century state, with the original owner's furnishings and memorabilia intact. Hiram Penniman, an early Walnut Creek pioneer, acquired portions of a Mexican land grant in the early 1850s. Here he planted 320 acres in fruit and nut trees. It's believed that Hiram built the homestead for his eldest, unmarried daughter who died, unfortunately, six years after the house was completed. The house and 2.7 acres were passed down through family members, and in 1948, a foundation was set up to administer the estate. Donated to the City of Walnut Creek in 1970, it is now listed on the National Register of Historic Places. In the last few years, Shadelands has received some major improvements which make it an exceptional spot to have a wedding or reception. Repainted in its original soft burgundy with cream trim, the house is really inviting, with broad steps that lead to a veranda that sweeps around one side of the building. The grounds have been nicely landscaped, with shade trees, roses and flowering annuals. In the back, a new gazebo, designed in keeping with the house, awaits the bridal party. Red roses cling to the posts, and the shady interior is perfect for sunny days. Expansive emerald lawns, beautifully maintained, surround the gazebo. For receptions, you can set up tables with umbrellas on either lawns or a medium-sized patio adjacent to the house. If you'd like to get married in an outdoor environment that is both pretty and pleasant, plus has an old-world appeal, Shadelands is worth a visit.

CAPACITY: Inside, the house can accommodate 50 guests. Outside, 250 guests.

FEES & DEPOSITS: A $100 non-refundable deposit (which is applied toward the rental fee) plus a refundable $200 cleaning/security fee secures your date. Both are payable when reservations are confirmed. Indoors or outdoors rents for $95/hour. Use of both is $180/hour. Use of the kitchen is $35/event and an optional custodian is $50/event.

AVAILABILITY: Year-round, any day from 8am–10pm. The house interior is not available 1pm–4pm on Sundays.

SERVICES/AMENITIES:

Restaurant Services: no

Catering: BYO

Kitchen Facilities: minimal

Tables & Chairs: BYO, some provided

Linens, Silver, etc.: BYO

Restrooms: wca

Bride's Dressing Area: CBA

Parking: large lots

Overnight Accommodations: no

Telephone: house phone

Outdoor Night Lighting: yes

Outdoor Cooking Facilities: CBA

Cleanup: renter or caterer

Dance Floor: patio

RESTRICTIONS:

Alcohol: BYO

Smoking: outside only

Music: amplified within reason

Wheelchair Access: yes

Insurance: proof of liability required

Other: no candles indoors, no rice

Need a caterer, cake maker, florist? The Service Directory starting on page 412 features the best in the business.

Campbell

MARTHA'S RESTAURANT AND CAFE

1875 S. Bascom Avenue #2400
Campbell, CA 95008
(408) 377-1193
Reserve: 3 months in advance

Martha's Restaurant & Cafe is located on the second floor of the PruneYard where it overlooks the landscaped courtyard below. This newly designed restaurant, with a color scheme in alabaster, teal and magenta has a bright, cheerful ambiance. Fine contemporary art is tastefully displayed on interior walls. The greenhouse terrace, glassed in on three sides and affording a view of surrounding hills and the courtyard's century-old palm, is one of the facility's best features. Dining here is enhanced by colorful murals, rattan furniture and glass tables on a terra cotta floor. Another popular space for small hors d'oeuvres celebrations is the Wine Room, with arched white ceiling and glass-encased wine racks. The Fireplace Lounge also accommodates smaller groups.

CAPACITY: The entire facility can accommodate 180 seated guests. The Wine Room can hold up to 40 standing guests; the Fireplace Room and Cafe up to 75 standing guests.

FEES & DEPOSITS: A $300 refundable deposit is due when reservations are confirmed. There is a rental charge of $50 if the group is under 15 guests. Per person rates are: luncheons $9–16, dinners $14–25 and hors d'oeuvres starting at $7.50. Tax and a 15% gratuity are additional. A special wedding package includes wedding buffet, champagne, disc jockey, wedding cake, flowers and non-alcoholic beverages. The package costs $3,250 for 100 guests, minimum.

CANCELLATION POLICY: With 3 month's notice, your deposit will be refunded.

AVAILABILITY: Year-round, everyday from 8am–1am except Sundays (unless the group is over 100 guests). Closed major holidays.

SERVICES/AMENITIES:

Restaurant Services: yes
Catering: provided, no BYO
Kitchen Facilities: n/a
Tables & Chairs: provided
Linens, Silver, etc.: provided
Restrooms: wca
Dance Floor: yes

Parking: large lot
Overnight Accommodations: no
Telephone: pay phone
Outdoor Night Lighting: access only
Outdoor Cooking Facilities: no
Cleanup: provided
Bride's Dressing Area : yes

RESTRICTIONS:

Alcohol: provided, corkage $8/bottle
Smoking: allowed
Music: amplified ok

Wheelchair Access: yes, elevator
Insurance: not required

Gilroy

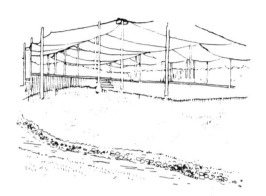

HECKER PASS
A Family Adventure

3050 Hecker Pass Highway
Gilroy, CA 95020
(408) 842-2121
Reserve for Events: 6–12 months in advance

Once the private park for Nob Hill Foods employees, this facility (located one and a half miles outside Gilroy) is now open for special events. There's a plant nursery on site, ensuring that Hecker Pass is beautifully landscaped, with a multitude of trees, shrubs and flowers. One of the big benefits of having a nursery here is that different kinds of plants can be arranged or moved to divide spaces, hence you can create different visual environments for your event. Say your vows on an emerald-green lawn under a white lattice arch, or under beautiful shade trees on the Creekside Patio. Three bridges cross a meandering creek which separates the ceremony site from the reception area, and nearby is a reception pavilion with an ivory-colored cloth canopy for protection on a warm day. This is a secluded, serene and peaceful spot at the base of the foothills. Water flowing gently down the creekbed provides the only sound.

CAPACITY: This facility has a minimum of 125 guests, but can accommodate up to 300 seated guests.

FEES & DEPOSITS: A non-refundable deposit of $500 is due when the contract is signed. 50% of the estimated event total is due 45 days before, and final payment is due 1 week prior to the event along with a final guest count. Five buffet menus are available, ranging $24–36/person, based on options selected. There is no service fee for a reception, but a fee of $300 is required for a ceremony. Tax is additional.

AVAILABILITY: April–October, everyday from 11am–8pm.

SERVICES/AMENITIES:

Restaurant Services: no
Catering: provided, no BYO
Kitchen Facilities: n/a
Tables & Chairs: provided

Parking: large lots
Overnight Accommodations: no
Telephone: pay phones
Outdoor Night Lighting: access only

Linens, Silver, etc.: provided
Restrooms: wca
Dance Floor: in Pavilion
Bride's Dressing Area: CBA

RESTRICTIONS:
Alcohol: BWC provided, no hard alcohol
Smoking: allowed
Music: amplified within limits

Outdoor Cooking Facilities: BBQ
Cleanup: provided
Other: wedding coordination

Wheelchair Access: yes
Insurance: not required
Other: no rice

Los Gatos

BYINGTON WINERY

21850 Bear Creek Road
Los Gatos, CA
(408) 354-1111 ext. 206
Reserve for Events: 3–12 months in advance

The Byington Winery and Vineyards are located up above Los Gatos, in one of the oldest grape growing regions in the U.S. Although a relative newcomer, Byington is already reserved well in advance for weddings because of its great location and wonderful amenities. For ceremonies, follow the brick path up to the 'wedding hill.' The path is bordered by vineyards and at the very top, guests are treated to a sensational panorama. You couldn't ask for more incredible views of the mountains and distant Monterey Bay. After taking your vows, descend to the winery. It's constructed of gray stone, with a terra cotta roof, and has several balconies dotted with blue umbrellas. Before the reception, greet guests in the VIP Room which features oak hardwood floors, black baby grand piano, a long bar, stone fireplace, overstuffed sofas and wingbacked chairs. For formal, seated functions, the VIP dining area with overhead chandelier sets the tone. For larger functions, both the Private Tasting Room and the Barrel Room are available. They overlook the wine cellar, which is filled with French oak barrels and large steel fermentation tanks. A real plus is the well-designed bride's changing room, which has a four-poster bed, full length mirror and its own bath. Byington is extremely service oriented. Only one wedding per day is scheduled so that staff can be flexible and provide brides and grooms with lots of personal attention.

CAPACITY: 150 seated guests; 250 for a standing reception.

FEES & DEPOSITS: A non-refundable deposit, due when the contract is signed, is one half of the rental fee. Rental fees are as follows: Friday, $1,550; Saturday or Sunday $1,550–2,450 depending on group size. Overtime is $150/hour. The other 50% is payable 3 months prior to the wedding. A $500 refundable security deposit is also required.

AVAILABILITY: All wedding functions are in 8-hour blocks Friday–Sunday until 10pm. Overtime hours are available upon request.

SERVICES/AMENITIES:

Restaurant Services: no

Catering: BYO, select from preferred list

Kitchen Facilities: ample

Tables & Chairs: provided

Linens, Silver, etc.: BYO

Restrooms: limited wca

Bride's Dressing Area: yes

Other: picnic area, baby grand piano

Dance Floor: CBA

Overnight Accommodations: no

Parking: 70 spaces, carpooling recommended

Telephone: pay phone

Outdoor Night Lighting: yes

Outdoor Cooking Facilities: BBQ

Cleanup: caterer

RESTRICTIONS:

Alcohol: provided, no BYO

Smoking: outside only

Music: amplified indoors only

Wheelchair Access: limited

Insurance: proof of insurance required

Other: no confetti, no rice or birdseed

MIRASSOU CHAMPAGNE CELLARS

300 College Ave.
Los Gatos, CA 95032
(408) 395-3790
Reserve: 1–3 months in advance

This is one lovely spot. Mirassou Champagne Cellars is housed on the grounds of the Sacred Heart Novitiate, an old Jesuit seminary with stone walls, large winery, huge shade trees and lots of privacy. The road leading up to this site is through a pretty residential neighborhood, but once you go through the Novitiate's stone and wrought iron gates, you leave the world behind. It was on top of this knoll that Jesuits began missionary work in the late 1860s. The first seminary was built here in 1888, giving way to a more permanent winery building in 1893. The latter is a fine example of a 19th century gravity-flow winery, with the top floor built for receiving and crushing harvested grapes. The Jesuits stopped making Novitiate wines in 1985 and have now leased the winery to Mirassou. The original winery building still stands, forming the core of the present-day Champagne Cellars. Both indoor and outdoor spaces are available for weddings. The tasting room and Blanc de Noir room hold small receptions. However, it's the entry, La Cave, that's unique. It actually resembles a cave, with vaulted, stone ceiling and champagne bottles stacked on end for riddling along one wall. Antique wine and champagne-making equipment and photos depicting the history of the Novitiate Winery are on the other side of La Cave. It's dimly lit, cool and very old world. A gentle slope with wide runner of red carpet leads bride and groom to the doorway arch, under which they can take their vows. Outdoors there's a sunny, quiet courtyard terrace, with an ivy-planted bank on one side and trees on the other. Recessed into the bank is a stepped, wooden platform, perfect for ceremonies or musicians. You couldn't ask for a more tranquil and beautiful environment for a wedding.

CAPACITY:

Area	*Seated*	*Reception*
Lower terrace	120	200
Tasting Room	75	150
Blanc de Noir Room	120	150

For a ceremony and/or champagne reception, 2 hours are allowed; with seated meals, 4 hours. The Tasting Room can be used in conjunction with the Lower Terrace for evening weddings and receptions.

FEES & DEPOSITS: A refundable deposit of 50% of the estimated facility fee is payable when reservations are confirmed. The balance and a refundable $300 security deposit are required 1 month prior to the event. Use fees (not including meals) range from $7–10/person with a $500 minimum for a 2-hour ceremony/champagne reception or $15–18/person, with a $900 minimum for a 4-hour function that includes ceremony, reception and all wine and champagne. Both options feature Mirassou wines and champagnes. Your final guest count is due 1 month prior to the event. A 1-hour rehearsal is included in the facility use fee and can be scheduled 9am–5pm, weekdays only.

CANCELLATION POLICY: With 6 months' notice, your deposit will be refunded.

AVAILABILITY: Year-round, everyday from 11am–9:30pm curfew.

SERVICES/AMENITIES:

Restaurant Services: no

Catering: preferred list

Kitchen Facilities: no

Tables & Chairs: provided up to 120 guests

Linens, Silver, etc.: provided

Restrooms: wca

Bride's Dressing Area: yes

Other: wedding coordination

Parking: several lots

Overnight Accommodations: no

Telephone: pay phone

Outdoor Night Lighting: yes

Outdoor Cooking Facilities: no

Cleanup: caterer

Dance Floor: outdoor patio or tasting room

RESTRICTIONS:

Alcohol: WC provided by Mirassou

Smoking: outside only

Music: amplified ok

Wheelchair Access: yes

Insurance: certificate required

Other: no rice, no hard alcohol

OPERA HOUSE

140 W. Main Street
Los Gatos, CA 95030
(408) 354-1218
Reserve: 6–12 months in advance

For large weddings, The Opera House is now the only game in town. Occupying a 1904 landmark building in historic Los Gatos, it offers 8,000 square feet with a seating capacity of up to 500 guests! The restored exterior facade is an attractive brick with crisp, white trim. Enter the downstairs foyer and wind your way up the formal, sweeping staircase to the main event floor. Highly detailed Bradbury & Bradbury wallpaper adorns the stairway in blues, creams and golds. Antique light fixtures abound and walls and ceilings are covered with original pressed tin in 15 different Victorian motifs. The grand ballroom has a 24-foot ceiling, with a rectangular skylight in the center which helps bring in natural light. Up above is the Balcony which overlooks the ballroom, great for those who want to look down on dancing below or as a place from which to toss your bouquet. The lower portion of the room is called the Mezzanine, which has a wall of windows facing north. Soft pastels, creams and taupes predominate and a large mural on an upper wall facing the Ballroom depicts the Opera House's original theater curtain. Because of the way this facility is configured, groups of 100 need not feel dwarfed in this space. Additional enhancements are a movable dance floor and separate cocktail bars. If you haven't been able to whittle down your invitation list, we think The Opera House is a must see.

CAPACITY:	*Seated*	*Standing*	*Reception*
Entire Facility	500	750	
Mezzanine	130	300	
Balcony	90	200	
Main Event Floor	320	500	

FEES & DEPOSITS: A non-refundable deposit totaling one quarter of the event cost is required within 1 week of confirming reservations. A second deposit, the amount dependent on size and type of event, is due 60 days prior to the event. The balance for entire event, including a $500 refundable damage deposit is due 1 week prior to your function. A $200/hour overtime charge is applied when appropriate. An optional wedding package for more than 250 guests is available including: food service, wine, champagne toast, flowers for church, bridal party and parents, DJ for 4 hours, wedding cake, photographer, limo for 3 hours for approximately $58/person plus tax and 15% gratuity. Without the package, the cost is approximately $40–60/person which includes food service, setup, cleanup, chairs, dance floor, linens, china and valet parking. Beverage packages are available from no host bars to hosted bars at $5–14/person. Tax and 15% gratuity are additional.

AVAILABILITY: Year-round. Mon–Fri 6pm-midnight. Sat and Sun 10–3pm or 7pm–midnight. All-day functions can be negotiated depending on the time of year.

SERVICES/AMENITIES:

Restaurant Services: no

Catering: select from preferred list

Kitchen Facilities: prep only

Tables & Chairs: provided for 350 guests

Linens, Silver, etc.: provided

Restrooms: wca

Dance Floor: yes

Other: event coordination

Parking: valet and attendant parking

Overnight Accommodations: no

Telephone: pay phone

Outdoor Night Lighting: access only

Outdoor Cooking Facilities: no

Cleanup: provided

Bride's Dressing Area: yes

RESTRICTIONS:

Alcohol: provided, no BYO

Smoking: allowed

Insurance: not required

Wheelchair Access: yes, elevator

Music: amplified ok

Other: decorations restricted

VILLAGE HOUSE AND GARDEN RESTAURANT

320 Village Lane
Los Gatos, CA 95030
(408) 354-1040
Reserve: 2 weeks in advance

The first thing you notice about the Village House and Garden Restaurant is the large outdoor patio, a wonderful area for al fresco dining during warm weather. Trees and flowers border the patio, while a trellis provides shade and the added beauty of hanging plants and wind chimes. The restaurant's interior also conveys a feeling of spring. Decorated in white and green, the ambiance is fresh and relaxed. The main dining room and patio combined make a popular setting for weddings receptions. The Copper Corner, a smaller room with brick fireplace and copper "hood," is suitable for groups of up to 36 people and is often used for wedding shower luncheons.

CAPACITY:	*Area*	*Season*	*Seated*	*Minimum Required*
	Main Dining Room	all	90	50 (days), 60 (eves)
	Copper Corner	all	36	16
	Inside/Outside	Oct 1–May 14	130	100
	Inside/Outside	May 15–Sept 30	130	100

For standing receptions, up to 200 guests, May 15–September 30.

FEES & DEPOSITS: For weekday functions, no deposit is required. A confirmed guest count is due 4 days prior to the event. For evening or Saturday functions, a non-refundable $250 deposit is required when reservations are confirmed. No rental fees are required for evening functions if food is served; Saturday reception rental is $350 for 3 hours, ceremony and reception is $500 for 4 hours. Each additional hour runs $100. The balance is due at the end of the event. Per person rates: luncheons $14 (Saturday luncheons start at $17.50), dinners at $25. Hors d'oeuvres by arrangement. Sales tax and 15% gratuity are additional.

AVAILABILITY: Year-round, Mon–Fri 9am–3pm; Saturday 11am–6pm. Closed Sundays, major holidays and the week between Christmas and New Year's day.

SERVICES/AMENITIES:

Restaurant Services: yes
Catering: provided, no BYO
Kitchen Facilities: n/a
Tables & Chairs: provided
Linens, Silver, etc.: provided
Restrooms: no wca
Dance Floor: yes

Parking: street, public parking lot nearby
Overnight Accommodations: no
Telephone: pay phone
Outdoor Night Lighting: access only
Outdoor Cooking Facilities: no
Cleanup: provided
Bride's Dressing Area: yes

RESTRICTIONS:

Alcohol: WBC only, corkage $5/bottle
Smoking: patio only
Music: amplified ok

Wheelchair Access: yes
Insurance: not required
Other: no bird seed or rice, $50 cleanup fee

Morgan Hill

OAK VALLEY VINEYARDS

Address withheld
Morgan Hill, CA
(408) 292-3100
Reserve: 6–12 months in advance

Oak Valley Vineyards is a place you'd never discover on your own. Hidden away in a small Morgan Hill valley, this ten-acre residential parcel includes lawns, a large pond and acres of vineyards. From the front, the light gray contemporary home doesn't suggest what's to come. Guests enter along the side of the house, facing the vineyards, and follow the brick path around back to a wisteria-covered arbor. They'll be pleasantly surprised by the rustic-chic garden that greets them. A series of brick steps lead guests to the pond's edge; other meandering paths, bordered by multi-colored roses, lavender and hundreds of bright annuals, define the event spaces. A brick patio supporting a huge barbecue is wonderful for al fresco cooking and dining; tables can be arranged on an emerald-green lawn overlooking the water. Adjacent to the lawn is another spot for tented buffets. Ceremonies are often held under a wood lath gazebo or post and beam arbor, with the pond and surrounding tree-covered hills as background. Secluded and quiet, this informal garden getaway has to be seen to be appreciated.

CAPACITY: If guests park on site, 120 guests, maximum. With off-site shuttle parking, up to 200 guests.

FEES & DEPOSITS: Half the rental fee acts as a refundable deposit, and is required to secure your date. The rental fee is $1,500 for Saturday, $1,250 for any other day. The fee covers a 12-hour block. The rental balance, along with a refundable $500 cleaning/security deposit, are due 30 days in advance of the event.

CANCELLATION POLICY: With 90 days' notice, the deposit is refunded in full.

AVAILABILITY: May through October, everyday from 8am–10pm.

SERVICES/AMENITIES:
Restaurant Services: no
Catering: select from preferred list
Kitchen Facilities: setup only
Tables & Chairs: some provided
Linens, Silver, etc.: BYO
Restrooms: no wca
Dance Floor: no

Parking: on site, off-site shuttle CBA
Overnight Accommodations: no
Telephone: emergency only
Outdoor Night Lighting: yes
Outdoor Cooking Facilities: yes
Cleanup: caterer or renter
Bride's Dressing Area: yes

RESTRICTIONS:
Alcohol: BYO
Smoking: outside only
Music: amplified ok

Wheelchair Access: limited
Insurance: certificate required

San Jose

THE BRIAR ROSE

897 East Jackson Street
San Jose, CA 95112
(408) 279-5999
Reserve: 2–4 weeks in advance

The Briar Rose Inn is a very attractive old Victorian home located in a quiet residential neighborhood five minutes from downtown San Jose. You enter under a vine-covered trellis and stroll up the rose-lined walkway past a small, white pitched-roof gazebo shaded by an old elm in the front yard. With a decorative wrought iron fence, lace curtains and pastel-painted exterior, the Inn presents an inviting face. Wide stairs lead you past the veranda into a warm and comfortable interior with lots of charm and Victorian detailing. The back yard has a well-tended garden and amenities for outdoor ceremonies—in fact, garden weddings are a Briar Rose specialty. Beautifully restored by its present owners, the Inn offers a variety of carefully appointed rooms for small receptions and overnight guests.

CAPACITY: The Inn can hold up to 50 guests indoors; 150 outdoors. The total capacity is 150.

FEES & DEPOSITS: A $500 non-refundable deposit is required when reservations are confirmed. The rental fee is $1,250 for 4 hours, with $200 per each additional hour. The total balance is payable 1 week prior to the function. Wedding meals can be provided at about $18.50/person.

AVAILABILITY: Year-round, everyday.

SERVICES/AMENITIES:

Restaurant Services: no
Catering: provided
Kitchen Facilities: setup only
Tables & Chairs: provided
Linens, Silver, etc.: provided
Restrooms: no wca
Dance Floor: brick portico
Bride's Dressing Area: provided

Parking: street
Overnight Accommodations: 5 guestrooms, 2 cottages
Telephone: guest phones
Outdoor Night Lighting: yes
Outdoor Cooking Facilities: no
Cleanup: provided
Other: event coordination

RESTRICTIONS:

Alcohol: WCB only, provided or BYO
Smoking: outside only
Music: no amplified

Wheelchair Access: garden only
Insurance: sometimes required

FAIRMONT HOTEL
San Jose

170 South Market Street
San Jose, CA 95113
(408) 998-1900 ext. 3520
Reserve: 8–12 months in advance

This luxury hotel, built in 1987, is a splendid addition to downtown San Jose. It's a facility that offers a myriad of spaces for special events: ballrooms, bistros, classy restaurants and an upscale luncheon eatery called the Fountain. The exterior and interior are designed with understated colors and quality materials: soft apricot hues, arched windows, marble floors, chandeliers, antiques, original artwork and granite columns. The entry lobby is both impressive and inviting. The lobby lounge is recessed, attractive with overstuffed, comfortable sofas and chairs and huge planters. Of special note is the Club Regent, a space designed like a nightclub. With stage lighting, dance floor, bistro seating and great acoustics, Club Regent is a sensational, sophisticated space for parties. The octagonal layout insures intimacy even though the room is very spacious. Several ballrooms and other nicely appointed spaces are available for ceremonies, receptions and rehearsal dinners—so ask for the full tour to examine all your options. For comfort, style and flexibility, the Fairmont is hard to beat.

CAPACITY:

Room	Seated Guests	Room	Seated Guests
The Crystal Room	150	The Club Regent	230
The Gold Room	150	Imperial Ballroom	500–1,000
The Regency Ballroom	450	Other Rooms	varying capacities

FEES & DEPOSITS: A $1,000–3,000 non-refundable deposit is required to secure your date. Food service is provided. Seated meals run $40–65/person, hors d'oeuvres receptions $12–20/person and buffets $45–70/person. Tax and a 17% service charge are additional.

AVAILABILITY: Year-round, any day until 2am.

SERVICES/AMENITIES:

Restaurant Services: yes
Catering: provided, no BYO
Kitchen Facilities: n/a
Tables & Chairs: provided
Linens, Silver, etc.: provided
Restrooms: wca
Bride's Dressing Area: yes
Other: wedding coordination

Parking: large lot and valet
Overnight Accommodations: 550 guestrooms
Telephone: pay phones
Outdoor Night Lighting: no
Outdoor Cooking Facilities: no
Cleanup: provided
Dance Floor: yes

RESTRICTIONS:

Alcohol: provided, no BYO
Smoking: designated areas
Insurance: not required

Wheelchair Access: yes
Music: amplified ok

HOTEL DE ANZA

233 West Santa Clara Street
San Jose, CA 95113
(800) 843-3700 or **(408) 286-1000**
Reserve: 2–6 months in advance

This place is a treasure. A recent infusion of $10 million dollars has brought the Hotel De Anza back to its original Art Deco splendor—it now shines both as a restored historic hotel and as one of San Jose's most beautiful event facilities. Every detail here has been considered. Guests who are new to the De Anza will be more than impressed by the lobby, with gold accents, etched glass and distinctive fixtures. It is a refined space, with limestone floors that have green-black marble insets. Walls are nicely hand painted to match the floor. The Hotel elevator's interior is striking, with mirrors and bird's-eye maple incised with ebony. Around the corner is the Hedley Club, the De Anza's classic lounge. It is, in a word, extraordinary. The ceiling is highly detailed, painted in golds, raspberries and blues. An enormous stone fireplace glows in winter. Large paintings, eclectic furnishings and a glass-backed bar create a sensational spot for pre-party cocktails. French doors lead to the adjacent Palm Court Terrace, which offers a splendid limestone patio, complete with three fountains, terra-cotta colored walls, palm trees and white umbrellas. Multi-color impatiens dot the patio and gray-blue tiles back the wall fountains. A white lattice screen separates the patio from the street on one side, a large white canopy (which can be erected or left down depending on the weather) is at the other. For indoor receptions, guests will be dazzled by the De Anza Room. This large space is richly magnificent. Walls are painted a warm gold— hand-stenciled with gold leaf leaves, edged with a cranberry-colored shadow. The ceiling's concrete beams are intricately painted in golds, burgundies, blues and greens. A beautiful mural, created on a self-standing screen, adds color across one end of the space. Tables are dressed up with white linens; comfortable chairs come with arm rests and seats with a lovely floral pattern. In a day and age when 'luxurious' and 'elegant' are buzzwords, the Penthouse atop the De Anza truly is stunning. This is a divine spot for a honeymoon. A marble bar, living room and foyer are designed in a neoclassic style, with beautiful furnishings and art. Nearby, one of the most sumptuous baths we've encountered beckons you with black marble floors, marble counters and a whirlpool bath large enough for four. A wall of mirrors and glass enclosed shower/steam room are special features. Two small decks for sunning or breakfasting offer views of downtown San Jose and are entirely private. We can't say enough about the Hotel De Anza. If you haven't seen it yet, we urge you to take a tour, including the on-premises restaurant, La Pastaia. Be prepared to spend some time here—the Hotel De Anza is a one-of-a-kind place that needs to be savored to be fully appreciated.

CAPACITY:	*Room*	*Seated*	*Reception*
	Boardroom	16	n/a
	De Anza	70	100
	San Jose	40	60
	Palm Court Terrace	120	170
	La Pastaia Restaurant	150	150

FEES & DEPOSITS: A room rental fee of $0–800 may apply, depending on the details of your function. Catering is provided by La Pastaia, with prices ranging from $25–50/person. Menus can be customized. Half of the estimated food and beverage total is due when the contract is signed; the balance is payable one week prior to the event. Tax and a 17% service charge are additional. The Palm Court outdoor canopy setup charge is $250.

CANCELLATION POLICY: With more than 30 days' notice, your deposit is refundable.

AVAILABILITY: Year-round. Everyday, anytime.

SERVICES/AMENITIES:

Restaurant Services: yes

Catering: provided, no BYO

Kitchen Facilities: n/a

Tables & Chairs: provided

Linens, Silver, etc.: provided

Restrooms: wca

Bride's Dressing Area: CBA

Other: wedding coordination & referrals, wedding cakes

Parking: nearby lots and valet

Overnight Accommodations: 100 rooms & penthouse

Telephone: pay phone

Outdoor Night Lighting: yes

Outdoor Cooking Facilities: no

Cleanup: provided

Dance Floor: CBA, extra fee

RESTRICTIONS:

Alcohol: provided

Smoking: outside only

Music: amplified ok

Wheelchair Access: yes

Insurance: not required

HOTEL SAINTE CLAIRE

302 South Market Street
San Jose, CA 95113
(408) 271-3350 Catering
Reserve: 6–12 months in advance

Welcome back! The Hotel Sainte Claire, a national historic landmark, has received a painstaking architectural restoration. Located across the street from the Convention Center, it offers a sumptuous, old-world ambiance for wedding receptions and rehearsal dinners. The entry lobby is lovely, with marble floors, large patterned rugs, a hand-painted ceiling and gold leaf accents. Exceptionally bright and inviting during the day, the wide corridor that leads from the lobby to the Ballroom has arches rimmed with gold leaf, and a fabulous light and dark checkered terrazzo floor. At the end of the corridor is the Ballroom, a formal, eye-appealing and understated room. Mirrors amplify the light that floods in through French doors and reflect the sparkle from multiple chandeliers overhead. A decorative carpet in teal and soft terra cotta colors complements cream and café au lait walls. You can rent the Ballroom separately, or in combination with the connecting open-air courtyard. Designed in a 1930s Mediterranean motif, the courtyard is an intimate spot for a quiet and secluded ceremony. A shade canopy protects guests from direct sun; two small wall fountains murmur gently. Brick pavers in different patterns and colorful, ornate tiles add detail and texture. We think the Hotel Sainte Claire is a jewel in the heart of downtown San Jose. If you need more of an incentive to preview this site, note that an additional culinary benefit is that Il Fornaio, well known for its authentic Tuscan cuisine, caters all functions.

CAPACITY:

Room	Seated	Reception
Grand Ballroom	280	450
Ballroom	192	300
Courtyard	80	180
Sainte Claire Room	120	200

FEES & DEPOSITS: A non-refundable $300–1,500 food and beverage deposit is required 15 days after you book your event. No rental fee is required. Menus are finalized 6 weeks prior to the function. Full payment is due 10 days in advance and a final guest count 3 days prior to the wedding. Luncheons run $20–30/person, dinners $30–50/person. Tax and a 17% service charge are additional.

AVAILABILITY: Year-round, daily. On Saturdays, there are two time frames for weddings: 10am–4pm and 6pm–1am.

SERVICES/AMENITIES:

Restaurant Services: yes
Catering: provided, no BYO
Kitchen Facilities: n/a
Tables & Chairs: provided
Linens, Silver, etc.: provided
Restrooms: wca
Dance Floor: yes

Parking: valet, street parking
Overnight Accommodations: 170 guestrooms
Telephone: pay phone
Outdoor Night Lighting: yes
Outdoor Cooking Facilities: no
Cleanup: provided
Bride's Dressing Area: CBA

RESTRICTIONS:

Alcohol: provided, corkage $10/bottle
Smoking: allowed
Music: amplified ok

Wheelchair Access: yes
Insurance: not required

LA PASTAIA

233 West Santa Clara Street
San Jose, CA 95113
(408) 286-8686
Reserve: 1–3 months in advance

For those of you who want to have an upscale wedding reception in the South Bay, take heart! The new La Pastaia, located in the recently refurbished Hotel De Anza, is a sophisticated, contemporary setting for both prenuptial dinners and receptions. La Pastaia (which means pastamaker in Italian) is a feast for the eyes. Designed in a Northern Italian mode, La Pastaia is serious about food, yet slightly irreverent. (The woman on the classic-looking logo proudly flourishes what appears to be a flag. Upon closer inspection, we notice it's a fork topped with wind blown pasta.) Slate tile in a subtle gray with green overtones covers many of the outer surfaces, including banquettes, booths and the softly curving arches that help divide the restaurant's spaces. Lemony yellow walls are hand painted in a faux marble pattern and the stone floor is broken up into subdued greens, browns and ochres. Black lacquered chairs contrast nicely with white linens, and enlivening the perimeters are large, framed Italian posters from the 1920s and 30s. The exhibition kitchen area is compelling. Laden with delectable desserts and fresh baked bread, the long marble counter draws guests in for a closer look. Linger here a while and watch the chefs work with a wood burning oven that glows continuously at one end of the counter. Small alcoves and a mixture of banquettes and tables create cozy, intimate spaces. Treat your wedding guests to genuine Italian cuisine—fresh pastas, lively appetizers and Italian country-style entrees—or design your own menu. La Pastaia's staff is extremely flexible. No matter what you select, your guests will appreciate the great food, professionally served in a Tuscan-chic atmosphere.

CAPACITY: 150 seated guests with dance floor; 175 without. For private parties, a guaranteed 70-guest minimum is required. Private rooms and patio are available for smaller groups.

FEES & DEPOSITS: A refundable deposit of $250 is required to secure your date, due when reservations are confirmed. With food service, no rental fee is required. La Pastaia can customize any menu, with prices ranging from $25–50/person. Half of the estimated food and beverage total is payable when the contract is signed; the balance is due one week prior to the event. Tax and 17% service charge are additional.

CANCELLATION POLICY: With two weeks' notice, your deposit will be refunded.

AVAILABILITY: Year-round, except Christmas Day.

SERVICES/AMENITIES:

Restaurant Services: yes

Catering: provided, no BYO

Kitchen Facilities: n/a

Tables & Chairs: provided

Linens, Silver, etc.: provided

Restrooms: wca

Bride's Dressing Area: CBA

Other: wedding cakes, coordination & referrals

Parking: nearby lots

Overnight Accommodations: Hotel De Anza

Telephone: Hotel pay phone

Outdoor Night Lighting: no

Outdoor Cooking Facilities: no

Cleanup: provided

Dance Floor: yes

RESTRICTIONS:

Alcohol: provided

Smoking: not allowed

Music: amplified ok

Wheelchair Access: yes

Insurance: not required

Other: no birdseed or rice

O'CONNOR MANSION

596 South Second Street
San Jose, CA 95112
(408) 286-2057 or **(408) 297-9501**
Reserve: 3–6 months in advance

The O'Connor Mansion, built in the late 1800s by one of the city's leading citizens, Myles O'Connor, was a splendid Victorian masterpiece. The Mansion, which has been part of Notre Dame High School since 1927, is no longer a Victorian from the outside (the exterior was drastically remodeled in the 1920s), however the interior has retained its original glory. The ground floor has majestic, sixteen-foot ceilings; the floors are highly polished hardwood. Detailed dark woodwork and lovely doors are a testament to the craftsmanship of the era. The Grand Hall and two main parlors have oriental carpets and all rooms have ornate fireplaces, mostly imported from Europe at the turn of the century. In 1991, when this was the location for the San Jose Symphony Auxiliary Showcase, most of the rooms were redecorated. As a result, the Green Room (painted in shades of green) has hand-painted clouds on its ceiling, green foliage on the walls. Everywhere you look, there are interesting details, such as faux marble surfaces and rag and sponge painting. The Grand Hallway ceiling, Florentine in design and highly detailed in execution, features Bradbury & Bradbury wallpaper, resplendent in blues, salmons and burgundies. Throughout the Mansion, you'll see lincrusta, an ornate Victorian wall stamping technique. Upstairs is the Grand Ballroom with stained glass windows, swag-draped windows and hardwood floors. Most guests eat downstairs and come upstairs to dance in the Ballroom. In front of the building, the landscaped courtyard is shaded and cool during summer months. Semi-enclosed, it offers shelter for mingling while enjoying hors d'oeuvres and champagne.

CAPACITY: The Mansion can hold up to 200 guests, maximum. The Grand Ballroom 100 guests at tables, 150 row seating.

FEES & DEPOSITS: The rental fee is a non-refundable $150/hour. Half of the anticipated fee is required when your contract is finalized, along with a $250 cleaning deposit, $200 of which is refundable if the Mansion is left in good condition. The rental balance is due 2 months before the event.

CANCELLATION POLICY: For a cleaning deposit refund, written notice is required no less than 60 days prior to the function.

AVAILABILITY: Year-round, weekday evenings and weekends until 1am.

SERVICES/AMENITIES:

Restaurant Services: no
Catering: preferred list, licensed caterer
Kitchen Facilities: big setup areas, minimal utilities
Tables & Chairs: provided, extra fee
Linens, Silver, etc.: caterer
Restrooms: wca limited

Parking: large lot available
Overnight Accommodations: no
Telephone: office phone
Outdoor Night Lighting: access only
Outdoor Cooking Facilities: no
Cleanup: caterer

Dance Floor: yes
Other: grand piano, wood altar

Bride & Groom's Dressing Area: yes

RESTRICTIONS:

Alcohol: BYO
Smoking: outside only
Music: amplified inside only

Insurance: required
Wheelchair Access: limited
Other: no birdseed or rice

SAN JOSE ATHLETIC CLUB

196 North Third Street
San Jose, CA 95112
(408) 292-1281
Reserve: 12–18 months in advance

Located in the heart of historic downtown San Jose, the San Jose Athletic Club is a striking and stately Neoclassic structure. It has large columns, enormous urns and broad granite steps leading up to the impressive front doors. Inside you'll find a variety of rooms available for private parties. Most often, receptions are held in the Corinthian Room, which is a stunning space. Its faux marble finish and intricately detailed high ceilings are extraordinary. The decor is tasteful, with attractive appointments and huge palm trees that grace the main floor. For formal or informal events, the San Jose Athletic Club is an impressive building with interior spaces to match.

CAPACITY:

Room	Standing	Seated	Room	Standing	Seated
Columns Lounge	250	100	Corinthian Room	400	100–300
Olympia Room	100	80	Gold, Silver, Bronze Rm	200	150

FEES & DEPOSITS: A deposit secures your date and is due when the reservation is made. Full payment is due prior to your event. The fee for the Corinthian Room is $250–1,000 based on the number of guests, for a 5-hour block. Other rooms range from $75–500. The Athletic Club provides full service catering, which can be customized for your function—you'll have to inquire for current prices. An 18% service charge and sales tax are applied to the final total.

CANCELLATION POLICY: The deposit is only refundable if the event date can be rebooked.

AVAILABILITY: All rooms are available everyday, from 6am–1am.

SERVICES/AMENITIES:

Restaurant Services: yes
Catering: provided, no BYO
Kitchen Facilities: n/a
Tables & Chairs: provided
Linens, Silver, etc.: provided
Restrooms: wca
Dance Floor: yes

Parking: street or nearby garage, complimentary on weekends & weekdays after 6pm
Overnight Accommodations: no
Telephone: pay phone
Outdoor Night Lighting: yes
Outdoor Cooking Facilities: BBQ
Cleanup: provided

Special: poolside parties

RESTRICTIONS:
Alcohol: provided
Smoking: allowed
Music: amplified ok

Bride's Dressing Area: CBA

Insurance: not required
Wheelchair Access: yes
Other: no helium balloons in Corinthian Room,
no confetti, seed or rice

SAN JOSE
HISTORICAL MUSEUM

Kelley Park between Story & Tully on
Senter Road
San Jose, CA 95112
(408) 287-2290 Events Dept.
Reserve: 1–3 months in advance

Housed on 25 acres in the southernmost section of Kelley Park, the Historical Museum Complex offers a unique glimpse of the old homes and businesses that once graced the streets of early San Jose. This is a recreation of old San Jose, with historically significant buildings and exhibits depicting the history of Santa Clara Valley. Whether restored or reconstructed, each building in Kelley Park is placed as nearly as possible in its original relation to other structures. The Museum Complex features an operating, turn-of-the-century trolley with costumed conductor, a scaled-down 115-foot high replica of the San Jose 1881 Electric Light Tower, a 1927 gas station and a decorative, 1890-style park bandstand. In addition to various outdoor spaces for parties, there are facilities in the Firehouse and Pacific Hotel for indoor functions. This is an interesting and unusual site for a wedding. Dress up and arrive in style aboard a vintage trolley or horse-drawn carriage! The Museum staff can help you be creative—period costumes, trolley rides, museum tours and ice cream parlor parties can be arranged.

CAPACITY: The Pacific Hotel's reception room can hold up to 40 seated guests, 80 standing, and the Firehouse upstairs reception room can accommodate 60 seated guests, 125 standing. For outdoor functions, up to 1,000 can be accommodated.

FEES & DEPOSITS: A non-refundable deposit of 50% of the estimated use fee is required when the reservation is made. A refundable maintenance deposit of $150 (indoor events) or $250 (outdoor events) is due 30 days prior to your function and is returned 2–3 weeks afterwards.

Indoor Functions: $50/hour 8am–5pm, $75/hour 5pm–midnight, for a 3-hour minimum block. For security, one off-duty police officer is required, rate varies.

Outdoor Functions:

Guest Count	Ceremony Only	Ceremony & Reception or Reception Only
	8am–6pm (4 hrs. max)	8am–10pm (8 hrs. max)
0-100	$350	$525
101-150	425	640

151–200	500	750
201–250	575	865
251–300	650	975
over 300	quoted	quoted

For outdoor security, one or more off-duty police officers is required, rate varies. The total balance is due 5 days prior to the event.

AVAILABILITY: Indoor functions: 8am–5pm or 5pm–midnight. Outdoor events: 8am–6pm or 10pm, depending on type of function.

SERVICES/AMENITIES:

Restaurant Services: no
Catering: BYO
Kitchen Facilities: minimal
Tables & Chairs: some provided
Linens, Silver, etc.: BYO
Restrooms: wca varies
Dance Floor: at plaza outside, indoors CBA
Bride's Dressing Area: CBA

Parking: large lots
Overnight Accommodations: no
Telephone: pay phone
Outdoor Night Lighting: yes
Outdoor Cooking Facilities: BBQs
Cleanup: caterer
Other: trolley, costumes & tours CBA

RESTRICTIONS:

Alcohol: BYO, BWC only, permit required
Smoking: outside only
Music: amplified restricted, permit required

Wheelchair Access: yes
Insurance: sometimes required

SAN JOSE MUNICIPAL ROSE GARDEN

Naglee and Dana
San Jose, CA 95126
(408) 277-5561
Reserve: 2–9 months in advance

Roses, roses everywhere. The City's Rose Garden, located in a quiet residential neighborhood just ten minutes from downtown San Jose, is laid out in tight, geometric patterns with rose beds in rectangles, triangles and squares. If you'd like to get a sense of color, peak times for blooms are from Mother's Day through the summer. At the garden's center lies a white, bubbling, two-tier fountain flanked by stone benches—a perfect area for a wedding ceremony or picture-taking backdrop. Another great spot is the stage/terrace where tall redwoods form a deep green background for bride and groom. A heavy timber, rose-covered arbor creates a formal entry into the rose garden and makes a nice approach for the wedding party entourage. The San Jose Rose Garden is also worthy of mention because, for those watching pennies, your celebration won't cost you an arm and a leg.

CAPACITY: Ceremonies only: fountain area 100 guests; stage/terrace 200.

FEES & DEPOSITS: A $250 refundable deposit and a $125 rental fee (for 2 hours use) are payable when reservations are made.

CANCELLATION POLICY: With more than 30 days' notice, the deposit will be refunded less 25% or $25 maximum. With less notice, 50% or $50 maximum will be subtracted.

AVAILABILITY: Year-round. Everyday 8am to dusk.

SERVICES/AMENITIES:

Restaurant Services: no

Catering: BYO

Kitchen Facilities: no

Tables & Chairs: BYO

Linens, Silver, etc.: BYO

Restrooms: wca

Bride's Dressing Area: no

Parking: on street

Overnight Accommodations: no

Telephone: emergency only

Outdoor Night Lighting: no

Outdoor Cooking Facilities: no

Cleanup: caterer or renter

Dance Floor: no

RESTRICTIONS:

Alcohol: not allowed

Smoking: allowed

Music: no amplified

Wheelchair Access: yes

Insurance: not required

Santa Clara

ADOBE LODGE FACULTY CLUB

Santa Clara University
Santa Clara, CA 95053
(408) 554-4059
Reserve: 12 months in advance

In the heart of Santa Clara University sits the Adobe Lodge. Now the Santa Clara University Faculty Club, it is the only structure to have survived the 1926 fire and remains the single structural remnant of the original 1822 Mission Santa Clara. It has been remodeled extensively, but still has a Mission-era flavor. To reach the Club, you stroll through the Old Mission Gardens, under an ancient, wisteria-laden pergola. This particular vine deserves mention because it's breathtaking, with 150-year old trunks the size of small trees. In the spring, the pergola overflows with color. In fact, all of the landscaping flanking the entry path is delightful. Everything from the palms dotting the lawns to the multi-hued roses and pansies is perfectly maintained. There is no traffic noise in this interior garden, only the sound of the birds. The Spanish-tiled Faculty Club building is surrounded by a vine-covered porch, and inside there's a main dining room which is formally resplendent in creams and golds. The Club's outdoor patio is inviting and intimate, with Chinese elms providing dappled shade overhead. These indoor and outdoor spaces create one of the most attractive reception and ceremony sites we've ever seen. For a wedding, it's one of our favorite places in the Santa Clara Valley.

CAPACITY: Main dining room, 100 seated guests; two adjacent dining rooms, 12 seated guests each; with porch and patio, up to 300 for receptions during warmer months.

FEES & DEPOSITS: A $600 rental fee, which includes a refundable $50 damage deposit, is due when the rental contract is submitted. The fee covers a 4 to 4-1/2 hour time frame. A final guest count is due 1 week prior to the wedding. Food services are provided. Special wedding menus, with prices ranging from $12.50–16.50/person, are available. The bartender's fee is $15/hour for a minimum of 6 hours. Tax and 15% service charge are additional. The balance is due at the conclusion of the reception.

CANCELLATION POLICY: A 90-day written notice is required for a refund. With less than 90 days, the rental fee deposit is pro-rated.

AVAILABILITY: Year-round. Saturday and Sunday, 10am–8:30pm.

SERVICES/AMENITIES:

Restaurant Services: no
Catering: provided, no BYO
Kitchen Facilities: n/a
Tables & Chairs: provided
Linens, Silver, etc.: provided
Restrooms: wca
Bride's Dressing Area: no

Dance Floor: yes
Parking: large lot
Overnight Accommodations: no
Telephone: pay phone
Outdoor Night Lighting: yes
Outdoor Cooking Facilities: CBA
Cleanup: provided

RESTRICTIONS:

Alcohol: WC provided, corkage $6.50/bottle
Smoking: outside only
Music: no amplified

Wheelchair Access: yes
Insurance: certificate required
Other: no rice, birdseed

DECATHLON CLUB

3250 Central Expressway
Santa Clara, CA 95051
(408) 738-8743 or **(408) 736-3237** Catering
Reserve: 6–18 months in advance

One of Silicon Valley's finest private athletic clubs, the Decathlon Club is ingeniously designed to accommodate private parties without disturbing its membership. As you enter, there is a shaded garden setting with a bubbling stream which flows through the building, beautifully separating the social-function spaces from the Club's athletic areas. Guests for weddings can be ushered into the party spaces without having to mingle with Club members. The dining area is large and open, yet it gives wedding guests a feeling of privacy. It opens onto a wide deck overlooking a lush, sloping lawn and tennis court below. Adjacent to the dining area is a raised, hardwood dance floor. For a large wedding party, the Decathon Club offers appealing spaces, in-house catering and assistance in putting it all together.

CAPACITY: Indoors, the Club can hold 600 guests for receptions with dancing; 400 seated. The outdoor stadium tennis court and outside deck areas can hold 500 guests.

FEES & DEPOSITS: A minimum guest count of 100 is required to book reservations. The $800 rental fee covers a 4-1/2 hour period. Overtime is available at an additional charge. A non-refundable $500 deposit, applied to final bill, is due when your reservation is confirmed. Thirty days before the event, 75% of the estimated food & beverage total is due. The balance of fees and rental is due upon conclusion of your party. Food service is provided. Per person rates: luncheons and dinners from $10–30, buffets from $20–35, hors d'oeuvres from $15–30 and BBQs at $18. Tax and an 18% service charge are additional.

AVAILABILITY: Year-round, everyday, 4-1/2 hour time blocks. Closed major holidays. Premises must be vacated by 1am.

SERVICES/AMENITIES:

Restaurant Services: yes
Catering: provided, no BYO
Kitchen Facilities: n/a
Tables & Chairs: provided
Linens, Silver, etc.: provided
Restrooms: wca
Dance Floor: yes
Bride's Dressing Area: yes

Parking: large lots
Overnight Accommodations: no
Telephone: pay phone
Outdoor Night Lighting: yes
Outdoor Cooking Facilities: BBQ
Cleanup: provided
Other: event coordination

RESTRICTIONS:

Alcohol: provided, no BYO
Smoking: outside deck only
Music: amplified ok

Wheelchair Access: yes
Insurance: not required
Other: no birdseed or rice

MADISON STREET INN

1390 Madison Street
Santa Clara, CA 95050
(408) 249-5541
Reserve: 2 weeks in advance

The Madison Street Inn is an inviting bed and breakfast establishment offering an unusual blend of 1890s Victorian charm with modern amenities. The house, with its white picket fence, antique furnishings, authentic wallpaper and lace curtains, maintains its period authenticity. Soothing colors, an intimate parlor with fireplace and a warm and airy dining area make wedding guests feel right at home. The grounds offer a more contemporary setting, with swimming pool and brick patio. In the summer, the white trellis over the patio is ablaze with colorful flowers—perfect for ceremonies. The adjacent lawn area is suitable for small, outdoor receptions.

CAPACITY: The Inn can hold up to 30 guests indoors and 75 outdoors.

FEES & DEPOSITS: A non-refundable $200 deposit, applied toward the rental fee, is required when reservations are confirmed. The rental fee is $100–400 depending on the total guest count. The total estimated balance of both rental and food service is due 1 week before the event. The Inn provides catering: hors d'oeuvres run $5–20/person, luncheons $10–15/person and dinners $15–25/person. Tax and gratuity are additional.

AVAILABILITY: Year-round, everyday 11am–7pm for weddings.

SERVICES/AMENITIES:

Restaurant Services: no

Catering: provided or BYO with approval

Kitchen Facilities: setup only

Tables & Chairs: some provided

Linens, Silver, etc.: some provided

Restrooms: wca

Dance Floor: yes

Bride's Dressing Area: CBA

Parking: on street

Overnight Accommodations: 5 guestrooms

Telephone: house phone

Outdoor Night Lighting: limited

Outdoor Cooking Facilities: BBQ

Cleanup: caterer

Other: event coordination

RESTRICTIONS:

Alcohol: BYO, BWC only

Smoking: outside only

Music: no amplified

Wheelchair Access: limited to garden

Insurance: not required

Saratoga

CHATEAU LA CRESTA
At The Mountain Winery

14831 Pierce Road
Saratoga, CA 95070
(408) 741-0763
Reserve: 2 weeks in advance

Chateau La Cresta, located within the Mountain Winery (home of the Paul Masson Summer Series), is situated high in the Santa Cruz Mountains, surrounded by vineyards. This is a lovely outdoor setting with majestic oaks and unbeatable views of the Santa Clara Valley. The winery building and Chateau La Cresta, Paul Masson's home, were built in 1905 of stone masonry. These historic ivy-covered structures feature large wood beams and oak casks—the appealing aroma of aging wine lingers in the air. The Chateau, built to entertain Masson's peers such as John Steinbeck and Charley Chaplan, represents a fine example of French country architecture. Outdoor ceremonies and receptions are held on lawns, or on a large wood terrace overlooking the valley floor; the Chateau and Great Winery Hall are available for indoor weddings. At 1,400 feet up, this "vineyard in the sky" provides a tranquil and unusual setting for an unforgettable wedding celebration.

CAPACITY: Chateau La Cresta can accommodate 50–1,500 guests, depending on how the facility is used. Areas available for wedding events: Deck, Wishing Well, Chateau and the Great Winery Hall.

FEES & DEPOSITS: The rental fee, contract and confirmed guest count are required when the facility is reserved. Rehearsals cost $75/hour, Mon–Fri 9am–5pm. Meals are $15.50–25/person, plus tax and 17% service charge. Unlimited wine, beer and champagne is $10/person. The final balance is due 1 week prior to the event.

Guests	Fee	Guests	Fee
up to 50	$1,200	126–150	$1,500
51–75	1,275	151–175	1,575
76–100	1,350	176–200	1,650
101–125	1,425		

Guests	Fee	Guests	Fee
up to 50	$2,000	126–150	$3,000
51–75	2,250	151–175	3,250
76–100	2,500	176–200	3,500
101–125	2,750	200–250	4,000

These fees include 2-hour rental, linens, glassware, chairs, tables and setup, 45 minutes of champagne service.

These fees include 5-hour rental, linens, glassware, china, silver, chairs, tables and setup.

AVAILABILITY: Year-round with some restrictions for the Paul Masson Summer Series which runs June–September.

SERVICES/AMENITIES:

Restaurant Services: yes
Catering: provided
Kitchen Facilities: n/a
Tables & Chairs: provided
Linens, Silver, etc.: provided
Restrooms: limited wca
Parking: large lot

Overnight Accommodations: no
Telephone: pay phone
Outdoor Night Lighting: yes
Outdoor Cooking Facilities: BBQ
Cleanup: provided
Dance Floor: CBA
Bride's Dressing Area: yes

RESTRICTIONS:

Alcohol: provided, WC only, no BYO
Smoking: outside only
Music: amplified with volume control

Wheelchair Access: limited
Insurance: certificate required
Other: no rice, confetti

Need a caterer, cake maker, florist? The Service Directory starting on page 412 features the best in the business.

SARATOGA FOOTHILL CLUB

20399 Park Place
Saratoga, CA 95070
(408) 867-3428 Dianna
Reserve: 9–12 months in advance

In a spot you'd never expect, on a quiet residential street near the crossroads of Big Basin and Sunnyvale/Saratoga Roads, lies the Foothill Club. This decorative 1915 Arts and Crafts-style historic landmark was designed by Julia Morgan as a women's club. The old-fashioned brown-shingled facade has a wisteria-covered trellis framing unusually shaped windows. An adjoining paved courtyard is dotted with Japanese maples. It's small but very pretty and private. The Club's formal entry is all in redwood, and ushers you into a room that is perfect for a buffet arrangement. The interior's largest room has 30-foot high ceilings, a raised platform stage, hardwood floors and an elaborate window through which glorious sunlight filters and sets the room aglow. A buffet table can be situated in front of the window, creating a special and highlighted place for the wedding cake and cutting ceremony. The Foothill Club offers a formal entry space, two interior rooms and an exterior courtyard for reception celebrations. All are pleasant, intimate spaces. The final impression is one of old-world comfort and warmth.

CAPACITY: From November–May, the Club's indoor and outdoor combined maximum capacity is 150 guests. From June–October the combined capacity is 185. The indoor maximum seated capacity is 126 guests.

FEES & DEPOSITS: A $200 refundable security deposit is required when reservations are made. For weddings, the rental fee is $500 for a 4-hour block.

AVAILABILITY: Tuesday through Sunday, 9:30am–9pm.

SERVICES/AMENITIES:

Restaurant Services: no
Catering: BYO
Kitchen Facilities: moderate
Tables & Chairs: provided
Linens, Silver, etc.: BYO
Restrooms: wca
Dance Floor: yes
Bride's Dressing Area: yes

Parking: adjacent church lot, $50 donation
Overnight Accommodations: no
Telephone: house phone
Outdoor Night Lighting: access only
Outdoor Cooking Facilities: no
Cleanup: caterer
Other: baby grand available

RESTRICTIONS:

Alcohol: BYO, WC only
Smoking: outside only
Music: amplified restricted

Wheelchair Access: no
Insurance: liability required

VILLA MONTALVO

15400 Montalvo Road
Saratoga, CA 95071
(408) 741-1524
Reserve: 1 month in advance

The Villa is a stately, Mediterranean-style estate nestled against a wooded slope in the private and secluded Saratoga hills. Built in 1912 as the private home of one of San Francisco's former mayors, Villa Montalvo, with its terra cotta tile roofs and light stucco exterior, is now an arboretum and a center for the arts. The Villa is approached from below by a narrow, one-way road offering a striking view of the structure as you round the last turn. An amphitheater with stage and a lovely patio with lawn are situated in back of the Villa. This open-air courtyard, called the Oval Garden, is surrounded by a wisteria-draped pergola and is a delightful place for a ceremony. The acoustics are fabulous in this quiet setting. For Montalvo Circle members, the Villa's main floor and surrounding areas are available for receptions, including the Spanish Courtyard, another smaller, wisteria-laden courtyard. The outdoor tiled and paved verandas are also very impressive spots for holding a reception. These have sweeping views down the grand steps and main lawn corridor to the Love Temple. Reserve well in advance. Villa Montalvo is an extraordinary site for an elegant and sophisticated wedding.

CAPACITY: Wedding ceremonies are held outdoors. The maximum capacity of the Oval Courtyard is 200 guests. Indoor capacity is 150–175 seated guests.

FEES & DEPOSITS: In order to have a reception here, you must be a Montalvo Circle member. Member prices range from $5,000 to $7,000. All amounts in excess of $2,500 are tax deductible. Membership also permits you one 8-hour event and a more immediate date confirmation. For ceremonies, a non-refundable 50% deposit of the total fee is required when you book your event date. A $500 security deposit is payable 30 days prior to the event and is usually returned 2 weeks after the wedding. The fees to have a ceremony here are as follows:

Guests	Fee	Guests	Fee
up to 50	$750	100–149	$1,250
51–99	975	150–200	1,500

Changes to the final guest count must be delivered, in writing, to the wedding coordinator 1 week prior to the event. The final balance is due, together with any other additional fees, 30 days prior to the wedding. Rehearsals, 45-minutes maximum, must be scheduled 1 month in advance of the event and are held the Thursday or Friday afternoon preceding your ceremony.

AVAILABILITY: Ceremonies, held between April and September, take place between 9am–11am, noon–2pm and 3pm–5pm. Receptions can be held year-round from 8am–11:30pm.

SERVICES/AMENITIES:
Restaurant Services: no
Catering: BYO, select from list

Parking: 125 cars, carpooling encouraged
Overnight Accommodations: no

Kitchen Facilities: ample
Tables & Chairs: provided
Linens, Silver, etc.: caterer
Restrooms: no wca
Dance Floor: required indoors, extra charge

RESTRICTIONS:
Alcohol: BYO, BWC only
Smoking: discouraged, not allowed inside Villa
Music: amplified with restrictions until 10:30pm

Telephone: pay phone
Outdoor Night Lighting: yes
Outdoor Cooking Facilities: no
Cleanup: caterer
Bride's Dressing Area: yes

Wheelchair Access: yes
Insurance: certificate required

Alexander Valley

CHATEAU SOUVERAIN

Independence Lane
Alexander Valley, CA 95441
(707) 433-3141
Reserve: 2–6 months in advance

Located seventy miles north of the Golden Gate Bridge, Chateau Souverain is beautifully situated on a vine-covered hill, commanding a spectacular view of Sonoma's Alexander Valley. Recognized for its contemporary French and American cuisine, it's one of the few California premium wineries to offer year-round gourmet dining. When you arrive, a grand staircase leads you from a tree-lined drive below to the large upper courtyard and fountain. The winery buildings are architecturally striking, designed in the shape of hop kilns with high-peaked slate roofs and extensive window detailing. The interior of the café is dynamic, with vibrant wall murals painted by a local artist and a large hanging fabric sculpture. Chateau Souverain's two formal dining rooms are connected by double glass doors. The Main Dining Room, with its large, fireplace and cathedral ceilings, opens onto a split-level terrace, while the Front Dining Room, a semi-private area, has a view of the fountain. The latter is great for semi-private events. Both are decorated in soft colors and are well-adorned with stunning floral arrangements. A bit off the beaten path, this winery makes a lovely setting for a Wine Country wedding reception.

CAPACITY, FEES & DEPOSITS: A refundable deposit of $300 is required to secure a date. A deposit of $15/person for lunch or $25/person for dinner, plus a room rental fee, is required a month prior to your event. These deposits are credited to the final bill. A final guest count guarantee is needed 1 week prior to your function. Sales tax and an 18% service charge are additional. Payment is due in full the day of the event. Luncheons start at $25/person, dinners at $40. Outside wedding cakes may be brought in with prior agreement; cake cutting is $2.50/person.

Area	Rental Fee	Seated	Standing	Hours
Main Dining Room	$500	90	—	
Front Dining Room	250	40	—	Hours vary
Outdoor Terrace	1,500 (1 tent, heating & lighting)	150	250	according to
	2,200 (2 tents, heating & lighting)	150	250	the event.
Cafe	varies	80	120	

CANCELLATION POLICY: With 30 days' written notice in advance of your function, your reservation deposit will be refunded.

AVAILABILITY: Private parties outdoors can take place during the time frames shown above. For indoor parties during regular business hours (approx. 11:30am–9:30pm) or with 75 guests or more, the restaurant can be opened beyond regular business hours.

SERVICES/AMENITIES:

Restaurant Services: yes
Parking: large lot
Catering: provided, no BYO
Kitchen Facilities: n/a
Tables & Chairs: provided
Linens, Silver, etc.: provided
Restrooms: wca

Dance Floor: CBA
Bride's Dressing Area: no
Overnight Accommodations: no
Telephone: pay phone
Outdoor Night Lighting: yes
Outdoor Cooking Facilities: no
Cleanup: provided

RESTRICTIONS:

Alcohol: provided, WC only
Smoking: outside only
Music: amplified indoors only until 9:45pm

Wheelchair Access: yes
Insurance: indemnification clause required
Other: decorations may be restricted

Calistoga

MOUNT VIEW HOTEL

1457 Lincoln Ave.
Calistoga, CA 94515
(707) 942-6877
Reserve: 2–6 months in advance

When you need a place for a wedding reception which also can provide overnight accommodations in the wine country—call the Mount View Hotel. Here, you can have the ceremony, the reception and your honeymoon. This recently renovated landmark hotel has both indoor and outdoor spaces for seated parties, a full service, upscale restaurant *plus* plenty of guestrooms for out-of-town guests. For indoor dining, Valeriano's (the Hotel's in-house restaurant) is a splendid reception spot. The decor is upscale contemporary. Colors are in creams and tans with white trim. Gold framed pictures, textured walls and cane chairs with rush seats make Valeriano's visually appealing. For al fresco receptions, try the Hotel's Poolside Grill and Patio Courtyard. Tables with umbrellas are arranged around the large, heated pool. Next to the pool, terra cotta sculptures with gurgling streams of water add to the ambiance. Inside, all the Hotel's rooms have all been renovated by interior designer Michael Moore, including the small but sweet cottages that are adjacent to the Hotel. Each cottage has a private courtyard and hot tub. What more could you ask for? Well, there is more—the Hotel's got a chic new European spa, all designed in marble and glass. It has every conceivable service your party needs to look their best. From facials to massage and herbal wraps to manicures, the spa's professional staff will make you feel as terrific as you look. And if you wonder why you should have a wedding in Calistoga, note that the Mt. View Hotel is in the heart of town—a stone's throw from golf, tennis, hot air ballooning, bicycling, glider rides and winery touring.

CAPACITY: Valeriano's 85 seated guests; the Poolside Patio 80–100 seated guests or 125 for a standing reception; the Private Dining Room 30 seated guests; Johnny's Cafe/Bar 60 seated guests, 80 standing.

FEES & DEPOSITS: A refundable $250 deposit is required to reserve your date and a 50% menu deposit is payable 30 days prior to the event. A final guest count is due 72 hours in advance. The rental fees are: Valeriano's $300, the Poolside Patio $500, Private Dining Room $150, Johnny's $250. The rental fee is payable 30 days in advance. Menus can be customized for your party and must be confirmed 2 weeks in advance. Luncheons start at $15/person, dinners and buffets start at $28/person. Tax and 15% service charge are additional. If you bring your own wedding cake, a cutting charge may apply.

CANCELLATION POLICY: If you cancel less than 14 days before an event, the menu deposit will be forfeited.

AVAILABILITY: Year–round. Everyday from 9am–10pm except Valeriano's, which is available from 9am–4pm.

SERVICES/AMENITIES:

Restaurant Services: yes
Catering: provided, no BYO
Kitchen Facilities: n/a
Tables & Chairs: provided
Linens, Silver, etc.: provided
Restrooms: wca
Dance Floor: yes
Other: full service wedding planning

Parking: on street, lot
Overnight Accommodations: 22 rooms, 8 suites, 3 cottages
Telephone: pay phones & room phones
Outdoor Night Lighting: yes
Outdoor Cooking Facilities: CBA
Cleanup: provided
Bride's Dressing Area: CBA

RESTRICTIONS:

Alcohol: provided, corkage $7.50–10/bottle
Smoking: designated areas
Music: amplified ok, outside until 10pm

Wheelchair Access: yes
Insurance: not required

Geyserville

TRENTADUE WINERY

19170 Geyserville Avenue
Geyserville, CA 95441
(707) 433-3104
Reserve: 6–12 months in advance

Trentadue Winery is located in the heart of the serene and exquisite Alexander Valley, just twenty minutes north of Santa Rosa. Framed by acres of vineyards, this family-owned winery provides a bucolic outdoor setting for a comfortable wine country wedding. A majestic weeping willow and latticed vine-covered arbors provide cool shade during summer months, and an expansive lawn is ringed by blooming flowers, redwoods and maples. Both ceremonies and receptions can be held on manicured lawns or under adjacent arbors, constructed in an old-world Italian style. Surrounded by panoramic views of Geyser Peak, Mt. St. Helena and Cobb Mountain, this winery garden retreat is conducive to great parties and relaxed family gatherings.

CAPACITY: The winery's outdoor spaces can accommodate up to 300 guests.

FEES & DEPOSITS: A non-refundable $400 deposit, applied toward the rental fee, is required when you make reservations. The rental fee balance, refundable $350 security deposit and a confirmed guest count are due 21 days prior to the event. There is a $625 minimum rental fee for use of the facility. Functions extending past 9pm need prior approval and will be charged an additional $75/hour. You will receive a 20% discount on all Trentadue varietal wines and champagne.

Guests	Champagne Plan/person	Chardonnay Plan/person
1–75	$16	$12.50
76–100	14	11
101–150	13	10
151–300	13.50	10.50

AVAILABILITY: Weddings and receptions can occur May–October, from 8am–9pm. Weddings are limited to a 5-hour block. Functions may extend until 11pm with prior approval.

SERVICES/AMENITIES:

Restaurant Services: no
Catering: preferred list, must be licensed
Kitchen Facilities: moderate
Tables & Chairs: provided
Linens, Silver, etc.: provided depending on plan selected
Restrooms: wca
Other: archway or gazebo, extra charge

Parking: large lot
Overnight Accommodations: no
Telephone: office phone, limited use
Outdoor Night Lighting: yes
Outdoor Cooking Facilities: no
Dance Floor: yes
Cleanup: provided
Bride & Groom's Dressing Area: yes

RESTRICTIONS:

Alcohol: WC provided
Smoking: outside only
Music: amplified ok

Wheelchair Access: yes
Insurance: liability required or CBA, extra fee
Other: children must be supervised

Need a caterer, cake maker, florist? The Service Directory starting on page 412 features the best in the business.

Guerneville

THE SURREY INN

16590 River Road
Guerneville, CA 95446
(707) 869-2002
Reserve: 6–12 months in advance

Less than two blocks from the center of town, this Russian River resort has been transformed into the best combination of indoor and outdoor spaces we've seen in this area. Totally private and enclosed by tall redwoods, the Surrey Inn is a three-and-a-half acre enclave featuring a pool, pool house, interior banquet spaces, tennis courts and lawns. Set back from River Road, the building's ordinary creme and gray-blue facade belies an exceptional interior. The largest space, designed for special events, has a high, vaulted ceiling, enormous wood-burning fireplace and skylights throughout. With this room, you don't have to worry about your guest list—it seats 350! Equally impressive are the outdoor facilities. The Surrey Inn has one of Sonoma's largest private swimming pools, with men's and women's changing areas, jacuzzi and spa. For more active guests, there are tennis courts, basketball court, horseshoes and volleyball. There's even play equipment for restless youngsters. On warm days and evenings, you can have a relaxed garden party arranged around the pool. Umbrellas provide shade and the outdoor bar is just a stone's throw away. If you've got a large guest list, you should make time to visit the Surrey Inn. This is a must-see location for Russian River weddings.

CAPACITY: Indoors, the Inn can hold 500 seated; 800 standing. Indoor and outdoor spaces up to 1,500 standing guests.

FEES & DEPOSITS: A non-refundable $500 security deposit is due when reservations are made. The rental fee is $500 for up to 100 guests, $2,000 for 500 guests and $4,000 for 1,500 guests. The rental fee covers a 5-hour period and is payable 30 days prior to the event. For parties over 200 guests, professional security guard(s) are required, to be hired at the renter's expense.

AVAILABILITY: Year-round, daily from 6am–2am.

SERVICES/AMENITIES:

Restaurant Services: no
Catering: provided or BYO
Kitchen Facilities: no
Tables & Chairs: BYO or CBA
Linens, Silver, etc.: BYO or CBA
Restrooms: no wca
Dance Floor: yes

Parking: large secured lot
Overnight Accommodations: no
Telephone: phone usage with approval
Outdoor Night Lighting: yes
Outdoor Cooking Facilities: BBQ
Cleanup: caterer or renter
Bride's Dressing Area: yes

RESTRICTIONS:

Alcohol: BYO

Wheelchair Access: yes

Smoking: outside only

Music: amplified ok indoors, limited outdoors

Insurance: liability required

Healdsburg

MADRONA MANOR

1001 Westside Road
Healdsburg, CA 95448
(707) 433-4231
Reserve: 2–12 months in advance

Madrona Manor is an exceptionally lovely Victorian house set high over the Dry Creek Valley of Sonoma County, surrounded by eight acres of wooded and landscaped grounds. Built in 1881 by John Paxton, a wealthy San Francisco businessman, the three-story stately Manor and adjacent buildings originally served as his summer home and weekend retreat. Now a country inn, the Manor complex provides its guests with an elegant country ambiance. The Manor's interior rooms come complete with antique furniture, Persian carpets and hand-carved rosewood detailing. A nearby Carriage House provides additional guestrooms. Outside, a sizeable deck overlooks a meticulously manicured lawn and flower beds, an herb, vegetable and citrus garden. All combine to create a wonderful environment for wedding parties. Madrona Manor offers an extensive wine list and beautifully prepared meals, containing ingredients that are always fresh. The Manor is so pleasant, pretty and tranquil, we guarantee you'll want to come back for more after the party's over.

CAPACITY: The Manor can accommodate up to 100 guests, 135 in good weather.

FEES & DEPOSITS: A $1,250 reservation fee is required when the contract is submitted, and includes the rental for 1 room for 2 nights. Food service is provided and runs about $30/person. Other fees will vary according to the needs of the group. Sales tax and 15% gratuity are applied to the total bill.

CANCELLATION POLICY: With 120 days' notice, your deposit will be refunded less $300.

AVAILABILITY: Weddings on Saturdays noon to 5pm. Sunday evenings, small groups up to 40 guests.

SERVICES/AMENITIES:

Restaurant Services: yes

Catering: provided, no BYO

Kitchen Facilities: n/a

Tables & Chairs: provided

Linens, Silver, etc.: provided

Restrooms: wca

Dance Floor: CBA

Bride's Dressing Area: guestroom

Parking: large lot

Overnight Accommodations: 21 guestrooms

Telephone: guestroom phones

Outdoor Night Lighting: yes

Outdoor Cooking Facilities: no

Cleanup: provided

Other: made-to-order special desserts

RESTRICTIONS:

Alcohol: provided, WBC only
Smoking: not in dining rooms
Music: no amplified

Wheelchair Access: yes
Insurance: not required
Other: decorating restrictions

VILLA CHANTICLEER

1248 North Fitch Mountain Road
Healdsburg, CA 95448
(707) 431-3301
Reserve: 12–24 months in advance

Atop a gentle slope, within a 17-acre park at the edge of Healdsburg, you'll find Villa Chanticleer, a casual, no-frills facility owned by the City of Healdsburg. The redwood tree setting is pleasant, quiet and cool. Built in 1910 as a lodge resort for San Franciscans, this one-story structure is surrounded on three sides by a wide veranda, shaded by a substantial trellis covered with wisteria. Follow the entryway which leads directly into a room containing a large, U-shaped bar with a southwest-style mural painted on the back wall. On either side of the bar are two more rooms: the Ballroom and the Dining Room, 3000 square feet each. Both have light-toned hardwood floors, redwood paneled walls and white ceilings. The Ballroom has a large stone fireplace at its center and a small elevated stage area built into one corner. The Dining Room has a more open, lighter ambiance and views of the adjacent hillside. These spacious rooms can accommodate a relaxed, down home party, or be dressed up for a formal affair. What's nice about this facility is that it can handle large crowds and the spaces are flexible. Consequently, Villa Chanticleer is extremely popular in this area—a great favorite among brides and grooms.

CAPACITY: The Dining Room and Ballroom hold 320 seated guests each; 300 each for a standing reception. The Annex accommodates 150 seated guests or 250 for a standing reception. Outdoor picnic facilities can accommodate up to 250 people. The bar area can hold up to 100 guests.

FEES & DEPOSITS: The Villa rents for $500 ($325 for Healdsburg residents) for a 10-hour block on weekdays or $750 ($475 for residents) for a 10-hour block on weekends. For each additional hour, $40 will be charged. The Villa Annex costs $40/hour to rent weekdays (residents $17.50/hour), and $50/hour weekends (residents $25/hour). Rental fees are due when reservations are confirmed. A $200 cleaning deposit is required for the Villa and a $100 cleaning deposit for the Annex. These are due 60 days prior to your event and will be refunded 30 days after the event. No deposit is required for use of the outdoor picnic facility. A $50 alcohol use fee is charged for all facilities.

AVAILABILITY: Year-round, seven days a week including holidays.

SERVICES/AMENITIES:

Restaurant Services: no
Catering: preferred list
Kitchen Facilities: ample

Parking: large lot
Overnight Accommodations: CBA
Telephone: pay phone

Tables & Chairs: provided
Linens, Silver, etc.: BYO linens
Restrooms: wca
Bride's Dressing Area: CBA
Dance Floor: yes

Outdoor Night Lighting: yes
Outdoor Cooking Facilities: BBQ
Cleanup: caterer
Special: dishes, glassware provided

RESTRICTIONS:

Alcohol: BYO, $50 use fee required
Smoking: allowed
Music: amplified ok

Wheelchair Access: yes
Insurance: required
Other: no rice, birdseed, metallic balloons, streamers

Kenwood

KENWOOD INN

10400 Sonoma Highway
Kenwood, CA 95452
(707) 833-1293
Reserve: 1–6 months in advance

The Kenwood Inn is an 'Italian pensione' with facilities for wedding receptions and prenuptial dinners as well as honeymoons. It's a bit hard to find, so keep your eyes open as you head into Kenwood from the South. This place has an old-world appearance and a romantic ambiance. The exterior of the building is very European, as is the interior. Walk right in. You'll find lovely slate floors, walls painted with fanciful motifs in rich shades of terra cotta and green. The style is Northern Italian Country. A medium-sized dining area is linked to the kitchen in an open, hospitable way. The kitchen has copper counters, burnt sienna-colored walls and modern amenities. All extend a subtle invitation to linger a while longer. There's even a fireplace here to warm guests in the evenings. To the left, there's a sitting room with another fireplace, also comfortably decked out with overstuffed couches, chairs and Mediterranean wrought-iron glass tables. Outside, a full-size pool and flagstone patio dominate the front garden, which is ringed by green lawn and rambling roses. This is a wonderful setting for a relaxed, poolside reception. At the Kenwood Inn, wedding guests can breath in fresh, country air while taking in the sights. From the Inn's windows and garden, you can marvel at the nearby hillsides covered with row upon row of grape vines. The Kenwood Inn is a fitting newcomer to the ever-beautiful Valley of the Moon.

CAPACITY: 125 guests, maximum. Guestrooms can accommodate 8 overnight.

FEES & DEPOSITS: A non-refundable $500 deposit is required 6 months prior to the event. For wedding receptions, all rooms must be reserved at the Inn, approximately $765 summer, $660 winter. An additional $1,700 fee is required for exclusive use of the premises plus a $200 refundable cleaning deposit.

CANCELLATION POLICY: With 6 months' notice, the deposit is refundable.

AVAILABILITY: Year-round, everyday.

SERVICES/AMENITIES:

Restaurant Services: no
Catering: provided or BYO, select from preferred list
Kitchen Facilities: ample
Tables & Chairs: BYO or provided
Linens, Silver, etc.: provided, extra fee
Restrooms: wca limited
Bride's Dressing Area: bridal suite

Dance Floor: poolside or dining room
Parking: lot provided
Overnight Accommodations: 4 guestrooms
Telephone: house phone
Outdoor Night Lighting: yes
Outdoor Cooking Facilities: BBQs
Cleanup: caterer

RESTRICTIONS:

Alcohol: BW provided
Smoking: outside only
Music: amplified ok

Wheelchair Access: no
Insurance: not required

LANDMARK VINEYARDS

101 Adobe Canyon Road
Kenwood, CA 95452
(707) 833-1144
Reserve: 1–6 months in advance

In the heart of the Valley of the Moon, at the junction of Adobe Canyon and Highway 12, you'll find Landmark Vineyards' new facility. Constructed in an early California style with shake roof and post-and-beam supports, the building encloses a very attractive patio courtyard with large fountain rimmed with blue tile. The courtyard is accented with terra cotta pots and pavers, and is well-situated to take advantage of the nice views of the adjacent vineyards and the hills beyond. You can set up umbrella-shaded tables or tenting during receptions. There's also a private dining room for smaller, more intimate parties, that comes with its own courtyard, accessible through multiple French doors. The structure also houses a large tasting room, with high beamed ceiling, terra cotta paved floors and windows overlooking the outdoor courtyard. A colorful mural, painted on the high wall over the tasting room bar, depicts a scene of the vineyard seen through a magnified grapevine. Landmark is designed for events, which makes it easy for planning purposes. And, it provides an in-house event coordinator for those who need assistance.

CAPACITY: Landmark can accommodate 115 seated guests or 100–200 for a standing reception indoors. The Dining Room holds up to 48 seated; the Tasting Room, after hours, can seat up to 67 guests. The maximum capacity outdoors is 500 guests seated or 600–700 standing.

FEES & DEPOSITS: Half of the facility use fee, which is applied toward the event, is required when reservations are confirmed. The balance of the fee plus a guaranteed guest count are due 7 days prior to the wedding.

Guests	_Use Fee_		_Guests_	_Use Fee_
1–40	$400		101+	$4.25/guest
41–100	$10/guest			plus $600 use fee

AVAILABILITY: Everyday, 7am–11pm. Outdoor use is seasonal.

SERVICES/AMENITIES:

Restaurant Services: no
Catering: preferred list, licensed & bonded
Kitchen Facilities: ample
Tables & Chairs: provided
Linens, Silver, etc.: BYO
Restrooms: wca
Bride's Dressing Area: CBA

Dance Floor: CBA, extra charge
Parking: lot provided
Overnight Accommodations: no
Telephone: pay phone
Outdoor Night Lighting: yes
Outdoor Cooking Facilities: BBQs
Cleanup: provided, cleaning fee for larger groups

RESTRICTIONS:

Alcohol: WC provided
Smoking: outside only
Music: amplified, some restrictions

Wheelchair Access: yes
Insurance: not required
Other: decorations restricted

Napa

BLUE VIOLET MANSION

443 Brown Street
Napa, CA 94559
(707) 253-2583
Reserve: 3–6 months in advance

This landmark bed and breakfast inn situated on a tree-lined street in historic Napa. The Blue Violet Mansion is a huge Victorian manor (appropriately painted a light blue) that offers special service for personalized weddings. Each event here is customized from the rehearsal dinner to the post-wedding gift baskets in guests' rooms. After many years of neglect, the 1886 Mansion has been fully restored to its former grandeur by the current owners, Kathy and Bob Morris. Working diligently since 1989, they've added turn-of-the-century fixtures, oriental carpets and Victorian antiques. The downstairs parlors and dining room, with twelve-foot ceilings and ornate fireplaces, can be used for rehearsal dinners or small receptions. The outside lawns are more appropriate for larger parties. For ceremonies, there's a lovely, hand-made white gazebo surrounded by annuals and hundred-year-old trees in front of the Mansion. Whether you arrange a candlelit dinner for a few or a garden party under umbrellas for a crowd, the key elements here are comfort and service.

CAPACITY: The interior parlors can hold up to 49 guests; the grounds up to 100 for a reception. For ceremonies, using the gazebo garden, 100 guests.

FEES & DEPOSITS: A non-refundable cleaning/damage deposit is due when you make reservations. After the event, the deposit is returned less the cleaning fee and any damage charges. The rental fees are due 30 days prior to the event. Ceremony and reception spaces are rented separately. All 8 guestrooms can be rented at a total cost of $1,350/night.

	Gazebo Garden	Parlors	Grounds Saturday	Grounds Sunday-Friday
Rental fee	$200	$200	$500	$350
Cleaning fee	100	100	250	250

CANCELLATION POLICY: If you cancel within 30 days of the event, refunds must be negotiated.

AVAILABILITY: The indoor parlors are available daily, year-round from 1pm–5pm. The grounds are available spring and summer from 1pm–5pm. If you book all 8 guestrooms, you may hold your event at anytime of day or night for up to 6 hours.

SERVICES/AMENITIES:

Restaurant Services: no
Catering: preferred list
Kitchen Facilities: n/a
Tables & Chairs: CBA or BYO
Linens, Silver, etc.: CBA or BYO
Restrooms: no wca
Dance Floor: outdoors CBA

Parking: valet and small lot
Overnight Accommodations: 8 guestrooms
Telephone: pay phone
Outdoor Night Lighting: no
Outdoor Cooking Facilities: BBQ
Cleanup: provided
Bride's Dressing Area: CBA

RESTRICTIONS:

Alcohol: provided, corkage $6.50/bottle
Smoking: outdoors only
Music: amplified outside until 6pm, inside until 9pm

Wheelchair Access: outside only
Insurance: certificate required
Other: no red wine indoors, no rice or birdseed, children must be supervised

CHIMNEY ROCK WINERY

5350 Silverado Trail
Napa, CA 94558
(707) 257-2641 Kathy Higgins
Reserve: 6 months in advance

Chimney Rock is located on the Silverado Trail near Yountville. It's a relatively new winery, set among 75 acres of vineyards in the famed Stags Leap District, known for its superlative wine growing conditions. Bordered by a stand of tall Lombardy poplars, the Hospitality Center was built for both wine tasting and special events. Designed in a Cape Dutch style, the building is tastefully appointed, with huge fireplace, beamed cathedral ceiling and hardwood floors. French doors lead to a large outdoor patio. The garden here is enclosed, sheltered on all sides by the walls of the buildings. On the upper portion of the winery building, facing guests as they enter the garden, is an impressive relief of Ganymede, cupbearer to the Gods. Sun plays with the relief's shadows during the day and at night when lit, the relief is stunning. For ceremonies, the interior garden with a lush lawn, divided in half by a falling cascade, is a Chimney Rock favorite. Pretty and private, this outstanding winery is well suited for both wedding ceremonies and receptions.

CAPACITY: Indoors, the facility can hold up to 60 seated guests; outdoors up to 250 seated. The winery barrel room can hold up to 100 seated guests. The winery maximum is 250 guests.

FEES & DEPOSITS: A non-refundable $750 deposit and signed contract are required to secure your date. The balance is due 1 week prior to the event. The winery use fee is $35/person (minimum $800) and includes all wine (limited quantity/person), wine service staff, glassware (including champagne flutes), tables, chairs, setup and cleanup.

AVAILABILITY: Year-round, except for Christmas and Thanksgiving. Receptions from 5pm–11pm.

SERVICES/AMENITIES:

Restaurant Services: no
Catering: preferred list
Kitchen Facilities: fully equipped
Tables & Chairs: provided
Linens, Silver, etc.: caterer
Restrooms: wca
Dance Floor: CBA
Bride's Dressing Area: yes

Parking: large lot
Overnight Accommodations: no
Telephone: business phone
Outdoor Night Lighting: yes
Outdoor Cooking Facilities: CBA
Cleanup: Chimney Rock and caterer
Other: wedding coordination, service referrals, bar staff provided

RESTRICTIONS:

Alcohol: W provided, champagne CBA, $8/bottle corkage, no hard alcohol
Music: amplified ok

Wheelchair Access: yes
Insurance: not required
Smoking: outside only

CHURCHILL MANOR

485 Brown Street
Napa, CA 94559
(707) 253-7733 Joanna
Reserve: 3–12 months in advance

Set back from a tree-lined street by an expansive green lawn dotted with annuals and a formal fountain, Churchill Manor is very impressive. Built in 1889 in the heart of historic residential Napa, the Manor has had a 100-year history of hosting weddings. Now a Victorian bed and breakfast inn, it features an antique-appointed interior, wide verandas and lovely landscaped grounds. The main entry doors with their detailed leaded glass inset panels lead into several parlors, each with a grand fireplace, period furnishings, fine woodwork, original brass and crystal fixtures and ornate ceilings. The airy white-painted solarium adjacent to the main buffet room is very inviting, with large leaded glass windows that overlook the garden, mosaic marble tile floor and white furniture. Churchill Manor's interior spaces all combine to make you feel like you've stepped back in time to a slower, more gracious period. The Manor's innkeeper takes great pains to assist with every detail, even down to arranging winery tours and rehearsal dinners. You can even reserve all 10 guestrooms and have the entire Manor exclusively for your yourself, your friends and family!

CAPACITY: In winter, the Manor accommodates a maximum of 75 guests inside. In spring and fall, including veranda, 125 guests. In summer, including garden and veranda, 150 guests.

FEES & DEPOSITS: A refundable damage deposit of $500 is required and will be returned if no damages are incurred. For a full-service wedding on Saturday, the rental fee is $1500. For Sunday–Friday events the rental fees vary: under 30 guests, $600; 31–75 guests, $600 plus $20/guest over 31 guests; and over 75 guests, $1,500. If you wish to seat over 125 guests, there's an extra setup charge of $2.50/guest. Food service is provided; any menu can be customized. A buffet reception costs approximately $17.50–22.50/person including an extensive hors d'oeuvres table and buffet meal. Sales tax and 15% gratuity are additional. The total balance, with a final guest count, is due 10 days prior to the wedding date.

If you reserve all 10 guestrooms, the total guestroom fee is $1,090/night plus tax, including a full breakfast. Note that if the event occurs on a Saturday, guestrooms must be booked for a minimum of 2 nights.

AVAILABILITY: If you reserve all 10 guestrooms, your party can extend, in a 6-hour block, from 11am to 9pm. If you don't reserve the entire Manor, you are restricted to a 4-1/2 hour time block between the hours of noon–5pm for both ceremony and reception.

SERVICES/AMENITIES:

Restaurant Services: no

Catering: provided, no BYO

Kitchen Facilities: n/a

Parking: 20 car lot, on street

Overnight Accommodations: 10 guestrooms

Telephone: house phone, guestroom phones

Tables & Chairs: provided
Linens, Silver, etc.: provided
Restrooms: wca
Dance Floor: yes, inside only
Bride's Dressing Area: CBA

Outdoor Night Lighting: yes
Outdoor Cooking Facilities: CBA
Cleanup: provided
Other: baby grand piano, wedding coordination

RESTRICTIONS:

Alcohol: BYO, WCB only
Smoking: outside only
Music: acoustic outside until 7pm, inside until 9pm

Wheelchair Access: limited
Insurance: not required
Other: children discouraged, must be supervised

INN AT NAPA VALLEY
Crown Sterling Suites

1075 California Blvd.
Napa, CA 94559
(707) 253-9160 Catering
Reserve: 1–12 months in advance

The Inn at Napa Valley, located near downtown Napa, offers spacious and varied accommodations for any size wedding party. This Mediterranean-style hotel, with pastel walls, red tile roof and stone arches, greets entering guests with fountains and a circular, palm-tree-lined driveway. Moving through one of the outdoor courtyards, with a working wood mill and mill pond with waterfowl, lush plantings and small waterfalls, you step into an interior restaurant atrium resplendent in Mexican tile pavers, potted trees and high ceilings. The Inn's facilities for wedding parties adjoin the atrium. The pre-function atrium offers high ceilings, large tropical plants, terra cotta tile floors, skylight and indoor fountain. The surrounding rooms can be combined to expand in any way to meet your guest requirements. And, if you wish to honeymoon here, the Inn has saunas, spas and both indoor and outdoor pools in addition to distinctive suites with fireplaces and wet bars.

CAPACITY: The Inn has a variety of spaces available and can accommodate a range from 25 to 200 seated or 200 standing guests.

FEES & DEPOSITS: A non-refundable $500 deposit, which is applied toward the event balance, is required when you reserve your date. Per person rates: luncheons are approximately $14, seated dinners $18 and buffet service $20. Sales tax and a 17% service charge are additional. The total balance is due 72 hours prior to your event and any remaining balance is payable at the event's conclusion. For ceremonies, use of the gazebo is $350. If multiple rooms are reserved, the use fee is $300; if your party can be contained in 1 room, there's no charge. Bartender service is $50/function.

AVAILABILITY: Year-round, 6am to 2am everyday

SERVICES/AMENITIES:

Restaurant Services: yes
Catering: provided, no BYO
Kitchen Facilities: n/a
Tables & Chairs: provided
Linens, Silver, etc.: provided
Restrooms: wca
Dance Floor: yes
Bride's Dressing Area: CBA

Parking: large lots
Overnight Accommodations: 205 suites
Telephone: pay phones
Outdoor Night Lighting: limited
Outdoor Cooking Facilities: no
Cleanup: provided
Other: grand piano

RESTRICTIONS:

Alcohol: provided, CW only, corkage $8/bottle
Smoking: allowed
Insurance: not required

Music: amplified ok
Wheelchair Access: yes

MacDONALD FARM

Address withheld to maintain privacy
Napa, CA 94558
(707) 226-8985
Reserve: 3 months in advance

Don't be misled by the name. It's not really a farm. The MacDonald's have a friendly-looking white farm house—simple yet homey. The pleasant surprise is that it sets in front of a gorgeous garden, featuring a circle of lush green lawn ringed by a profusion of annuals and perennials. The brilliant floral display is framed by a semi-circle of very tall conifers which provide a background tapestry of green. On the lawn's edge, a white lath archway with roses and other flowering vines provides the perfect setting to take your vows. After the ceremony, tables and chairs with white umbrellas can be loosely or formally arranged on the lawn for seated receptions. Off to one side of the garden is another semi-enclosed area containing a small, irregular shaped pool where guests can mingle and, with champagne in hand, engage in intimate conversation. If you'd like to get married in a more woodsy setting, a small lawn under an enormous bay tree, on the other side of the house, is available. This mini-glade provides a sheltered, private clearing for a small ceremony. The owners of this garden retreat, Art and Barbara MacDonald are delightful and warm hosts, inviting guests to enjoy the house and grounds for the day. If your wedding vision is of a private, sunlit garden, with an emerald green lawn surrounded by trees and multi-colored flowers, you couldn't pick a better spot than MacDonald Farm in Napa.

CAPACITY: 150 guests, maximum.

FEES & DEPOSITS: A non-refundable $300 rental deposit plus a refundable $400 cleaning/damage deposit are required to reserve your date. Up to 75 guests, the rental fee is $750. From 75–150 guests, $1,100. The balance is due 7 days prior to the event.

CANCELLATION POLICY: If you cancel, only the cleaning/damage deposit will be returned.

AVAILABILITY: From May 15 through October.

SERVICES/AMENITIES:

Restaurant Services: no

Catering: BYO

Kitchen Facilities: yes

Tables & Chairs: BYO

Linens, Silver, etc.: BYO

Restrooms: wca limited

Dance Floor: CBA

Parking: private lot

Overnight Accommodations: no

Telephone: emergency only

Outdoor Night Lighting: CBA

Outdoor Cooking Facilities: CBA

Cleanup: caterer or renter

Bride's Dressing Area: yes

RESTRICTIONS:

Alcohol: BYO

Smoking: garden area only

Music: amplified restricted, 10pm limit

Wheelchair Access: limited

Insurance: proof of liability required

NAPA RIVER BOAT

Napa Valley Marina
1200 Milton Road
Napa, CA 94559
(707) 226-2628 Judy
Reserve: 3–6 months in advance

Plan your wedding or rehearsal dinner aboard the authentic sternwheeler 'City of Napa' and return to a slower-paced, gentler period. Your memorable wedding cruise can be as formal as an antebellum plantation ball or as casual as a relaxed weekend picnic. Antique lighting, oak bar and rich mahogany paneling grace the interior. Meals are served on crisp linens and beautifully presented on settings of gleaming crystal and china. You can relax here. The captain or clergy of your choice can perform the ceremony on the upper deck to the accompanying music of splashing water from the Napa River Boat's paddlewheel.

CAPACITY: The entire vessel holds up to 100 standing or 90 seated guests.

FEES & DEPOSITS: A deposit of 25% of the estimated total fee is required when your contract is returned. For boat rental only, the fee is $250/hour for a 2-hour minimum cruising time. Rental plus food service runs $24–46/person, depending on whether it is a brunch or a 4-course gourmet seated meal. The rental fee is for a 3-hour period. Tax and a 15% gratuity are added to the final bill which is due 3 working days prior to the event.

CANCELLATION POLICY: With 30 days' notice your deposit is fully refundable; with less than 30 days' notice, 80% is refundable if the date can be rebooked.

AVAILABILITY: Any day, anytime.

SERVICES/AMENITIES:

Restaurant Services: no

Catering: provided

Parking: marina lots

Overnight Accommodations: no

Kitchen Facilities: full galley
Tables & Chairs: provided
Linens, Silver, etc.: provided or BYO if hourly rental
Restrooms: no wca
Dance Floor: yes
Bride's Dressing Area: no

RESTRICTIONS:

Alcohol: provided, corkage $5/bottle
Smoking: outside decks only
Music: amplified ok, space limited

Telephone: radio
Outdoor Night Lighting: yes
Outdoor Cooking Facilities: no
Cleanup: caterer
Other: captain performs ceremonies, wedding coordination, remote pick-ups

Wheelchair Access: lower deck only
Insurance: not required

VERSANT VINEYARDS

1945 Mt. Veeder Road
Napa, CA 94558
(415) 567-4077 or **(415) 346-6066**
Reserve: 2–12 months in advance

Versant Vineyards is a special place for a personalized garden wedding. This is a private estate nestled in the hills west of Napa Valley, about six miles from downtown Napa. From Mt. Veeder, take the steep road to the top of the private drive and you'll find yourself in a quiet, informal garden setting, punctuated by large redwoods. Stone retaining walls and steps define and enclose the landscape. Paths weave in and around the terraces and a wide range of plant materials provide a multi-hued backdrop for picture taking. In spring and summer, the garden is a profusion of color. Versant Vineyards has something we've never seen before—a long, linear area beneath eighty-foot redwoods that serves as an event space. Many couples set up a row of tables under this living canopy, which provides a shady, intimate spot for a reception. The deep green foliage contrasts nicely with white linens; crystal, silver flatware and flowers make the tables festive. Down the way, a wider space forms a natural cathedral for the ceremony. You can take your vows under huge redwoods, while savoring a vista of vineyards and the Napa hills beyond.

CAPACITY: 250 guests, maximum.

FEES & DEPOSITS: Half the rental fee of $1,600 is the refundable deposit required to secure your date. The remaining rental balance, along with a refundable $400 security deposit, are due 30 days in advance prior to the event. The fee covers a site manager for the day, valet services, some tables and chairs and PA system. With more than 150 guests, additional valet services and restrooms may be required. Other available items: wedding arch for $100, bandstand for $100, additional outdoor restrooms at $120/each, dance floor in sections at $14/section. Additional tables run $8/each and chairs $2/each.

CANCELLATION POLICY: With 90 days' notice, $400 of the rental deposit will be returned.

AVAILABILITY: Late April through mid-October from 7am–10:30pm. Guests must leave by 10pm; all service providers by 10:30pm.

SERVICES/AMENITIES:

Restaurant Services: no

Catering: BYO, must be licensed

Kitchen Facilities: setup only

Tables & Chairs: some provided, extra fee

Linens, Silver, etc.: BYO

Restrooms: wca

Dance Floor: CBA, extra fee

Other: site manager, PA system

Parking: valet provided

Overnight Accommodations: no

Telephone: emergency only

Outdoor Night Lighting: yes

Outdoor Cooking Facilities: large BBQ

Cleanup: caterer

Bride & Groom's Dressing Area: yes

RESTRICTIONS:

Alcohol: BYO

Smoking: designated areas

Music: amplified until 10pm

Wheelchair Access: yes

Insurance: certificate required

Other: no rice, pets; decorations need approval

Petaluma

FAIRBANKS MANSION

758 D Street

Petaluma, CA 94952

(707) 765-2105

Reserve: 2–6 months in advance

Possibly one of Petaluma's most celebrated homes, this historic three-story mansion is a Victorian of grand proportions. Built in 1890 by Hiram T. Fairbanks, one of California's most prominent lumber barons, it sits on a handsome street lined by stately homes. Set back from the street by expansive lawns, the building and grounds are impressive. With its five-sided tower, fishscale shingles, swept dormer windows and wide veranda, it is an extraordinary example of Queen Anne-style architecture. Notice the magnificent entry. Come up to the ornate door and step inside. The Mansion's foyer features original curved glass windows, a romantic mural and player piano. The ground floor has spacious rooms that are beautifully detailed with marble, oak and other hardwoods. From the foyer, a grand mahogany staircase leads upstairs, illuminated by an eleven-foot stained glass window at the top. Off to the left is an intimate Victorian library and to the right are the formal dining room and parlor. Both have high ceilings, and a grand piano and organ are available for functions. There's even a gourmet kitchen guaranteed to make any caterer ecstatic. From the kitchen windows, you can peek out into the garden where ceremonies are held under the lovely canopy of a wisteria-covered pergola. Guests can be seated on the lawns or around the entry drive for receptions. During relaxed garden parties, you can play croquet or lawn tennis. If you'd like to return to a slower, more gracious time, the Fairbanks Mansion offers old world grandeur at its best.

CAPACITY: Inside the Mansion: 80 seated (concert style), 60 for seated meals, 120 for a standing reception. The gardens can accommodate 250 standing, 200 concert-style or 100 for a seated meal.

FEES & DEPOSITS: A $500 non-refundable security deposit (applied toward the rental fee) is required when reservations are confirmed. Rental fees range from $650–4,000 depending on the date, use and number of guests. For the Mansion's first floor, $1,000 is required for a 4-hour minimum rental. The upper floor dressing room for the bride is an additional $300. Security guards are occasionally required.

CANCELLATION POLICY: Deposits will only be refunded if the date can be rebooked with a party of comparable size.

AVAILABILITY: Year-round, any day from 8am. Guests and caterer must vacate premises by midnight.

SERVICES/AMENITIES:

Restaurant Services: no
Catering: select from preferred list
Kitchen Facilities: ample
Tables & Chairs: BYO
Linens, Silver, etc.: BYO
Restrooms: wca
Dance Floor: yes
Other: carriage service CBA

Parking: on street
Overnight Accommodations: no
Telephone: restricted
Outdoor Night Lighting: yes
Outdoor Cooking Facilities: BBQ
Cleanup: caterer or renter
Bride's Dressing Area: yes

RESTRICTIONS:

Alcohol: provided, no BYO
Smoking: outside only
Music: amplified within limits

Wheelchair Access: limited inside
Insurance: required
Other: decorations restricted

GARDEN VALLEY RANCH

498 Pepper Road
Petaluma, CA 94952
(707) 795-0919   Robert Galyean
Reserve: 6–12 months in advance

If you are a rose lover, gardening or horticulture buff, Garden Valley Ranch, located three miles north of Petaluma, is the perfect location for an outdoor celebration. And if you just want your ceremony or reception held amidst roses, this is a terrific spot. This seven-acre ranch contains some 4,000 rose bushes cultivated for the sale of their blooms and a one-acre garden where fragrant plants are grown for potpourri blends. Several Victorian-style structures, a large lawn and adjacent gardens are available for large functions. Tents, canopies, tables with umbrellas and dance floor can be set up on lush, green lawns, creating a comfortable environment for the ultimate garden wedding.

CAPACITY: The facility can accommodate up to 250 guests for outdoor functions.

FEES & DEPOSITS: A non-refundable security deposit totaling 50% of the rental fee is payable when reservations are confirmed. A refundable security deposit of $400, the remaining 50% of the rental fee and equipment fees are due 2 weeks prior to the function. Rental rates: up to 50 guests $750, 51–100 guests $950, 101–150 guests $1,150, 151–200 guests $1,350, 201–250 guests $1,550. Extra time is available for an additional fee.

AVAILABILITY: May–October, Wednesday–Sunday 10am–8pm, one event per day.

SERVICES/AMENITIES:

Restaurant Services: no

Catering: BYO

Kitchen Facilities: moderate

Tables & Chairs: provided, extra charge

Linens, Silver, etc.: BYO

Restrooms: wca

Dance Floor: at Belvedere structure

Bride's Dressing Area: yes

Parking: large lots

Overnight Accommodations: no

Telephone: emergency only

Outdoor Night Lighting: minimal

Outdoor Cooking Facilities: BBQ with approval

Cleanup: caterer or CBA extra fee

Other: tents CBA extra fee

RESTRICTIONS:

Alcohol: BYO

Smoking: allowed

Music: amplified ok

Wheelchair Access: yes

Insurance: suggested

Other: children must be supervised, decorations restricted

Rutherford

AUBERGE DU SOLEIL

180 Rutherford Hill Road
Rutherford, CA 94573
(707) 963-1211
Reserve: 3–6 months in advance

On a Napa hillside, near the Silverado Trail, rests the lovely Mediterranean-style Auberge du Soleil. This is an outstanding facility for an elegant party. The entrance is upstairs, through an exquisite garden courtyard complete with a tastefully designed fountain and shaded canopy of gray olive trees. The beautifully appointed, yet understated lobby is all in light pastels. A curved staircase leads down to the private banquet rooms. The smaller room is circular and is appropriately named The Black Room because it really is painted black. But don't worry—the black walls highlight the many French doors and windows overlooking the valley below and the upholstered chairs and couches in black, green and pink floral patterns contrast well with the dark walls. Wood ceilings and floors and a large stone fireplace make this a very comfortable room. The Black Room serves as a cocktail area, expanded dinner seating room or as a place for band and dancing. It's also ideal for small group gatherings and dinners. The adjacent banquet room, the White Room, is large and airy with white walls and furniture plus excellent views. The gravel Terrace, just outside these two rooms, has unparalleled views and, on warm days or evenings, can be set up for outdoor dining with tables and white umbrellas. The Auberge sets the tone for a really upscale, California-style wedding.

CAPACITY: The Black Room holds up to 50 standing, or 30 seated guests. The White Room holds up to 80; the Terrace 50 guests.

FEES & DEPOSITS: A deposit is due 2 weeks from the booking date, with 50% of the estimated event total due 30 days prior to the event. The rental charge is $300–500. The total balance is due upon departure. Per person rates for in-house catering: buffets $25–55, luncheons $27–35 and dinners $45–60. Sales tax and a 20% gratuity are applied to the final bill.

CANCELLATION POLICY: If the space(s) can be rebooked, the initial deposit will be refunded.

AVAILABILITY: Everyday, from 11am–5pm and 6pm–1am.

SERVICES/AMENITIES:

Restaurant Services: yes
Catering: provided, no BYO
Kitchen Facilities: n/a
Tables & Chairs: provided
Linens, Silver, etc.: provided
Restrooms: wca
Dance Floor: yes

Parking: valet
Overnight Accommodations: 48 guestrooms/suites
Telephone: pay phone
Outdoor Night Lighting: yes
Outdoor Cooking Facilities: no
Cleanup: provided
Bride's Dressing Area: CBA

RESTRICTIONS:

Alcohol: provided
Smoking: allowed
Music: on approval

Wheelchair Access: elevator
Insurance: not required

RANCHO CAYMUS INN

1140 Rutherford Road (Hwy 128)
Rutherford, CA 94573
(707) 963–1777 or **(800) 845–1777**
Reserve: 3–6 months in advance

The Rancho Caymus Inn is a Spanish Mission–style inn, complete with big cacti, mosaics, red tile roof, stucco walls, arched windows, interior patios and abundant landscaping. You can take your vows within the interior brick-paved courtyard, surrounded by wisteria-laden arbors or have your outdoor rehearsal dinner or reception here. The building encircles your guests—small tables with umbrellas, a large, river-rock fireplace and the sound of trickling water from a fountain add to the ambiance. For indoor parties, the Mont. St. John Room, adjacent to the patio, has a large wood bar, hardwood floors, handsome stone fireplace, piano and stained glass windows. And if you'd like to start your honeymoon here, the Inn has a variety of lovely suites from which to choose.

CAPACITY: The garden patio can accommodate 60 guests; the Mont. St. John Room can hold up to 55 seated or 115 in combination with the patio.

FEES & DEPOSITS: A deposit equal to the rental fee is required to secure your date. The rental fee is $500. Per person rates for food service: modest hors d'oeuvres reception $9, a full buffet $20–30 and seated dinner $20–45. Sales tax and a 15% gratuity are additional.

CANCELLATION POLICY: With 4 weeks' notice, the deposit is refundable.

AVAILABILITY: Everyday, from 5pm.

SERVICES/AMENITIES:

Restaurant Services: yes
Catering: provided, no BYO
Kitchen Facilities: n/a
Tables & Chairs: some provided
Linens, Silver, etc.: some provided
Restrooms: wca
Dance Floor: yes
Bride's Dressing Area: CBA

Parking: large lot
Overnight Accommodations: 26 suites
Telephone: house phone, local only
Outdoor Night Lighting: yes
Outdoor Cooking Facilities: no
Cleanup: provided
Other: event coordination services

RESTRICTIONS:

Alcohol: BWC provided, corkage $7.50/bottle
Smoking: allowed
Insurance: not required

Music: amplified until 10pm
Wheelchair Access: yes

Santa Rosa

CHATEAU DEBAUN WINERY

5007 Fulton Road
Santa Rosa, CA 95403
(707) 571-7500 John Burton
Reserve: 3 months in advance

Imagine an impressive French chateau-style winery, surrounded by acres of vineyards and walnut trees. The Chateau's elegant banquet room features brass chandeliers, French provincial furnishings, fireplace and a skylight in the vaulted, thirty-five foot ceiling. Outdoors, the spacious courtyard patio is framed by fragrant roses and features a gazebo. This is a sizeable space, conducive to large gatherings. The vineyard and distinctive architecture make Chateau DeBaun an unusual setting in the Wine

Country for rehearsal dinners, luncheons or wedding receptions.

CAPACITY:

Area	*Seated*
Harmony Hall (Banquet Room)	160
Concerto Courtyard	350
Medley Meadows	800
VIP Room	20
Symphony Hall (Tasting Room)	60

FEES & DEPOSITS : A non-refundable facility fee in the amount of 25% of the estimated total is required to secure your date. The remaining 75% is due 1 week prior to your function. For events Friday–Sunday, the facility fee starts at $25/person. A minimum guest count of 60 is required. The facility fee is for a 5-hour function and includes all setup and cleanup, tables, chairs, linens, china, glassware and beverage service.

AVAILABILITY: Everyday, except for major holidays. Individual areas (except Tasting Room) are available for events from 10am–1am. The entire facility is available for rental after 5pm.

SERVICES/AMENITIES:

Restaurant Services: no
Catering: select from preferred list
Kitchen Facilities: ample
Tables & Chairs: provided
Linens, Silver, etc.: provided
Restrooms: wca
Dance Floor: yes
Bride's Dressing Area: yes

Parking: large lot and on private road
Overnight Accommodations: no
Telephone: pay phone
Outdoor Night Lighting: yes
Outdoor Cooking Facilities: BBQ
Cleanup: caterer and staff
Other: limo, carriage and tents CBA

RESTRICTIONS:

Alcohol: provided, WC only
Smoking: outside only
Music: amplified ok

Wheelchair Access: yes
Insurance: not required

Need a caterer, cake maker, florist? The Service Directory starting on page 412 features the best in the business.

MARK WEST LODGE

2520 Mark Springs Road
Santa Rosa, CA 95404
(707) 546-2592
Reserve: 3–6 months in advance

It's impossible to miss Mark West Lodge—an enormous grape arbor which spans the entire highway lets you know you've arrived. Planted over 150 years ago, these gnarled vines grow up through the lodge's deck and, according to Ripley's "Believe It or Not," are the largest in the world. Once an important stage stop between San Francisco and the Northwest, the Lodge is now a traditional French restaurant. The main dining room is French Provincial, with ornate chandeliers, gold-framed mirrors and gold-toned drapes. Large 18th-century portraits add an old-world, European flavor. At the end of the room, light filters through stained glass panels with a grapevine and flower motif, illuminating a bubbling fountain. Two other rooms are available for smaller receptions, prenuptial dinners or cocktails. The real treat here, though, is the back patio. Sheltered on three sides by the restaurant, it's an idyllic spot for an afternoon or evening reception. Guests can enjoy the surrounding tree-covered hills, shielded from the bright sun by a colorful parachute suspended overhead. And if you'd like to get married here, a gazebo ringed by lawn and flowers has been provided for ceremonies. Cocktails and dancing can also take place in the bar area, where guests often wander out onto the deck and relax under the grapevine canopy. Owned and operated by French chef, Robert Ayme, Mark West Lodge offers affordable French cuisine and hospitality just a few minutes from Santa Rosa.

CAPACITY:

Area	Seated	Standing	Area	Seated	Standing
Banquet Room	20–60	100	Patio	130	200
Dining Room	70–200	500	Patio w/lawn	200	300

FEES & DEPOSITS: A $200 non-refundable deposit is required at the time of booking. An additional 80% of the total anticipated cost is due 2 weeks prior to the event, and the final guest count is due 1 week before the event. Any remaining balance is due at the conclusion of the event. Per person food costs are $9–$13 for seated luncheons, $18 for buffets and $15–25 for seated dinners. Alcoholic beverages, tax and gratuity are additional. If the entire restaurant needs to be closed for the event, a $200–$500 facility use fee may apply.

CANCELLATION POLICY: The initial $200 deposit is not refundable. Refunds given within the 2 weeks prior to the event depend on the amount of preparations already completed.

AVAILABILITY: Year-round, Tuesday through Sunday, 9am to midnight.

SERVICES/AMENITIES:

Restaurant Services: yes
Catering: provided
Kitchen Facilities: n/a
Tables & Chairs: provided
Linens, Silver, etc.: provided
Restrooms: wca
Dance Floor: yes

Parking: ample
Overnight Accommodations: CBA
Telephone: pay phone
Outdoor Night Lighting: yes
Outdoor Cooking Facilities: BBQ
Cleanup: provided
Bride's Dressing Area: large restroom

RESTRICTIONS:

Alcohol: provided, corkage $5.50/bottle
Smoking: outside & lounge only
Music: limited amplified ok

Wheelchair Access: yes
Insurance: not required

Sonoma

BUENA VISTA WINERY

18000 Old Winery Road
Sonoma, CA 95476
(800) 926-1266
Reserve: 3–12 months in advance

The Buena Vista Winery, founded in 1857 by Count Agoston Haraszthy, is generally acknowledged as the birthplace of premium wines in California. The Old Winery is a striking two-story stone building in a grotto of eucalyptus, redwoods and lush greenery. The main tasting room has exposed stone walls, very high ceilings and a second story gallery displaying local artwork. The extended bank of wine racks, the long bar and the historic displays give the room a friendly and convivial ambiance and a wood-burning stove warms chilly evenings. Outside is a large paved courtyard, dotted with huge, old wooden wine kegs. The dappled sunlight from the tall canopy of trees provides a comfortable and relaxing atmosphere for outdoor ceremonies and dining. A second, vine-covered stone building provides an impressive backdrop to the fountain courtyard.

CAPACITY: The winery requires a minimum of 50 guests. Indoor facilities can seat 100 guests. Outdoor spaces can accommodate up to 200 guests for a seated dinner or 400 for a standing reception.

FEES & DEPOSITS: A $250 refundable security deposit is required to reserve a date. The deposit is returned within 2 weeks after the event. The facility fee is $25–30/person and is due one week prior to the event. The fee includes setup and cleanup, 2/3 bottle of wine/person, tables, chairs and staff.

CANCELLATION POLICY: With 90 days' notice, the deposit will be refunded less 20%.

AVAILABILITY: Everyday, 6:30pm–10:30pm.

SERVICES/AMENITIES:

Restaurant Services: no
Catering: select from preferred list
Kitchen Facilities: n/a
Tables & Chairs: most provided
Linens, Silver, etc.: caterer
Restrooms: no wca
Dance Floor: yes, outdoor floor CBA

Parking: large lot
Overnight Accommodations: no
Telephone: pay phone
Outdoor Night Lighting: yes
Outdoor Cooking Facilities: no
Cleanup: provided
Bride's Dressing Area: CBA

RESTRICTIONS:
Alcohol: provided, WC only
Smoking: outside only
Music: amplified & acoustic ok until 10pm

Wheelchair Access: yes
Insurance: not required

DEPOT 1870 RESTAURANT

241 First Street, West
Sonoma, CA 95476
(707) 938-2980 Gia Ghilarducci
Reserve: 6–9 months in advance

Originally a private home, Depot 1870 has played an active role in Sonoma's past as a bar, restaurant and hotel. It is currently housed in an historic stone building near the Plaza in downtown Sonoma. Enter through the fireplace parlor, comfortably furnished with overstuffed chairs and couches. The crisp white walls, luxurious burgundy upholstery and simple bar make the room cheerful and homey. Glass doors lead out onto a covered terrace encircling the formal garden. The garden is serene and secluded, landscaped with flowers, hedges and a large reflecting pool. An elegant and comfortable dining area adjacent to the bar is enlarged by a glass-enclosed garden room. Here you have the benefits of indoor dining while feeling that you're outdoors. The Depot offers the services of Chef Ghilarducci, who received the prestigious national award, Grand Master Chef of America.

CAPACITY: The Depot can accommodate up to 140 guests.

FEES & DEPOSITS: A $200 deposit is required when you make your reservation and is applied towards the food and beverage cost. There is no rental fee. Food service is provided, and prices range from an hors d'oeuvres reception at $13–19/person to seated meals at $10–30/person. All event costs are payable by the day of your party.

CANCELLATION POLICY: The deposit will only be refunded if your date can be rebooked.

AVAILABILITY: Smaller functions, anytime; larger parties (over 30 guests) on weekends from noon to 4pm, or anytime on Monday or Tuesday.

SERVICES/AMENITIES:
Restaurant Services: yes
Catering: provided, no BYO
Kitchen Facilities: n/a
Tables & Chairs: provided
Linens, Silver, etc.: provided
Restrooms: wca
Dance Floor: outside

Parking: large lots
Overnight Accommodations: no
Telephone: pay phone
Outdoor Night Lighting: yes
Outdoor Cooking Facilities: BBQ
Cleanup: provided
Bride's Dressing Area: CBA

RESTRICTIONS:

Alcohol: provided, corkage $8/bottle
Smoking: allowed
Music: amplified ok

Wheelchair Access: yes
Insurance: not required

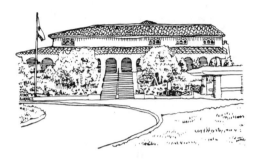

GLORIA FERRER
CHAMPAGNE CAVES

23555 Highway 121
Sonoma, CA 95476
(415) 897-2798   Carol Furr
Reserve: 2–12 months in advance

Set back from Highway 121, Gloria Ferrer Champagne Caves is a Spanish-style hacienda with old-world hospitality. Drive up the long road through rolling hills dotted with vineyards to the top of a knoll. The main building is impressive, with red tile roof and wide entry steps. Inside, the tasting room, called the Sala de Catadores, is a warm and inviting space highlighted by a stunning mahogany bar and fireplace of matching wood and stone. Adjoining the Sala is a terrace that takes full advantage of the panoramic view of Sonoma Valley and the Ferrer vineyards below. On a warm, windless day, this is a great spot for a ceremony. Intimate and elegant, with dark mahogany wood accents, the Executive Dining Room has windows that look out onto a colorfully landscaped promenade. This winery is a hidden, very private getaway for a wedding.

CAPACITY: The Sala de Catadores holds up to 90 seated; 150 for a standing reception. The Executive Dining Room seats 40.

FEES & DEPOSITS: Half of the rental fee is required as a non-refundable deposit and is due 2 months prior to the event. The balance is due the day of the event.

Guests	Rental Fee	Guests	Rental Fee
1–49	$700	76–100	$1,300
50–75	1,050	101–150	1,500

The sparkling wine fee is a required 2-case minimum purchase of Gloria Ferrer Brut ($336) for up to 75 guests, a 3-case minimum ($504) for 75–100, and a 4-case minimum ($672) for 101–150 guests. Additional wine may be purchased for $14/bottle. Tax is additional.

AVAILABILITY: Everyday, 6:30pm–11:30pm. Closed Thanksgiving, Christmas and New Year's days.

SERVICES/AMENITIES:

Restaurant Services: no
Catering: BYO, must be licensed
Kitchen Facilities: ample
Tables & Chairs: some provided
Linens, Silver, etc.: BYO
Restrooms: wca

Parking: large lot
Overnight Accommodations: no
Telephone: house phone
Outdoor Night Lighting: minimal
Outdoor Cooking Facilities: no
Cleanup: caterer

Bride's Dressing Area: yes
Other: wedding coordinator

Dance Floor: yes

RESTRICTIONS:

Alcohol: Ferrer Champagne only,
W corkage $5/bottle
Music: amplified inside only

Wheelchair Access: yes
Smoking: outside only
Insurance: not required

LAS CASTAÑAS

2246 Sobre Vista Road
Sonoma, CA 95476
(707) 996-5742
Reserve: 1–2 months in advance

Up from the Valley of the Moon, down a private road flanked by oaks, bays and redwoods, you get the feeling that your destination will be very special. Once the Spreckels family's private estate, the 40 acres of grounds and buildings are an arrestingly beautiful hybrid of casual, country charm with a touch of formal elegance. The outdoor spaces here are sensational—some of the best we've ever seen. A large concrete and flagstone patio meanders through and around the huge indigenous redwoods and is surrounded by rock-terraced lawns and lush flower beds. The grounds here are gorgeous. From the estate's greenhouses come flowers that line virtually every pathway. Stones that form the winding terrace walls that define gardens and sloping lawns have been unearthed from the surrounding vineyards. Las Castañas also has a tennis court and lovely swimming pool with brick patio—perfect for an afternoon reception. Indoor celebrations are held in the main Tudor-style house. The large dining room has a brick fireplace, a high cathedral ceiling framed with wood beams, handsome wood floors adorned with orientals and large windows overlooking the Valley's vineyards and orchards. An adjacent room, jutting out from the main building, is surrounded by windows with terrific views. This site is attractive, private, spacious and flexible. All in all, Las Castañas is a wonderful addition to Sonoma Valley.

CAPACITY:	*Area*	*Seated*	*Standing*		*Area*	*Seated*	*Standing*
	Main Room	75	100		Redwood Terraces	300	500
	Sun Room	40	75		Pool & Patio	75	150

FEES & DEPOSITS: The base rental fee for use is $1,500, which includes 10 guests for 1 overnight stay, use of the pool house, main house, honeymoon cottage, tables and chairs and release of doves with over 100 guests. The non-refundable guest fee, which is in addition to the base fee, is $25/guest for up to 100 guests and $15/guest for over 100 guests. Valet parking, security guards and setup/break-down are additional. Half of the base rental and guest fees are required as a non-refundable deposit and is due when you book your date. A $1,000 refundable damage/security deposit is required 7 days before the function. The fee balance is due 30 days prior to the event. A purchase of estate Chardonnay, 1/2 bottle/

guest, is requested.

AVAILABILITY: Year-round, daily from 9am–9pm.

SERVICES/AMENITIES:

Restaurant Services: no
Catering: BYO or CBA
Kitchen Facilities: ample
Tables & Chairs: provided
Linens, Silver, etc.: BYO or CBA
Restrooms: wca
Bride's Dressing Area: yes
Other: event coordination CBA

Parking: large lot
Overnight Accommodations: 7 guestrooms
Telephone: use with approval
Outdoor Night Lighting: yes
Outdoor Cooking Facilities: CBA
Cleanup: renter or caterer
Dance Floor: outdoor terrace

RESTRICTIONS:

Alcohol: estate wine or corkage $5/bottle
Smoking: designated areas only
Music: amplified within reason

Wheelchair Access: limited
Insurance: certificate required
Other: no hard alcohol

MISSION SAN FRANCISCO SOLANO DE SONOMA

First Street East and Spain
Sonoma, CA 95476
(707) 938-0151 Department Park & Rec.
Reserve: 2 weeks in advance

The site of the Mission was selected and consecrated by Father Jose Altimira on July 4, 1823. In 1840, General Vallejo supported the construction of the Mission Chapel to provide Sonoma with a parish church. The Chapel, available for non-denominational ceremonies, is quite charming. It is long and somewhat narrow with a hand-laid brick floor. The side walls are decorated with the Stations of the Cross and a colorful Indian design border. The altar, delineated by a low, dark railing, is adorned with a beautiful cross and colorful figures of the saints. Windows in the Chapel are high and small, filtering in a subdued light—all is peaceful and serene. The Mission is available for ceremonies only.

CAPACITY: 100 guests, standing only.

FEES & DEPOSITS: A $225 rental fee is required to reserve a date. One hour is allowed for setup.

AVAILABILITY: Year-round, from 10am–5pm.

SERVICES/AMENITIES:

Parking: limited, on street
Kitchen Facilities: no
Restrooms: no wca
Bride's Dressing Area: no

Tables & Chairs: no
Telephone: no
Cleanup: renter

RESTRICTIONS:

Alcohol: no food or drink
Smoking: not allowed
Music: must have advance approval

Wheelchair Access: yes
Insurance: sometimes required

SONOMA MISSION INN AND SPA

Highway 12 and Boyes Boulevard
Sonoma, CA 95476
(707) 938-9000
Reserve: 6 months in advance

Amidst 8 acres of eucalyptus trees, manicured lawns and colorful gardens, the Sonoma Mission Inn & Spa is an ideal setting for special celebrations. The Inn offers a variety of reception rooms, most with high ceilings, muted colors and natural sunlight. The largest of these rooms, the Sonoma Valley Room, has an inviting fireplace for cold winter evenings and French doors that open onto terraces during warm weather. Banquet menus range from simple hors d'oeuvres to elegant, seated dinners and theme buffets. To help with your event, the Inn provides a professional, efficient and courteous staff. They will oversee all aspects of the wedding, from initial party setup to overnight accommodations for your guests. With the Spa's full range of beauty services helping the wedding party to look and feel their best, it's no wonder that this spot is so popular.

CAPACITY, FEES & DEPOSITS: The rental fee is used as a refundable deposit to reserve a date. Another non-refundable deposit of half the estimated event total is payable 90 days prior to your function. Fees vary:

Room	Standing	Seated	Fees
Sonoma Valley Room	275	135–150	from $750
Harvest/Carneros Suites	50	24	from 525
(with guestroom)	25	10	—
Kenwood Room	—	32	from 250

Food service is provided. Meals start at $30/person with bar service and bartender additional. Tax and a 20% gratuity are applied to the final bill, due the day of the event.

CANCELLATION POLICY: With 180 days' notice, your deposit will be refunded in full.

AVAILABILITY: Any day, anytime.

SERVICES/AMENITIES:

Restaurant Services: yes
Catering: provided, no BYO
Kitchen Facilities: n/a
Tables & Chairs: provided
Linens, Silver, etc.: provided
Restrooms: wca

Parking: large lot, complimentary valet
Overnight Accommodations: 170 guestrooms
Telephone: pay phone
Outdoor Night Lighting: yes
Outdoor Cooking Facilities: yes
Cleanup: provided

Dance Floor: yes
Bride's Dressing Area: yes

RESTRICTIONS:
Alcohol: provided, corkage $8.50/bottle
Smoking: restricted
Music: amplified until 11pm

Other: event coordination, wedding cakes

Wheelchair Access: yes
Insurance: not required

VALLEJO HOME

3rd Street West and Spain
Sonoma, CA 95476
(707) 938-0151   Department of Parks & Rec.
Reserve: 2 weeks in advance

For one-hour ceremonies, the grounds of the Vallejo Home are serene, beautiful and romantic. General Mariano Vallejo built his family home at the foot of the Sonoma hills in 1850. He named his estate Lachryma Montis, mountain tears, after the free-flowing spring which once ran next to the building. The house is a rare Carpenter's Gothic style, with twin porches, dormer windows and elaborately carved wood trim. It is surrounded by carefully maintained lawns and colorful flowers. Directly in front of the house is a circular gravel courtyard where many ceremonies are performed, and at the far end of the yard is an intimate setting in front of a small lattice and vine-covered cottage featuring a quaint swan fountain.

CAPACITY: The courtyard, up to 100 guests; the swan fountain area, up to 50.

FEES & DEPOSITS: The $225 rental fee is required to secure your date.

AVAILABILITY: Available for ceremonies only, year-round, 10am–noon.

SERVICES/AMENITIES:
Parking: limited space
Telephone: no
Tables & Chairs: BYO

Restrooms: wca
Bride's Dressing Area: no
Cleanup: renter

RESTRICTIONS:
Alcohol: not permitted
Smoking: not allowed
Music: must be approved in advance

Wheelchair Access: yes
Insurance: sometimes required
Other: no food or drink permitted

Prices and policies <u>do</u> change. Call each facility and confirm everything you read in Here Comes The Guide.

VIANSA WINERY

25200 Arnold Dr. (Highway 121)
Sonoma, CA 95476
(707) 963-1664 Wine Country Weddings
Reserve: 1–6 months in advance

Viansa is one of the best and most professionally designed new facilities we've seen in a while. The owner has taken great care to develop a site that is both visually appealing and workable for events. Located on a knoll, overlooking vineyards and the northernmost part of San Francisco Bay, this Tuscan-style winery has a remarkably warm ambiance. With terra-cotta-colored walls, dark green shutters and tile roofs, it makes you feel comfortable, as though you're in Northern Italy. It's the details, such as decorative ironwork, intricate paintings on wine tanks, murals, herringbone brick floors and exceptional lighting, that make Viansa special. The interior tasting room, which includes a state-of-the-art area for food setup, is perfect for large parties. For smaller receptions, there is a wine cellar with large oak barrels and arched ceilings and a small dining room with lovely, patterned concrete floors. Outside is a circular courtyard surrounding a small, water-filled cistern. Terra cotta pots with flowers abound. The 'loggia' adjacent to the courtyard has French doors, a working fireplace and dark green cafe tables and chairs which match the shutters—a fine spot to chat with guests while sampling Viansa wines. There's even a hillside garden where Viansa grows its own vegetables, ensuring that everything served here is absolutely fresh. The professional staff can handle simple ceremonies and all aspects of a wedding celebration, from catering to flowers. We can't say enough about Viansa. We're very impressed by this relative newcomer and urge you to take a look for yourself.

CAPACITY: Maximum indoor seated capacity 112 guests; for indoor standing receptions, using both the tasting room and wine cellar, 275 guests.

FEES & DEPOSITS: A non-refundable $350 deposit is due when the contract is submitted. Two weeks prior to the event, 50% of the remaining balance is payable along with a $500 security deposit. Final payment is due one week prior to the event. There is a facility fee of $975 plus $4/person over 48 people. Food and wine service is provided. Four-course dinners start at $64/person and include a before-dinner reception with hors d'oeuvres and wine, wine with each dinner course, custom-printed menus, glasses, table settings and flowers. Tax and a 7.5% gratuity are additional.

CANCELLATION POLICY: If you cancel less than 2 weeks prior to your event, only the $500 security deposit will be refunded.

AVAILABILITY: Everyday after 5:30pm.

SERVICES/AMENITIES:

Restaurant Services: no
Catering: provided, no BYO
Kitchen Facilities: professional
Tables & Chairs: provided
Linens, Silver, etc.: provided
Restrooms: wca
Bride's Dressing Area: CBA

Parking: ample
Overnight Accommodations: no
Outdoor Night Lighting: yes
Outdoor Cooking Facilities: no
Cleanup: provided
Telephone: pay phone
Dance Floor: yes

RESTRICTIONS:

Alcohol: wine provided, no BYO
Smoking: outside only
Music: amplified requires approval

Wheelchair Access: yes
Insurance: not required

St. Helena

CHARLES KRUG WINERY

2800 Main Street
St. Helena, CA 94574
(707) 963-5057
Reserve: 3–6 months in advance

Charles Krug, the oldest winery in the Napa Valley, is just two miles north of St. Helena on Highway 29. It occupies a prime location on the valley floor, surrounded by vineyards. The winery has an expansive two-acre lawn which can easily accommodate more than 1,500 guests for an outdoor wedding! The lawn spreads south from the Carriage House and is generously dotted by huge, hundred-year-old oaks and conifers. On the grounds are a permanent stage, with tall posts set for lighting and sound equipment and a large outdoor barbecue sheltered by a post and beam trellis structure. For more intimate gatherings indoors, the historic Carriage House, built in 1881, offers a wonderful change of pace. This California historical landmark is a remarkable structure with arched windows and doors, multiple roof lines and stone and concrete architectural elements. Inside, wine barrels and a wine library provide an interesting backdrop for a memorable wedding reception.

CAPACITY: Carriage House lawn, from 100 to more than 1,500 guests. Carriage House, 120 seated guests, 200 for a buffet reception.

FEES & DEPOSITS: A $500 refundable rental deposit is required to secure your date. For use of the lawn or the Carriage House, the rental fee is $15/person for groups up to 120 with a $600 minimum rental fee required. For groups of 121–300, the rental fee is $12/person; $10/person for groups of 301 or more. If both spaces are used, the fee is an additional $5/person with a $1,000 minimum required. The rental fee balance, with a $250 cleaning deposit, is payable 30 days in advance of the function. Note that wine must be purchased from Charles Krug and is available at 33% off retail cost with a minimum purchase of 2 cases for groups of 50 or less. Wine service is $10/person per staff person charged on an hourly basis.

CANCELLATION POLICY: With 120 days' notice, the deposit is refunded in full. With less notice, the deposit will only be refunded if the event date can be rebooked.

AVAILABILITY: Carriage House lawn, from May–October, 9am to 10pm. The Carriage House is available year-round, 9am–12:30pm.

SERVICES/AMENITIES:

Restaurant Services: no
Catering: select from preferred list
Kitchen Facilities: minimal
Tables & Chairs: some provided
Linens, Silver, etc.: caterer
Restrooms: wca
Dance Floor: no, CBA

Parking: large parking lot
Overnight Accommodations: no
Telephone: pay phone at Visitor Center
Outdoor Night Lighting: yes
Outdoor Cooking Facilities: BBQ
Cleanup: caterer or renter
Bride's Dressing Area: CBA

RESTRICTIONS:

Alcohol: Charles Krug wine only. BYO CB
Music: indoors until midnight, outdoors until 9:30pm
Smoking: outside only

Wheelchair Access: yes
Insurance: certificate required
Other: no bird seed or rice

MEADOWOOD RESORT

900 Meadowood Lane
St. Helena, CA 94574
(707) 963-3646
Reserve: 12 months in advance

Driving into the Meadowood Resort is indeed a pleasure. You follow a narrow, tree-shaded lane, flanked by immaculately tended vineyards and forested hillsides, to the sophisticated resort complex, complete with wine school, executive conference center and first-rate recreational facilities. The superbly designed buildings are reminiscent of New England during the early 1900s with white balconies, gabled roofs and gray clapboard siding. All is secluded on 250 acres of densely wooded Napa Valley landscape. The sprawling, multi-tiered Clubhouse accommodates private parties. It's set high, overlooking lush, green fairways and manicured lawns. The large Vintner Room and Woodside Room are available for indoor wedding receptions. The Vintner Room is fabulous, with high ceilings and stone fireplace, decks with umbrella-shaded tables and outstanding views. The nearby lawn slopes down to steps adjacent to a dry creek bed planted with willows, leading to a footbridge which crosses over to golf fairways. For outdoor celebrations, Meadowood arranges tables and tents on the lawns next to the Vintner Room. There is something very special about this facility. It provides top flight cuisine prepared by French chefs, deluxe accommodations and an environment to match. It ranks high on our list of wedding locations.

CAPACITY: The Vintner Room seats 110 guests indoors and, with the lawn area, another 140 guests. The Woodside Room seats 60 guests, plus lawn area another 20 more.

FEES & DEPOSITS: A deposit is required to secure your date. The facility fee ranges from $15–25/ person and includes ceremony and reception setup and table settings. Catering services are provided. Per person rates: 3-course luncheon $35; a 4-course dinner $45; buffets and barbecues start at $42. Tax and an 18% gratuity are applied to the final total.

CANCELLATION POLICY: If you cancel within 6 months of your date, and the date can be rebooked for a function of equal or greater value, 50% of your deposit will be refunded.

AVAILABILITY: Year-round, everyday. Sunday–Thursday, 11am–4pm and 6pm–10pm; Friday–Saturday 11am–4pm and 6pm–11pm.

SERVICES/AMENITIES:

Restaurant Services: yes

Catering: provided, no BYO

Kitchen Facilities: n/a

Tables & Chairs: provided

Linens, Silver, etc.: provided

Outdoor Cooking Facilities: CBA

Cleanup: provided

Other: referrals to wedding services, spa & fitness center

Overnight Accommodations: 82 guestrooms plus suites

Restrooms: wca

Dance Floor: Vintner yes, Woodside CBA

Parking: multiple lots, no valet

Bride's Dressing Area: CBA

Outdoor Night Lighting: CBA

Telephone: pay phones

RESTRICTIONS:

Alcohol: provided, corkage fee if BYO

Smoking: allowed

Music: amplified indoors only

Wheelchair Access: yes

Insurance: not required

Other: no rice, seeds, tacks or staples

MERRYVALE VINEYARDS

1000 Main Street
St. Helena, CA 94574
(800) 326-6069   Director of Special Events
Reserve: 1–12 months in advance

For an experience that's really memorable, have your reception or rehearsal dinner in Merryvale's Cask Room. It features antique casks made in San Francisco in the late 1800s. The historic casks lining the walls hold up to 2,000 gallons, and the ones framing the steps as you enter hold an astonishing 16,000 gallons. These remarkable redwood wine barrels must be at least 16 feet in diameter! Candle-lighted prenuptial dinners and weddings are especially lovely in here. Behind the winery is the renovated "schoolhouse," an appealing Victorian-looking building with an old world aura. It's also a great spot for ceremonies and receptions, with a wide, wisteria-framed veranda painted in crisp white.

CAPACITY: Indoor and outdoor areas hold up to 160 guests, maximum.

FEES & DEPOSITS: A non-refundable deposit of 20% of the estimated total winery fees and signed contract are due within 1 month of making a reservation. Winery fees include: rental, wine with ceremony reception, 1/2 bottle wine/person for dinner, tables, chairs, glassware, wine service staff and candelabras. Catering can be provided, approximately $25–35/person for dinner. Tax and gratuity are additional. The balance is due the day of the event.

AVAILABILITY: Year-round. Everyday 6:30pm to midnight, except for Christmas and Thanksgiving.

SERVICES/AMENITIES:

Restaurant Services: no
Catering: CBA or BYO with approval
Kitchen Facilities: ample
Tables & Chairs: provided
Linens, Silver, etc.: some provided
Restrooms: wca
Dance Floor: yes

Parking: large lot
Overnight Accommodations: no
Telephone: business phone
Outdoor Night Lighting: yes
Outdoor Cooking Facilities: no
Cleanup: Merryvale and caterer
Bride's Dressing Area: yes

RESTRICTIONS:

Alcohol: provided, no BYO, no hard alcohol or beer
Smoking: outside only
Music: amplified ok

Wheelchair Access: yes
Insurance: not required

V. SATTUI WINERY

White Lane at Highway 29
St. Helena, CA 94574
(707) 963-1664 Rebecca Kingsley
Reserve: 1–12 months in advance

V. Sattui Winery, located in the heart of Napa Valley, is a small, family winery founded in 1885. It occupies a massive stone building reminiscent of California's early wineries and is surrounded by two acres of tree-shaded picnic grounds, lush lawns, giant oak trees and 35 acres of vineyards. The surrounding scenery is really lovely, with extensive vineyards and vistas of the Napa Valley hills beyond. Wedding guests can dine in a castle-like cellar lined with oak barrels and filled with the pungent aromas of aging wines. Through a stone archway are four caves where wines are aged behind heavy wrought iron gates. A second cellar provides a more intimate setting for smaller gatherings. Hand-hewn stone walls, heavy ceiling timbers and wine barrels create an old-world atmosphere suitable for elaborate formal buffets, cozy luncheons or rehearsal dinners. A great outdoor ceremony spot is in the front of the winery, where there is a small patio with steps leading down to a lawn. Services can be performed on the top step using the building as a colorful, picturesque backdrop.

CAPACITY: The large cellar can hold 200 seated guests, the small cellar, 50 guests; 250 total. The outside lawn and terraces can accommodate up to 350.

FEES & DEPOSITS: A $350 deposit is required to secure your date. The rental fee is $975 plus $4/person. Rental fees plus a final guest count are due 1 week prior to the event. All weddings are coordinated by Wine Country Weddings, for which there is a consulting fee.

CANCELLATION POLICY: The deposit is refundable only if the date is rebooked.

AVAILABILITY: Everyday, from 6pm–midnight.

SERVICES/AMENITIES:

Restaurant Services: no

Catering: select from preferred list

Kitchen Facilities: minimal

Tables & Chairs: provided

Linens, Silver, etc.: caterer

Restrooms: wca

Dance Floor: yes

Other: wedding coordinator, one bar staffperson

Parking: large lot

Overnight Accommodations: no

Telephone: pay phone

Outdoor Night Lighting: yes

Outdoor Cooking Facilities: BBQ

Cleanup: provided

Bride's Dressing Area: CBA

RESTRICTIONS:

Alcohol: V. Sattui wine only, champagne corkage $5/bottle

Music: amplified ok

Smoking: outside only

Wheelchair Access: ramp and lift

Insurance: certificate required

Other: no hard liquor

WHITE SULPHUR SPRINGS RESORT AND SPA

3100 White Sulphur Springs Road
St. Helena, CA 94574
(707) 963-8588
Reserve: 2–12 months in advance

In the heart of Napa Valley, nestled in a secluded canyon, is California's first and oldest resort. Established in 1852, White Sulphur Springs is composed of eight white cottages, an inn, small hotel, dining room and lodge. It's reached by a road that starts from Spring Street in downtown St. Helena, and quickly narrows, winding into the foothills. White Sulphur Springs Creek meanders through the resort site and there is actually a warm sulphur pool and large outdoor heated spa available to guests. Wedding ceremonies are usually performed in the Redwood Grove, a shaded glen adjacent to a trickling creek. There are rustic wood picnic tables and chairs, wrought-iron benches and BBQs plus a log foot-bridge to Indian Meadow, another great wedding spot. The Resort can accommodate a variety of outdoor activities including volleyball, basketball, horseshoes, badminton, croquet and hiking to year-round waterfalls. Indoor functions take place in the newly renovated Lodge, large dining room or smaller lounges. You're out in the country here and it's very quiet. The natural grounds, historic buildings and the attentive care of the owners make this place an ideal weekend wedding getaway.

CAPACITY:	*Area*	*Standing*	*Seated*
	Redwood Grove	300	250
	Lodge	200	150
	Reception/Dining Room	150	100

FEES & DEPOSITS: A $500 non-refundable deposit is required to hold your date which becomes the security/cleaning deposit once all other fees are paid. It is refundable within 14 days following the wedding. During the peak season, all 37 guestrooms must be reserved for a 2-day, 2-night minimum. The rate for the entire resort is $8,000 for the weekend. The owners have developed a gracious method of reimbursing the bride and groom as guests confirm room reservations. After guests have paid for their lodging, the cost to the wedding couple for use of the entire resort for 2 days is under $2,000. During the off-season, there's no minimum overnight stay and the facilities rental is $1,000–1,600/event.

AVAILABILITY: Year-round. April 1–November 30, on weekends, the entire resort must be booked for 2 days and nights. December 1–March 31 and weekdays, no minimum is required.

SERVICES/AMENITIES:

Restaurant Services: no

Catering: provided or BYO

Kitchen Facilities: limited

Tables & Chairs: provided

Linens, Silver, etc.: caterer

Restrooms: no wca

Dance Floor: in Lodge & outdoors

Other: mineral springs, spa services

Parking: large lots

Overnight Accommodations: 37 units

Telephone: pay phone

Outdoor Night Lighting: yes

Outdoor Cooking Facilities: BBQs

Cleanup: caterer

Bride's Dressing Area: CBA

RESTRICTIONS:

Alcohol: provided or BYO, no hard alcohol

Smoking: outside only

Music: amplified ok until midnight

Wheelchair Access: limited

Insurance: proof of insurance

Other: no rice

Yountville

CAFE KINYON!

6525 Washington Street
Yountville, CA 94599
(707) 944-2788
Reserve: 1–6 months in advance

Cafe Kinyon! is an upscale restaurant located in the Vintage 1870 complex. Converted from what was once a working winery, the restaurant is housed in an architecturally significant structure featuring lovely old brick walls and heavy timbers. For wedding receptions, it's an excellent choice. The main dining room has French doors and multiple windows overlooking a garden area, making it light and airy. Soft pink and rose colors predominate. It has a large skylight and more doors leading into the adjacent garden. The smaller dining room is also appealing, with a terra cotta colored brick wall and softwood floors. Overall, the decor is clean and fresh, expressing sophistication and a touch of elegance.

CAPACITY: Cafe Kinyon! can accommodate 150 seated, 250 standing inside. Including the outdoor spaces, 400 seated.

FEES & DEPOSITS: A $500 deposit is required to hold your date. To rent the restaurant, there is a $5/ person rental charge. Per person rates: luncheons from $15, dinners start at $20. Extravagant buffets slightly higher. Half of the estimated food and beverage total is required with a returned contract, and the balance is payable at the end of the event. Tax and a 17% service charge are additional.

CANCELLATION POLICY: If the event space can be rebooked, the deposit will be refunded.

AVAILABILITY: Year-round, everyday from 8am–1am.

SERVICES/AMENITIES:

Restaurant Services: yes
Catering: provided, no BYO
Kitchen Facilities: n/a
Tables & Chairs: provided
Linens, Silver, etc.: provided
Restrooms: wca
Dance Floor: yes

Parking: multiple lots
Overnight Accommodations: yes, within complex
Telephone: pay phones
Outdoor Night Lighting: yes
Outdoor Cooking Facilities: BBQ
Cleanup: provided
Bride's Dressing Area: no

RESTRICTIONS:

Alcohol: provided, corkage $8/bottle
Smoking: allowed
Music: amplified ok

Wheelchair Access: yes
Insurance: sometimes required

Need a caterer, cake maker, florist? The Service Directory starting on page 412 features the best in the business.

Clearlake

WINDFLOWER ISLAND

Clearlake, CA 95422
(707) 542-1235 ESP Event Planners
Reserve: 90 days in advance

Windflower Island is the place for those who want something extraordinary—a totally private tropical garden setting surrounded by water. Set at the base of Clearlake's twin volcanoes, this two and a half acre island paradise is often likened to Maui yet is only a 2-1/2 hour drive from San Francisco. A leisurely boat ride transports you in minutes to this secluded island estate. What awaits you are manicured lawns with sweeping lake views, an open-air gazebo, flagstone patios and lush landscaping. Several spots are ideal for ceremonies. The island's custom-designed home has a 360 degree panorama of the Clearlake Basin, and is perfect for wedding nights and romantic honeymoon getaways. A beach for sun bathing and swimming, boat docks and outdoor barbecues areas are additional amenities. If honeymooners are interested in active water sports, jet skiing, windsurfing and waterskiing are available nearby. More leisurely excursions include lake cruises, fishing and canoeing. One of the more unique and lovely locations we've encountered, Windflower Island is a rare find.

CAPACITY: The island can accommodate 60 guests.

FEES, DEPOSITS & CANCELLATION POLICY: Call for current pricing, deposit requirements and cancellation policies.

AVAILABILITY: Daily, March 1–November 15, from 8am to sunset.

SERVICES/AMENITIES:
Restaurant Services: no
Catering: provided
Kitchen Facilities: n/a
Tables & Chairs: provided
Linens, Silver, etc.: provided
Restrooms: no wca
Dance Floor: no
Other: transportation to island provided, wedding coordination, sound system available

Parking: several lots
Overnight Accommodations: 2 guestrooms or Konocti Harbor Resort
Telephone: emergency only
Outdoor Night Lighting: access only
Outdoor Cooking Facilities: no
Cleanup: provided
Bride's Dressing Room: yes

RESTRICTIONS:
Alcohol: provided or BYO
Smoking: outdoors only
Music: amplified ok

Wheelchair Access: no
Insurance: liability required
Other: children must be supervised, limited electrical outlets, minors must wear life vests on boats

Aptos

THE VERANDA

8041 Soquel Drive
Aptos, CA 95003
(408) 685-1881
Reserve: 1 week–3 months in advance

The Veranda is a restaurant occupying the main floor of the vintage 1878 Victorian Bayview Hotel in historic Aptos Village. All has been restored with attention to detail. The interior boasts two glass-walled verandas as well as a main dining room and outstanding bar. Muted colors in roses, off-whites and pinks blend to create a visually appealing space. The bar is in a separate room, accessible by double doors. There's a newly designed and constructed patio for outdoor events with brick pavers, roses and white lattice. Note, the food here is distinctive and very good. For ceremonies or receptions, The Veranda creates an environment of casual elegance.

CAPACITY: Capacities are as follows: the Veranda indoors accommodates 80 seated guests, main dining room 36, side veranda 28, front veranda 20, anteroom 10. The garden patio holds up to 50 seated guests or 125 standing. The entire facility holds up to 150–175 guests.

FEES & DEPOSITS: A refundable $300 deposit is required when reservations are confirmed. For groups, luncheons start at $12/person, dinners at $22/person and hors d'oeuvres at $13/person. The rental fee for use of the garden and interior dining room is $300/event; either space rents for $200/event. A confirmed guest count is required 48 hours prior to your function and your event balance is payable by the end of the event.

CANCELLATION POLICY: Your deposit will be refunded with 30 days' notice or if the space can be rebooked.

AVAILABILITY: Year-round, every day, by arrangement.

SERVICES/AMENITIES:

Restaurant Services: yes
Catering: provided, no BYO
Kitchen Facilities: n/a
Tables & Chairs: provided
Linens, Silver, etc.: provided
Restrooms: wca
Dance Floor: CBA

Parking: large lot
Overnight Accommodations: 8 guestrooms
Telephone: pay phone
Outdoor Night Lighting: yes
Outdoor Cooking Facilities: yes
Cleanup: provided
Bride's Dressing Area: CBA

RESTRICTIONS:

Alcohol: provided, no BYO
Smoking: only in bar or outside
Music: amplified, DJs ok

Wheelchair Access: yes
Insurance: not required

Ben Lomond

HIGHLANDS HOUSE
AND PARK

8500 Highway 9
Ben Lomond, CA 95005
(408) 425-2696 Parks Department
Reserve: 2–12 months in advance

The Highlands House is a former private residence built in the 1940s. Set in a public park, surrounded by large redwoods, the 2-story white wood house is available for weddings and receptions. The house sits quite a way below Highway 9, ensuring quiet and a sense of privacy. The setting is lovely with expansive lawns, huge magnolia and pine trees, well-maintained landscaping and nearby pool. Framed by several tall palms, the Highland House is an attractive and pleasant spot for a celebration.

CAPACITY: The facility can accommodate 200.

FEES & DEPOSITS: Fees and deposits are required when reservations are made. For bookings made less than 45 days in advance, a $50 surcharge applies. The rental fee for county residents is about $550, non-county residents, about $700. The cleaning deposit is $200 with alcohol use, $100 without. These fees are for an 8-hour block.

CANCELLATION POLICY: With 30 days' notice, all fees will be returned less a $100 cancellation charge. With less than 30 days, only the cleaning deposit will be returned.

AVAILABILITY: Year-round. Friday and Saturday 10am–12am, Sunday, 10am–10pm.

SERVICES/AMENITIES:

Restaurant Services: no
Catering: BYO
Kitchen Facilities: ample
Tables & Chairs: some provided
Linens, Silver, etc.: BYO
Restrooms: wca
Dance Floor: yes
Bride's Dressing Area: yes

Parking: large lot, fee on summer weekends
Overnight Accommodations: no
Telephone: pay phone
Outdoor Night Lighting: access only
Outdoor Cooking Facilities: BYO BBQ
Cleanup: renter's responsibility
Other: spinet available

RESTRICTIONS:

Alcohol: BYO, WBC only
Smoking: outside only
Music: amplified to 75 decibels

Wheelchair Access: yes
Insurance: not required

Santa Cruz

BABBLING BROOK INN

1025 Laurel Street
Santa Cruz, CA 95060
(408) 427-2437
Reserve: 3 months in advance

The Babbling Brook Inn, the oldest and largest bed and breakfast inn in the Santa Cruz area, has one of the most delightful ceremony spots we've seen. Tucked behind wood-shingled structures belonging to the Inn, the wedding deck features a white, wrought-iron gazebo which is delicate and fanciful, yet large enough to hold a medium-sized wedding party underneath. It was created by U.C. Santa Cruz students for a Shakespeare production and was scheduled for dismantling. Babbling Brook's owner purchased the gazebo and had it installed on a redwood deck overlooking the Inn's terraced garden setting, complete with creek and footbridge. All is incredibly green here. This is an enclosed, private spot—a very beautiful setting with moss, ferns and lush foliage. A small brook trickles, cascades and splashes through the site, creating pleasant sounds. Although you can't hold a large reception here, the small brick patio has tables with umbrellas if you'd like to drink a toast, cut some cake or sample modest hors d'oeuvres. Note that the Inn offers very pretty honeymoon accommodations, too.

CAPACITY: 40 seated guests, maximum.

FEES & DEPOSITS: A deposit of one half the estimated total fee is due when reservations are made. The rental fee for use of the garden and gazebo only is $250. To have a ceremony plus a small reception, the fee is $650, which includes the use of 2 rooms. Wedding rehearsal is limited to 1 hour and is included in the rental fee. Overtime charges are $75 per half hour. A $100 cleaning/damage deposit is also required. The balance of fees is payable 30 days prior to the function.

CANCELLATION POLICY: The deposit is fully refundable with 60 days' notice; between 30 and 60 days $150 will be retained; less than 30 days, no refund. The security and damage deposit is usually returned 1 week after the wedding.

AVAILABILITY: Every day, between 12:30 and 3:30pm.

SERVICES/AMENITIES:

Restaurant Services: no
Catering: BYO, select from preferred list
Kitchen Facilities: no
Tables & Chairs: provided, limited amount
Linens, Silver, etc.: BYO
Restrooms: wca
Bride's Dressing Area: CBA

Parking: valet required for over 25 guests
Telephone: house or guest phones
Overnight Accommodations: 12 guestrooms
Outdoor Night Lighting: access only
Outdoor Cooking Facilities: no
Cleanup: caterer

RESTRICTIONS:
Alcohol: provided or BYO, WC only, corkage $2.50/bottle
Smoking: outside only
Music: no amplified

Wheelchair Access: no
Insurance: recommended
Other: children must be supervised, no rice

CHAMINADE
at Santa Cruz

1 Chaminade Lane
Santa Cruz, CA 95065
(408) 475-5600, (408) 475-5676 Catering
Reserve: 1–6 months in advance

Chaminade is a lovely Mediterranean-style resort and conference center retreat set high on a mountain bluff overlooking rolling hills and forest with a panoramic view of Monterey Bay. The original Mission-style buildings, constructed in the 1930s as a boys' school, have been expanded and remodeled into a well-designed complex that includes two restaurants, a 14,000 square foot Executive Fitness Center, ten banquet rooms, and a beautiful ocean-view wedding ceremony lawn. The red tile roofs and stucco exteriors, along with the Mediterranean landscape, reflect the original architectual character of the old school. Here, you can take advantage of ocean views, the balmy, coastal weather and colorful sunsets from the multiple decks, balconies, patios and expansive lawn areas. Chaminade, with its careful attention to service and culinary excellence, make it an ideal, private setting for a sophisticated wedding celebration.

CAPACITY: From 25–225 guests; with dance floor 180.

FEES & DEPOSITS: A non-refundable deposit is required with a returned contract. The balance is due the day of the event. The Ceremony site fee is $750; the Wedding Reception site fee for the Greenhouse/Sunset Patio is $450; and the Santa Cruz Ballroom with dance floor is $750. For menu pricing, call Chaminade for current rates.

AVAILABILITY: Any day, morning through evening. Luncheons until 4:30pm; dinners 6:30–1am.

SERVICES/AMENITIES:
Restaurant Services: yes
Catering: provided, no BYO
Kitchen Facilities: n/a
Tables & Chairs: provided
Linens, Silver, etc.: provided
Restrooms: wca
Dance Floor: charge for setup

Parking: complementary valet & shuttle
Overnight Accommodations: 152 guestrooms
Telephone: pay phone
Outdoor Night Lighting: limited
Outdoor Cooking Facilities: no
Cleanup: provided
Bride's Dressing Area: complimentary w/ceremony

RESTRICTIONS:
Alcohol: provided, no BYO
Smoking: allowed
Music: amplified restricted outdoors

Wheelchair Access: yes
Insurance: not required
Other: no rice, birdseed

COCOANUT GROVE

400 Beach Street
Santa Cruz, CA 95060
(408) 423-5590
Reserve: 12 months in advance

As unlikely as it may seem, this historic site is available for private functions. Built in 1907 as one of the first amusement parks and casino complexes, Cocoanut Grove still sits at the water's edge next to the famous Santa Cruz Beach Boardwalk. Inside there are several party spaces worth considering. The Bay View Room is ample-sized with dance floor and bay windows overlooking the ocean, beach and Boardwalk. It's adjacent to the expansive Ballroom, which has black ceilings, decorative lights, suspended and rotating mirrored ball and hardwood dance floors. Both of these rooms are terrific dining and dance party spaces! The Bay View Bar and Lounge is connected to the Ballroom and Bay View Room and comes with oak curved bar, red carpets and great ocean views. The Sun Room is like a solarium with a retractable glass ceiling which rolls back to beckon in the ocean breezes. With a garden atmosphere and pastel colors, the Sun Room offers guests a really pleasant indoor/outdoor dining environment. Some rooms can be rented separately or in combination, so make sure you get the full tour in order to choose those most appropriate for your event.

CAPACITY: For large gatherings, the Ballroom and Balcony hold up to 400 guests, the Bay View Room, 200. The combined capacity is 600 guests. Note that the Bay View Room Lounge adjoins both of these rooms and is included as part of the rental. The Sun Room can accommodate up to 275 seated guests and up to 325 by using the adjoining Sun Room Terrace.

FEES & DEPOSITS: A non-refundable deposit of $750 is required for the Ballroom or Bay View Room, $500 for the Sun Room. The deposit is payable when you sign your rental agreement. No rental fees are required when a guaranteed minimum number of meals is served. Per person food service rates: luncheon buffets start at $12 and dinner buffets at $15. There's also a special bar and beverage package for private parties, so ask for rates. Sales tax and 15% gratuity will be added to the final bill.

AVAILABILITY: Saturdays, 8am–4pm and 6pm–1am. On Sundays, the Bay View Room and Ballroom are available from 2pm–10pm for dinners and receptions.

SERVICES/AMENITIES:

Restaurant Services: yes
Catering: provided, no BYO
Kitchen Facilities: n/a
Tables & Chairs: provided
Linens, Silver, etc.: provided
Restrooms: wca
Dance Floor: yes
Bride's Dressing Area: CBA

Parking: discount at Boardwalk parking lot
Overnight Accommodations: no
Telephone: pay phone
Outdoor Night Lighting: access only
Outdoor Cooking Facilities: no
Cleanup: provided
Other: ceremony $175 for setup, 2 pianos

RESTRICTIONS:

Alcohol: provided, corkage $4.50/bottle
Smoking: allowed, no cigars, clove cigarettes
Music: amplified ok

Wheelchair Access: yes
Insurance: sometimes required
Other: decorating restrictions, no rice or birdseed

HOLLINS HOUSE

20 Clubhouse Road
Santa Cruz, California 95060
(408) 459-9177 Margy Seifert
Reserve: 6–12 months in advance

The Hollins House, built in 1929 by championship golfer Marion Hollins, is located in the Pasatiempo Golf Course Complex in the Santa Cruz Mountains, not far from Highway 17. Approached through acres of green fairways, the house is situated atop a knoll and has impressive views of Monterey Bay. You can reserve either the entire facility or just the Hollins Room and patio. The main dining room is very long, with high ceilings, big mirrors and picture windows with views of the garden and ocean beyond. There's also a fireplace and hardwood parquet dance floor. The Tap Room is a more informal space, with a long wood bar, fireplace and windows overlooking garden and ocean. The adjacent garden is narrow with a lawn bordered by profusely blooming impatiens. A medium-sized patio surrounded by wisteria and situated next to the Hollins Room is a picturesque place for an outdoor reception. The Hollins Room is small, with a big mirror over the fireplace, chandelier, rounded bay windows with bench seat and a vista of the Pacific Ocean framed by nearby oak trees. The house staff aim to please and will assist you with all of your event arrangements, from flowers to specialized menus.

CAPACITY: The entire facility can accommodate up to 250 guests maximum in the summer and fall, 175 guests during cooler months. The Hollins Room and patio combined can accommodate 45 guests.

FEES & DEPOSITS: When reservations are made, a non-refundable deposit of $7 per person, based on an anticipated number of guests, is required. The rental fee for the entire Hollins House is $5 per person. For the Hollins Room and patio it's only $1.50 per person. The ceremony setup fee is $125. Per person rates: hors d'oeuvres/buffets are approximately $20 and seated meals vary from $13–21. These fees do not include sales tax or 15% gratuity. You may customize your menu with help from the chef and/or wedding coordinator. There is also a cake service charge of approximately $40/100 guests. The total balance is due in full by the end of your event.

AVAILABILITY: For the entire Hollins House; Monday–Saturdays 11am–4pm and Sundays 4pm–9pm. For the Hollins Room and patio; 6pm–midnight Saturdays and 10am–2pm Sundays.

SERVICES/AMENITIES:

Restaurant Services: yes
Catering: provided, no BYO

Parking: large lots
Overnight Accommodations: no

Kitchen Facilities: n/a
Tables & Chairs: provided
Linens, Silver, etc.: provided
Restrooms: wca
Dance Floor: yes

Telephone: pay phone
Outdoor Night Lighting: yes
Outdoor Cooking Facilities: BBQ CBA
Cleanup: provided
Bride's Dressing Area: yes

RESTRICTIONS:

Alcohol: provided, corkage fee $70/case
Smoking: allowed
Music: amplified ok if entire facility rented

Wheelchair Access: ramp
Insurance: not required

TERRACE HILL HOUSE AND GARDENS

Address withheld to maintain privacy.
Santa Cruz Mountains, CA 95030
(408) 353-5022
Reserve: 6 months in advance

Way up in the Santa Cruz Mountains, just minutes from Highway 17, are two private gardens, both highly suitable for weddings. What makes these two gardens so appealing, besides the attractive settings, are the caterers: Sandra, Gay and Bev. They offer extraordinarily personalized, creative wedding receptions. The Terrace Hill location is Sandra's home. This place is quiet and very relaxing. As you enter the site from a private driveway, you'll follow brick paths to lawn and patios with umbrella-shaded tables. Her garden sits on a gentle slope, with lots of terraces. For ceremonies, we particularly like the old-fashioned rose-covered arbor with its panoramic vistas of the mountains beyond. The other private garden, Maison du Lac, is located about a mile away. A narrow gravel road flanked by meadows and oaks leads to a wide opening where you'll encounter an idyllic setting, complete with large pond ringed by rocks, lawn and multi-color annuals and perennials. Ducks and other wildlife abound. Tall redwoods and a rambling house with stone fireplace act as a backdrop to this pastoral setting. A small trellis is perfect for ceremonies, with seating on the lawn adjacent to the pond. Sandra, Gay and Bev serve their edibles from tables laden with flowers and colorful glass and dinnerware. Everything is a visual delight. Note that much of what you see or eat comes directly from the owner's multi-level vegetable and flower terraces. Although a bit off the beaten path, we think Terrace Hill House and Maison du Lac Garden are worth a visit if you're looking for someplace that feels intimate and gives you a sense of well-being.

CAPACITY: Terrace Hill Garden up to 75 guests; Maison du Lac Garden from 75–200 seated guests.

FEES & DEPOSITS: A $200 refundable deposit is required to hold your date. The rental fee is about $1,000 for a 4-hour block, and will vary depending on the site selected. The buffet wedding package starts at $40/person and includes food, flowers, service, non-alcoholic beverages and all table setup and cleanup. Special menus can be arranged. Half of the estimated total is payable 2 months prior to the event; the balance 1 week in advance.

CANCELLATION POLICY: The deposit is refundable with 90 days' notice.

AVAILABILITY: May–September, any day from 10am–sunset.

SERVICES/AMENITIES:

Restaurant Services: no
Catering: provided, no BYO
Kitchen Facilities: n/a
Tables & Chairs: provided
Linens, Silver, etc.: provided
Restrooms: no wca
Bride's Dressing Area: CBA
Dance Floor: outdoor patio & lawns

Parking: small lots
Overnight Accommodations: no
Telephone: emergency only
Outdoor Night Lighting: no
Outdoor Cooking Facilities: BBQs
Cleanup: provided
Other: event coordination

RESTRICTIONS:

Alcohol: BYO or CBA
Smoking: designated areas only
Music: amplified limited

Wheelchair Access: limited
Insurance: recommended

Carmel

HIGHLANDS INN

Highway 1
Carmel, CA 93921
(408) 624-3801
Reserve: 6–12 months in advance

Built in 1916 in the Carmel Highlands just south of Carmel, the Highlands Inn is one of the most sought-after wedding locations in California. Noted for its breathtaking views and extraordinary cliffside setting, the Inn provides an idyllic environment for one of life's great moments. After its multi-million-dollar, award-winning renovation, Highlands Inn is more stunning than ever. Commanding one of the world's most spectacular vistas, with exploding waves crashing two hundred feet below, the Inn offers a variety of first class facilities for special affairs. For outdoor ceremonies, a redwood deck complete with contemporary gazebo is perched just above the rocky cliffs overlooking the Pacific. During inclement weather, ceremonies take place in front of one of two large fireplaces in the Fireside Room. The Room has a refined Arts and Crafts period feel, with hardwood floors, rough wool upholstery against butter-soft leathers and brass and polished granite appointments. A grand piano is also available for functions. After the ceremony, guests are ushered into a variety of reception areas—each is elegant, with comfortable furnishings and outstanding views. The Inn's chefs are renowned for culinary excellence and the wine and champagne list is extensive. The staff can organize a traditional affair or a more creative event for the adventuresome. If you are looking for a very special place, the incomparable Highlands Inn should be high on your list.

CAPACITY:

Area	Standing	Seated	Area	Standing	Seated
Yankee Point Room	—	50	Gazebo & Deck	100	65
Monarch Room	—	10	Wine Room	—	40
Surf Room	—	100	Groves North & South	80	60
Fireside Room	180	—			

FEES & DEPOSITS: The space rental fee is the deposit and is payable when the wedding date is reserved. The rental fees are: Gazebo & Deck, $350; Monarch Room $150; Yankee Point Room $400; Wine Room $150; Grove Room $250 and Surf Room $550. A dance floor is an extra $125; wedding cakes vary in price. Average per person rates for food service: luncheons $22 and dinners $36. Sales tax and 17% gratuity are additional. Half the estimated total bill is due 4 weeks before and the balance is due 7 working days prior to the event. A final confirmed guest count is required 3 working days in advance of the wedding.

CANCELLATION POLICY: The deposit will be fully refunded if the date can be rebooked with an equal number of guests. A partial refund may be negotiated. With less than 6 weeks' notice, the deposit is forfeited.

AVAILABILITY: Any day, any time.

SERVICES/AMENITIES:

Restaurant Services: yes
Catering: provided, no BYO
Kitchen Facilities: n/a
Tables & Chairs: provided
Linens, Silver, etc.: provided
Restrooms: wca
Dance Floor: extra charge

Parking: complementary valet
Overnight Accommodations: 142 guestrooms
Telephone: pay phone
Outdoor Night Lighting: limited
Outdoor Cooking Facilities: BBQs
Cleanup: provided
Other: wedding cakes & coordination services

RESTRICTIONS:

Alcohol: provided
Smoking: allowed
Music: amplified restricted

Wheelchair Access: limited
Insurance: not required

LA PLAYA HOTEL

Camino Real and 8th Street
Carmel, CA 93921
(408) 624-6476
Reserve: 2–9 months in advance

Occupying several acres in the heart of residential Carmel, just two blocks from the beach, La Playa is one of the loveliest and most inviting places we've seen. Originally built in 1904 as a private residence, La Playa was converted and expanded into a hotel in 1916. Boasting an exceptionally beautiful Mediterranean style, with terra cotta tile roofs, soft pastel walls and formal gardens, this full-service resort hotel offers a contemporary freshness as well as romantic old-world appeal. For outdoor celebrations, the wrought-iron gazebo is the spot, set amid brick patios, fountain, technicolor annuals, manicured lawns and climbing bougainvillea. The entire setting is lush and private. Inside are rooms of various size for private functions, with antiques, lithographs and memorabilia of early Carmel. Tasteful furnishings, French doors, big windows and magnificent views are standard amenities. This is a wonderful site for a ceremony or reception and an equally great location for a honeymoon.

CAPACITY, FEES & DEPOSITS:

Room	Deposit	Rental Fee	Standing	Seated
Garden Room	$250	$75	50	36
Fireside Room	250	50	30	18
Poseidon Room	500	200	150	100

Deposits must be submitted within 10 days of making your reservation. All deposits are applied to the total food and beverage bill. 70% of the estimated event total is due 60 days prior to the function and the remaining balance, within 30 days after the event. Per person rates: reception buffets about $25, seated meals about $25–30. Sales tax and 16% gratuity are additional.

CANCELLATION POLICY: Refunds are given with 4 months' or more notice.

AVAILABILITY: Every day, any time.

SERVICES/AMENITIES:

Restaurant Services: yes

Catering: provided, no BYO

Kitchen Facilities: n/a

Tables & Chairs: provided

Linens, Silver, etc.: provided

Overnight Accommodations: 75 guestrooms, 5 cottages

Bride's Dressing Area: CBA

Restrooms: wca

Dance Floor: portable

Parking: on street

Telephone: pay phones, guest phones

Outdoor Night Lighting: limited

Outdoor Cooking Facilities: no

Cleanup: provided

RESTRICTIONS:

Alcohol: provided, corkage $12/bottle

Smoking: allowed

Music: booked thru La Playa, over by 10pm

Wheelchair Access: yes

Insurance: not required

MISSION RANCH

26270 Dolores
Carmel, CA 93923
(408) 624-3824
Reserve: 1–15 months in advance

Mission Ranch has been a Carmel tradition for over 50 years. Once a working dairy, the Ranch is a delightful and rustic retreat, extensively renovated in 1992. Situated on the grounds are a turn-of-the-century farmhouse, a bunkhouse, rustic cottages, hotel rooms and triplex cottages with spectacular views of Carmel Beach and rugged Point Lobos. These historic buildings, surrounded by 100-year-old cypress trees and natural landscaping, offer the kind of quiet and peaceful ambiance not found in nearby bustling downtown Carmel. Ceremonies are often held on the brick patio of the Patio Party Barn or under the huge cypress trees on the lawns. The Party Barns are known for their friendly bars and great dance floors. The Patio Party Barn has a wall of full-length wood-framed glass doors opening onto a brick patio with a restful view of meadows and wetlands rolling down to Carmel River Beach. The Large Party Barn is ideal for larger wedding parties with its lofty, three-story ceiling. Both barns feature stages for live music, upright pianos and high, open truss ceilings. The structures are appropriately painted white with barn red trim. The Ranch Catering Department prides itself in designing specialty menus for any occasion. If you're looking for a place to hold a relaxed wedding in a classic country setting, this is it.

CAPACITY: The Patio Party Barn accommodates up to 150 guests seated and 200 standing. The Large Party Barn holds up to 180 seated and 300 standing guests. There is a required minimum of 50 guests in the barns.

FEES & DEPOSITS: The Party Barn rental fee ($650/Large Party Barn; $850/Patio Party Barn) is required to reserve a date. A 60% deposit on all estimated services is due 60 days prior to the event, with the remaining estimated balance due 10 days prior. Party Barn rental fees cover a 5-hour period. Additional overtime charges are billed at $100/hour. Buffet and dinner prices start at $21/person. A 16% gratuity and tax are additional.

AVAILABILITY: Every day, any time. (Note that live music is allowed Thursday–Saturday until 11pm and Sunday until 6pm.)

SERVICES/AMENITIES:

Restaurant Services: yes

Catering: provided, no BYO

Linens, Silver, etc.: basics provided

Restrooms: wca

Dance Floor: in Barns

Parking: large lot

Overnight Accommodations: 31 guestrooms

Bride's Dressing Area: no

Kitchen Facilities: n/a

Tables & Chairs: provided

Telephone: pay phones

Outdoor Night Lighting: CBA

Outdoor Cooking Facilities: CBA

Cleanup: provided

Other: full wedding planning services

RESTRICTIONS:

Alcohol: provided, no BYO

Smoking: not allowed in rooms

Music: amplified with restrictions

Wheelchair Access: yes

Insurance: not required

Carmel Valley

THE RIDGE RESTAURANT
at Robles Del Rio Lodge

200 Punta Del Monte
Carmel Valley, CA 93924
(408) 659-0170
Reserve: 2 weeks–3 months in advance

Getting to the Ridge Restaurant is half the fun. It's located up a beautiful, winding road leading to a hilltop where the restaurant overlooks Carmel Valley. Charming and rustic in appearance, The Ridge is actually part of the old Robles Del Rio Lodge which has the best ambiance and views at twilight, when the sun sets and the lights come up in the Valley. Seated meals are generally the rule inside. The interior of the restaurant has two main dining areas, one with a glassed-in terrace with terrific panoramas of the Valley. The Fireside Room, which has a grand piano, adjoins the dining room and there's a full service cantina. Outdoor functions are a delight. Sizable groups can have cocktails and hors d'oeuvres, barbecues or more formal receptions on the lawns or the Lodge's garden patios. For smaller receptions or prenuptial dinners, the private Oak Meadow Cottage, with large outdoor terrace, is available for up to 60 guests.

CAPACITY: The main dining room can hold up to 60 seated guests; the deck, 50, Fireside Room, 40 and outdoor areas, 200–300 standing guests.

FEES & DEPOSITS: A non-refundable deposit secures your date. For small groups staying overnight, the deposit is sometimes waived. Half of the estimated food and beverage cost is due 30 days prior to the function and the balance is due on the day of the event. Per person rates: luncheons start at $7.50, dinners start at $16, buffets range from $10–40 and Sunday brunch from $16. Tax and an 18% gratuity are added to the final bill.

CANCELLATION POLICY: Confirm the cancellation policy at the time you book your function to be clear about obtaining a refund.

AVAILABILITY: Year-round, daily.

SERVICES/AMENITIES:

Restaurant Services: yes

Catering: provided, no BYO

Kitchen Facilities: n/a

Tables & Chairs: mostly provided

Linens, Silver, etc.: mostly provided

Restrooms: wca

Dance Floor: several areas

Parking: large lots

Overnight Accommodations: 33 guestrooms

Telephone: pay phone

Outdoor Night Lighting: yes

Outdoor Cooking Facilities: BBQ

Cleanup: provided

Bride's Dressing Area: CBA

Cleanup: provided

Other: full event coordination

RESTRICTIONS:

Alcohol: provided, corkage $10–12/bottle for W&C

Smoking: allowed

Music: amplified, DJs ok

Wheelchair Access: yes

Insurance: not required

Need a caterer, cake maker, florist? The Service Directory starting on page 412 features the best in the business.

Monterey

MONTEREY BAY AQUARIUM

886 Cannery Row
Monterey, CA 93940
(408) 648-4928
Reserve: 6–18 months in advance

If you've already been to the sensational Monterey Bay Aquarium you'll be delighted to learn that it's available for private events. If you haven't been here yet, then this is a great opportunity to see one of the most beautifully designed buildings in the United States. Constructed on the site of the old Hovden Cannery on the water's edge in the heart of Monterey's historic Cannery Row, this facility is unsurpassed in its range of Monterey Bay displays and exhibits. One extraordinary feature is a three-story tank complete with kelp forest swaying in rhythm with tidal undulations. Some of the touch-and-learn exhibits, where you can pet swimming bat rays or multi-colored sea stars, are open at night and there are countless other exotic-looking sea creatures to see. The nicely appointed Portola Cafe is also available, and as an added dimension to an already exceptional setting, aquarium guides will be available during your exclusive evening event. What a treat for your wedding guests! No one will turn down an invitation to join in the festivities if you decide to hold your party here. Reserve early—this is a much sought-after place.

CAPACITY:

Area	Standing	Seated
Kelp Forest	100	100
Marine Mammals Gallery	300	200-250
Portola Cafe	80	80
Entire Aquarium	2,000	—

FEES & DEPOSITS: An initial deposit is required 6 months in advance of the event and complete payment is required one month prior to the event. Admission fees will be quoted at the time of your inquiry. Per person food service rates: an hors d'oeuvres reception $15–30, a seated dinner or buffet $28–60. Breakfast, lunch and coffee-break menus are also available. Sales tax and 16% gratuity are applied to the final bill.

CANCELLATION POLICY: With 6 months' notice, your deposit will be fully refunded; 3–6 months, 50% will be refunded; less than 3 months, no refund.

AVAILABILITY: Every evening, 7pm–11pm. Closed Christmas.

SERVICES/AMENITIES:

Restaurant Services: yes
Catering: provided, no BYO
Kitchen Facilities: n/a

Parking: City lots
Overnight Accommodations: no
Telephone: pay phones

Tables & Chairs: provided
Linens, Silver, etc.: provided
Restrooms: wca
Dance Floor: yes
Bride's Dressing Area: yes

Outdoor Night Lighting: yes
Outdoor Cooking Facilities: no
Cleanup: provided
Other: full range of wedding services

RESTRICTIONS:

Alcohol: provided, corkage $8/bottle
Smoking: outside only
Music: amplified ok
Wheelchair Access: yes

Insurance: extra liability required
plus indemnification clause
Other: decoration restrictions

OLD WHALING STATION

391 Decatur St.
Monterey, CA 93940
(408) 375-5356
Reserve: 2 weeks–3 months in advance

This historic adobe structure reflects the character and history of early Monterey. Most sources indicate that the Old Whaling Station was built in 1847 by a Scottish adventurer as a home for his wife and daughter. In 1855, The Old Monterey Whaling Company began using the building for on-shore whaling operations, hence the unusual name. Local legend has it that whalers kept their lookout from the upstairs windows which have an unimpeded view of the Bay. When the whaling business waned at the turn of the century, the building fell into disrepair. Now leased by the Junior League of Monterey County, Inc., the property has undergone an extensive restoration and the result is an appealing facility and technicolor garden available for small, private events.

CAPACITY: The Station can hold up to 50 inside; the garden up to 100 seated guests. The facility's total capacity is 150 guests.

FEES & DEPOSITS: Rental fees are $500 for the general community and $250 for non-profit organizations. A non-refundable booking deposit of $250, which will be applied to the rental fee, must be submitted with a signed contract within 10 working days of making a tentative reservation. The balance of the rental fee, if any, is due 21 days in advance of the rental date. A refundable $200 security deposit is due when keys are transferred to the renter. If you'd like an additional half day rental for setup or cleanup, the fee is $150.

CANCELLATION POLICY: Rental fee payments are non-refundable. With 6 week's notice, the booking deposit may be transferred to another date within 12 months of the original contract, subject to availability.

AVAILABILITY: Year-round, every day from 9am to midnight.

SERVICES/AMENITIES:

Restaurant Services: no
Catering: BYO
Kitchen Facilities: full kitchen
Tables & Chairs: some provided
Linens, Silver, etc.: some provided
Restrooms: wca limited
Dance Floor: CBA by renter

RESTRICTIONS:

Alcohol: BYO
Smoking: outside only
Music: amplified restricted

Parking: Heritage Harbor lots
Overnight Accommodations: no
Telephone: house phone
Outdoor Night Lighting: yes
Outdoor Cooking Facilities: CBA by renter
Cleanup: renter
Bride's Dressing Area: yes

Wheelchair Access: no
Insurance: not required
Other: no pets

Pacific Grove

MARTINE INN

255 Oceanview Blvd.
Pacific Grove, CA 93950
(408) 373-3388 Marion
Reserve: 1 week–1 year in advance

The Martine Inn is set high, right on the edge of Monterey Bay, overlooking the rocky coastline of Pacific Grove. Originally designed as an oceanfront Victorian mansion in 1899, it was remodeled as a Mediterranean Villa by James and Laura Park (of the Park Davis pharmaceutical company) when Victoriana went out of style in the early 1900s. Although the exterior is Mediterranean, the Inn's decor is strictly Victorian, in rose and pink hues. There are elegantly furnished rooms complete with museum-quality American antiques, and from interior windows, guests have wonderful views of waves crashing against the cliffs. The Martines can help you design your event to meet your specific requirements and will even provide a staff consultant to plan for food, music, decorations or entertainment.

CAPACITY: The Parlor can hold 30–50 guests and the courtyard up to 125. If you rent the entire Inn for your party, it can accommodate 125 guests indoors.

FEES & DEPOSITS: For under 10 guests, there's a $100 deposit; for 10–35 guests, a $250 deposit is required. If there are more than 35 guests, you must reserve the entire Inn for which there is a $500 deposit. All deposits are non-refundable. Reserving the entire house costs approximately $3,000/night. For groups of fewer than 35 guests, there is a 2-night minimum stay for weekend events (either Fri/Sat night or Sat/Sun night). For groups of 35 or more, if the event occurs on Saturday, you must book half the guestrooms on Friday night, all the guestrooms on Saturday night and half the guestrooms on

Sunday night. Arrangements for payment of the balance due are made individually. Call for current catering costs.

CANCELLATION POLICY: Cancellation refunds are handled individually.

AVAILABILITY: The Inn accommodates weddings year-round. Call to investigate dates. If you book the entire Inn, the event hours are negotiable. If you reserve only a portion of the Inn, the hours are usually 1pm–4pm.

SERVICES/AMENITIES:

Restaurant Services: no
Catering: provided, no BYO
Kitchen Facilities: n/a
Tables & Chairs: provided
Linens, Silver, etc.: provided
Restrooms: wca
Dance Floor: yes
Bride's Dressing Area: guestroom

Parking: on street, medium lot
Overnight Accommodations: 19 guestrooms
Telephone: guest phone
Outdoor Night Lighting: minimal
Outdoor Cooking Facilities: BBQ
Cleanup: provided
Other: full wedding services

RESTRICTIONS:

Alcohol: provided, no BYO, WBC only
Smoking: restricted
Music: amplified with volume limit

Wheelchair Access: yes
Insurance: not required

Pebble Beach

BEACH AND TENNIS CLUB

Pebble Beach, CA 93953
(408) 624-3811 ext. 283
Reserve: 24 months in advance

Just two quick minutes from the Lodge at Pebble Beach is the resort's private Beach and Tennis Club which has tennis courts, pool, spa and fitness center. Although this is a private club, you don't have to be a member to reserve the banquet facilities! And that's a good thing because the Surf Room is one of the most wonderful places for a reception we've run across. The location and ambiance rivals—no, surpasses—The Lodge at Pebble Beach in providing outstanding views in an intimate setting. The main dining room juts out almost to the ocean's edge. And since three of the four dining room walls are glass, the vistas over Carmel Bay, nearby fairways and cliffs are unparalleled. With muted pastel colors, white linens and brass and mirror details, the Surf Room is sophisticated yet comfortable. The adjacent poolside patio can be tented for outdoor dancing, bar service or buffet meals. Another room that's available is the Terrace Room, which has a working black marble-faced fireplace and is decorated in whites and cream colors. This room is primarily for small, seated functions or it can be used for buffet table service when guests are seated in the Surf Room.

CAPACITY: The Surf Room holds 200–250 for a seated party (depending on use of the dance floor), the Terrace Room holds up to 50 seated guests and the Patio can hold up to 80 seated guests.

FEES & DEPOSITS: A refundable $1,500 deposit is due within 2 weeks after you make your reservation. A $1,500 rental fee reserves the entire club. Food service is provided. Wedding buffets start at $44/person and dinners range from $45–50/person. Sales tax and 17% service charge are applied to the final bill. The total is due 14 days in advance of your party.

CANCELLATION POLICY: With 6 months' notice, the deposit will be refunded.

AVAILABILITY: Monday–Tuesday, Friday–Sunday, from 6pm until midnight. This is a private club, consequently availability is limited.

SERVICES/AMENITIES:

Restaurant Services: yes
Catering: provided, no BYO
Kitchen Facilities: n/a
Tables & Chairs: provided
Linens, Silver, etc.: provided
Restrooms: wca
Dance Floor: yes
Bride's Dressing Area: no

Parking: large lot
Overnight Accommodations: at Lodge
Telephone: pay phone
Outdoor Night Lighting: yes
Outdoor Cooking Facilities: CBA
Cleanup: provided
Other: tents for patio CBA, extra charge

RESTRICTIONS:

Alcohol: provided, corkage $10/bottle
Smoking: allowed
Music: amplified ok

Wheelchair Access: yes
Insurance: not required

THE INN AT SPANISH BAY

17 Mile Drive
Pebble Beach, CA 93953
(408) 647-7500
Reserve: 1–6 months in advance

Right off of the famous 17 Mile Drive, this new resort stands at the edge of the Del Monte Forest, barely 300 yards from the ocean's edge. The Inn is designed in the Old Monterey and Spanish California style, with sloping roofs, arched windows and light stucco walls. The Inn is surrounded by lush golf fairways and wind-swept dunes sloping down to the ocean. Inside, the Inn offers guests fireplaces, tasteful appointments in soft colors and various special amenities. This is a large complex, featuring 270 guestrooms, restaurants, retail shops, recreation facilities as well as banquet accommodations. A wide range of rooms is available for private parties including the sizeable Ballroom and the Bay Club Restaurant.

CAPACITY: The Bay Club Restaurant, available on Saturdays for lunch only, seats 60 guests. The Ballroom seats 300 guests comfortably and the Fairway Patio can hold 250 guests for a standing reception.

FEES & DEPOSITS: A non-refundable $500–1,000 deposit, depending on the size of the room, is due when you book your reservations. For events, per person rates: luncheons $22–30, buffets start at $35, and dinners at $38. Sales tax and 17% gratuity are additional.

CANCELLATION POLICY: If you cancel less than 2 months prior to your event, your deposit will be forfeited unless the Inn can rebook the date.

AVAILABILITY: Any day, until 2am.

SERVICES/AMENITIES:

Restaurant Services: yes
Catering: provided, no BYO
Kitchen Facilities: n/a
Tables & Chairs: provided
Linens, Silver, etc.: provided
Restrooms: wca
Dance Floor: yes

Parking: large lots
Overnight Accommodations: 270 rooms
Telephone: pay phones
Outdoor Night Lighting: CBA
Outdoor Cooking Facilities: BBQs
Cleanup: provided
Bride's Dressing Area: CBA

RESTRICTIONS:

Alcohol: provided, no BYO
Smoking: allowed
Music: amplified ok

Wheelchair Access: yes
Insurance: not required

Prices and policies do change. Call each facility and confirm everything you read in Here Comes The Guide.

THE LODGE AT PEBBLE BEACH

17 Mile Drive
Pebble Beach, CA 93953
(408) 624-3811
Reserve: 12 months in advance

Since opening in 1919, the Lodge has served as the hub of one of the world's premier and most challenging golf courses. The emerald-green, meticulously manicured fairways follow the serpentine edge of Carmel Bay and lie directly below the Lodge. With its sweeping ocean panoramas, setting and relaxed elegance, the Lodge is one of Northern California's favorite spots for weddings and receptions. Inside are a variety of rooms suitable for private parties that have great views and are well appointed. Plus, there's a conference center which can seat up to 330 guests. For those with limited time to coordinate an event, The Lodge's professional and courteous staff can assist you with every detail of your function.

CAPACITY, FEES & DEPOSITS:

Room	Seated Capacity	Room	Seated Capacity
Pebble Beach Room	120–150	Conference Center	330
Library Room	60	Card Room	30

The exterior lawn can be rented for croquet games and lawn parties. Call for individual quotes. A refundable deposit of approximately $500 is due within 2 weeks after making your reservation. Per person rates for food: hors d'oeuvres start at $25, luncheons start at $22–27 and dinners at $40–50. Sales tax and 17% gratuity are additional. For ceremonies on the lawn overlooking the ocean, the setup fee is $1,500.

CANCELLATION POLICY: With 6 months' notice, the deposit will be refunded.

AVAILABILITY: Any day, any time until midnight.

SERVICES/AMENITIES:

Restaurant Services: yes
Catering: provided, no BYO
Kitchen Facilities: n/a
Tables & Chairs: provided
Linens, Silver, etc.: provided
Restrooms: wca
Dance Floor: yes
Bride's Dressing Area: yes

Overnight Accommodations: 161 guestrooms
Telephone: pay phone
Outdoor Night Lighting: limited
Outdoor Cooking Facilities: CBA
Cleanup: provided
Other: tents for outdoor lawn parties CBA
Parking: large lots

RESTRICTIONS:

Alcohol: provided, corkage $10/bottle
Smoking: allowed
Music: amplified outside until 11pm

Wheelchair Access: yes
Insurance: not required

Amador City

IMPERIAL HOTEL

14202 Highway 49
Amador City, CA 95601
(209) 267-9172
Reserve: 2 weeks–6 months in advance

Built originally as a mercantile store, this building was developed into a hotel in 1879 because the town had insufficient lodging. In 1988, after a 51-year hiatus, the Imperial Hotel was restored by its present innkeepers. It has a restaurant and bar in addition to overnight accommodations. The dining room is simple yet stylish, with high ceilings, white walls and contemporary art which gives the interior an art-gallery ambiance. The bar is also appealing, with features reminiscent of an Egyptian oasis. A favorite place for ceremonies is in front of a waterfall which flows between two century-old rock walls. Receptions can be held outside on the patio, surrounded by lots of potted flowers, ferns and trees. With outstanding food and an environment to match, the Imperial is a splendid destination for a creative celebration.

CAPACITY: The dining room can hold up to 55 seated guests for dinner and up to 60 for lunch. The patio can accommodate 50 for a seated reception.

FEES & DEPOSITS: The facility rental fee is $100. If meal service is provided, the charge is waived. Food service starts at $10/person for lunch, and dinners start at $14/person. A non-refundable deposit of 50% of the estimated event cost is due 7 days in advance of the function. The balance is due at the end of the event.

AVAILABILITY: Year-round, every day except during Sunday brunch from 10am to 2pm. Most Friday and Saturday group events are scheduled between 5pm and 7pm.

SERVICES/AMENITIES:

Restaurant Services: yes
Catering: provided, no BYO
Kitchen Facilities: n/a
Tables & Chairs: provided
Linens, Silver, etc.: provided
Restrooms: wca
Dance Floor: no

Parking: on street, parking lot
Overnight Accommodations: 6 guestrooms
Telephone: house phone
Outdoor Night Lighting: no
Outdoor Cooking Facilities: no
Cleanup: provided
Bride's Dressing Area: yes

RESTRICTIONS:

Alcohol: provided, no BYO
Smoking: allowed
Music: amplified restricted

Wheelchair Access: yes
Insurance: sometimes required

Auburn

AUBURN VALLEY COUNTRY CLUB

8800 Auburn Valley Road
Auburn CA 95603
(916) 269-2775
Reserve: 6 months in advance

The Auburn Valley Country Club is one of those unexpected gems. You drive down a curvy scenic road for miles, wondering if the destination at the end will be worth the drive. Well, this one is. Set atop a knoll, the Club overlooks a gorgeous golf course studded with lakes, rolling hills and deep green trees. The view is breathtaking, and the surroundings so peaceful that all you hear are the birds and the breeze. The dining room faces this picture-book valley through floor-to-ceiling windows, providing a light and airy space for a wedding event. A large, nicely landscaped patio is also a great place for outdoor functions.

CAPACITY:

Area	Seated	Standing
Patio	250	400
Lounge	100	—
Dining Room	200	175

FEES & DEPOSITS: The facility rental fee is $500. A $500 deposit is due at the time of booking. 90% of all costs and a guaranteed guest count are due 1 week prior to the event. The balance is payable on departure. Per person catering fees run about $16–30 for sit-down meals and buffets.

CANCELLATION POLICY: A refund is only given with 30 or more days' notice.

AVAILABILITY: Every day, 4pm–midnight in the winter, 5pm–midnight during the rest of the year.

SERVICES/AMENITIES:

Restaurant Services: yes
Catering: provided
Kitchen Facilities: n/a
Tables & Chairs: provided
Linens, Silver, etc.: provided
Restrooms: wca
Dance Floor: yes

Parking: lot
Overnight Accommodations: no
Telephone: pay phone
Outdoor Night Lighting: yes
Outdoor Cooking Facilities: BBQ
Cleanup: provided
Bride's Dressing Area: CBA

RESTRICTIONS:

Alcohol: provided or BYO CW, corkage $6/bottle
Smoking: allowed
Music: amplified ok

Wheelchair Access: yes
Insurance: not required

POWER'S MANSION INN

164 Cleveland Ave.
Auburn, CA 95603
(916) 885-1166
Reserve: 3–6 months in advance

One of Auburn's landmarks, this century-old Victorian bed and breakfast inn can host small events. The large dining room and adjoining parlors are often used for receptions. The Inn has been completely restored with custom wallpaper, antiques, period fixtures and beautiful colors. The elegant interior, terraced garden patio, wrap-around porches and decks make this a lovely spot for wedding parties.

CAPACITY: Dining room 35, two parlors 40; the entire facility, 75 guests total.

FEES & DEPOSITS: One third of the estimated charges are due at the time of booking. The balance is due the day of the event. The facility rents for $400/day if no lodging is reserved, and there is a $50 credit for each room reserved. Catering is handled by the Inn and runs $9–15/person for lunch and $16–25/person for dinner.

CANCELLATION POLICY: With partial rental, you will receive a full refund with 2 weeks' notice. If you have reserved the entire Inn, 1 month's notice is required.

AVAILABILITY: Year-round, every day.

SERVICES/AMENITIES:
Restaurant Services: breakfast only
Catering: provided, no BYO
Kitchen Facilities: n/a
Tables & Chairs: provided
Linens, Silver, etc.: provided
Restrooms: wca
Dance Floor: yes
Bride's Dressing Area: guestroom

Parking: on and off street
Overnight Accommodations: 11 guestrooms
Telephone: guest phones
Outdoor Night Lighting: yes
Outdoor Cooking Facilities: no
Cleanup: provided
Special Services: valet service

RESTRICTIONS:
Alcohol: provided, corkage $3/bottle
Smoking: outside only
Music: no restrictions if you rent entire Inn

Wheelchair Access: 1st floor only
Insurance: not required

Need a caterer, cake maker, florist? The Service Directory starting on page 412 features the best in the business.

Columbia

ANGELO'S HALL

State Street
Columbia, CA 95310
(209) 532-5134   Columbia House Restaurant
Reserve: 1–6 months in advance

A Mother Lode dance hall, this has also been used as Columbia's town hall and for community gatherings over the last 70 years. Historic Angelo's Hall is a pleasant yet unassuming wood structure with one large room. Because of its hardwood floors and spacious interior, it is one of the most popular dance halls around. The Hall is a very flexible space and can support rehearsal dinners, ceremonies, receptions or even square dancing.

CAPACITY: The Hall can hold 199 people standing, 150 seated.

FEES & DEPOSITS: A $50 maintenance fee and the estimated rental total is due when reservations are booked. If the Columbia House provides the catering, the rental fee is $1/person, otherwise it's $2/person. Average per person meals are $5/breakfast, $8.50/lunch and $14.50/dinner, including tax and gratuity. Any additional balance is payable the day of the event.

CANCELLATION POLICY: With 30 days' notice, fees are fully refundable.

AVAILABILITY: Year-round, any day until midnight.

SERVICES/AMENITIES:

Restaurant Services: yes
Catering: provided or BYO
Kitchen Facilities: no
Tables & Chairs: provided
Linens, Silver, etc.: BYO
Restrooms: wca
Dance Floor: yes

Parking: rear lot
Overnight Accommodations: no
Telephone: no
Outdoor Night Lighting: no
Outdoor Cooking Facilities: no
Cleanup: caterer or renter
Bride's Dressing Area: no

RESTRICTIONS:

Alcohol: BWC provided or BYO w/some restrictions
Smoking: outside only
Music: some restrictions

Wheelchair Access: limited
Insurance: sometimes required

AVERY RANCH

Forest Service Road 3N03
Columbia, CA 95310
(209) 533-2851 or **(415) 752-6434**
Reserve: 1–6 months in advance

Getting here is part of the fun. Avery Ranch, a full-service wilderness resort, is set in a remote and beautiful meadowland overlooking the Stanislaus River Canyon, forty minutes from historic Angel's Camp. You can elect to arrive by car, air-conditioned van, helicopter or by boat! Avery Ranch is at an elevation of 2,700 feet, encircled by thousands of acres of Stanislaus National Forest. Once an old homestead, the site still has the original Avery cabin, complete with stone fireplace. The spacious Main Lodge serves as the center for dining and entertaining, plus there are private cottages and log cabins for overnight guests. Here you'll find the perfect blend of rustic comfort and really good food. Everything is homemade yet prepared with attention to variety and creativity. Versatility, a commitment to good fun and good friends makes this place a rare treat. The Ranch can handle everything from spectacular theme parties, private events, stage shows, dances, group retreats to secluded 'hide-outs' for famous entertainers. This is a superb and tranquil setting for ceremonies and receptions. Recreation activities abound; river rafting, hiking, bicycling, horseback riding, swimming and fishing. Avery Ranch provides an extraordinary, peaceful and relaxed environment.

CAPACITY: The Avery Cabin can hold 20–30 seated guests, the Lodge dining room 75. A maximum of 250 guests can be accommodated in conjunction with the outdoor spaces.

FEES & DEPOSITS: A $100 refundable deposit secures your reservation and is due when the reservation is booked. 25% of the estimated total is due 1 week prior to the event and the final 75% is due at the end of the event. Each function is unique, so charges vary. The normal range is $25–75/person per day. Call to make specific arrangements.

CANCELLATION POLICY: With 4 weeks' notice, you'll receive a full refund.

AVAILABILITY: Year-round, every day.

SERVICES/AMENITIES:
Restaurant Services: no
Catering: provided, can BYO extra charge
Kitchen Facilities: full industrial
Tables & Chairs: provided
Linens, Silver, etc.: provided
Restrooms: limited wca, CBA
Dance Floor: yes
Bride's Dressing Area: CBA

Parking: lots
Overnight Accommodations: 15 guestrooms
Telephone: radio phone
Outdoor Night Lighting: CBA
Outdoor Cooking Facilities: BBQ
Cleanup: provided
Other: outdoor stage, wedding consulting

RESTRICTIONS:
Alcohol: provided, corkage $2/bottle
Smoking: outside only
Music: amplified ok

Wheelchair Access: limited, CBA
Insurance: sometimes required
Other: no pets

CITY HOTEL

Main Street
Columbia, CA 95310
(209) 532-1479
Reserve: 1–3 months in advance

Built in 1856 and located in Columbia State Historic Park, four miles north of Sonora, the City Hotel still provides hospitality on a daily basis. Small and intimate, the hotel appears to have been left intact as a remnant of California's gold-mining past when Columbia had 5,000 residents, 150 saloons and shops. The parlor rooms upstairs are furnished with antiques and open directly onto the main sitting parlor. Dining here is a memorable event; the food is terrific and the wine list extensive. For wedding receptions, the Main Dining Room and adjacent Morgan Room are perfectly suited for luncheons and/ or dinners. If you want to stay overnight there are 10 guestrooms upstairs and additional rooms in the nearby Fallon Hotel, operated by the same management. The City Hotel can also arrange for other Columbia lodgings. Note that adjacent to the Hotel is the Columbia Gazebo and nearby Fallon Garden, both of which make great spots for a ceremony. The stagecoach is also a crowd pleaser, shuttling wedding guests from churches nearby.

CAPACITY: The Main Dining Room can seat 60 guests; 100 standing. The Morgan Room can hold a maximum of 25 seated. An additional 20 can be seated in the adjacent historic saloon.

FEES & DEPOSITS: A refundable deposit is required, due within 2 weeks of making the reservation. For the Morgan Room and Main Dining Room, the day and evening deposits are $50/200 and $100/ 200 respectively. For luncheon or dinner events, food service is provided. Lunch starts at $11/person, dinners at $19/person. Tax and a 15% gratuity are added to the total bill which is payable at the end of the event.

CANCELLATION POLICY: With more than 2 weeks' notice, you will receive a full refund less $50.

AVAILABILITY: Every day; from 8am to 11pm, depending on the type of function arranged.

SERVICES/AMENITIES:
Restaurant Services: yes
Catering: provided, no BYO
Kitchen Facilities: n/a
Tables & Chairs: provided
Overnight Accommodations: 10 guestrooms
Telephone: pay phone
Outdoor Night Lighting: limited
Bride's Dressing Area: guestroom

Linens, Silver, etc.: provided
Restrooms: limited wca
Dance Floor: no
Parking: lot behind Hotel
Outdoor Cooking Facilities: no
Cleanup: provided
Other: on-staff minister, historic tours, stagecoach, gold panning

RESTRICTIONS:
Alcohol: provided, corkage $7/bottle
Smoking: restricted
Music: restricted

Wheelchair Access: limited
Insurance: not required
Other: no pets

Foresthill

MONTE VERDE INN

18841 Foresthill Road
Foresthill, CA 95631
(916) 888-8123
Reserve: 3–12 months in advance

If you're looking for a very special place, it's in Foresthill, a small hamlet about 40 minutes northeast of Sacramento. Here you'll find the historic Monte Verde Inn which is, in a word, wonderful. The property was originally a gathering spot for Indians, and after gold was discovered in the 1850s, it became a toll station and respite for travelers. In the 1890s, the National Hotel was built here. Although it burned down in 1920s, some of the original structure survived forming the foundation for the Monte Verde Inn. Constructed during the depression, this stately Georgian-style manor is an old fashioned, gracious reminder of the past. A glassed-in conservatory covers the front of the manor house, and is used for dancing in winter months. Inside, rooms are large and open. French doors, antiques, high ceilings and lots of labor-intensive detailing make the interior inviting. Unlike many old homes, it's bright and cheerful, with an eclectic selection of both new and old elements—a sophisticated yet playful environment. Outdoors, you'll feel like you're in the middle of an English country estate with lush manicured lawns and a veritable tapestry of flowers (changed seasonally according to the whim of the owners). The long entry drive, lined with venerable old cedars, draws you back in time. For ceremonies, try the patios surrounded by very tall cedars which form an informal outdoor cathedral. At night, 'fairy lights' and turn-of-the-century street lights create a glittering halo around dancing couples. Hundred-year-old quince trees, a fountain dating back to 1890s and a granite pond filled with large koi contribute to Monte Verde Inn's successful mix of rustic and country elegance.

CAPACITY: Inside, 75 guests maximum. Outdoors, up to 250 seated.

FEES & DEPOSITS: A refundable $500 cleaning/damage deposit is required to secure your date. Rates run $35–40/person, which includes rental for 5 hours, all setups for ceremony and reception, floral centerpieces, wedding cake and coffee, floral arch for outdoor weddings, floral baskets for indoor weddings and full buffet. Note that all food is prepared from fresh ingredients on the premises by a European-trained chef. Tax is additional. If the site is left in good condition, the cleaning/damage deposit will be refunded 1 week after the event.

CANCELLATION POLICY: If you cancel and the event date can be rebooked with a function of comparable value, 90% of all deposits are refunded.

AVAILABILITY: Inside, year-round. Outdoor facilities from May 15th–October 15th.

SERVICES/AMENITIES:

Restaurant Services: no   *Parking:* large lot

Catering: provided, no BYO
Kitchen Facilities: n/a
Tables & Chairs: provided
Linens, Silver, etc.: provided
Restrooms: wca only outdoors
Dance Floor: yes

RESTRICTIONS:
Alcohol: provided, BWC only
Smoking: outside only
Music: amplified ok

Overnight Accommodations: carriage house
Telephone: emergency only
Outdoor Night Lighting: yes
Outdoor Cooking Facilities: yes
Cleanup: provided
Bride's & Groom's Dressing Area: yes

Wheelchair Access: yes, outdoors only
Insurance: not required
Other: decorations restricted

Jackson

WINDROSE INN

1407 Jackson Gate Road
Jackson, CA 95642
(209) 223-3650 Sharon & Marv Hampton
Reserve: 4–8 months in advance

The Windrose Inn lies just outside of downtown Jackson. This is a beautiful, restored Victorian which sits on a magnificent piece of property. There's a trickling stream and bridge you cross as you make your way up to the front door. Well-manicured lawns dotted with white lawn furniture, an old-fashioned gazebo, colorful flowers, fish pond, large shade trees and genuine, personal attention by the owners complete the picture of this idyllic country house. For sensational surroundings for ceremonies or receptions (or a romantic honeymoon), the Windrose is a must if you plan to celebrate with friends and family in the Gold Country. This spot just feels good. We urge you to arrange a site visit to 'feel' it for yourself.

CAPACITY: For outdoor weddings; 100 guests. The indoor capacity is 15–20.

FEES & DEPOSITS: Half of the estimated total is due when you book your event. The balance is due 30 days prior to you function. Rental fees for a 2-hour minimum: 1–25 people $100/hour; 26–100 guests $150/hour.

CANCELLATION POLICY: With 30 days' notice, you'll receive a full refund; 15–29 days a 50% refund; less than 14 days, no refund.

AVAILABILITY: Every day; hours are negotiable.

SERVICES/AMENITIES:
Restaurant Services: no

Parking: lot, on street

Catering: CBA or BYO from list
Kitchen Facilities: moderate
Tables & Chairs: BYO or CBA
Linens, Silver, etc.: BYO or CBA
Restrooms: no wca
Dance Floor: CBA
Bride's Dressing Area: guestroom must be rented

RESTRICTIONS:
Alcohol: WBC only, server needs license
Smoking: outside only
Music: amplified ok before 7pm

Overnight Accommodations: 8 guestrooms
Telephone: house phone
Outdoor Night Lighting: yes
Outdoor Cooking Facilities: BBQ
Cleanup: caterer, CBA for extra fee
Other: event consulting

Wheelchair Access: yes
Insurance: some required
Other: no pets

Jamestown

HISTORIC NATIONAL HOTEL

77 Main Street
Jamestown, CA 95327
(209) 984-3446
Reserve: 2 weeks–6 months in advance

One of the ten oldest continuously operating hotels in California, The National is a good example of 1860s Mother Lode architecture. Its rooms have been authentically restored to convey a feeling of the past. Of special note is the saloon which has the Hotel's original bar, dating back to 1859! Here you'll find wainscotting, period furnishings, oak stools and a convivial ambiance popular with the locals. Receptions can be held in the Hotel's dining rooms, or outside on the garden courtyard. When the weather's warm, it's a festive spot, with white furniture and blue Campari umbrellas. Overhead is an arbor with lush vines and latticework detailing. Another main attraction is the National's cuisine, touted by Bon Appetit and Motorland magazines. The food is great and their award-winning wine list is extensive. The hotel is a delightful place to stay overnight, and if you need additional accommodations, their staff will arrange it for you. Although the National has added some new amenities, it has successfully retained its quaint, 19th-century charm.

CAPACITY: The dining room holds 60 seated, and 100 standing. The courtyard accommodates 50 seated, 75 standing.

FEES & DEPOSITS: A refundable deposit in the amount of 20% of the total estimated bill is due when reservations are made. Food service is provided. Luncheons range from $9–11/person and dinners from $15–18/person. Tax and service charge are included. The event balance is due the day of the function.

CANCELLATION POLICY: A full refund is given with 30 days' notice.

AVAILABILITY: Year-round, any time.

SERVICES/AMENITIES:

Restaurant Services: yes
Catering: provided, no BYO
Kitchen Facilities: n/a
Tables & Chairs: provided
Linens, Silver, etc.: provided
Restrooms: no wca
Dance Floor: no
Bride's Dressing Area: guestroom

Parking: on street
Overnight Accommodations: 11 guestrooms
Telephone: pay phone
Outdoor Night Lighting: yes
Outdoor Cooking Facilities: no
Cleanup: provided
Other: wedding coordination

RESTRICTIONS:

Alcohol: provided, corkage $3–5/bottle
Smoking: bar only
Music: amplified ok

Wheelchair Access: downstairs only
Insurance: not required

JAMESTOWN HOTEL

18153 Main Street
Jamestown, CA 95327
(209) 984-3902
Reserve: 2 weeks–4 months in advance

The restored Jamestown Hotel rests in the center of this historic Gold Rush town. With brick exterior and flower boxes, it feels homey and old fashioned. For those that want to relax before the festivities, the comfortable lounge has period furniture, an inviting fireplace and nicely detailed oak bar with large mirror. The main dining room has light floral wallpaper and is an attractive room with both bench seating and individual tables. Right outside there's a garden patio—a wood deck which is enclosed by overhead lattice and side screens. On a warm day this is a pleasant place for a reception. For ceremonies, use the white, Victorian gazebo in the town's center, about a block away, and then arrange for a horse-drawn carriage back to the Jamestown Hotel for the celebration. And, if you're from out of town, note that your group can stay overnight in cozy rooms upstairs, all nicely furnished with Gold Rush-era antiques.

CAPACITY: The dining room holds 64 seated, the lounge 36 seated and the garden patio 84 seated. The total capacity for a standing reception is 140 guests.

FEES & DEPOSITS: A $100 deposit which is applied to the final bill is required when reservations are made. No rental fees are required if food service is provided. Per person rates: luncheons range $9–11, buffet lunches start at $10, seated dinners at $20 and dinner buffets at $15. These prices generally include tax and gratuity.

CANCELLATION POLICY: With 2 weeks' notice, you'll receive a full refund.

AVAILABILITY: Year-round, every day.

SERVICES/AMENITIES:

Restaurant Services: yes
Catering: provided, no BYO
Kitchen Facilities: n/a
Tables & Chairs: provided
Linens, Silver, etc.: provided
Restrooms: wca
Dance Floor: no
Bride's Dressing Area: CBA

Parking: lot nearby, on street
Overnight Accommodations: 8 guestrooms
Telephone: pay phone
Outdoor Night Lighting: yes
Outdoor Cooking Facilities: BBQ
Cleanup: provided
Other: event coordination, horse-drawn carriage CBA

RESTRICTIONS:

Alcohol: provided, corkage $3–5/bottle
Smoking: dining room is non-smoking
Music: amplified ok

Wheelchair Access: yes
Insurance: not required

RAILTOWN 1897

Sierra Railway Depot
Fifth Avenue at Reservoir Rd.
Jamestown, CA 95327
(209) 984-3953
Reserve: 2–6 months in advance

Ride a steam train and relive the past! Railtown provides an authentic glimpse of the era when America steamed innocently into the 20th Century. This is a living museum, with vintage steam locomotives which have served the Sierra Railway since its inception in 1897. Railtown, a working facility that maintains and dispatches its historic equipment for excursion rides and filming operations, has contributed to nearly 200 feature movies, television shows and commercials. Steam engine #3, Hollywood's favorite, has become the most photographed locomotive in the world. Your group can charter one car or an entire train, depending on the nature of your celebration. Special events have included a mystery train tour, pumpkin tours at Halloween and train dance parties. Now a 26-acre State Historic Park, including a large picnic area for receptions, Railtown remains much the same as it was at the turn of the century.

CAPACITY, FEES & DEPOSITS: Railtown offers a variety of train excursion and picnic options. Train excursions can accommodate up to 450 guests, and the picnic area up to 325. Rates for adults range from $8 for a 1-hour train ride to $34.50 for a train ride with BBQ and entertainment. Call for train schedules, private charter and childrens' rates.

A 50% deposit is required when reservations are made. The balance is due the day of the event. Groups of 10 or more are required for group reservations.

CANCELLATION POLICY: With 48 hours' advance notice, you'll receive a full refund.

AVAILABILITY: Every day, year-round, depending on the type of event planned.

SERVICES/AMENITIES:

Restaurant Services: no

Catering: provided

Kitchen Facilities: no

Tables & Chairs: some provided, BYO

Linens, Silver, etc.: BYO

Restrooms: wca

Dance Floor: dance train car

Bride's Dressing Area: no

Parking: large lot

Overnight Accommodations: no

Telephone: pay phone

Outdoor Night Lighting: yes

Outdoor Cooking Facilities: BBQs

Cleanup: caterer or renter

Other: full event coordination, live band CBA

RESTRICTIONS:

Alcohol: provided, BWC only, no BYO

Smoking: outside only

Music: amplified restricted

Wheelchair Access: yes

Insurance: sometimes required

Groveland

THE IRON DOOR SALOON

18761 Main Street
Groveland, CA 95321
(209) 962-5947
Reserve: 1 month in advance

On your way to Yosemite, you probably passed the oldest operating saloon in California without knowing it. Built in 1852, The Iron Door Saloon was initially called the 'Granite Store' most likely because the front and back walls are made of solid granite. The sidewalls are of rock and mortar, and the roof consists of three-foot-thick sod covered with tin. Inside are reminders of the region's colorful past: bullet holes, pictures of the pre-dam Hetch Hetchy Valley and Old West paraphernalia. Although moose heads and deer antlers adorn the walls, the interior feels more like a natural history museum; the owners are ecology-minded and provide information about the status of these animals. Outside, don't miss the outstanding mural on the building's front—a collage of western scenes depicting miners, mountain men, Indians, wild horses and stampeding buffalo along with a portrait of John Muir. Peter and Betticke Barsotti refurbished The Iron Door in 1985, after falling in love with the historic lore of the building. The staff is efficient and friendly, and since both owners are producers for Bill Graham Presents, events are handled very professionally. This is a fun spot to have a wedding party.

CAPACITY: The indoor capacity is 150 for a reception, 75 guests seated.

FEES & DEPOSITS: A non-refundable $500–750 deposit for Friday–Saturday night or $500 for Sunday–Thursday is due when reservations are confirmed. The rental fee is $250–500/event; however, it may be waived depending on the total amount of services requested. Both deposit and rental fee vary depending on the time of year. Per person rates: dinners start at $20, luncheons at $10, hors d'oeuvres at $10 and buffets at $15. The balance is due the day of event; tax and a 15% gratuity are additional.

AVAILABILITY: Year-round. Weekends, from 10am–4pm; weekdays anytime.

SERVICES/AMENITIES:
Restaurant Services: yes
Catering: provided, no BYO
Kitchen Facilities: n/a
Tables & Chairs: provided
Linens, Silver, etc.: provided
Restrooms: no wca
Dance Floor: yes
Bride's Dressing Area: yes

Parking: medium lot
Overnight Accommodations: no
Telephone: pay phone
Outdoor Night Lighting: no
Outdoor Cooking Facilities: no
Cleanup: provided
Other: full event coordination

RESTRICTIONS:
Alcohol: provided, no BYO

Wheelchair Access: yes

Smoking: allowed
Music: amplified ok

Insurance: sometimes required

Oakhurst

ESTATE BY THE ELDERBERRIES
Erna's Elderberry House and
Chateau du Sureau

48688 Victoria Lane
Oakhurst, CA 93644
(209) 683-6800 or **(209) 683-6860**
Reserve: 6 months in advance

If you're like many Californians, half your wedding party hails from the north, the other half from the south. We've found a place midway that's guaranteed to make everyone happy—the Estate by the Elderberries. Nestled in the hills near Oakhurst, not far from Yosemite's south gate and forty-five minutes from Fresno, this is a place that's worth the trip—from anywhere. The seven-and-a-half-acre estate, which contains the Elderberry House Restaurant and Chateau du Sureau (the French word for elderberry), offers guests a chance to sample both an old-world European ambiance and a sublime culinary experience. The Elderberry House, renowned for its innovative prix fix menus (arguably the best cuisine in Central California) has four dining rooms. Dressed up with fine linens, crystal and fresh flowers, each provides an exceptional environment for a sophisticated wedding reception. Ceremonies, framed by a cascading fountain and towering pines, can be held outdoors during warmer months. Smaller weddings can take place in the nearby Chateau de Sureau, a castle-like inn, with turret and stone walls. There's even a small chapel inside, with enough pews to seat nine guests. Designed and furnished to resemble a nineteenth-century French country estate, this manor house has wrought-iron balconies imported from Paris, stone and red clay tile floors and hand-carved doors. For honeymooners, the Chateau's rooms have canopied beds with goosedown comforters and are furnished with antiques, tapestries and pieces of art. Bathrooms are extraordinary—all marble and hand-painted French tiles with deep, sunken tubs big enough for two. Ahhh. You can finally relax. Warm yourself in front of a roaring fire. Let yourself be pampered by the Chateau's caring staff. The Estate by the Elderberries is where you can make your fantasy wedding come true.

CAPACITY: Indoors, the Elderberry House can seat 100 guests. With garden and terrace areas, the total capacity is 165 guests.

FEES & DEPOSITS: Both the Restaurant and Chateau require a 50% deposit of the estimated food, beverage and lodging total. The Restaurant's rental fee is $500/event. Dinners range from $35–75/person, luncheons from $18–35/person, tax and gratuity included. The remaining balance is due the day of event.

AVAILABILITY: Year-round, with the exception of the first 3 weeks in January.

SERVICES/AMENITIES:

Restaurant Services: yes
Catering: provided
Kitchen Facilities: n/a
Tables & Chairs: provided
Linens, Silver, etc.: provided
Restrooms: wca
Dance Floor: outdoor terrace
Bride's Dressing Area: CBA

Parking: estate lot
Overnight Accommodations: 9 guestrooms
Telephone: guest phones CBA
Outdoor Night Lighting: yes
Outdoor Cooking Facilities: no
Cleanup: provided
Other: event coordination

RESTRICTIONS:

Alcohol: provided, corkage $10/bottle
Smoking: outside or in wine cellar only
Music: amplified within reason

Wheelchair Access: yes
Insurance: not required

Yosemite

YOSEMITE FACILITIES

Yosemite Park and Curry Company
Yosemite National Park, CA 95389
(209) 372-1122
Reserve: 12 months in advance

Have your wedding in the most beautiful place on earth—Yosemite. It never fails to leave its visitors with a sense of awe and wonder. The park's unparalleled beauty is an inspiring backdrop for any function, whether it's a rehearsal dinner, wedding shower or reception. Here you'll find the classically elegant and sophisticated Ahwahnee, the versatile Yosemite Lodge, the well-equipped Curry Village and the old-world Wawona Hotel. After the festivities, enjoy a multitude of summer and winter activities. Savor Yosemite. It can transform your wedding into a special celebration.

CAPACITY:

THE AHWAHNEE		YOSEMITE LODGE		WAWONA HOTEL	
Dining Room	*Capacity*	*Dining Room*	*Capacity*	*Dining Room*	*Capacity*
Winter Club Room	10–45	Mt. Room Broiler	60	Sunroom	75
Mural Room	10–45	Redwood Room	40	Lawns	150
Solarium	40–125	Mt. Broiler & Redwd	100		
		Cliff Room	75		
		Falls Room	75		
		Cliff & Falls Rooms	150		

The Ahwahnee can accommodate any combination of the above totalling 168 seated or 300 guests for a standing reception.

FEES & DEPOSITS: A $300 refundable deposit is required within 1 month after booking. There is no room rental fee for the first 3 hours of a reception. A room rental fee of $125/hour is charged for every additional hour. Menu selection for groups is to be submitted at least 6 weeks in advance and a final guest count must be submitted 72 hours prior to your party. The estimated total is due 4 weeks prior to the event and the final balance is payable before departure. Overnight accommodations vary. Call for rates.

CANCELLATION POLICY: With less than 90 days' notice, the deposit is forfeited.

AVAILABILITY: Year-round.

SERVICES/AMENITIES:

Restaurant Services: various choices

Catering: provided, no BYO

Kitchen Facilities: n/a

Tables & Chairs: provided

Linens, Silver, etc.: provided

Restrooms: wca

Dance Floor: several locations

Bride's Dressing Area: CBA

Parking: large lots

Overnight Accommodations: wide range

Telephone: pay phones

Outdoor Night Lighting: no

Outdoor Cooking Facilities: no

Cleanup: provided

Other: event coordination

RESTRICTIONS:

Alcohol: all alcohol through Yosemite Park & Curry Co.

Smoking: restricted areas

Music: subject to approval, no amplified outdoors

Wheelchair Access: yes

Insurance: not required

Other: no rice, birdseed, helium balloons, no horse-drawn carriages

---

Need a caterer, cake maker, florist? The Service Directory starting on page 412 features the best in the business.

Rancho Murieta

RANCHO MURIETA COUNTRY CLUB

7000 Alameda Drive
Rancho Murieta, CA 95683
(916) 354-3400
Reserve: 1–12 months in advance

Golfers from all over the country come here and think they've gone to heaven. What's surprising is that Rancho Murieta Country Club is also popular as a wedding and reception location. Built in a Spanish Hacienda style, the Clubhouse has unadorned cream walls, dark, wood-beamed ceilings and numerous arches. Large receptions are held in the Murieta Room which features a high, vaulted ceiling, mammoth beams, and a striking stained-glass window. Comfortable seating surrounds a central dance floor, and strings of tiny Christmas lights add sparkle overhead. A glass wall dominates the room, providing not only light, but a direct view of the 18th green. The California Room can accommodate a small rehearsal dinner, or offer a convenient and private getaway for the bridal party. Its dark wood paneling and ceiling are lightened by an expansive view of the golf course. The main attraction at the club has to be the terrace, a curved brick patio that is wonderful for outdoor receptions or ceremonies. From here, the rolling hills of the golf course spread out endlessly in all directions. Oaks dot the landscape, and a wild turkey is occasionally spotted amongst the trees. Meticulously landscaped rock gardens border the terrace, and in spring, they're covered with brilliantly colored blooms. And for tennis aficionados, there are six lighted tennis courts. More than a golfer's paradise, Rancho Murieta Country Club is an unexpected place for weddings, just a half hour and a million miles from downtown Sacramento.

CAPACITY:

Room	Seated	Standing	Room	Seated	Standing
Murieta Room	200	350	California Room	40	60
(w/o full dance floor)	250	350	Terrace	200	300
Club Rancho Room	100	150			

FEES & DEPOSITS: Rental is for the entire facility. A deposit of $750 is required at booking, and is applied to the total balance. The facility rental fee is $1,000 for a reception only, and $1,750 for both the ceremony and the reception. The total estimated balance is due 10 days prior to the event. A minimum of 150 guests is required April through November, and the final guest count is due 72 hours before the event. Seated luncheons start at $9.95/person, seated dinners at $17.95/person. Buffet luncheons start at $11.95/person, buffet dinners at $16.95/person. Beverages, tax and a 20% service charge are additional. Note that a honeymoon suite and chauffeured Lincoln Towncar are included in the facility fee.

CANCELLATION POLICY: With more than 90 days' notice, your deposit is fully refunded. With less notice, refunds are only given if the space can be rebooked.

AVAILABILITY: Year-round, everyday, except some major holidays from 11am–1am.

SERVICES/AMENITIES:

Restaurant Services: yes
Catering: provided, no BYO
Kitchen Facilities: n/a
Tables & Chairs: provided
Linens, Silver, etc.: provided
Restrooms: no wca
Dance Floor: yes
Other: wedding coordination, pre- and post-wedding golf/tennis CBA

Parking: 2 large lots, valet CBA
Overnight Accommodations: CBA
Telephone: pay phone
Outdoor Night Lighting: yes
Outdoor Cooking Facilities: BBQ
Cleanup: provided
Bride's Dressing Area: CBA

RESTRICTIONS:

Alcohol: provided, corkage $6/bottle
Smoking: designated areas only
Music: limited amplified ok

Wheelchair Access: yes
Insurance: sometimes required
Other: decorations must be approved

Rocklin

FINNISH TEMPERANCE HALL

4090 Rocklin Road
Rocklin, CA 95677
(916) 632-4100 Diana
Reserve: 3–12 months in advance

This recently remodeled 1905 hall is a surprisingly fresh and inviting space. Light pouring through tall win-dows with stained glass panels makes the room bright and cheerful. Painted off-white and light olive green with clean, straight lines, the hall succeeds in creating a warm, eye-pleasing environment. A raised stage, beautiful maple flooring, and overhead spot lighting add to the room's ambiance.

CAPACITY: The Hall can accommodate 144 seated guests or 309 for a standing reception.

FEES & DEPOSITS: A $250 refundable deposit is due when the contract is submitted and the rental fee is due 15 days prior to the function. A $15 service fee is included in the rental totals below. Any hours over 12 will be billed at the hourly rate.

Hourly Rate	3 Hour min.	6 Hours	7 Hours	8 /9 Hours
$30	$150	$255	$295	$330

CANCELLATION POLICY: With 31 days' notice, 25% of the rental fee will be forfeited. With less notice, 50% will be retained; less than 10 days, 100%.

AVAILABILITY: Year-round, everyday, anytime.

SERVICES/AMENITIES:

Restaurant Services: no
Catering: BYO
Kitchen Facilities: fully equipped
Tables & Chairs: provided
Linens, Silver, etc.: BYO
Restrooms: wca
Dance Floor: yes
Bride's Dressing Area: no

Parking: adjacent lot
Overnight Accommodations: no
Telephone: pay phone
Outdoor Night Lighting: no
Outdoor Cooking Facilities: no
Cleanup: renter or caterer
Special Services: stage

RESTRICTIONS:

Alcohol: BYO, some restrictions apply
Smoking: allowed
Music: amplified with approval

Wheelchair Access: yes
Insurance: not required
Other: decorations restricted

SUNSET WHITNEY COUNTRY CLUB

4201 Midas Ave.
Rocklin, CA 95677
(916) 624-2402 Social Coordinator
Reserve: 6–12 months in advance

While its main claim to fame may be its golf course, the Sunset Whitney Country Club is also a popular place for parties and wedding receptions. Both the Sunset and Whitney Rooms have vaulted, wood-beamed ceilings, and stone, wood and glass construction. They are spacious, airy, and a nice refuge from the heat in summer. The Whitney Room has a unique 4-sided fireplace that creates a warmth and intimacy in all corners of the room during cooler weather. It also opens out onto a large tree-shaded patio with pool—a delightful area to set up tables outdoors. Out of the main metropolitan area, the Sunset Whitney Club is a relaxed and versatile facility.

CAPACITY, FEES & DEPOSITS:

Room	Maximum Guests	Room Charge
Sunset Room	200	$450
Whitney Room	120	400
Whitney Room & Patio	300	600
Gazebo & Lawn	200	150 *(with reception)*
Gazebo & Lawn	200	300 *(without reception)*

A deposit equal to the room charge is due when reservations are confirmed and is applied to the total. The estimated event cost is due 1 week prior to the event; the balance is payable at the end of the function. The room charge includes setup, cleanup, tables, chairs, linens, etc. for 4 hours use. Extra hours can be arranged for $100/hour. Food service per person: buffets start at $10, luncheons at $8, dinners at $12 and hors d'oeuvres at $7. Tax and a 15% gratuity are additional.

CANCELLATION POLICY: If the space can be rebooked or with 3 months' notice, the deposit is refundable.

AVAILABILITY: Year-round, everyday from 7am–midnight. Closed Christmas and Thanksgiving days.

SERVICES/AMENITIES:

Restaurant Services: yes
Catering: provided, no BYO
Kitchen Facilities: n/a
Tables & Chairs: provided
Linens, Silver, etc.: provided
Restrooms: wca
Cleanup: provided
Special Services: piano

Parking: large lots
Bride's Dressing Area: yes
Overnight Accommodations: no
Telephone: pay phones
Outdoor Night Lighting: yes
Outdoor Cooking Facilities: BBQ
Dance Floor: yes

RESTRICTIONS:

Alcohol: provided, no BYO
Smoking: allowed
Music: amplified ok

Insurance: required
Wheelchair Access: yes
Other: decorations restricted, no confetti or open flames

Roseville

HAMAN HOUSE RESTAURANT

424 Oak Street
Roseville, CA 95678
(916) 791-2545 Office
Reserve: 2 weeks–6 months in advance

This old redwood-shaded Victorian has been transformed into a restaurant and art gallery, combined. The restaurant is on the ground floor and is a wonderful place for receptions and parties. The front parlor has a bay window, chintz curtains, dark rose ceilings and white walls. Tables are covered with pink and white linens, and art livens up the walls. Two more rooms have similar appeal, and all three flow into each other, creating a feeling of intimacy. A wide veranda winds around the house, providing outdoor seating. The art gallery upstairs is accessible during all events. The word "charming" is often overused, but for the Haman House it's perfectly appropriate.

CAPACITY:

Area	Seated	Reception
Restaurant	50	65–70
Veranda	30–35	30–35
Garden	200	300

FEES & DEPOSITS: A $150 cleaning deposit and a $250 refundable damage deposit are required when the date is confirmed. The rental deposit is applied to the rental balance. On Saturday and Sunday the house, grounds and gazebo cost $225/day for groups under 50 guests and $550 for groups over 50. Monday–Friday, the house and grounds cost $65–115/day. The balance is due 2 weeks prior to the event. Per person rates: brunch $8.50–12.50, hors d'oeuvres $8–12, seated luncheons $6-8, buffet luncheons $8.50–12, seated dinners $10–26, dinner buffets $8.50–22.50. Tax and 15% gratuity are additional.

CANCELLATION POLICY: With 90 days' notice, deposits are refunded.

AVAILABILITY: Year-round, everyday 8am–midnight. Closed Christmas and New Year's day plus all major holidays.

SERVICES/AMENITIES:

Restaurant Services: yes
Catering: provided, no BYO
Kitchen Facilities: n/a
Tables & Chairs: provided or BYO
Linens, Silver, etc.: provided or BYO
Restrooms: no wca
Dance Floor: no
Bride's Dressing Area: no

Parking: adjacent City lot
Overnight Accommodations: no
Telephone: office & lobby phone
Outdoor Night Lighting: yes
Outdoor Cooking Facilities: no
Cleanup: provided
Other: event coordination, piano

RESTRICTIONS:

Alcohol: WBC provided, BYO ok
Smoking: outside only
Music: amplified ok

Wheelchair Access: no
Insurance: certificate required
Other: decorations restricted

MAIDU
COMMUNITY CENTER

1550 Maidu Drive
Roseville, CA 95661
(916) 781-0690
Reserve: 1–12 months in advance

This large, ultra-modern facility is the City of Roseville's brand new community center. Built to serve every segment of the community, it houses space for parties, ceremonies and receptions. The interior is fresh, airy and well designed. The lobby is impressive with a high vaulted ceiling, and windows around the top let in lots of sunlight. A spacious patio with a gazebo in back is enclosed by a high brick fence that provides privacy and quiet. Surrounded by undeveloped park land, the center also enjoys a peaceful, natural environment.

CAPACITY, FEES & DEPOSITS:

Room	Seated	Reception	Cleaning Deposit	Security Deposit	Rental Fees/Hour
Reception Hall	280	450	$200	$200	$22–88
Meeting Rooms 1 & 2 Combined	130	150	100	100	12–39
Senior Meeting Room	50	70	50	50	5–19
Senior Activity Room	50	85	50	50	4–14

Rental fees vary depending on residential status plus a few other factors. A non-refundable security deposit, applied to the rental fee, is required when reservations are confirmed. The cleaning deposit and rental balance are due two weeks prior to the event. The cleaning deposit is usually returned after the event if the facility is left in clean condition.

CANCELLATION POLICY: The security deposit is only refunded if the space(s) can be rebooked.

AVAILABILITY: Year-round, Sunday–Thursday 6am–11pm, Friday–Saturday 6am–1am. Closed major holidays.

SERVICES/AMENITIES:

Restaurant Services: no
Catering: BYO
Kitchen Facilities: setup only
Tables & Chairs: provided
Linens, Silver, etc.: BYO
Restrooms: wca
Dance Floor: yes
Parking: large lot

Overnight Accommodations: no
Telephone: pay phone
Outdoor Night Lighting: yes
Outdoor Cooking Facilities: BYO
Cleanup: caterer or renter
Other: PA system; podium; portable bar, extra fee; tot lot
Bride's Dressing Area: CBA

RESTRICTIONS:

Alcohol: BYO
Smoking: outside only
Music: amplified ok

Wheelchair Access: yes
Insurance: required
Other: decorations restricted, no open flames

ROSEVILLE OPERA HOUSE

Lincoln and Main
Roseville, CA 95678
(916) 773-0768
Reserve: 2 months in advance

From the street, you might never know that this facility exists. You enter through a door on the side of an old Roseville building and walk upstairs to a large ballroom. Recently redecorated, the room is painted light pink with a cream colored ceiling and deep green trim. Drapes are artfully hung over the windows, adding softness to an otherwise unadorned space. Hardwood floors and a stage make the room adaptable to both ceremonies and receptions.

CAPACITY: The Opera House can accommodate 250 seated guests and 320 for a reception.

FEES & DEPOSITS: A refundable $200 cleaning deposit is required when the date is confirmed. The rental fee for Friday–Sunday is $450 for a 24-hour period. Hourly rates are available for Monday–Thursday. The rental balance is due 1 month prior to the event.

CANCELLATION POLICY: With 60 days' notice, the deposit is refunded.

AVAILABILITY: Year-round, everyday, anytime.

SERVICES/AMENITIES:

Restaurant Services: no
Catering: BYO
Kitchen Facilities: minimal
Dance Floor: yes
Parking: adjacent lot
Overnight Accommodations: no
Telephone: no
Bride's Dressing Area: yes

Tables & Chairs: provided
Linens, Silver, etc.: BYO
Restrooms: no wca
Outdoor Night Lighting: access only
Outdoor Cooking Facilities: no
Cleanup: renter or caterer
Other: event coordination

RESTRICTIONS:

Alcohol: BYO, any sale requires license
Smoking: not allowed
Music: amplified ok

Wheelchair Access: no
Insurance: certificate required
Other: no red wine or punch, no candles

Sacramento

AMBER HOUSE

1315 22nd Street
Sacramento, CA 95816
(916) 444-8085
Reserve: 1 week–2 months in advance

Shaded by towering elm trees, Amber House is an elegant yet comfortable Craftsman-style inn. The warmth of wood in the beamed ceilings, staircase, wainscotting and floors blends well with the serenity of the interior. Antiques, oriental carpets and a brick fireplace make you feel right at home. Adjacent to the Amber House is a beautifully restored Mediterranean-style home featuring beveled and leaded glass, Grecian columns and elaborate wood mouldings. It also provides an intimate setting for smaller weddings and receptions. And if you're looking for a lovely honeymoon spot, Amber House offers nicely appointed suites with marble tiled baths and jacuzzi tubs for two.

CAPACITY: The facility accommodates up to 65 people.

FEES & DEPOSITS: Rates start at $300 and vary with time required, guest count and services provided. A deposit of 50% of the rental fee is required when reservations are confirmed.

CANCELLATION POLICY: For weddings, 30 days' notice is required. Less 30 days', the deposit will be forfeited unless the space is rebooked.

AVAILABILITY: Everyday, anytime.

SERVICES/AMENITIES:

Restaurant Services: no
Catering: BYO, licensed
Kitchen Facilities: adequate
Tables & Chairs: provided
Parking: on street, lot
Telephone: guest phones
Outdoor Night Lighting: no
Bride's Dressing Area: yes

Linens, Silver, etc.: caterer
Outdoor Cooking Facilities: no
Restrooms: no wca
Dance Floor: no
Overnight Accommodations: 8 guestrooms
Cleanup: caterer
Other: full event coordination

RESTRICTIONS:

Alcohol: BYO
Smoking: outside only
Music: no amplified

Wheelchair Access: no
Insurance: not required

CALIFORNIA STATE RAILROAD MUSEUM

111 I Street
Old Sacramento, CA 95814
(916) 445-7387
Reserve: 12 months in advance

For those of you who harbor a secret passion for trains, the Railroad Museum is nirvana. Home to 21 locomotives and cars, it is the finest train museum in North America. Lighting throughout is subdued, imbuing these historical gems with a certain mystery. The largest locomotive here weighs over a million pounds while the oldest dates back to 1862. Many of the trains are displayed in the Roundhouse, a stark, vaulted structure that serves as a train "hangar". Events take place here, guests mingling among these monuments to railroad ingenuity. This is definitely one of the more unusual wedding locations we have seen.

CAPACITY: The Museum accommodates 600 standing or 400 seated guests.

FEES & DEPOSITS: A refundable $250 cleaning deposit is due when reservations are confirmed. The basic rental fee is $1,250. If engines need to be moved, however, there is an added charge of $750 for the first one and $250 for the second. All fees are payable 30 days prior to the event.

CANCELLATION POLICY: With two weeks' notice, the deposit is refunded.

AVAILABILITY: Everyday, 5pm–11pm except Thanksgiving and Christmas week.

SERVICES/AMENITIES:

Restaurant Services: no
Catering: BYO
Kitchen Facilities: no
Tables & Chairs: BYO
Linens, Silver, etc.: BYO
Restrooms: wca
Dance Floor: in Roundhouse

Parking: on street, lot
Overnight Accommodations: no
Telephone: pay phone
Outdoor Night Lighting: no
Outdoor Cooking Facilities: no
Cleanup: renter or caterer
Bride's Dressing Area: CBA

RESTRICTIONS:

Alcohol: BYO, license required for sales
Smoking: outside only
Music: amplified ok

Wheelchair Access: yes
Insurance: liability required
Other: food restricted to Roundhouse

CAPITOL PLAZA HALLS

1025 Ninth Street, Suite 201
Sacramento, CA 95814
(916) 443-4483
Reserve: 1 week–12 months in advance

When walking through this facility's undistinguished entrance, you wonder what it could possibly have to offer. A quick trip up the elevator, however, reveals an extraordinary pair of rooms which are perfect for weddings and receptions. Over 100 years old, both halls have 29-foot hand-painted ceilings restored by a local artist. The colors—teal green, pink, mauve, blue and gold leaf—are exquisite. Tall draped windows and chandeliers complete the feeling of elegance. Downstairs is another hall used for large events. It's more contemporary, with wood paneled walls and subdued lighting. These halls are worth seeing even if you don't have your wedding here!

CAPACITY:

Room	Seated	Standing
Fraternity Hall	300	450
Temple Hall	300	450
Silver Room	300	500

FEES & DEPOSITS: Weekend rates run $900–1,100. Weekday rates are negotiable. For weddings, a $300 deposit is due when reservations are confirmed and the balance is due 15 days prior to the event.

CANCELLATION POLICY: The deposit will be refunded with 90 days' notice.

AVAILABILITY: Everyday.

SERVICES/AMENITIES:

Restaurant Services: no
Catering: provided or BYO
Kitchen Facilities: minimal
Tables & Chairs: provided
Linens, Silver, etc.: provided for fee
Restrooms: wca
Dance Floor: yes
Bride's Dressing Area: yes

Parking: on street, valet, garage
Overnight Accommodations: no
Telephone: pay phone
Outdoor Night Lighting: access only
Outdoor Cooking Facilities: no
Cleanup: provided
Special Services: event planning

RESTRICTIONS:

Alcohol: provided or BYO
Smoking: foyers or outside only
Music: amplified ok

Wheelchair Access: yes
Insurance: liability required
Other: decoration restrictions

CASA DE LOS NIÑOS

2760 Sutterville Road
Sacramento, CA 95820
(916) 452-2809
Reserve: 3–12 months in advance

You might not expect much from a restaurant run by volunteers, but in the case of Casa de los Niños you'd be mistaken. Operated for the benefit of the Sacramento Children's Home, the restaurant is a delightful place to have your wedding reception. From the moment you walk through the vine-laden entryway, you're impressed by the meticulously maintained grounds. Branches form a delicate canopy over the walkway, bordered by ferns, bushes and clusters of impatiens. An outdoor terrace is surrounded by magnolias, oaks, sycamores and redwoods, and a variety of flowers weave color throughout the garden. The terrace is a versatile space that can be set up for a ceremony, al fresco dining or dancing. Indoors, the Garden Room overlooks the terrace, and tall windows on three sides provide each guest with a garden view. A vaulted ceiling, light peach walls and chintz valences give the room an airy, pleasant ambiance, while black lacquer chairs, white linens and pink carnations add a touch of formality. For small receptions or prenuptial dinners, the Patio Room offers a more intimate space, overlooking yet another lush landscape. A little deck with flower pots and a white wrought iron table and chairs brings the freshness of the garden into the dining room. In addition to hosting a wide range of events, Casa de los Niños also serves as an art gallery, featuring a different artist's work every two months.

CAPACITY:	*Area*	*Seated*	*Standing*
	Garden Room	93	150
	Patio Room	36	—
	Terrace	30	50

FEES & DEPOSITS: A $300 deposit, which is applied to the final bill, is required at the time of booking. There is no rental fee for a 3-hour reception, but a $200 fee is charged for each additional hour. And if the ceremony is performed on site, there is a $100 wedding facility fee which covers an additional 30 minutes. Rehearsals are $50 each. There is an 80 person minimum, and per person food costs are $12.50 for hors d'oeuvres or a seated luncheon, and $17.50 for a buffet. A full dinner (including hors d'oeuvres, dessert and nonalcoholic beverage) can also be served in the Garden Room for $15/person. Tax and gratuity are additional (any gratuity is tax deductible). The food balance is due 10 working days before the event. Beverages, damages and fees are billed after the event.

CANCELLATION POLICY: The deposit is fully refundable up to 3 months before the event.

AVAILABILITY: Year-round, everyday except major holidays, 7am–9pm.

SERVICES/AMENITIES:
Restaurant Services: yes
Catering: provided

Parking: large lot
Overnight Accommodations: no

Kitchen Facilities: n/a
Tables & Chairs: provided
Linens, Silver, etc.: provided
Restrooms: wca
Dance Floor: terrace or indoor CBA

RESTRICTIONS:
Alcohol: WCB only provided
or $5/bottle corkage
Smoking: terrace only
Music: amplified ok

Telephone: courtesy phone
Outdoor Night Lighting: yes
Outdoor Cooking Facilities: no
Cleanup: provided
Bride's Dressing Area: yes, two areas

Wheelchair Access: yes
Insurance: not required
Other: no rice or birdseed

DRIVER MANSION INN

2019 21st Street
Sacramento, CA 95818
(916) 455-5243 Sandi & Richard Kann
Reserve: 3–12 months in advance

Built in 1899, this colonial revival mansion is one of Sacramento's most significant Victorian residences. Set back on a grassy slope, the Inn appears regal and imposing as you walk up the steps to the entrance. Once inside, however, the warmth and airiness make you feel at home. The Garden Suite is spacious and lovely with hardwood floors, tall windows and lots of natural light. Oriental carpets, a working fireplace and antique fixtures add to the feeling of relaxed elegance. The Dining Room, with its dark peach walls, lace curtains and high ceilings is also a comfortable space for small get-togethers. For outdoor events, the Inn has a large garden patio shaded by an enormous picture-perfect oak tree. Located in a residential neighborhood, the Driver Mansion Inn provides wedding guests with quiet and privacy.

CAPACITY: The facility can accommodate 100 guests.

FEES & DEPOSITS: A non-refundable deposit of $250–800, depending on the type of event, is required. Rental fees range from $250–2,000 depending on guest count, day of week, time of day and space(s) reserved.

AVAILABILITY: Year-round, everyday.

SERVICES/AMENITIES:
Restaurant Services: no
Catering: provided
Kitchen Facilities: n/a
Tables & Chairs: provided
Linens, Silver, etc.: provided
Restrooms: no wca
Dance Floor: no

Parking: on street
Overnight Accommodations: 9 guestrooms
Telephone: guest phones
Outdoor Night Lighting: no
Outdoor Cooking Facilities: BBQ
Cleanup: provided
Bride's Dressing Area: CBA

RESTRICTIONS:

Alcohol: provided by caterer
Smoking: outside only
Music: amplified indoors only

Wheelchair Access: no
Insurance: not required

FAIRYTALE TOWN

1501 Sutterville Road
Sacramento, CA 95822
(916) 264-7061
Reserve: 2–12 months in advance

Most of us have harbored an occasional desire to be someone else, but Fairytale Town is one of the few places we know of that actively encourages you to indulge your fantasy—especially if you're partial to fairytale heroes and heroines. Get married here as Cinderella and her Prince, or King Arthur and Queen Guinevere. Where else could you say your vows on a drawbridge over a castle moat? Be Robin Hood and Maid Marion, and have your ceremony in Sherwood Forest. Then host a reception for your band of merry friends on the lawn near Mother Goose. Fairytale Town is a one-of-a-kind wedding spot, and if you've got an active imagination, it's a terrific place to tie the knot.

CAPACITY: After 6pm, the grounds can accommodate up to 3,500 guests until dusk.

FEES & DEPOSITS: A refundable cleaning/security deposit of $100 is required when the application is submitted. The rental fee is $100/hour for a 2-hour minimum with the rental balance due 10 days prior to the event. There may be an additional deposit required if alcohol is included in your event.

CANCELLATION POLICY: With 30 days' notice, the deposit is refunded.

AVAILABILITY: Year-round, everyday after 6pm. Closed when raining and on Christmas day.

SERVICES/AMENITIES:

Restaurant Services: no
Catering: provided or BYO
Kitchen Facilities: no
Tables & Chairs: BYO
Linens, Silver, etc.: BYO
Restrooms: wca
Dance Floor: grass area or BYO

Parking: large lot
Overnight Accommodations: no
Telephone: pay phone across street
Outdoor Night Lighting: yes
Outdoor Cooking Facilities: BBQ
Cleanup: renter or caterer
Bride's Dressing Area: CBA

RESTRICTIONS:

Alcohol: BYO, permit required
Smoking: outside only
Music: amplified within limits, permit required

Wheelchair Access: yes
Insurance: required w/alcohol

GOVERNOR'S MANSION

1526 H Street
Sacramento, CA 95814
(916) 323-3047
Reserve: 6 months in advance

This is certainly one impressive Victorian. Built for Albert Gallatin in 1877 at the corner of 16th and H Streets, the ornate Italianate mansion was the official residence of thirteen California governors for sixty-four years. Now a registered landmark and museum housing historic California artifacts, the grounds, interior foyer and mansion steps are available for ceremonies and receptions. Follow the black, wrought iron perimeter fence (with gold-tipped points) to the front of the Mansion. Its massive entry steps are a dramatic spot for a picture-perfect ceremony. Once up the steps, go through the etched glass doors and enter the foyer. Here floors are a shiny hardwood covered with multi-colored orientals. Descend the grand staircase curving down to the foyer and take your vows. All the interior parlor rooms leading from the foyer are just as ornate as the Mansion's exterior. Many walls are curved and have elaborate moldings and period chandeliers. However, these spaces are roped off to guests. From this vantage point, your guests can take in original furnishings, historic photos on the walls, high ceilings and a marble fireplace in every room. Outside, near the carriage house, manicured lawns, roses and large shade trees offer an environment conducive to receptions. Tables with umbrellas can be set up in either the brick-paved courtyard adjacent to the pool or in the one between the Mansion and carriage house. An evening reception would be lovely here on a warm night. Note that mansion tours are available during your event.

CAPACITY: Indoors, 35 seated guests; 60 for a standing reception. The foyer holds up to 65 standing guests. Outdoors, the patio accommodates 200 maximum for a standing reception.

FEES & DEPOSITS: A $250 refundable security/cleaning deposit is due upon booking your reservation. The $700 rental fee is due in full two weeks prior to the event. The security/cleaning deposit is returned within 2 weeks after the event if the facility is left clean and undamaged.

AVAILABILITY: Year-round, everyday from 5pm to 11pm, including setup and take down.

SERVICES/AMENITIES:

Restaurant Services: no
Catering: BYO
Kitchen Facilities: minimal
Tables & Chairs: BYO
Linens, Silver, etc.: BYO
Restrooms: wca
Bride's Dressing Area: CBA
Other: guided tours through mansion

Parking: on street
Overnight Accommodations: no
Telephone: no
Outdoor Night Lighting: limited
Outdoor Cooking Facilities: BYO BBQ
Cleanup: caterer or renter
Dance Floor: patio and carriage house

RESTRICTIONS:

Alcohol: BYO
Smoking: outside only
Insurance: required

Wheelchair Access: 1st floor only
Music: amplified within reason to 11pm
Other: no flash photos inside mansion

HYATT REGENCY SACRAMENTO
at Capitol Park

1209 L Street
Sacramento, CA 95814
(916) 443-1234
Reserve: 3–6 months

The Hyatt may be the busiest hotel in Sacramento. It has every kind of event space you can think of, including a terrace on the 12th floor and access to the lovely park across the street. The lobby sets the tone—light, airy and soothing to the eye. Soft shades of grey, dusky pink, teal and mauve, touches of marble and an abundance of glass create a tasteful and distinctive environment. The Ballroom has an intricately patterned 16-foot ceiling and special lighting and mirrors which add sparkle. And for outdoor events, the hotel can arrange your wedding event among the trees on the Capitol grounds. For variety, elegance and all the amenities a cosmopolitan hotel can offer, the Hyatt is an excellent choice.

CAPACITY:	*Room*	*Seated*	*Reception*
	Golden State	100	100–150
	Big Sur & Carmel	80	80
	Trinity, Ventura, Santa Barbara & Tahoe	40–50	40–50
	Busby Berkeley Lounge	60	200
	Poolside Area	80	200
	Regency Ballroom (has 6 sections)	1,075	1,650

FEES & DEPOSITS: A non-refundable deposit ranging from $200–$1,000 is required, the rate dependent on room(s) reserved. The deposit is due when the contract is submitted. Per person rates: buffet brunches $15, luncheons $16, buffet luncheons $18, dinners $24, buffet dinners $28 and hors d'oeuvres start at $12/person. The estimated balance plus a final guest count are required 48 hours prior to the function. Tax and 17% gratuity are additional. If food and beverage service is provided, all or a portion of any room rental may be waived.

CANCELLATION POLICY: With 90 days' notice, the deposit will be refunded. With less notice, it will only be refunded if the space can be rebooked.

AVAILABILITY: Year-round, everyday, anytime.

SERVICES/AMENITIES:

Restaurant Services: yes
Catering: provided, no BYO
Kitchen Facilities: n/a
Tables & Chairs: provided
Linens, Silver, etc.: provided
Restrooms: wca
Parking: adjacent lots
Bride's Dressing Area: CBA

Overnight Accommodations: 500 guestrooms
Telephone: pay phones
Outdoor Night Lighting: yes
Outdoor Cooking Facilities: yes
Cleanup: provided
Dance Floor: yes
Special Services: event coordination, wedding cakes

RESTRICTIONS:
Alcohol: provided, no BYO
Smoking: allowed
Music: amplified w/in limits

Wheelchair Access: yes
Insurance: sometimes required

MCKINLEY PARK ROSE GARDEN

33rd and H Streets
Sacramento, CA 95816
(916) 277-6060
Reserve: 6–12 months in advance

For ceremonies only, the McKinley Rose Garden offers a lovely, colorful place to get married when the roses are in full bloom. The garden is located on one end of a large park, surrounded by an attractive, older residential neighborhood. With a palm tree in the center, the rose garden is laid out in concentric ovals, with eight rings of rose beds radiating from the center of the garden to its edges. Large shade trees dot the site. Walk arm-in-arm down the lawn 'paths' and take your vows under a rose-covered arbor. In the middle of all these blooms, the smell is heavenly. If you're looking for a picture-perfect backdrop, this is a wonderful choice. Because this site is the ultimate 'bargain', reserve early—Saturdays during the peak season book up fast.

CAPACITY: 200 guests, maximum.

FEES & DEPOSITS: The non-refundable rental fee is the deposit required to secure your date. For under 200 guests the fee is $10, for over 200 guests the fee is $15. The fee covers a 2-hour time period.

AVAILABILITY: Year-round, any day from 8am–8pm in 2-hour blocks.

SERVICES/AMENITIES:
Parking: on street
Tables & Chairs: not recommended
Bride's Dressing Area: CBA
Outdoor Night Lighting: no
Cleanup: renter

Telephone: in community center
Restrooms: wca in park
Kitchen Facilities: no
Outdoor Cooking Facilities: BBQ in park

RESTRICTIONS:
Alcohol: BYO
Smoking: allowed
Insurance: not required

Wheelchair Access: yes
Music: amplified ok
Other: ceremonies only

Need a caterer, cake maker, florist? The Service Directory starting on page 412 features the best in the business.

THE PENTHOUSE

2901 K Street
Sacramento, CA 95816
(916) 448-8520
Reserve: 2–6 months in advance

The Penthouse, located on the top floor of the Sutter Square Galleria, is a striking, super-modern structure housing a collection of trendy shops. A relatively new facility, it's already become a popular spot for special events. It's a large, multi-function room that has been custom-designed down to the tables and chairs to provide maximum comfort and flexibility. Eye-soothing tones of mauve and teal green, and an immaculate and fresh appearance make this space very inviting. The management specializes in providing impeccable service, so for a wedding reception in Sacramento, this is an excellent choice.

CAPACITY: Suite A holds 150 seated or 200 standing; Suite B holds 80 seated or 100 standing. These rooms can be combined for a total 240 seated or 300 standing guests.

FEES & DEPOSITS:

Room	Saturday Events, 5 Hrs.	Sunday Events, 5 Hrs.
Suite A	$ 850	$550
Suite B	550	350
Suites A&B	1,200	800

Fees for weekday events vary with the number of guests and time requested. A holding deposit of $500 is required at the time of booking and will be subtracted from the room rental fee. A $400 refundable security deposit is due with the balance of fees 2 weeks prior to the event.

CANCELLATION POLICY: With 120 days' notice, the deposit will be refunded.

AVAILABILITY: Friday 6pm-midnight; Saturday and Sunday, 11am–5pm and 6:30–midnight. These time frames include some setup time.

SERVICES/AMENITIES:

Restaurant Services: 6 located in Galleria
Catering: provided, no BYO
Kitchen Facilities: adequate
Tables & Chairs: provided
Linens, Silver, etc.: provided
Restrooms: wca
Dance Floor: yes
Special Services: event planning

Parking: garage
Bride's Dressing Area: restrooms
Overnight Accommodations: no
Telephone: pay phone
Outdoor Night Lighting: no
Outdoor Cooking Facilities: no
Cleanup: provided

RESTRICTIONS:

Alcohol: provided or BYO, license required for sales
Smoking: outside only
Music: amplified ok

Wheelchair Access: yes
Insurance: not required

RADISSON HOTEL
Sacramento

500 Leisure Lane
Sacramento, CA 95815
(916) 922-2020 or **(800) 333-3333**
Reserve: 3 months in advance

The Radisson Hotel underwent a 30-month, $40-million-dollar renovation in 1990. Born as the Woodlake Inn in 1957, this sprawling complex has meeting, dining and lodging accommodations built around an 18-acre site off Canterbury Road and Highway 160. Remodeled in a contemporary, comfortable, Mediterranean style with tile roof, light stucco walls and Mexican pavers, it offers a multitude of choices for weddings and receptions. In the main building, the Grand Ballroom is the largest of the Radisson event spaces. Divisible into six separate rooms, it can expand or contract to fit your group size. Designed in a light apricot, the Ballroom has stage, superb lighting and plenty of room for seated functions. In fact, the room is perfect for those who can't seem to whittle down their guest list. Its pre-function area, including the lakefront terrace, is 6,000 square feet! Outdoors, the most notable feature of this site is a small lake, complete with fountain that shoots 40-foot sprays into the air. You can rent a deck adjacent to the lake or an outdoor patio called the Grove. Guests who want to have fun can rent paddleboats for a quick spin on the water. Also for outdoor weddings is the Conference Plaza in front of the two-story clocktower building. The Plaza is geometric in design, with round fountain and rectangular lawns on all sides. Here you can have your seated reception outside, under umbrella-shaded tables. If you need lots of flexibility or you've got an overly large gathering of friends and family, the Radisson will come to the rescue.

CAPACITY:

Area	Seated	Reception
Grand Ballroom Total	1,000	1,800
Conference Plaza	100	140

FEES & DEPOSITS: The Radisson offers two wedding packages. The first includes reception room, butler service for cake cutting and toast and a lakeside honeymoon room with champagne for $350. The second includes a rehearsal and ceremony spot, reception room, butler service and deluxe lakeside suite with champagne and fruit basket for $550. The deposit for a reception room for up to 250 guests is $850. For a wedding space for up to 120 guests, the deposit is $325. These deposits are applied to the final bill and are due three months prior to your event. Per person food service starts at $11.75 for luncheons, $15.75 for dinners, $23 for buffets and $11.75 and $15.75 for luncheon and dinner hors d'oeuvres, respectively. Two thirds of the estimated total cost is due 30 days before and the balance, due three days prior to the event date.

CANCELLATION POLICY: With more than 30 day's notice, your deposit and fees are refunded. With 30 or less days' notice, refunds are given only if the space is rebooked.

AVAILABILITY: Year-round, everyday, 11am to 4pm or 6pm to 1am. Outdoor ceremony space is available only during summer months.

SERVICES/AMENITIES:

Restaurant Services: yes
Catering: provided, no BYO
Kitchen Facilities: n/a
Tables & Chairs: provided
Linens, Silver, etc.: provided
Restrooms: wca
Bride's Dressing Area: CBA
Other: wedding coordination, pianos, ice carvings, candelabras

Parking: large lot
Overnight Accommodations: 320 guestrooms
Telephone: pay phone
Outdoor Night Lighting: yes
Outdoor Cooking Facilities: BBQ
Cleanup: provided
Dance Floor: yes, extra fee

RESTRICTIONS:

Alcohol: provided, corkage $5/bottle
Smoking: allowed
Insurance: not required

Wheelchair Access: yes
Music: amplified ok
Other: decorations must be approved

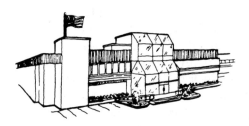

RANCHO ARROYO

9880 Jackson Road
Sacramento, CA 95827
(916) 364-7980
Reserve: 1–12 months in advance

Rancho Arroyo Sports Complex literally has something for everyone. The Bar and Lounge area has a dance floor, suspended video screen and sound system. The Restaurant down the hall is spacious and has a glass wall overlooking the lagoon at the entrance of the facility. Rancho Arroyo may seem modest in size at first glance, but when you explore the place you are in for a surprise. In addition to all the "regular" event spaces, there are indoor tennis courts and an olympic-size swimming pool where Olympic Gold Medalist Mark Spitz trained. When the courts are removed, this indoor area can accommodate 4,000 people! The only complex in the area with so much to offer, Rancho Arroyo is quite a unique facility for wedding receptions.

CAPACITY, FEES & DEPOSITS:

Room	Seated	Reception	Fee/5 hours
VIP Room	25	—	$ 125
Restaurant	250	500	950
Poolside	500	1,000	1,500
Bar & Lounge	200	300	1,250
Indoor Tennis Courts	2,400 all 8 courts	6,000 all 8 courts	$500/court
	300 each	750 each	500/court

A refundable security deposit of $75–250, depending on which space(s) is reserved, is required when reservations are confirmed. The estimated total food and beverage balance is payable 48 hours prior to the event. Per person rates: seated luncheons $8–15, dinners $10–20, brunches $12–15, hors d'oeuvres $7–17 and buffets $13–20. Tax and a 17% gratuity are additional. Sometimes an additional security fee is required.

CANCELLATION POLICY: With 30 days' notice, the deposit will be refunded.

AVAILABILITY: Year-round, everyday until 2am except some major holidays.

SERVICES/AMENITIES:

Restaurant Services: yes

Catering: provided, no BYO

Kitchen Facilities: n/a

Tables & Chairs: provided

Linens, Silver, etc.: provided

Dance Floor: yes

Parking: large lot

Bride's Dressing Area: CBA

Overnight Accommodations: no

Telephone: pay phone

Outdoor Night Lighting: yes

Outdoor Cooking Facilities: yes

Restrooms: wca

Cleanup: provided

Special Services: event coordination, piano, bartenders

RESTRICTIONS:

Alcohol: provided, corkage $5/bottle

Smoking: designated areas

Music: amplified ok

Wheelchair Access: yes, elevators

Insurance: sometimes required

Other: decorations restricted

RIVERBOAT DELTA KING

1000 Front Street
Old Sacramento, CA 95814
(800) 248-4354 or **(916) 444-5464**
Reserve: 2–6 months in advance

The last of the true California paddlewheelers, the Delta King is the impressive result of 5 years of painstaking restoration at a cost of 9 million dollars. During her heyday in the 20s and 30s, the Delta King and her twin, the Delta Queen, made their famous nightly passages between San Francisco and Sacramento to the music of jazz bands and the gentle swish of the paddlewheel. When this era ended, the boat went into gradual decline and finally sank in 1981. Looking at her now, it's hard to believe she was ever anything but graceful, elegant and luxurious. Fully restored, with 5 decks, meeting rooms, a theater, lounge, restaurant and hotel, the Delta King can accommodate almost any kind of event. Teak, mahogany, brass appointments, antique lanterns and nautical touches preserve the ship's original ambiance. The Captain's Quarters, located in the original wheel house, makes a wonderful honeymoon suite. Add to this an extended view of the river, balmy breezes and royal treatment by staff and you have an exceptional location for a rehearsal dinner, ceremony and/or wedding reception!

CAPACITY:

Area	Seated	Area	Seated
Theater	115	Mark Twain Salon	150
Landing (Outdoors)	150	Paddlewheel Saloon	100
Jenny Lind	60	Yosemite	40
Chrysopolis	12		

FEES & DEPOSITS: For special events, a deposit of $300–500 is due within 14 days of confirming reservations. Room rental fees run $200–400 and catering about $12–18/person for lunch or buffets; $17–29/person for seated dinners. The balance, including all food costs, is due 10 days prior to the event.

CANCELLATION POLICY: A refund is given only if the space can be rebooked with a comparable event.

AVAILABILITY: Banquet/dining rooms anytime.

SERVICES/AMENITIES:

Restaurant Services: yes
Catering: provided
Kitchen Facilities: n/a
Tables & Chairs: provided
Linens, Silver, etc.: provided
Restrooms: wca
Dance Floor: yes

Parking: on street, lot, valet
Overnight Accommodations: 44 staterooms
Telephone: guest phones
Outdoor Night Lighting: yes
Outdoor Cooking Facilities: no
Cleanup: provided
Bride's Dressing Area: CBA

RESTRICTIONS:

Alcohol: provided
Smoking: allowed
Music: amplified w/restrictions

Wheelchair Access: yes
Insurance: not required

SACRAMENTO ASSOCIATION OF REALTORS' BUILDING

2003 Howe Avenue at Cottage Way
Sacramento, CA 95816
(916) 922-8294 or **(916) 922–7711**
Reserve: 6–12 months in advance

Housed in the Sacramento Association of Realtors' building is a very large, contemporary room, designed in neutral teals and beige, which can hold quite a crowd. The structure, itself, is relatively new and is designed in a Mediterranean–California style with light stucco walls and red tile roof. Entering guests come through the generous-sized lobby, light and airy featuring a two-story ceiling, large staircase (great for wedding photos) and chandeliers. The Association's auditorium is available for private parties and has turned out to be very popular for wedding receptions. For smaller receptions, the room can be partitioned in half. If you have a particularly difficult time paring down your guest list, you may want to come by and take a look.

CAPACITY: The entire room can seat 325 guests; half the room can seat about 160.

FEES & DEPOSITS: A $200 refundable cleaning/security deposit is required to hold your date. The rental fee, due 30 days prior to the event, is $500 for a 4-hour block, $800 for up to 12 hours. Each additional hour is $75. Half the room costs $325 for 4 hours, $500 for up to 12 hours. Each additional hour is $50. The renter is given 2 free hours of setup time, 1 free hour of cleanup; each additional hour is $20. The fee for kitchen use is $100. Association family members are allowed a 20% discount.

CANCELLATION POLICY: With 6 months' notice, half the deposit will be forfeited; with 60 days' notice, the entire deposit. If you cancel with 30 days' notice, you will have to pay the entire rental fee. All cancellations must be made in writing.

AVAILABILITY: Year-round, from 8am to 2am.

SERVICES/AMENITIES:

Restaurant Services: no
Catering: BYO
Kitchen Facilities: fully equipped
Tables & Chairs: provided
Linens, Silver, etc.: BYO
Restrooms: wca
Bride's Dressing Area: yes
Other: portable bar

Parking: large lot
Overnight Accommodations: no
Telephone: pay phone
Outdoor Night Lighting: access only
Outdoor Cooking Facilities: no
Cleanup: caterer or renter
Dance Floor: yes

RESTRICTIONS:

Alcohol: BYO
Smoking: outside only
Insurance: proof of liability required

Wheelchair Access: yes
Music: amplified ok
Other: decorations restricted, no rice, no red wine or punch

SACRAMENTO GRAND BALLROOM

629 J Street
Sacramento, CA 95814
(916) 446-9491
Reserve: 2–6 months in advance

The simple, unadorned lobby of this building does not prepare you for what comes next. Turn the corner and, voilà—you stand open-mouthed, gazing into the Grand Ballroom. And grand it is! New owners have unveiled the Ballroom after it was submerged for years under carpets, wall separators and a bank facade. Its soaring, forty-five foot high ceiling once again greets you in all its gold leaf splendor. The height and ornate detail take your breath away. High above, a multitude of plaster cast moldings have been painted, predominantly in gold, with dark teal highlights. Around the cornices are more detailed moldings painted in tans, creams and rich cocoa. Suspended from the ceiling are eight original light fixtures, all as enormous and detailed as the room. At the far end of the room, an elegant brass revolving door is ready to bring in guests and nearby, old fashioned teller windows bring back memories of banking days past. The former 'Paying' and 'Receiving' windows, dressed in shiny brass and beveled glass, now function as the front of a spacious bar area. A light marble floor, ringed with a black marble border, is in keeping with the grand style. Several raised areas are perfect for buffet setups or band. For smaller parties, check out the Board Room upstairs. Again, the ceiling here is outstanding, with intricate detailing in painted plaster. Gold leaf and trim highlight raised patterns. A white, hand-carved marble fireplace with large overhead mirror is the center focus of the Board Room. Dark, rich wood paneling and decorative wall friezes add warmth. This is a sensational room which must be seen to be appreciated. Downstairs is a women's restroom that is one of the best we've seen. Brand new, but designed with the same refined quality as the Ballroom, the marble-clad women's room is gorgeous. As a bride's dressing area, it can't be beat. For those interested in an elegant wedding in Sacramento, you're in luck. We're glad this neoclassic ballroom has been brought back to life.

CAPACITY: 500 seated guests; 700 for a standing reception.

FEES & DEPOSITS: A non-refundable $250 reservation fee and a $250 security deposit are required to secure your date. The rental fee balance is due seven days prior to the event. Additional hours beyond the contracted time period will be billed at $75 per hour. Rental fees range from $800–1,500 depending on date, time and space(s) selected.

CANCELLATION POLICY: If notice of cancellation is given 45 or more days prior to the scheduled date, the security deposit will be refunded. If notice is given less than 45 days in advance, $500 will be retained.

AVAILABILITY: Year-round, everyday from 8am to 2am.

SERVICES/AMENITIES:

Restaurant Services: no
Catering: BYO or CBA
Kitchen Facilities: minimal, extra fee
Tables & Chairs: provided
Linens, Silver, etc.: BYO
Restrooms: wca
Bride's Dressing Area: yes
Other: wedding coordination

Parking: public lots nearby
Overnight Accommodations: no
Telephone: pay phone
Outdoor Night Lighting: no
Outdoor Cooking Facilities: no
Cleanup: some provided and caterer
Dance Floor: yes

RESTRICTIONS:

Alcohol: BYO
Smoking: outside only
Insurance: sometimes required

Wheelchair Access: yes
Music: amplified ok
Other: no rice or confetti

SACRAMENTO HISTORY CENTER

101 I Street
Old Sacramento, CA 95814
(916) 449-2057
Reserve: 1 month in advance

The old fashioned brick facade of this museum belies its totally modern interior. Only 5 years old, it houses displays and information about much of Sacramento's local history. The lobby is intriguing with its high reflective metal ceiling, slate floor and huge mural peopled by anonymous folks from the region's past. The museum has an open design—various galleries flow together and are visible to each other from different levels. All exhibits are accessible during your event. The museum's pride and joy is its 1928 kitchen, complete with stove, pantry, table and chairs, apron and dozens of period details. And if you want to combine a few history lessons with your wedding, docents are available. The History Center is a fascinating place, certain to enhance any event.

CAPACITY: The facility accommodates 700 people.

FEES & DEPOSITS : Call for information regarding fees.

AVAILABILITY: Special events Tues–Sun, 5pm to a negotiable hour.

SERVICES/AMENITIES:

Restaurant Services: no
Catering: preferred list or BYO w/approval
Kitchen Facilities: minimal
Tables & Chairs: BYO
Linens, Silver, etc.: BYO
Restrooms: wca
Dance Floor: no

Parking: on street, lot
Overnight Accommodations: no
Telephone: pay phone
Outdoor Night Lighting: limited
Outdoor Cooking Facilities: no
Cleanup: caterer
Bride's Dressing Area: no

RESTRICTIONS:

Alcohol: BYO
Smoking: outside only
Music: amplified ok

Wheelchair Access: yes
Insurance: liability required

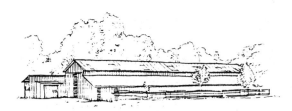

SACRAMENTO HORSEMEN'S ASSOCIATION

3200 Longview Drive
Sacramento, CA 95660
(916) 483-2845 or **(916) 421-9060**
Reserve: 6–12 months in advance

Even if you're not a horse lover, the Sacramento Horsemen's Association Clubhouse may appeal to you. Here, you feel like you're in the country—not in urban Sacramento. As you drive in, you'll see a large red barn, corrals, horse paddocks and picnic areas. Located in Del Paso Park, on the other side of Haggin Oaks Municipal Golf Course, you can just make out the outline of fairways through a grove of stately oak trees. For weddings and receptions, the Clubhouse is the spot. It's not fancy, but it does have an informal charm. Inside, the Clubhouse decor is western-style rustic. The largest room has an open beam ceiling with knotty pine paneling. Adjacent is the bar area, with brick fireplace, and doors which open to a patio surrounded by lawn. The outdoor facilities back up onto a creek area with lots of large shade trees. Surprise your friends and arrive in a horse drawn carriage! The Horsemen's Association Clubhouse is perfect for relaxed gatherings of friends and family.

CAPACITY: Inside, the facility can hold 175 guests; outside 200. The maximum capacity is 200 guests.

FEES & DEPOSITS: A refundable $100 cleaning/security deposit is required to hold your date. The rental fee varies depending on the type of event and the day of the week.

CANCELLATION POLICY: Cancellations are handled individually.

AVAILABILITY: Year-round, everyday from noon to midnight.

SERVICES/AMENITIES:
Restaurant Services: no
Catering: preferred list or BYO
Kitchen Facilities: fully equipped
Tables & Chairs: provided
Linens, Silver, etc.: BYO
Restrooms: wca
Bride's Dressing Area: yes

Parking: large lot
Overnight Accommodations: no
Telephone: pay phone
Outdoor Night Lighting: yes
Outdoor Cooking Facilities: BBQs
Cleanup: caterer or renter
Dance Floor: yes

RESTRICTIONS:
Alcohol: BYO
Smoking: outside only
Insurance: required

Wheelchair Access: yes
Music: amplified ok

A SHOT OF CLASS
and Bon Marche Ballroom

1020 11th Street
Sacramento, CA 95814
(916) 447-5340
Reserve: 6–12 months in advance

A Shot of Class Restaurant is housed in a classic 1930s structure which used to be the Bon Marche Department Store. Fronting Cathedral Square, the building has planter boxes and a gray and white awning which extends far enough to shade the entry and several interior rooms. Yes, you can reserve the entire dining room for your private function. All is presented in a grand Art Deco motif. Twenty-three foot high walls are painted in a soft pink; large black urns, Erte-like sculpture and artwork on walls are also of 1930s vintage. Stylish linen-clad tables show off white linen napkins tucked vertically into wine glasses and a baby black grand piano is a permanent part of the dining experience. Popular for rehearsal dinners, the Alcove Room has a black lacquered screen that can totally or partially separate guests from the main dining room. Next door, in what was once the Better Women's Wear section of the old store, is the sizeable Bon Marche Ballroom with high ceiling, 1930s fixtures, art and soft colors. Here you'll find a dance floor, raised stage and plenty of space for a band. Adjacent to this is the Petite Room, a very small room with custom-designed furnishings, perfect for rehearsal dinners or wedding showers for up to twelve guests. The nicest thing about both the Restaurant and Ballroom is that A Shot of Class is the caterer as well as the event coordinator. Do you need an ice sculpture that looks like your father-in-law? Decorations for a Carmen Miranda theme wedding? No problem. A Shot of Class is multi-talented, extremely service oriented and very professional.

CAPACITY:	*Room*	*Seated*	*Standing Reception*
	Shot of Class Dining Room	250	400
	Alcove Room	60	75
	Bon Marche Ballroom	250	400
	Petite Room	12	—

FEES & DEPOSITS: A non-refundable $500 deposit, which is credited to the final bill, is required to secure your date. The room rental fee is $1/person per hour with a $400 minimum. A refundable security/cleaning fee is required. Food service is provided. Wedding buffets start at $12/person and seated dinners at $15/person. Tax and a 15% service charge are additional. Half of the estimated total is due two weeks prior to the wedding; the final balance is due on the event day.

AVAILABILITY: Year-round, everyday from 9am–1am.

SERVICES/AMENITIES:

Restaurant Services: yes
Catering: provided, no BYO
Kitchen Facilities: n/a
Tables & Chairs: provided

Parking: nearby lot, valet CBA
Overnight Accommodations: no
Telephone: pay phone
Outdoor Night Lighting: yes

Linens, Silver, etc.: provided

Restrooms: wca

Bride's Dressing Area: CBA

Other: wedding coordination & ceremonies, floral arrangements, ice carvings, wedding cakes

RESTRICTIONS:

Alcohol: provided, no BYO

Smoking: allowed

Insurance: not required

Outdoor Cooking Facilities: CBA

Cleanup: provided

Dance Floor: yes

Wheelchair Access: yes

Music: amplified ok

THE SPIRIT OF SACRAMENTO & THE MATTHEW MCKINLEY

1207 Front St., #18
Sacramento, CA 95814
(800) 433-0263 or **(916) 552-2933**
Reserve: 1–12 months in advance

Aptly named, the snappy red and white Spirit of Sacramento is hard to resist. Built in 1942, this paddlewheeler has graced the rivers of the west in a variety of roles—most notably as a "movie star" in the film *Blood Alley*. Today, she not only offers dining cruises, but is available for weddings and receptions. Want to get married on board? No problem. The captain can perform the ceremony, and you can have your reception on one of two climate-controlled decks. The upper deck offers fabulous atrium seating—no matter where you sit, you're surrounded by the river and the sky. Photos of *Blood Alley* stars, John Wayne and Lauren Bacall, adorn the walls. White and burgundy linens add color and a touch of elegance. The second deck has an interior dining room with a river view from every table. The tongue-in-groove oak ceiling, red flock wallpaper and historical riverboat photos provide a glimpse of the golden days of riverboat travel. And for a treat, take a walk on the bow and let the sun and river breezes caress you as The Spirit gently wends its way up and down the Sacramento River. Newer than her sister ship, the Matthew McKinley is perfect for smaller receptions. Have your ceremony on the bow or the upper deck, and your party below. Rows of windows just above the water line bring the river almost to your table. If you're looking for an unusual place to tie the knot, these two paddlewheelers can deliver an experience you and your guests will long remember.

CAPACITY: The Spirit of Sacramento can seat 350; standing 350. The Matthew McKinley can seat 150; standing 150 guests.

FEES & DEPOSITS: Half the estimated total or rental fee is due as a deposit 15 days after the reservation is made. The balance is payable 15 days prior to departure. Per person food rates run $6–12 for hors d'oeuvres, $15–20 for buffets and $22–24 for dinners. Bar, tax and a taxable 15% service charge are additional. Rental rates are as follows:

	Time	Weekday	Weekend
Spirit of Sacramento	3 hours	$3,450	$4,200
	4 hours	4,450	5,350
	each add. hour	975	1,100
Half of the Spirit of Sacramento	3 hours	1,950	2,375
	4 hours	2,500	3,000
	each add. hour	550	625
Matthew McKinley	3 hours	1,000	1,400
	4 hours	1,450	1,850
	each add. hour	350	400

CANCELLATION POLICY: The deposit is refundable with 60 days' notice.

AVAILABILITY: Year-round, 7 days a week, 24 hours a day.

SERVICES/AMENITIES:

Restaurant Services: no
Catering: provided
Kitchen Facilities: n/a
Tables & Chairs: provided
Linens, Silver, etc.: provided
Restrooms: Sp. of Sac is wca, MM is limited wca
Dance Floor: yes

Parking: on street, public garage
Overnight Accommodations: CBA w/special discount
Cleanup: provided
Telephone: emergency only
Outdoor Night Lighting: yes
Outdoor Cooking Facilities: no
Bride's Dressing Area: no

RESTRICTIONS:

Alcohol: provided, corkage $7.50/bottle, wine & champagne only
Smoking: outside decks only
Music: amplified ok, select from preferred list or by special permission only

Wheelchair Access: yes
Insurance: not required
Other: light decorations only, children must be supervised

STERLING HOTEL

1300 H Street
Sacramento, CA 95814
(800) 365-7660 or **(916) 448-1300**
Reserve: 3 months in advance

The Sterling Hotel is one of the most charming hotels in Sacramento. Close to downtown, but on a tree-lined residential street, this white Victorian accommodates both weddings and receptions. The elegant tone is set by dusky pink and cream walls, marble floors, high ceilings and striking light fixtures. You can have your ceremony in the intimate living room or in the completely private all-glass garden conservatory. For honeymoons, several spacious hotel suites are also available. Chanterelle, the hotel's 4-star restaurant, caters all functions and can provide a contemporary space for small rehearsal dinners and receptions.

CAPACITY: The Living Room can hold 48 seated or 110 standing; the Glass Garden 110 seated or 200 standing and the four Suites, 15 seated guests each.

FEES & DEPOSITS: A non-refundable deposit of 75% of the rental cost is due when reservations are confirmed, with the balance due the day of the function. Daytime rental fees for the Living Room are $775 for 5 hours. The Glass Garden rental fee is $995 for 5 hours. For small receptions, there is an additional charge of $275 for the first hour and $150 for each additional hour. Catering is done through the Chanterelle Restaurant; the entire catering fee is due the day of the event.

AVAILABILITY: Everyday.

SERVICES/AMENITIES:

Restaurant Services: yes

Catering: provided

Kitchen Facilities: n/a

Tables & Chairs: provided

Linens, Silver, etc.: provided

Restrooms: wca

Parking: on and off street, lot

Dance Floor: portable

Overnight Accommodations: 12 suites

Telephone: guest phones

Outdoor Night Lighting: no

Outdoor Cooking Facilities: no

Cleanup: provided

Bride's Dressing Area: CBA

RESTRICTIONS:

Alcohol: provided, corkage $5/bottle

Smoking: outside only

Music: some restrictions

Wheelchair Access: yes

Insurance: not required

Other: decorations restricted

TOWE FORD MUSEUM

2200 Front Street
Sacramento, CA 95818
(916) 442-6802 Kristin
Reserve: 1–2 months in advance

This is not an ordinary place to hold a wedding! Essentially a car museum, this warehouse (located 1 mile south of Old Sacramento) is an automobile lover's paradise. While antique Fords are the car of choice here, many other vintage varieties are also on display. The building itself is spare—cement floor, bare-bulb lighting and a domed roof overhead are the only amenities. However, a special events area has recently been created with multi-level risers for seating guests. This space will be equipped with a new stage area within the next year. And anyway, when you have hundreds of gorgeous vehicles surrounding you, how much more do you need?

CAPACITY: The Museum can accommodate 300 seated guests or 500 standing guests for a reception.

FEES & DEPOSITS: A refundable $100 cleaning deposit is required 1 month prior to the event. The rental fee is $500 for 6pm–midnight use of the building, payable in advance of the function.

CANCELLATION POLICY: If the Museum is left in clean condition, the deposit is refunded.

AVAILABILITY: Year-round, everyday from 6pm to midnight. Closed Christmas, Thanksgiving and New Year's holidays.

SERVICES/AMENITIES:

Restaurant Services: no

Catering: BYO

Kitchen Facilities: no

Tables & Chairs: provided

Linens, Silver, etc.: BYO

Restrooms: wca

Parking: large lot

Dance Floor: CBA, extra fee

Overnight Accommodations: no

Telephone: office phone

Outdoor Night Lighting: yes

Outdoor Cooking Facilities: BYO

Cleanup: renter or caterer

Bride's Dressing Area: in restroom

RESTRICTIONS:

Alcohol: BYO, any sales need permit

Smoking: outside only

Music: amplified ok

Wheelchair Access: yes

Insurance: certificate required

THE TRAVELER CENTRE

428 J Street
Sacramento, CA 95814
(916) 736-1000
Reserve: 2 weeks–6 months in advance

This large lobby is a throw-back to the 1920s. A crystal chandelier sparkles overhead in the main entryway. The floor is reminiscent of Grandma's house with miniature white and grey hexagonal tiles throughout. In the center of the lobby is a fountain, and as you glance up at the high ceiling, you notice the elaborate molding with gold leaf and white fixtures from the period. The mezzanine floor railing is wrought-iron filigree covered with gold. Lighting here is very subdued and is best suited to evening affairs.

CAPACITY: The Lobby can accommodate 300 guests, total.

FEES & DEPOSITS: A refundable $250 deposit is required when the contract is submitted. The rental fee is $500–700 per day, depending on guest count. A payment schedule with several payments is required prior to the function; the balance is due 3 weeks prior to the event.

CANCELLATION POLICY: With 2 months' notice, the deposit is refunded.

AVAILABILITY: Year-round, Monday–Friday 5:30pm–2am, weekends anytime until 2am.

SERVICES/AMENITIES:

Restaurant Services: no
Catering: BYO
Kitchen Facilities: no
Tables & Chairs: BYO
Linens, Silver, etc.: BYO
Restrooms: wca
Parking: adjacent lots
Bride's Dressing Area: no

Dance Floor: Lobby floor
Overnight Accommodations: no
Telephone: office phones
Outdoor Night Lighting: no
Outdoor Cooking Facilities: no
Cleanup: renter, caterer & janitorial staff
Special: 24-hour security guard provided

RESTRICTIONS:

Alcohol: BYO, any sales need permit
Smoking: allowed
Music: amplified ok

Insurance: certificate required
Wheelchair Access: yes
Other: decorations restricted

WILLIAM LAND PARK AMPHITHEATER

William Land Park
Sacramento, CA 95822
(916) 277-6060
Reserve: 3–6 months in advance

Ducks swim on an emerald green pond. A fountain sprays glistening jets of water into the morning sun. Redwoods, sycamores and oaks cast dappled shade on gently rolling lawns. And framed by tall, slender evergreens, the amphitheater itself sets serenely in the midst of all this beauty. Terraced rows of low benches lead the eye down to a small stage, and provide seating with a clear view for everyone in the audience. After the ceremony, your guests can meander through a California natives garden, or stroll through the park. Although the site is open to the public, the most notable visitors we saw were groups of birds who seemed to be enjoying their surroundings as much as we were.

CAPACITY: 150 seated.

FEES & DEPOSITS: The rental fee is $25/hr on weekdays and $35/hr on weekends, with a 2-hour minimum. Payment in full is due upon booking. A permit is required for amplified sound which costs $25 on weekdays and $40 on weekends.

CANCELLATION POLICY: The rental fee is fully refundable; permit fees are not.

AVAILABILITY: September through May, everyday, from dawn until dusk.

SERVICES/AMENITIES:

Restaurant Services: no
Catering: BYO
Kitchen Facilities: no

Parking: limited
Overnight Accommodations: no
Telephone: pay phone 1 block away

Tables & Chairs: CBA for fee
Linens, Silver, etc.: BYO
Restrooms: 3/4 block away (wca)
Dance Floor: dancing on stage

RESTRICTIONS:
Alcohol: not allowed
Smoking: allowed
Music: limited amplified ok after 5pm

Outdoor Night Lighting: access only
Outdoor Cooking Facilities: no
Cleanup: renter
Bride's Dressing Area: no

Wheelchair Access: limited
Insurance: not required

Yuba City

HARKEY HOUSE

212 C Street
Yuba City, CA 95991
(916) 674-1942 Lee Limonoff & Bob Jones
Reserve: 2–4 months in advance

Harkey House is not only a bed and breakfast inn, but a delightful spot for weddings and receptions. The house is a creamy yellow, classical Italian Victorian over 100 years old. In back, there is a wonderful brick patio with willow tree furniture and a covered trellis providing shade. A spa, pool and brick patio are added options. The Dining Room has a black and white tile floor, fireplace and high windows, providing light and privacy. The Living Room has a marble fireplace, comfortable seating and a unique piano that traveled all the way around the Cape. Each guestroom has a different theme and the entire house is fresh and inviting. Note that this is a great spot for a honeymoon, too.

CAPACITY: The facility can accommodate 40 guests inside and 125 outdoors (total 165).

FEES & DEPOSITS: A refundable security deposit of $125 and the rental fee are due 4 weeks prior to the event. The rental fee for use of either the inside or outdoor space is $200; rental of the entire facility costs $400. Guestroom rates are $75–100 for a double and $65–90 for a single.

CANCELLATION POLICY: A full refund will be given with 1 month's notice. With less than a month's notice the deposit will be refunded only if rebooked.

AVAILABILITY: Everyday except Christmas.

SERVICES/AMENITIES:
Restaurant Services: no
Catering: BYO
Kitchen Facilities: adequate
Tables & Chairs: some provided
Linens, Silver, etc.: caterer

Parking: on street
Overnight Accommodations: 4 guestrooms
Telephone: guest phones
Outdoor Night Lighting: yes
Outdoor Cooking Facilities: BBQ

Restrooms: no wca
Dance Floor: outside patio

RESTRICTIONS:
Alcohol: BYO
Smoking: outside only
Music: amplified ok

Cleanup: caterer
Bride's Dressing Area: CBA

Wheelchair Access: no
Insurance: not required

MOORE MANSION

560 Cooper Avenue
Yuba City, CA 95991
(916) 674-8559
Reserve: 1 week–6 months in advance

Built in the early 1920s, this craftsman-style bungalow is a distinctive bed and breakfast inn. Built by Charles Moore, owner of the Omega Gold Mine located near Grass Valley, the house was purchased by Peggy Harden in 1979, who is the current innkeeper. This 17-room, historically rich home has retained its original character. Of note is the Sutter Buttes Room, a perfect honeymoon spot for the newlyweds. Each of the Mansion's five rooms is designed differently, many with antique furnishings. The front rooms on the main floor are very adaptable for private parties. The Parlor is an airy, pleasant room with a fireplace, oak paneled walls and comfortable furniture. The most charming room, however, is the Dining Room. It has its own large fireplace and a wall hutch full of glassware and china. The walls are painted in a soft peach and teal and a colorful border has been painted just below the ceiling. A closed-in porch at the front of the house is appointed with antique white wicker. Outdoors is a lawn ringed by large sycamore trees which provide shade during warm summer months and old fashioned pink roses border the wrought-iron fence which runs along the yard's perimeter. Centrally located between Chico and Sacramento, the Moore Mansion offers convenience, comfort and hospitality.

CAPACITY: The facility can accommodate 60 guests, maximum, indoors.

FEES & DEPOSITS: A refundable $100 deposit is required to secure the date and is applied towards the rental fee. For indoor/outdoor functions, you must reserve the entire Mansion. The rental fee of $675 covers 4pm to 11am the next day, including a bridal suite for honeymooners. The rental balance is due 1 week prior to the event.

CANCELLATION POLICY: With 30 days' notice, the half of the deposit is refunded.

AVAILABILITY: Year-round, everyday.

SERVICES/AMENITIES:
Restaurant Services no
Catering: BYO
Kitchen Facilities: set up only

Restrooms: no wca
Dance Floor: library or outdoors
Overnight Accommodations: 5 guestrooms

Tables & Chairs: some provided
Linens, Silver, etc.: BYO or CBA
Outdoor Night Lighting: access only
Cleanup: caterer or renter

RESTRICTIONS:
Alcohol: BYO
Smoking: outside only
Music: amplified limited

Parking: small parking lot
Telephone: house phone
Outdoor Cooking Facilities: BBQ
Bride's Dressing Area: CBA

Wheelchair Access: outside only
Insurance: sometimes required

Need a caterer, cake maker, florist? The Service Directory starting on page 412 features the best in the business.

Ryde

GRAND ISLAND INN

14340 Highway 160
Ryde, CA 95680
(916) 776-1318
Reserve: 2 weeks–12 months in advance

Now the Grand Island Inn, the historic Ryde Hotel was once owned by film star Lon Chaney's family. It was built as a classy gambling house to cater to the riverboat crowd coming from San Francisco and was a famous speakeasy and casino during prohibition. The 4-story hotel, with pink stucco and navy blue canvas awnings, is designed in a classic California 1930s style. Inside it's all Art Deco with potted palms, small Egyptian statues, black lacquered ceiling fans and large Erte 30s-style posters. Available for private parties, the Inn provides distinctive spaces for any type of gathering. Ceremonies and receptions can be held indoors or in the outdoor garden area.

CAPACITY: The inside capacity, main level, is 100 seated guests, 150 for a reception; lower level (Cabaret) 250 seated, 350 for a reception. Combined with outdoor areas, the capacity is 700 guests, depending on the season.

FEES & DEPOSITS: A $200 deposit is required to hold your date; 90 days prior to the function, the deposit increases by $800.

Event rental fees: $50/hour for a 4-hour block; each additional hour is $100. Buffets or lunch/dinner entrees range from $13–20/person. Tax and 15% gratuity are added to the final total.

CANCELLATION POLICY: With 90 days' notice, the deposit is fully refundable.

AVAILABILITY: Year-round, every day from 8am–1am.

SERVICES/AMENITIES:

Restaurant Services: yes, seasonally
Catering: provided, no BYO
Kitchen Facilities: n/a
Tables & Chairs: provided
Linens, Silver, etc.: provided
Restrooms: limited wca
Dance Floor: yes
Bride's Dressing Area: yes

Parking: large lot
Overnight Accommodations: 50 guestrooms
Telephone: pay phone
Outdoor Night Lighting: limited
Outdoor Cooking Facilities: CBA
Cleanup: provided
Other: swimming pool, recreation & docking facilities

RESTRICTIONS:

Alcohol: provided, corkage $5/bottle
Smoking: allowed
Music: amplified ok, DJ ok

Wheelchair Access: yes
Insurance: not required

Walnut Grove

GRAND ISLAND MANSION

13415 Grand Island Road
Walnut Grove, CA 95690
(916) 775-1705
Reserve: 2 weeks–12 months in advance

On Grand Island, in the heart of California's lush Delta, lies an impressive, 58-room mansion. Surrounded by miles of orchards, the Grand Island Mansion has 4 stories, a terra cotta roof, spacious balconies with intricate iron railings and an entrance highlighted by enormous Corinthian columns. A cypress-lined circular driveway adds to the extraordinary setting. The estate faces a waterway and has its own yacht facility. Inside, the expertise of imported European craftsmen is seen everywhere: the white marble entrance hall, featuring a sweeping circular stairway, the ballroom with hardwood floors, beveled mirrored walls, sculptured fireplace, gold-gilded columns and crystal chandeliers. French doors lead to a brick courtyard surrounding a tiled swimming pool and spa. This place has it all: an 18-seat cinema, billiards room, a regulation bowling lane with new AMF automatic pinsetter and a charming old fashioned soda fountain. Both a lovely garden and ballroom locations are available for ceremonies.

CAPACITY: The inside capacity is 200 seated, buffet setup 500 guests, and combined with outdoor areas, 1,000 guests, depending on the season. There is a 100-guest minimum for an event.

FEES & DEPOSITS: A $200 deposit is required to secure your date; 90 days prior to the function, the deposit amount increases by $800. There are no rental fees if meal service is provided. Per person rates: luncheons range $19–25, dinners $22–26, buffets $22–25 and hors d'oeuvres start at $19.50. Tax and 15% gratuity are added to the final total. Functions are usually allowed a 5-hour block with $200 for each extra hour.

CANCELLATION POLICY: With 90 days' notice, the deposit is fully refundable.

AVAILABILITY: Year-round, every day. Weddings and receptions usually take place between 11am–4pm or 6pm–11pm.

SERVICES/AMENITIES:

Restaurant Services: no
Catering: provided, no BYO
Kitchen Facilities: n/a
Tables & Chairs: provided
Linens, Silver, etc.: provided
Restrooms: no wca
Dance Floor: yes

Parking: driveway, large lot
Overnight Accommodations: no
Telephone: house phone
Outdoor Night Lighting: yes
Outdoor Cooking Facilities: CBA
Cleanup: provided
Bride's Dressing Area: yes

RESTRICTIONS:

Alcohol: provided, WBC only, corkage $5/bottle

Smoking: outside only

Music: amplified ok, DJ ok

Wheelchair Access: limited

Insurance: not required

Lodi

JAPANESE PAVILION AND GARDENS
Micke Grove Park

11793 Micke Grove Road
Lodi, CA 95240
(209) 953-8800 or **(209) 331-7400**
Reserve: 6–12 months in advance

Sheltered by large pines, bamboo, azaleas and camellias, the Japanese Pavilion is an unexpected sight in Micke Grove Park. Located in a separate, fenced area within the park, it is evocative of the Far East. The Pavilion resembles a tastefully designed pagoda, with wood floors, simple wood detailing and decks plus a distinctive high pitched roof that slopes upward at the edges. Adjacent to the structure is a small pool with fountain and red footbridge. In the front, a generous expanse of lawn leads to several wide steps up to the Pavilion; in the back, a gentle ramp leads back into the garden. A popular location for receptions, the Pavilion has a special ambiance.

CAPACITY: Pavilion and garden 175 guests; inside seating 50 guests; garden alone can hold up to 175.

FEES & DEPOSITS: There is a $50–200 cleaning deposit for indoor use, $50–600 for outdoor use. The amount is based on guest count. The Pavilion and garden rental fee is $125 per 4-hour block and the garden alone rents for $65 per 2-hour block. Vehicle entry into the park is $2/car weekdays and $3/car on weekends; group passes can be purchased in advance. Fees and deposits are due within 2 weeks of making a reservation. The cleaning deposit is returned 20 days after the event. Note that there may be some restrictions regarding setup areas for food and alcohol.

CANCELLATION POLICY: With 21 days' notice, rental fees and cleaning deposit will be refunded. There's a cancellation fee of $25.

AVAILABILITY: Year-round, anytime except for Christmas day.

SERVICES/AMENITIES:
Restaurant Services: no
Catering: BYO or CBA
Kitchen Facilities: no
Tables & Chairs: provided
Linens, Silver, etc.: BYO
Restrooms: wca nearby
Dance Floor: no dancing
Bride's Dressing Area: no

Parking: large lots
Overnight Accommodations: no
Telephone: pay phones
Outdoor Night Lighting: no
Outdoor Cooking Facilities: no
Cleanup: caterer or renter
Other: decorating CBA

RESTRICTIONS:
Alcohol: BYO, sales require permit
Smoking: outside only
Music: amplified ok, DJ ok

Wheelchair Access: yes
Insurance: not required

WINE AND ROSES COUNTRY INN

2505 West Turner Road
Lodi, CA 95242
(209) 334-6988
Reserve: 2 weeks–3 months in advance

Secluded on a magnificent 5-acre setting with towering trees, the Wine and Roses Country Inn is an outstanding destination for special celebrations. Lush lawns and old fashioned flower gardens surround the lovely, 90-year-old home that has been converted into a 10-room country inn. Ceremonies take place on the garden lawn under the white, lattice arch. The Inn's courtyards and terrace are great for outdoor receptions and the inside is tastefully decorated in soft rose, rich burgundy with cream trim and windows with lace curtains. All meals are prepared with the finest and freshest of ingredients by the chef, who is a graduate of the San Francisco Culinary Academy. The inn is family-owned and operated and the staff has expertise in coordinating all types of events. This is a very special place.

CAPACITY: The dining room can hold up to 65 seated and 90 standing guests. The sitting room holds up to 35 seated guests and the outside garden up to 400 guests.

FEES & DEPOSITS: A non-refundable deposit of 50% of the rental fee is required to secure your date. The rental fee is $200–500 November–April, $1,000 May–October. The remainder of the rental fee is due 6 weeks prior to the event along with 50% of the estimated catering total; the balance is due the day of the function. Buffets start at $12/person, seated meals at $13/person. Tax and service charges are additional.

CANCELLATION POLICY: If the Inn can be rebooked for a similar event, your deposit will be refunded less a $50 cancellation fee.

AVAILABILITY: Everyday, anytime.

SERVICES/AMENITIES:

Restaurant Services: yes
Catering: provided, no BYO
Kitchen Facilities: n/a
Tables & Chairs: provided
Linens, Silver, etc.: provided
Outdoor Night Lighting: yes
Outdoor Cooking Facilities: no
Cleanup: provided

Restrooms: wca
Dance Floor: courtyard or CBA extra fee
Parking: large lot
Overnight Accommodations: 10 guestrooms
Telephone: house phone
Other: baby grand piano, PA system
Bride's Dressing Area: yes
Special: wedding coordination

RESTRICTIONS:

Alcohol: provided, corkage $5/bottle
Smoking: outside only
Music: amplified/DJ until 10pm

Wheelchair Access: yes
Insurance: sometimes required

Stockton

BOAT HOUSE

Oak Grove Regional Park
4520 West Eight Mile Road
Stockton, CA 95209
(209) 953-8800 or **(209) 331-7400**
Reserve: 6–12 months in advance

This popular park, located between Interstate 5 and Highway 99, is an oasis on a hot summer's day. Lush green lawns, a meandering waterway, amphitheater, plus huge oaks and willows combine to create a wonderful destination for a private party. Large, colorful inflatables looking like tricycles on the water are available for rental. Of note is the Boat House, a simple wood structure with deck situated at the water's edge. With the adjacent BBQ and picnic tables, the Boat House can be used as an informal indoor/outdoor reception facility. For a small gathering of friends and family, this is an ideal spot for a fun wedding.

CAPACITY: The Boat House can accommodate 32 seated or 50 standing guests.

FEES & DEPOSITS: The cleaning deposit is $50. The Boat House rental fee is $50 per 6-hour block and $20 for each additional hour. Vehicle entry into the park is $2/car weekdays and $3/car on weekends; group passes can be purchased in advance. Fees and deposits are due within 2 weeks of making a reservation. The cleaning deposit is returned 20 days after the event. Note that there may be some restrictions regarding alcohol.

CANCELLATION POLICY: With 21 days' notice, rental fees and cleaning deposit will be refunded. There's a cancellation fee of $25.

AVAILABILITY: Year-round, any day.

SERVICES/AMENITIES:

Restaurant Services: no
Catering: BYO or CBA
Kitchen Facilities: minimal
Tables & Chairs: provided
Linens, Silver, etc.: BYO
Outdoor Night Lighting: yes
Outdoor Cooking Facilities: BBQs

Restrooms: wca
Dance Floor: no
Parking: large lots
Overnight Accommodations: no
Telephone: pay phones
Cleanup: caterer or renter
Bride's Dressing Area: no

RESTRICTIONS:

Alcohol: BYO, sales require permit
Smoking: outside only
Music: amplified ok, DJ ok

Wheelchair Access: yes
Insurance: not required

Big Bend

RAINBOW LODGE

Hampshire Rocks Road
Big Bend, CA 95728
(916) 426-3661
Reserve: 6–12 months in advance

Discover Rainbow Lodge. Here you can savor old Tahoe—where fireplaces were built of river rock, walls of granite and round, whole logs were used as posts and beams. This historic building, constructed in 1922, is located several miles west of Soda Springs on Donner Pass. It's a sturdy, handsome survivor of 1920s mountain architecture, now operating as a bed and breakfast. Parties are held in the Sierra Room, complete with stone walls, knotty pine ceiling and fireplace. The adjacent deck with umbrella-shaded tables overlooks the garden and gazebo, offering a sheltered spot to take your vows. With oversized rustic furnishings and fixtures, the lobby is a comfortable place for people to unwind and socialize. Around the corner is a friendly bar, sprinkled with locals who come in to share tales. We really like the Rainbow. Treat your wedding guests to one of the last authentic mountain lodges left in the Sierras.

CAPACITY: 120 seated guests; with outside spaces, 150 guests.

FEES & DEPOSITS: A $450 non-refundable rental fee is due when reservations are confirmed. Buffets run $14–25/person, seated meals $15–25/person. Half of the estimated food cost is payable 30 days prior to the event. The balance is due 7 days before the function along with a final guest count. Any remaining balance is due the day of the event. Tax and a 20% service charge on food are additional.

AVAILABILITY: Year-round, every day, any time.

SERVICES/AMENITIES:
Restaurant Services: yes
Catering: provided, no BYO
Kitchen Facilities: n/a
Tables & Chairs: provided
Linens, Silver, etc.: provided
Restrooms: no wca
Bride's Dressing Area: yes
Other: floral arrangements, wedding coordination and referrals

Parking: large lot
Overnight Accommodations: 30 guestrooms
Telephone: pay phone
Outdoor Night Lighting: yes
Outdoor Cooking Facilities: CBA
Cleanup: provided
Dance Floor: no

RESTRICTIONS:
Alcohol: provided, corkage $5/bottle
Smoking: allowed
Music: amplified ok

Wheelchair Access: yes
Insurance: not required

Carnelian Bay

GAR WOODS GRILL AND PIER

5000 N. Lake Blvd.
Carnelian Bay, CA 96140
(916) 546-3366
Reserve: 1–6 months in advance

Gar Woods is a restaurant located right on the rim of Lake Tahoe. For outdoor wedding receptions, there's a substantial deck complete with blue, yellow and red umbrellas, wind screens and heat lamps for chilly days. The deck has fabulous views of Gar Woods' private pier, the lake and the mountains beyond. If the weather is unfriendly, guests just relocate to the adjacent indoor dining room. Don't worry. The vistas through floor-to-ceiling windows make you feel like the water is only an arm's length away. The interior is easy on the eyes: a cascading waterfall surrounded by ferns greets you as you enter the restaurant, and the decor is in soft, muted taupe and cream. The private dining room upstairs is a favorite among local diners. More formal than the main dining room, it features floor-to-ceiling windows, light pine walls, hand-crafted chairs and historical color photos of boats on the lake. Dressed up for a wedding party, banquet or reception, Gar Woods presents a very pretty picture, inside and out.

CAPACITY: Indoors, the entire restaurant accommodates 220 seated guests and 300 for a standing reception. The upstairs private dining room holds 80 seated and 100 standing. The deck accommodates 150 seated, 200 for a standing reception.

FEES & DEPOSITS: A refundable deposit equaling 25% of the estimated food and beverage total is required to secure your date. If you want to change the table and chair arrangement, the setup fee is $100/room. Wedding buffets start at $16/person, seated luncheons at $12/person and dinners $16/person. The balance is due the day of the event. Tax and a 15%–20% service charge are additional.

CANCELLATION POLICY: With 60 days' notice, the deposit will be refunded.

AVAILABILITY: Year-round, every day from 11am–1am.

SERVICES/AMENITIES:

Restaurant Services: yes
Catering: provided, no BYO
Kitchen Facilities: n/a
Tables & Chairs: provided
Linens, Silver, etc.: provided
Restrooms: wca downstairs
Bride's Dressing Area: yes
Other: wedding referrals

Parking: large lot
Overnight Accommodations: CBA
Telephone: courtesy phone
Outdoor Night Lighting: yes
Outdoor Cooking Facilities: no
Cleanup: provided
Dance Floor: CBA

RESTRICTIONS:

Alcohol: provided
Smoking: allowed
Music: amplified limited

Wheelchair Access: yes
Insurance: not required

Norden

SUGAR BOWL RESORT

Sugar Bowl Ski Area
Norden, CA 95724
(916) 426-3651
Reserve: 2 weeks in advance

Grab your shades and sun block! If you're looking for an informal setting for a mountain wedding or rehearsal dinner, Sugar Bowl is the answer. Located off Interstate 80 at Donner Summit, this ski resort offers a high altitude deck (6900-foot elevation!) and creekside lawn for ceremonies and receptions. You can get married here summer or winter. The deck is really large—a sun worshiper's dream! Backed on one side by the lodge and open on the other to snow-topped mountains and stream, it offers plenty of space for dining, dancing and sunning. The deck comes equipped with numerous picnic tables and giant barbecues. During the summer, the flat, grassy area below the deck is highlighted by tall trees. We like it a lot because it's situated right next to a clear Sierra stream. Take your vows by the stream—then repair to the deck for a reception feast. At Sugar Bowl, blue sky, crisp mountain air and the smell of pine needles can make your celebration come to life.

CAPACITY: 400 guests maximum.

FEES & DEPOSITS: A non-refundable facility fee is required when reservations are confirmed. The fee is $450 for weddings of more than 100 guests. Buffets run approximately $9–23/person; seated service starts at $20. Half of the estimated event total is due 30 days in advance; the balance is payable the day of the function. Tax and a 15% gratuity are additional.

AVAILABILITY: Year-round, every day from 7am–10pm.

SERVICES/AMENITIES:

Restaurant Services: yes
Catering: provided, no BYO
Kitchen Facilities: fully equipped
Tables & Chairs: provided
Linens, Silver, etc.: CBA
Restrooms: wca limited
Bride's Dressing Area: yes
Other: wedding coordination and referrals

Parking: ample
Overnight Accommodations: 28 guestrooms
Telephone: pay phone
Outdoor Night Lighting: limited
Outdoor Cooking Facilities: BBQs
Cleanup: provided or renter
Dance Floor: deck or lounge

RESTRICTIONS:
Alcohol: provided
Smoking: designated areas
Music: amplified ok

Wheelchair Access: no
Insurance: not required

South Lake Tahoe

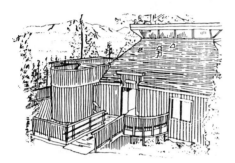

TALLAC VISTA

Ski Run Boulevard at David Lane
South Lake Tahoe, CA 96151
(916) 541-4975 summer or **(916) 542-4166** winter
Reserve: 1–3 months in advance

Situated on a high mountainside, within 12 acres of stately pines and massive boulders, Tallac Vista is a contemporary building, perfect for small, private weddings. Owned and operated by the California Tahoe Conservancy, a state agency that implements acquisition and land management programs to protect the environment, it's named after Mt. Tallac, one of the highest peaks in the Sierra. On a calm day, you can see Mt. Tallac mirrored in the still, dark blue waters below. Park a small distance from the site and a private shuttle bus will take you to the building. It has panoramic views of the lake, the mountains and surrounding tall pines. Take your vows indoors in front of windows overlooking Lake Tahoe; outdoor ceremonies can take place under the fragrant trees. The Tallac Vista building is light and open, with rustic beams and endless windows. Multi-level decks and verandas also have sweeping views. Isolated from traffic, this site is private, peaceful and quiet. Treat your guests to an evening reception, when incomparable sunsets on the lake create an extraordinarily beautiful ambiance.

CAPACITY: 75 guests, maximum.

FEES & DEPOSITS: A non-refundable $75 deposit is required when reservations are confirmed. Rental fee is $175 per hour. The rental balance is due 2 weeks prior to the event.

CANCELLATION POLICY: With less than 2 weeks' notice, service charges will apply.

AVAILABILITY: Year-round except January, February and March. Every day 9am–11pm.

SERVICES/AMENITIES:
Restaurant Services: no
Catering: BYO
Kitchen Facilities: no
Tables & Chairs: provided
Linens, Silver, etc.: BYO
Restrooms: wca
Bride's Dressing Area: yes
Other: wedding referrals

Parking: shuttle provided
Overnight Accommodations: no
Telephone: house phone
Outdoor Night Lighting: yes
Outdoor Cooking Facilities: no
Cleanup: caterer or renter
Dance Floor: no

RESTRICTIONS:

Alcohol: BYO
Smoking: not allowed
Music: amplified indoors only, restricted

Wheelchair Access: yes
Insurance: not required

VALHALLA

Highway 89
South Lake Tahoe, CA 96151
(916) 541-4975 summer or **(916) 542-4166** winter
Reserve: 6 months in advance

Valhalla is an historic estate home on the southwest shore of Lake Tahoe. Now owned and operated by the U.S. Forest Service, it sits near the water's edge along with several other large homes. Built in 1922 by the Heller family, it is a reminder of days past when wealthy San Franciscans brought their families here to while away the summers. Set among many tall, vertical pines and firs, Valhalla (which literally means 'heavenly place' in Norwegian) is a simple, yet large home made of local stone and wood. Lodge poles provide the support for the long veranda, and veranda railings are made from local trees with the bark intact. The interior is unique, to say the least. The Grand Hall has numerous windows along the lake view side, and a cavernous stone fireplace that takes up another. In fact, the fireplace is more like a room in itself. With an 'Etruscan' stone arch overhead, the opening spans some twenty feet. A second-floor gallery around the perimeter of the room gives guests a chance to watch events happening below. Ceremonies take place indoors. Receptions can be held indoors or on the green lawns that lead to the Lake. There are quite a few picnic tables and additional tables can be imported for special events. Although this is a no frills location, it does have a rustic elegance. If you'd like to have a Lake Tahoe wedding, with an old world ambiance, explore Valhalla.

CAPACITY: 125 guests, maximum.

FEES & DEPOSITS: A non-refundable $50 deposit is required when reservations are confirmed. The rental fee is $175 per hour. However, the rate may change shortly. A $50 cleaning fee is required. The rental balance is due 2 weeks prior to the event.

CANCELLATION POLICY: With less than 2 weeks' notice, service charges will apply.

AVAILABILITY: Year-round, daily 9am–11pm.

SERVICES/AMENITIES:

Restaurant Services: no
Catering: BYO
Kitchen Facilities: no
Tables & Chairs: some provided
Linens, Silver, etc.: BYO

Parking: several lots, 35 cars
Overnight Accommodations: no
Telephone: pay phone
Outdoor Night Lighting: no
Outdoor Cooking Facilities: BBQ CBA

Restrooms: no wca

Bride's Dressing Area: yes

Other: wedding referrals

RESTRICTIONS:

Alcohol: BYO

Smoking: not allowed

Music: amplified inside only

Cleanup: renter or caterer

Dance Floor: yes

Wheelchair Access: no

Insurance: not required

Other: no outdoor ceremonies

Squaw Valley

RESORT AT SQUAW CREEK

Squaw Valley, CA 96146

(916) 583-6300

Reserve: 1–24 months in advance

Wow! That's the simplest word we could come up with to describe how impressed we were by the year-round Resort at Squaw Creek. You've got to come for a visit—this splendid, multi-million dollar facility has to be seen to be fully appreciated. From its position slightly above the valley floor, views of the valley below and the surrounding mountains are refreshing. For a wedding, we can hardly think of a more suitable spot. It's got everything—ballrooms, multiple sun decks and restaurants, three pools and a 250-foot cascading waterfall, footbridge and stream. Dressed for success, this facility is aesthetically decked out in glass, wood and granite. Tasteful furnishings, fixtures and artwork accent beautifully designed interior spaces. Outdoor decks and patios are likewise appointed, with teak chairs and tables, huge umbrellas and distinctive paving underfoot. The level of detail here is awe-inspiring. Not only does the Resort offer top-notch spaces for events, but it also provides plenty of services to pamper wedding guests. Have a sauna or a leisurely dip in the spa. An adjacent salon and massage room come fully staffed to keep the bridal party relaxed and looking its best. No matter what your culinary tastes, the Resort can arrange any menu to satisfy your needs. In-house restaurants include the elegant Glissandi, with world-class French cuisine in a deco setting, the more casual Cascades, with California regional food, Hardscramble Creek Bar & Grille, a chic bistro cafe and Bullwhackers, a high Sierra pub. Overnight guests? The Resort's 405 guestrooms can accommodate any size wedding crowd, plus the bride and groom are treated to a complimentary honeymoon suite. Definitely ask for the full tour because there are numerous places for picture-perfect ceremonies as well as receptions. With great skiing and ice skating in winter, and in summer, golf course, swimming pools, tennis courts and horseback riding trails nearby, you can turn your wedding event into a vacation getaway. Your wedding guests will be eternally thankful for the introduction to and memories from the Resort at Squaw Creek.

CAPACITY:

Area	Seated	Reception	Area	Seated	Reception
Grand Sierra Ballroom	660	950	Glissandi Deck	75	100
Squaw Peak Ballroom	350	475	Bullwhackers Pub	80	120
Hardscramble Creek Bar & Grill	100	175	Cascades	240	—
Hardscramble Deck	250	325	Ice Skating Area	250	325
Glissandi	80	120	*(summer only)*		

FEES & DEPOSITS: A $500–1,000 deposit (depending on room size) is due when reservations are confirmed. There is no rental fee for receptions with food service. Ceremonies cost $100–300, depending on chair setup. Per person rates for luncheons range from $15–30, buffets and dinners begin at $32. Sales tax and 18% service charge are additional. The estimated event total is payable 3 days prior to the function.

CANCELLATION POLICY: With two months' notice, the deposit will be refunded if space can be rebooked.

AVAILABILITY: Year-round, everyday from 6am–2am.

SERVICES/AMENITIES:

Restaurant Services: yes
Catering: provided, no BYO
Kitchen Facilities: n/a
Tables & Chairs: provided
Linens, Silver, etc.: provided
Restrooms: wca
Bride's Dressing Area: CBA
Other: wedding coordination, cakes, salon, massage

Parking: valet
Overnight Accommodations: 405 guestrooms & suites
Telephone: pay phones
Outdoor Night Lighting: yes
Outdoor Cooking Facilities: BBQs
Cleanup: provided
Dance Floor: deck or indoors

RESTRICTIONS:

Alcohol: provided
Smoking: allowed
Music: amplified ok

Wheelchair Access: yes
Insurance: not required

Need a caterer, cake maker, florist? The Service Directory starting on page 412 features the best in the business.

Tahoe City

THE RIVER RANCH

Highway 89 at Alpine Meadows Road
Tahoe City, CA 95730
(916) 583-4264 or **(800) 535-9900**
Reserve: 3–12 months in advance

The River Ranch occupies an enviable location on the banks of the fast-flowing Truckee River. First called the Deer Park Inn in 1888, it grew into a fashionable watering hole when the narrow gauge railway deposited visitors right to its door. The Great Depression caused Deer Park to go under; subsequently it was abandoned and eventually fell into disrepair. In 1940, old timbers were cleared and a new structure, the River Ranch, was erected as a summertime fishing lodge and wintertime ski lodge. River Ranch is famous for its enormous patio on the Truckee's famous 'Big Bend'. Sit atop the perimeter river rock wall and watch the river rush by and the adjacent bank's tall pines sway in the wind. Brown and tan umbrellas shade guests from high altitude glare and heat lamps are provided to take the chill off. The patio, which has large pines growing right through it, comes fully equipped with several outdoor serving and bar stations plus sizeable barbecues for outdoor feasts. This is one great spot for a party! For indoor receptions the River Ranch has some attractive spaces, too. The bar area is light and large, with a lovely stone wall, hardwood floor and beamed ceiling. It has a circular edge with tables and tartan-covered chairs set beneath multi-paned windows facing the river. For intimate conversations, a cozy alcove is nestled next to the rock fireplace. Another dining room, which is long and narrow, has a large river rock fireplace graced by a large, mounted trout. French doors open right onto the patio, making a terrific indoor-outdoor event spot. If guests are from out of town, no problem. River Ranch offers cozy guestrooms for friends, family and honeymooners.

CAPACITY: Indoors, 100 seated guests; deck, 200 seated.

FEES & DEPOSITS: A non-refundable $200 deposit, which is applied to the total, is required to secure your date. 20% of the anticipated total is due one month prior to the event, and the balance is payable the day of the event. There is a 50-guest minimum. Wedding buffets start at $15/person, seated meals start at $20. Tax and an 18% service charge are additional.

CANCELLATION POLICY: Cancellations are handled individually.

AVAILABILITY: Year-round except July and August. Every day, noon–1am.

SERVICES/AMENITIES:

Restaurant Services: yes
Catering: provided, no BYO
Kitchen Facilities: n/a
Tables & Chairs: provided

Parking: large lot
Overnight Accommodations: 20 guestrooms
Telephone: pay phones
Outdoor Night Lighting: yes

Linens, Silver, etc.: provided
Restrooms: wca limited
Bride's Dressing Area: CBA
Other: wedding referrals

Outdoor Cooking Facilities: BBQs
Cleanup: provided
Dance Floor: deck

RESTRICTIONS:
Alcohol: provided, no BYO
Smoking: designated areas
Music: amplified ok

Wheelchair Access: yes
Insurance: not required

SUNNYSIDE
Restaurant and Lodge

1850 West Lake Blvd.
Tahoe City, CA 95730
(916) 583-7200
Reserve: 6–12 months in advance

Recreated to resemble a classic 1920s mountain lodge, Sunnyside is constructed of wood siding, dormers, large timbers and stone. All is designed to evoke a romantic image of old Tahoe. The charm extends to the inside where hunting trophies frame a huge river-rock fireplace, canoes hang from the ceiling and antique snow shoes tread across the walls. Light fixtures are craftsman-style brass, furnishings are rustic-chic 'twig' and antique oak. Three dining rooms (two with wall-to-wall windows facing the Lake) are available for private parties. Each is tastefully appointed and painted in soft colors. For sun lovers, Sunnyside's spacious deck is spectacular. You can't get much closer than this to the Lake—it's right on the water's edge. Vivid green, blue and red umbrellas unfold to shade guests from bright rays. All details here, down to the deck's railings of lodgepole pine, are designed to maintain the flavor of a traditional Sierra lodge. Below the deck, colorful vessels await launch during summer months. In winter, snow-capped roof and icicle drapes belie Sunnyside's cozy interior warmth. Have your ceremony on the sun-drenched deck or inside in the Lake Room. Popular for good reason, Sunnyside will impress your guests with a range of modern facilities presented with an ambiance of days gone by.

CAPACITY:

Room	Seated Guests	Room	Seated Guests
Lake Room	75–100	Emerald Room	50–75
Christ Craft	75	Deck	75

FEES & DEPOSITS: A refundable $500 deposit is due when reservations are confirmed. For weddings, a 100 guest minimum is required. A room rental fee of $100 plus a cleanup and setup fee of $2/guest are also required. Wedding buffets run approximately $15–25/person; rehearsal dinners from $18–26/person. Tax and an 18% gratuity are additional. The balance is due the day of the event.

CANCELLATION POLICY: With 2 weeks' notice, the deposit will be refunded.

AVAILABILITY: Mid-September through mid-May, Monday-Saturday. During warm weather months, dining room and deck receptions 11:30am–4pm. Rehearsal dinners from 5:30pm–9:30pm.

SERVICES/AMENITIES:

Restaurant Services: yes

Catering: provided, no BYO

Kitchen Facilities: n/a

Tables & Chairs: provided

Linens, Silver, etc.: provided

Restrooms: wca

Bride's Dressing Area: CBA

Other: wedding referrals

Parking: large lot

Overnight Accommodations: 28 guestrooms

Telephone: pay phone

Outdoor Night Lighting: yes

Outdoor Cooking Facilities: no

Cleanup: provided

Dance Floor: deck or indoors

RESTRICTIONS:

Alcohol: provided, corkage $5/bottle

Smoking: allowed

Music: amplified ok

Wheelchair Access: yes

Insurance: not required

WILLIAM B. LAYTON PARK
and Gatekeeper's Museum

130 West Lake Blvd.
Tahoe City, CA 96145
(916) 583-1762
Reserve: 6–12 months in advance

What a surprise to find this gem of a park just blocks from the bustling heart of Tahoe City. Walk through the hefty gates and you'll enter a hidden and enchanting spot. The Gatekeeper's Museum, surrounded by hundreds of daffodils and multi-colored tulips, is the focal point of the park. This hand-crafted log cabin overlooks three and a half acres of tall pines and grassy expanses that border the lake. The original 1910 structure was destroyed by arson fire in 1978, and was reconstructed with great care and attention to detail. For 60 years, the cabin served as the residence of "the gatekeepers", the men who regulated the water outflow from Lake Tahoe. Currently, it houses historic artifacts and displays. A secluded clearing in the trees, right on the shore, is a wonderful spot for a wedding and there's plenty of room under the pines for a lovely outdoor reception. A redwood lattice arch is available for ceremonies and picnic tables for informal receptions. For natural beauty, tranquility and a great lakeside location, this park is hard to beat. Reserve early—it's a popular spot.

CAPACITY: 300 plus seated guests.

FEES & DEPOSITS: A post-dated check, in the amount of the rental fee, is required to secure your date. A $50 cleaning deposit is also required. The rental fees vary depending on number of guests: ceremonies (only), $50–200; receptions, $100–300. A wedding arch is available for free; chairs, extra tables and canopies can be rented.

CANCELLATION POLICY: With 10 days' notice, deposits are refundable.

AVAILABILITY: June 1 through September 30th. Every day, 8am–5pm. After 5pm, extra charges apply.

CANCELLATION POLICY: With one month's notice, your deposit will be refunded.

AVAILABILITY: Year-round, every day from 9am–9pm.

SERVICES/AMENITIES:

Restaurant Services: yes
Catering: provided, no BYO
Kitchen Facilities: n/a
Tables & Chairs: provided
Linens, Silver, etc.: provided
Restrooms: no wca
Bride's Dressing Area: CBA
Other: wedding referrals

Parking: several lots
Overnight Accommodations: no
Telephone: restaurant phone
Outdoor Night Lighting: yes
Outdoor Cooking Facilities: no
Cleanup: provided
Dance Floor: deck or indoors

RESTRICTIONS:

Alcohol: provided, corkage $7/bottle
Smoking: allowed
Music: amplified ok

Wheelchair Access: yes
Insurance: not required

Tahoe Vista

LA PLAYA

7046 North Lake Blvd.
Tahoe Vista, CA 96148
(916) 546-5903
Reserve: 1-3 months in advance

The lake becomes a part of the experience at La Playa—a brilliant and ever-changing body of blue that makes a stunning backdrop for a wedding or reception. Have your ceremony in front of the fireplace or outdoors, on the lawn or sandy beach. The restaurant's dining rooms and outdoor patios have panoramic views of Lake Tahoe and the encircling mountains. Wind screens are provided for offshore breezes, and if it gets a bit chilly, move the reception indoors. La Playa's light interior is really attractive. It's an eclectic blend of styles and artifacts—sea-faring paraphernalia is part of the decor as is nice looking contemporary art on the walls. A huge fireplace (with pot-belly stove inside) dominates one end of the room, wall-to-wall glass the other. Tables, with white linens and flowers, can be arranged as you like—set up for formal, seated dinners or casual buffets. Create memories at La Playa, where wedding guests can enjoy a few hours in the sun and relax to the sound of waves lapping at the shore.

CAPACITY: Indoors, 100 seated guests; combined with outdoors, 175 seated guests.

FEES & DEPOSITS: A refundable deposit of 30% of the estimated food total secures your date and is due when reservations are confirmed. With food service, no rental fee is required. La Playa can customize any menu, with prices ranging from $18-42/person. The balance is payable by the end of the event. La Playa will close for a guaranteed minimum guest count.

CANCELLATION POLICY: With one month's notice, your deposit will be refunded.

AVAILABILITY: Year-round, every day from 9am-9pm.

SERVICES/AMENITIES:

Restaurant Services: yes
Catering: provided, no BYO
Kitchen Facilities: n/a
Tables & Chairs: provided
Linens, Silver, etc.: provided
Restrooms: no wca
Bride's Dressing Area: CBA
Other: wedding referrals

Parking: several lots
Overnight Accommodations: no
Telephone: restaurant phone
Outdoor Night Lighting: yes
Outdoor Cooking Facilities: no
Cleanup: provided
Dance Floor: deck or indoors

RESTRICTIONS:

Alcohol: provided, corkage $7/bottle
Smoking: allowed
Music: amplified ok

Wheelchair Access: yes
Insurance: not required

Tahoma

EHRMAN MANSION

Sugar Pine Point State Park
Tahoma, CA 96142
(916) 525-7982
Reserve: 2 weeks in advance

Experience the opulence of old Tahoe. The historic Ehrman mansion, completed in 1903, is one of the largest and most elegant estates on the Lake. In 1897, San Francisco businessman I.W. Hellman began buying property at Sugar Pine Point and by 1913 had acquired nearly 2,000 acres. His grand summer home, called Pine Lodge, is considered one of the finest in the high Sierra. (It has since been renamed for his daughter, Florence Hellman Ehrman, who inherited the estate.) This impressive brown-shingled home is multi-story, with stone foundation, fireplaces and walls. The inside is dark, with lots of woodwork and fancy beamed ceilings. Hollywood crews have been here—*Things Change* with Don Ameche and several segments of *The Young and the Restless* were filmed on the estate. The Mansion sits on a small rise. Consequently, ceremonies and hors d'oeuvres receptions on the porch have great lake vistas through huge pines. Other ceremony spots include a round, rustic, cedar gazebo and a grass croquet court near the lake. Receptions can be held on the estate lawns or in the nearby picnic area. Delight your friends and family with a period wedding by dressing up in turn-of-the-century costumes.

The Ehrman Mansion is a one-of-a-kind wedding location.

CAPACITY: 150 guests, maximum.

FEES & DEPOSITS: The rental fee, damage deposit and certificate of insurance are required when the application is submitted. For weddings on the Mansion's porch, the fee is $200 with a $200 damage deposit. For outdoor weddings, the fee is $100, with a $100 damage deposit, which includes park day use fees for the entire wedding party. With less than 15 guests, fees are waived. Parking for service vehicles needs approval.

CANCELLATION POLICY: With 48 hours' notice, the deposit will be refunded.

AVAILABILITY: June 15th–Labor Day, one wedding per day between 5pm–9pm.

SERVICES/AMENITIES:

Restaurant Services: no

Catering: BYO

Kitchen Facilities: no

Tables & Chairs: BYO

Linens, Silver, etc.: BYO

Restrooms: wca yes

Dance Floor: no

Overnight Accommodations: no

Telephone: no

Outdoor Night Lighting: no

Outdoor Cooking Facilities: BBQ in picnic area

Cleanup: caterer or renter

Bride's Dressing Area: CBA

Parking: designated areas

RESTRICTIONS:

Alcohol: BYO, permit required

Smoking: outside only

Music: no amplified

Wheelchair Access: yes

Insurance: certificate required

Truckee

COTTONWOOD RESTAURANT

10142 Rue Hilltop
Truckee, CA 96160
(916) 587-5711
Reserve: 1 week–3 months in advance

Cottonwood is wonderful. Located on a high bluff overlooking Truckee, this one-time railway stop, lumbermill and lodge was the site of the first ski area in California. Pictures of Charlie Chaplin and other notables grace one of the walls since *Gold Rush* and other films were shot here in the 1920s. Cottonwood preserves a bit of the Old West—nothing about this place is ordinary. Parts of the building are constructed of railroad ties, and remnants of the tracks that once ran in front of the structure are still visible. The road that takes you here is unpaved and the railing in front of Cottonwood is suggestive of old-time hitching posts. Inside, the entry rooms feature an old brick fireplace, a heavily beamed ceiling and stone and plank flooring on the diagonal. The main room, by contrast, has a more contemporary feeling of an art gallery. Large and airy, with an open truss ceiling, it offers a bird's-eye view of the city below through a wall of windows. Crisp white linens and flowers on every table add a touch of elegance. Wedding ceremonies are often held on the adjacent deck which is bathed in afternoon sun. At twilight, the mood becomes romantic as candles glow on each table and the lights from Truckee begin to twinkle.

CAPACITY: Indoors, 150 seated guests; with the deck, add an additional 80 guests.

FEES & DEPOSITS: The $200 rental fee is the deposit required to secure your date. Wedding buffets and seated meals run about $20/person. Tax and a 15% service charge are additional.

CANCELLATION POLICY: With 7 days' notice, your deposit will be refunded.

AVAILABILITY: Year-round. Every day, any time except Monday. Weekend weddings until 4:30 pm.

SERVICES/AMENITIES:

Restaurant Services: yes
Catering: provided, no BYO
Kitchen Facilities: n/a
Tables & Chairs: provided
Linens, Silver, etc.: provided
Restrooms: wca
Bride's Dressing Area: no

Parking: large lot
Overnight Accommodations: no
Telephone: pay phone
Outdoor Night Lighting: yes
Outdoor Cooking Facilities: CBA
Cleanup: provided
Dance Floor: yes

RESTRICTIONS:

Alcohol: provided, corkage $5/bottle
Smoking: bar or outside only
Music: amplified ok

Wheelchair Access: yes
Insurance: not required

NORTHSTAR

Highway 267 at Northstar Drive
Truckee, CA 96160
(916) 587-0265
Reserve: 3–5 months in advance

Although you may think Northstar is just a ski resort, think again. Here you'll find facilities that are well designed—plus comprehensive services that should appeal to anyone planning a wedding party. Designed as a self-contained village, Northstar can provide guests with winter and summer accommodations. Take your vows in the shade of pines and firs on a grassy area adjacent to the Village Clocktower building. After the ceremony, guests can step up to the umbrella-dotted sun deck, several yards away, for an outdoor, mountain-air reception. The deck sports a huge outdoor fireplace for informal barbecue feasts. Quiet and private, the wind through the trees and the birds provide the only sounds. If the weather is uncooperative, the indoor Alpine and Chaparral Rooms are great choices for an indoor party. Floor-to-ceiling windows allow light to flood in, affording glimpses of the deck and tall conifers beyond. The Alpine Room has a portable dance floor and bar. Dressed up with white linens and flowers, both rooms sparkle. As an added plus, Northstar's event staff will help coordinate all the essentials from music to photography. Chances are you never thought of Northstar for your wedding—now that you know, we urge you to take a closer look.

CAPACITY:

Area	Seated	Standing Reception
Deck	200	300
Chaparral Room	150	300
Alpine Room	150	200

FEES & DEPOSITS: A $100 refundable deposit, which is applied towards the balance, is due when reservations are booked. Luncheon buffets and seated meals run approximately $10–22/person. Northstar will customize any menu for your private party. Half of the food and beverage total is due 30 days in advance, with a $300 rental fee and event balance payable the day of the function. Tax and a 17% service charge are additional.

CANCELLATION POLICY: With 30 days' notice, the deposit is refundable.

AVAILABILITY: Every day, any time before November 15th and after April 1st.

SERVICES/AMENITIES:

Restaurant Services: yes

Catering: provided, no BYO

Kitchen Facilities: n/a

Tables & Chairs: provided

Linens, Silver, etc.: provided

Restrooms: wca

Bride's Dressing Area: CBA

Other: wedding coordination & referrals

Parking: large lot

Overnight Accommodations: 225 condos

Telephone: pay phone

Outdoor Night Lighting: limited

Outdoor Cooking Facilities: BBQ

Cleanup: provided

Dance Floor: yes

RESTRICTIONS:

Alcohol: provided, champagne corkage $10/bottle

Wheelchair Access: yes

Smoking: allowed

Insurance: not required

Music: amplified ok

Prices and policies <u>do</u> change. Call each facility and confirm everything you read in Here Comes The Guide.

ZINA'S!

10292 Donner Pass Road
Truckee, CA 96160
(916) 587-1771
Reserve: 1–3 months in advance

This Queen Anne Eastlake mansion, the C.B. White house, says welcome the moment you step across the threshold. Built in 1873, it's a Victorian reminder of Truckee's golden years at the turn of the century and has the distinction of being the only building in the Truckee area chosen for the National Register of Historic Places. Originally the home of Henry Kruger, the owner of a successful lumber mill, it was purchased by Bank of America executive Charles Bernard White in 1904. Restored with a great deal of care and filled with antique furnishings and fixtures collected by Zina, this stately house embraces you with a sense of place. Lace curtains filter incoming light through numerous windows. High ceilings give small rooms a spacious feeling. Subdued, patterned wallpapers, historic photographs, hanging plants and soft colors create a warm environment for a special occasion. A long, enclosed front porch, glassed in on three sides, offers a view of the mountains beyond. Glorious aromas waft in from the kitchen. Here Zina works her magic, preparing creative foodstuffs for parties. And, if you'd like to have an impressive wedding cake, Zina can concoct something truly special. Her intricate designs and ability to decorate with flowers sets these cakes apart from the ordinary. (They also taste divine.) Not for large celebrations, Zina's! is just right for rehearsal dinners and small, cozy receptions for friends and family.

CAPACITY: 50–75 seated guests, 90 for a standing reception.

FEES & DEPOSITS: As a refundable deposit, half of the estimated event total is due when reservations are confirmed. A $250 refundable security/cleaning deposit is due 1 week before the event. There is no room rental fee with food service. Food costs per person: luncheons start at $12, buffets and/or seated dinners, $22–50. Tax and 15% gratuity are additional. The balance is payable the day of the event.

CANCELLATION POLICY: With 30 days' notice, the deposit is refundable, less any expenses incurred.

AVAILABILITY: Year-round, everyday except Thanksgiving and Christmas days.

SERVICES/AMENITIES:

Restaurant Services: yes
Catering: provided, no BYO
Kitchen Facilities: n/a
Tables & Chairs: provided
Linens, Silver, etc.: provided
Restrooms: wca
Bride's Dressing Area: spacious restroom
Special: wedding cakes and custom desserts

Parking: several lots
Overnight Accommodations: no
Telephone: house phone
Outdoor Night Lighting: yes
Outdoor Cooking Facilities: BBQ CBA
Cleanup: provided
Dance Floor: on porch & patio
Other: wedding coordination

RESTRICTIONS:

Alcohol: provided, corkage $5/bottle
Smoking: outside only
Music: acoustic only

Wheelchair Access: yes
Insurance: not required
Other: no open flames

Here Comes The Guide's
Service Directory

The professionals listed in **Here Comes The Guide** *are special.*

They are unequivocally the best in the business—the people I'd recommend to my friends and business associates without hesitation. I personally endorse each individual or company represented in *Here Comes The Guide*, so when you call them, you can feel as confident as I do about their abilities.

How did I find them?

Actually, they found me. Since I don't "advertise" my service directory, they either discovered it by reading *Here Comes The Guide* or heard about it via word-of-mouth. Although my office receives many calls from vendors who'd like to be in our publication, I only accept the industry's top performers.

I turned away ad dollars! I must be crazy, right?

Not really. It's my way of guaranteeing that you get to choose from only the finest service providers in Northern California—including some who claim they never advertise. Those candidates who received consistent, rave reviews made it into the *Guide*. Everyone else was (nicely) turned down.

Getting into Here Comes The Guide *is tough.*

Because I *endorse* the vendors in this publication, I want to feel absolutely sure each one is top-notch. Since one-time satisfied customers are not the best qualified to evaluate my potential advertisers, we require a list of 10–30 *trade* references from each candidate. These are professionals in the events field who have worked with them over time, and are able to assess their level of expertise.

We call every single reference and ask about the professionalism, technical competency and service orientation of the advertisers in question. Each interview takes from 15–60 minutes. When you talk to that many people, you get a clear picture of who's doing a superb job and who isn't.

I've done the legwork so you won't have to worry.

I've spent an enormous amount of time putting the highest caliber service providers at your fingertips. If you call the companies and individuals listed in my directory, you'll eliminate a time-consuming search. And, because I've thoroughly checked the reputation of each, you won't have to worry. It's an honor to represent these professionals in *Here Comes The Guide* and a real pleasure to bring the best services in Northern California to your attention.

Ministers/Celebrants/Officiants

We've received many requests for ministers, rabbis and non-denominational officiants for wedding ceremonies, so we did some research on your behalf.

Like the other service providers we've endorsed in *Here Comes The Guide*, each individual or group ministry has gone through a rigorous reference check. They've all been given high marks for professionalism, superior performance and integrity by numerous wedding professionals.

Even though these people come highly recommended, you still have to choose a celebrant that fits your personality. Balance, inspired counsel, perspective, humor, spirituality, joy and trust were some of the qualities mentioned in the testimonials we received. If you select someone who understands your lifestyle, beliefs and traditions, you'll be more likely to have a flawless ceremony, with not a dry eye in the house.

Individual or Group Ministry

MINISTERS FOR WEDDINGS

Rev. Ward Atwood	Rev. Robin Phelps
Rev. Edward Caller	Rev. Roger Smith
Rev. John Ham	Rev. Virginia Surrell
Rev. Donald Morgan	Rev. Marvin Yarnold
Rev. Patricia-Alyce Parker	

ordained ministers • personalized ceremonies

HENRY S. BASAYNE

certified senior humanist minister • non-denominational and interfaith ceremonies • custom designed ceremonies • pre-nuptial counseling

REVEREND LESLIE DAVENPORT

spiritual/humanistic, non-denominational and interfaith ceremonies • personalized, traditional and non-traditional ceremonies • premarital counseling

ANN KEELER EVANS, M. DIV., A RITE TO REMEMBER

personalized ceremonies and vows which blend the traditional and the new • interfaith ceremonies • ceremonies of commitment • ordained, non-denominational minister

Area Served

(408) 275-6886

Santa Clara, Santa Cruz, Monterey, San Mateo, San Francisco, Solano, Alameda and Contra Costa Counties

(415) 567-7044

Marin, San Francisco, East Bay and Peninsula

(415) 459-4122

Marin, San Francisco, East Bay, Wine Country and Peninsula locations

(510) 655-2191

East Bay, San Francisco, North Bay, Half Moon Bay, and Peninsula locations

REVEREND ED HOLT, M. DIV.

unique, customized and traditional ceremonies •
non-denominational and interfaith marriages • creative
locations • pre-marital counseling • confidential license
available

(415) 595-4225
San Mateo, San Francisco,
Alameda and
Santa Clara Counties

JOAN NELSON, M.A., ED.D.

premarital and marital counseling • other non-denominational
life-transition ceremonies • counselor/chaplain American
Humanist Association • board certified clinical sexologist

(415) 453-6221
Greater Bay Area with
offices in Marin and San
Francisco

REVEREND JENNIFER LOVEJOY

non-denominational minister of the Universal Life Church •
traditional and non-traditional ceremonies • personalized
ceremonies • other ceremonies of commitment

(408) 479-7296
Santa Cruz, Monterey
Peninsula and San
Francisco

REVEREND TIMOTHY MILLS, M.DIV., PH.D.

inter-denominational and interfaith weddings • customized
ceremonies

(510) 782-8593
Wine Country, North Bay
and East Bay locations

MINISTERS OF MARRIAGE

Rev. Barbara A. Forbes	Rev. Nicholas Wittmayer
Rev. Jay Peterson	Rev. Lynda Hadley
Rev. Edwin Holt	Rev. Ted Comerford

Christian and non-religious ceremonies • sample vows
provided or write your own • keepsake script of the complete
wedding ceremony • rehearsal coordination

(510) 455-4327
Alameda, San Francisco,
Contra Costa, San Mateo,
and Santa Clara Counties

REVEREND H.P. (TERRY) SLOAN

ordained Presbyterian minister • certified pastoral
counselor • personalized traditional and non-traditional
wedding services • prenuptial consultation • sample
services/vows provided or created

(510) 526-9082
Bay Area and surrounding
locations

MR. JOSEPH T. STEINKE, S.T.L., M.A.

prenuptial counseling • personalized ceremonies • vows
written or provided • ceremony coordination • cordless lapel
microphone and speaker

(510) 471-3468
Alameda, Contra Costa, San
Francisco, San Mateo and
Santa Clara Counties

JOSIE TERESI, MINISTER
non-denominational, unique, personalized
ceremonies • pre- and post-nuptial counseling

(408) 335-5982
Northern California from
Sacramento to San Joaquin
Valley

T. MIKE WALKER, THE TRAVELING MINISTER
non-denominational • unique, personalized vows • printed
scripts • prenuptial consultation

(408) 425-5755
Santa Cruz, Monterey, Gilroy,
San Jose and Santa Clara

HELEN WILLS
non-denominational • spiritual and civil, traditional and
non-traditional ceremonies • custom ceremonies created •
sings wedding songs or leads guests in song

(408) 425-5755
greater Bay Area locations

FREDERICK WIGGLESWORTH
pre-wedding meeting • rehearsals • ceremonies

(408) 354-7296
San Francisco, Peninsula,
South Bay, Santa Cruz area

Bittersweet

Original Chocolate Celebration Cakes
by appointment only

415-921-8728
San Francisco

custom-designed
celebration cakes

distinctive & delicious

by appointment
415-239-1326
Maralyn Tabatsky

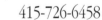

The Finest

Wedding Cakes

are created by

Katrina Rozelle

5931 College Avenue
Oakland

215 B Alamo Plaza
Alamo

510/655-3209

C A K E W O R K

CUSTOM · WEDDING · AND · PARTY · CAKES

CECILE GADY
415/863-4444
573 Hayes Street, San Francisco, CA 94102

Chestnut Tree Catering

A menu of your Choosing
& Imagination (helpful
Suggestions if you wish).
Delightfully excellent
And inconspicuous service.
Fastidiously prepared and
Presented.

(510) 849-0681

VISA

Trumpet Vine Catering Inc.

Serve California's Finest Cuisine

We plan everything for . . .
Weddings & Bar Mitzvahs
Hors d'oeuvres Receptions
Gourmet Suppers in a Box
Executive Lunches

In the Location of Your Choice

We arrange parties in . . .
Private Homes
Famous Museums
Quaint Victorians
Corporate Offices

Elegant, Delicious and Affordable
Please call us for a free consultation

510 ◆ 848 ◆ 7268
FAX: 510 ◆ 848 ◆ 7302
2533 Seventh Street, Berkeley, CA 94710

Still &
Always the
Best Around

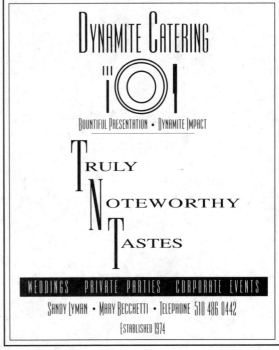

Dynamite Catering

Bountiful Presentation • Dynamite Impact

Truly
Noteworthy
Tastes

WEDDINGS   PRIVATE PARTIES   CORPORATE EVENTS

Sandy Lyman • Mary Becchetti • Telephone 510 486 0442

Established 1974

Now you can enjoy great food and so much more...

The talents of creative event designers.
Superb cuisine and dessert creations by talented chefs.
Gracious service and elegant presentations.

Your best choice is...

Taste

CATERING AND EVENT PLANNING

Call and speak to our Wedding Designer
for assistance when planning your special event.

Bay Park, 3450 Third Street 4D   Phone 415-550-6464
San Francisco, CA 94124   Fax 415-550-1858

Previously Taste and Edible Art. Two of Northern California's largest
and best-known catering and event design companies are now one.

FLOWERS

Michaele Thunen

W E D D I N G S   P A R T I E S   E V E N T S
P L A N N I N G — C O O R D I N A T I O N
510·527·5279   BERKELEY · CALIFORNIA

Laurie Stern Floral Art

Specializing in Romantic, Victorian, and English country styles, designed to set a unique and spectacular mood.

(510) 524-4895

Floral Design Studio

- Wedding Specialist
- Parties • Events
- Corporate Installation

Susan Groves
415- 328 -0658
Palo Alto, CA

An Occasional Arrangement

Unique and beautiful floral designs.

Specializing in weddings for nineteen years.

Laurie Chestnut
415-325-9926

Video

DISCOVER THE PROMISE OF BRIDAL BELLES.

*Creative excellence
in wedding
photography and portraiture.
Romantic bouquets
and wedding flowers
in fresh or preserved.
Artistically
designed cakes.
Veils, Millinery.
Consulting and
coordinating services.
Your complete wedding store.*

*1952 Armory Drive
Santa Rosa, California 95401*
707-525-1970

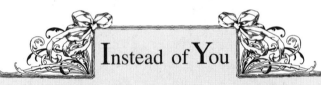

We get married every week...

and all that experience helps when you're planning the perfect wedding. We feature the services of a variety of wedding professionals in every field and we'll help with all or part of your wedding planning at no charge.

We offer a huge display of invitations plus...

- Photographers
- Video
- Site Video
- Caterers
- Flowers
- Bridal Accessories
- Musicians
- Cakes
- Favor & Party Supplies
- And much, much more!

THE ***Wedding Connection***
Wedding Consultant and Talent Agency

408 688-0355
9099 Soquel Drive ◆ No. 1 ◆ Aptos ◆ *(In the Redwood Village)*

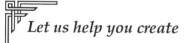

Overwhelmed Planning
Your Wedding?
Too Busy?
Filled with Anxiety?
On a Budget?
Need Assistance?
Call…

A Joyous Occasion
by GreMar

Free One Hour Consultation

Gretchen Coleman-Thomas
Marcia Coleman-Joyner
(408) 267-0773
Member, Association of
Bridal Consultants
Certified by Ann Nola's
Association of Certified
Professional Wedding Consultants

*Association of Certified
Professional Wedding Consultants*

*We're there when
you need us most!*

The Wedding Resource

**FULL SERVICE EVENT
PLANNING**

✤

FIND QUALITY SERVICES

✤

*STAY ORGANIZED AND
ON SCHEDULE*

✤

*DESIGN ADVISE
CEREMONY IDEAS*

✤

*RELAX WITH ON SITE
DIRECTION OF YOUR
REHEARSAL AND
WEDDING DAY*

✤

**CALL FOR BROCHURE
DIANE BREIVIS
(415) 626-8147**

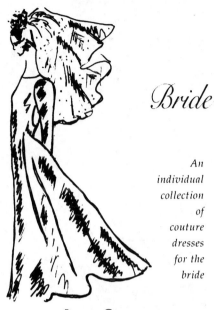

Bride

An
individual
collection
of
couture
dresses
for the
bride

JOAN GILBERT
BRIDAL COLLECTION
By appointment: 415/752-2456 in S.F.

Hair/Make-up

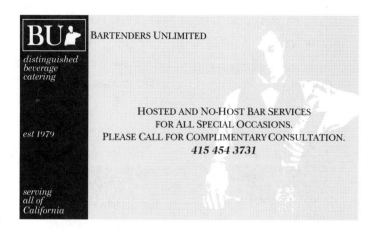

Entertainment

Photographers

PHOTOGRAPHY BY RUSTY ENOS

COORDINATOR & ASST. INCLUDED

LARKSPUR, CA (415) 924-3563

**CELEBRATIONS
PHOTOGRAPHY
AND VIDEO**
Specializing in Weddings

UNOBTRUSIVE STYLE
UNIQUE • REASONABLE • PROFESSIONAL
5999 WESTOVER DR. • OAKLAND, CA 94611 • 510-530-4480

When it's Forever...
DAVILA PHOTOGRAPHY
Oakland 510.547.7531 Santa Rosa 707.544.9151

Cherish the moment,
Capture the joy...

Richard Miller

PHOTOGRAPHY

(415) 388-3722

GENESIS
PHOTOGRAPHY

International, Award-winning Photography
Contemporary, State-of-the-art Studio
Relaxed, Elegant Atmosphere

We never forget
whose day it is!

See front cover

(415) 967-2301 • 185 Moffett Blvd., Mountain View, CA 94043

"Always a Flower Girl, Never a Bride"

Photography by

*Specializing in Wedding Photography
for over 25 years*

By appointment
(415) 491-4575
Photography by Bill Stockwell

LAWRENCE LAUTERBORN

P H O T O G R A P H Y

SAN FRANCISCO STUDIO (415) 863-1132

S U Z A N N E   P A R K E R

d i s t i n c t i v e   w e d d i n g   p h o t o g r a p h y

4 1 5 . 9 3 1 . 7 1 5 1

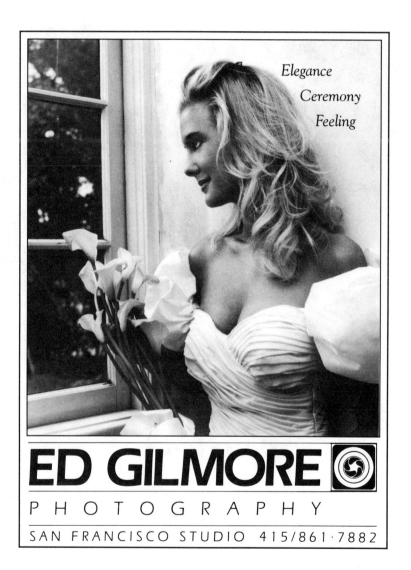

Elegance
Ceremony
Feeling

ED GILMORE
P H O T O G R A P H Y
SAN FRANCISCO STUDIO 415/861·7882

Index

DID YOU BORROW THIS BOOK?

If you want your very own copy, order one directly from Hopscotch Press!

And, if you'd like a copy of *PERFECT PLACES*, our 480-page party, special event and business function location guidebook, you can order one, too. In fact, if you purchase both, we'll make you a special offer of $5.00 OFF!

☐ _____ **YES! I want to receive my own copy of *HERE COMES THE GUIDE!***

Copies @ $24.00 each
(Includes tax, shipping & handling;
for more than 1 book, add $1.)   Total $_____

☐ _____ **YES! I want to receive a copy of *PERFECT PLACES!***

Copies @ $21.00 each
(Includes tax, shipping & handling;
for more than 1 book, add $1.)   Total $_____

☐ _____ **YES! I want to receive both *HERE COMES THE GUIDE* and *PERFECT PLACES!***

Both for $40.00 (that's $5.00 off the total and
includes tax, shipping & handling).   Total $_____

Mail my copies to:

Name_____

Address_____

City, State, Zip_____

Or just call us at 510/525-3379 and order your books over the phone!

HOPSCOTCH PRESS 1563 Solano Avenue, Suite 135 • Berkeley, CA 94707

Lynn Broadwell is a marketing professional
for the events industry. Her companies,
Lynn Broadwell & Associates and Hopscotch Press
provide consulting services, publications and products
which are designed to meet the needs of both the public and the event professional.
She has been featured in articles, on radio and TV throughout Northern California.

Hopscotch Press publishes *Perfect Places* and *Here Comes The Guide.*

Lynn is a graduate of UC Berkeley, with both an undergraduate degree in
landscape architecture and a masters degree in business.
She lives in the Berkeley hills with her husband, Doug, and son, Matthew.

DELANCEY STREET

600 Embacadero
San Francisco, CA 94107
(415) 957-9800
Reserve: 2–12 months in advance

LATE ADDITION!

Named after the part of New York City's Lower East Side where immigrants congregated at the turn of the century, Delancey Street has evolved over the last 20 years into "the world's greatest halfway house," occupying most of a city block. Constructed almost entirely by the residents, it includes a variety of spaces that are available for ceremonies and receptions. The Town Hall, a triangular-shaped auditorium with a vaulted pine ceiling and hardwood floor, is an airy and expansive place for large receptions. A huge sliding barn door opens onto a spacious patio. The Theatre features plush seating, a stage, and state-of-the-art lighting, screen and projector. In the Club Room, pool tables are transformed into buffet tables, and balcony doors open to sea breezes and a bird's-eye view of the Bay Bridge. The Dining Room is the fresh and functional heart of Delancey Street, enhanced by a stunning Tiffany-style stained glass window, designed and executed by the residents. Right outside, the Gallery is a wonderful open-air spot for either cocktails and hors d'oeuvres or al fresco dining. A vaulted skylight provides protection while keeping the space open to the sun and stars. And for an upscale dining experience, have your rehearsal dinner in one of Delancey Street Restaurant's private dining rooms.

CAPACITY:

	Town Hall	*Theatre*	*Club Room*	*Dining Room*	*Gallery*
Seated	50–300	150	80	250	60
Standing	500	—	80–200	—	100

FEES & DEPOSITS: Facility rental fees range from $600–1500. The Theatre rents for $125/hour. A non-refundable deposit (50% of the rental fee) is required when the booking is made. 80% of the event cost is due 2 weeks prior to the event; the balance is payable at the conclusion. Food costs run $14–50/person. Beverage, tax and a 15% gratuity are additional.

CANCELLATION POLICY: Cancellations are handled on an individual basis.

AVAILABILITY: Year-round, daily 8:30am–2am. Closed some holidays.

SERVICES/AMENITIES:

Restaurant Services: yes
Catering: provided or BYO
Kitchen Facilities: no
Tables & Chairs: some provided
Linens, Silver, etc.: BYO
Restrooms: wca
Dance Floor: Town Hall only

Parking: on street
Overnight Accommodations: no
Telephone: pay phone
Outdoor Night Lighting: Gallery, Town Hall patio
Outdoor Cooking Facilities: no
Cleanup: renter & Delancey Street
Bride's Dressing Room: yes

RESTRICTIONS:

Alcohol: provided or BYO, extra fee
Smoking: outside only
Insurance: not required

Wheelchair Access: yes
Music: amplified ok in Town Hall only
Other: decorations limited, children supervised

1409 SUTTER

1409 Sutter St.
San Francisco, CA 94109
(415) 561-0855 or **(415) 561-0856**
Reserve: 2–6 months in advance

LATE ADDITION!

You may think that 1409 Sutter is an odd name for an event site, but this is one address with a very long history. Built in 1881 by a forty-niner who made his fortune in business, this house is a Victorian treasure, surviving both the 1906 earthquake and subsequent fire. From the ornate, wrought iron fence encircling the front yard to the colorful mosaic landing at the foot of impressive front doors, 1409 Sutter is a great example of 1880 architecture. The formal, deep burgundy foyer has oak wainscotting, fifteen-foot ceilings, windows with stained glass panels at the top and inlaid hardwood floors. It leads directly into the Great Hall and the Parlor, which can be used independently or in combination for receptions. The Great Hall is a very large room with chandeliers, fireplace and a massive oak staircase. The Parlor is slightly smaller with a window alcove perfect for a band setup. Also on the event floor are the Main Bar, a room with a long, dark mahogany bar and intricate patterned wallpaper, and the Red Room Bar, which has striking cranberry wallpaper and a small bar. Around the corner is the Atrium, which has floor-to-ceiling glass at one end, making it the lightest room in the house. The third floor contains a professional kitchen which supports an in-house chef, available for all functions. Other caterers can be selected from a preferred list. If you're looking for a spacious mansion in San Francisco to host your reception, this is a new addition we'd recommend you preview.

CAPACITY: The entire main floor accommodates 150 seated guests, 275 for a standing reception.

FEES & DEPOSITS: Rental rates range from $100–2,000 based on guest count, hours and season. Ten percent of anticipated costs are required as a deposit to hold your date. The rental fee balance plus a $100–500 refundable security deposit are payable 60 days prior to the event.

CANCELLATION POLICY: With 45 days' notice, you'll receive a refund less a $50 cancellation fee. Food cancellations within 72 hours of the function will incur a 50% charge of quoted food cost.

AVAILABILITY: Year-round, daily.

SERVICES/AMENITIES:

Restaurant Services: no
Catering: provided or select from list
Kitchen Facilities: professional
Tables & Chairs: provided, extra fee
Linens, Silver, etc.: provided, extra fee
Restrooms: wheelchair access
Dance Floor: yes
Other: bar service available

Parking: on street, nearby garages, valet CBA
Overnight Accommodations: no
Telephone: pay phones
Outdoor Night Lighting: access only
Outdoor Cooking Facilities: no
Cleanup: caterer
Bride's Dressing Area: CBA

RESTRICTIONS:

Alcohol: wine & hard alcohol provided, corkage $7/bottle
Music: amplified ok until 11pm

Wheelchair Access: yes
Insurance: proof of liability may be required
Smoking: outside only

Our Free SERVICE!

Receive information about great wedding services for *FREE*!

Fill out this card and mail it back to us with a
<u>self-addressed, stamped (52¢) envelope</u>.
We'll send you *CUSTOMIZED* information about the *BEST*
wedding services and products in your area.

If you need a fantastic caterer, florist, cake-maker, photographer, etc.
JUST SEND IN THIS CARD!

Free Referral Service!

GO AHEAD — Tear out this card and mail it!

Name_____

Address_____

City, State, Zip_____Phone_____

My event is scheduled for:

☐ Jan–Mar 1993   ☐ July–Sept 1994

☐ Apr–June 1993   ☐ Oct–Dec 1994

☐ July–Sept 1993   ☐ Jan–Mar 1995

☐ Oct-Dec 1993   ☐ April–June 1995

☐ Jan-Mar 1994   ☐ July–Sept 1995

☐ Apr-June 1994   ☐ Oct–Dec 1995

My total estimated budget for this event is: $_____

I'll need these services:

☐ Wedding Coordination
☐ Catering
☐ Announcements/Invitations
☐ Florist
☐ Cake
☐ Professional Hair/Make-up
☐ Live Music or DJ (please circle one)
☐ Minister/Celebrant
☐ Valet or Limousine (please circle one)
☐ Photography
☐ Videography
☐ Bartender
☐ Wedding Dress
☐ Doves
☐ Other _____